Co

The Complete Book of Woodwork

Charles H. Hayward

Drake Publishers Inc, New York

ISBN 87749-162-3
Library of Congress Catalog Card Number 70-178805

Published in 1972 by
DRAKE PUBLISHERS INC
381 Park Avenue South
New York, N.Y. 10016

Printed in the United States of America

Contents

INTRODUCTION

WOODWORK is a subject with many branches, each of which calls for a book in itself if it is to be dealt with adequately. Hence the specialized range of WOODWORKER handbooks, of which a full list is given on page 345. Many men, however, need a general book which includes information on all the branches of woodwork which the home craftsman is likely to tackle. So this book was written. It does not pretend to cover any particular subject as fully as a book which specializes in that branch, but it does give all basic information, and in this sense it should be the best all-round book for the man who is a comparative beginner in the subject.

More men are doing woodwork as a hobby to-day than at any other period, and it is one of the most heartening signs of this age when the temptation to accept things ready-made is almost irresistible. Just as it is so much easier to listen to the music of radio or gramophone than to produce it yourself, so it is simpler to accept the product of the machine which in an effortless way turns out uniform items with a speed and regularity equalled only by its lack of individuality and feeling for the material it works in. Yet the fact that men are turning away from this robot-like production and are making things themselves, shows that they realize the cost of the modern trend to mechanization.

It may be that we are passing through a specially difficult phase. If men have more leisure to-day than ever before, there is so much more temptation to do nothing useful with it. Radio, television, motoring, and the cinema all have their place in the scheme of things, but only too often they claim far more than their share of a man's spare time, and leave little to show for themselves. Thus it is one hails this renaissance of handwork with relief, for through it comes the realization of what honesty of construction stands for, and an appreciation of the value of good design. And it is in this that the chief hope for the future lies.

SECTION I.

IN THE WORKSHOP

CHAPTER I

TOOLS–THE KIT

THE selection of tools depends to an extent upon the type of work generally to be done, but there is a fundamental range which is always needed. The choice of individual items may vary slightly with the stature and the age of the user, but the list given on pages 3–9 makes a good representative kit, and we have marked with an asterisk the items the beginner should start with. As he progresses the necessity for other tools will become obvious. He can obtain them as the need makes itself felt.

Do not buy a " complete box of tools." If you do you will be accepting what someone else thinks you ought to have, and you will have to take the whole without being able to exercise any judgment on the individual items. Quite likely, too, you will pay for some items which you will never use, or which may be unsuitable for you. The best plan is to go to a reliable tool dealer and tell him what you want, explaining that you do not want " cheap " tools (in fact they are not cheap in the long run). A good, sound tool should last you a lifetime (some last several lifetimes), and, though you pay more for it in the first place, it will easily repay its cost. It may easily happen that in buying a poor quality tool you may be handicapping yourself from the start. A plane or square which is inaccurate; a chisel or screwdriver which is soft; a stone which is liable to become hard; any of these may cause endless and quite unnecessary trouble in the future.

The choice of the tools on pages 3–9 has been made on the assumption that the reader is a comparative beginner, and as such is not likely to be considering at present the installation of any machines. Those who have had some experience will know that much backaching work can be saved by having a small machine, and we therefore give in Chapter VI some advice on the choice and

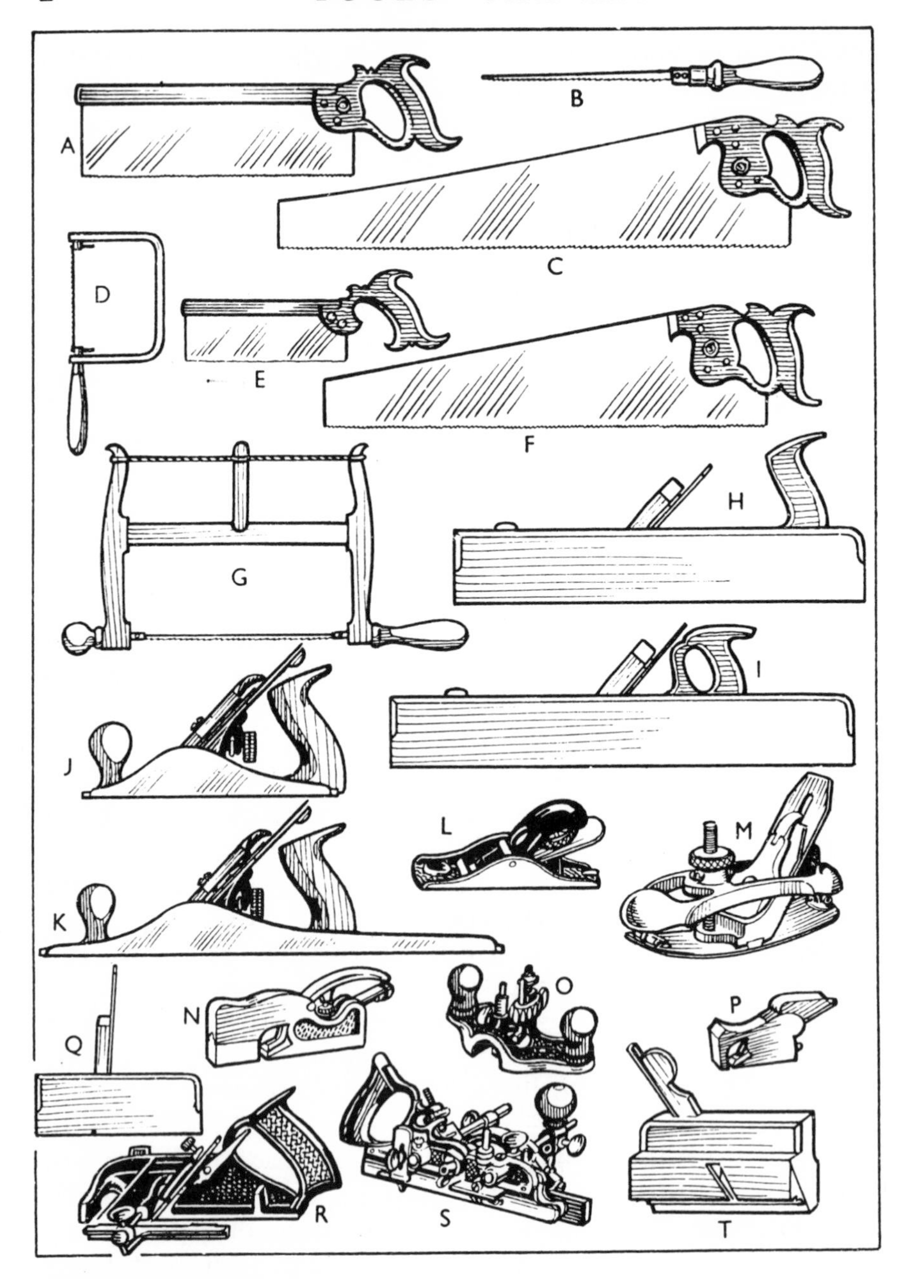

FIG. 1. SAWS AND PLANES USED IN GENERAL WOODWORK

Most of these tools are available in several sizes, and there are variations in detail in accordance with the particular make. If made by a reputable manufacturer they should be reliable.

installation of suitable machines. Those who propose to install a machine could modify the kit of hand tools in accordance with the operations the machine can tackle.

FUNDAMENTAL KIT OF TOOLS

Items marked with an asterisk are what we suggest the beginner should start off with.

Saws
(Fig. 1)

*(C) Cross-cut saw, 24 or 26 in., teeth 8 or 9 points per inch.
(F) Panel saw, 20 in., teeth 10–12 points per inch.
*(A) Tenon saw, 14 or 16 in., teeth 12 or 14 points per inch, brass or iron back.
(E) Dovetail saw, 8 in., teeth 18 to 22 points per inch, brass or iron back.

(If you wish to limit your kit you could substitute a 9 or 10 in. backsaw with teeth about 16 points per inch for the tenon saw and the dovetail saw. The two saws are the better choice, however.)

(G) Bow saw, 12 in.
(D) Coping saw, 6 in.
(B) Keyhole saw, about 11 in.

Planes
(Fig. 1)

*(H) Jack plane, wood, 16 in., $2\frac{1}{8}$ in. cutter.
*(J) Smoothing plane, adjustable metal, 9 in., 2 in. cutter.
(K) Fore plane, adjustable metal, 18 in., $2\frac{3}{8}$ in. cutter.
(I) Trying plane, wood, 22 in., $2\frac{3}{8}$ in. cutter.
(Q) Toothing plane, wood, 2 in. cutter, medium teeth.
(L) Block plane, $1\frac{1}{4}$ in. cutter.
(M) Compass plane, $1\frac{3}{4}$ in. cutter.
(R) Rebate plane, metal adjustable fillister, $1\frac{1}{2}$ in. cutter, or wood, $1\frac{1}{2}$ in. cutter. The metal fillister type recommended.
(P) Bullnose plane, 1 in. cutter.
(N) Shoulder plane, 1 in. or $1\frac{1}{4}$ in. cutter.

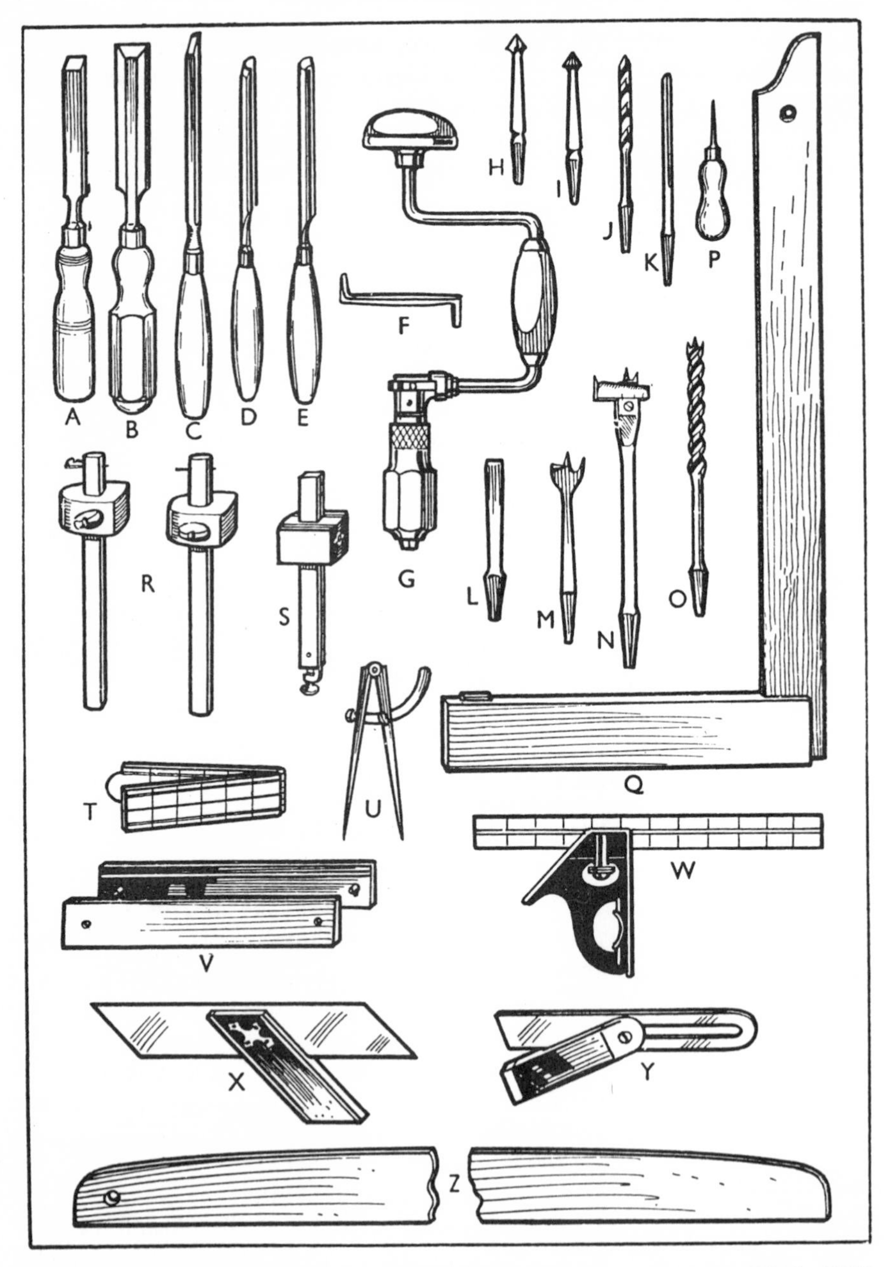

FIG. 2. CHISELS, BORING TOOLS, AND THOSE FOR MARKING AND TESTING

It is an economy in the long run to buy good tools. Bad design and poor materials soon make the working of a tool unsatisfactory or inaccurate.

(S) Plough plane, metal. Wide range available. Smallest works grooves, $\frac{1}{8}$ in., $\frac{3}{16}$ in., $\frac{1}{4}$ in. Larger sizes $\frac{1}{8}$ in. to $\frac{9}{16}$ in. Also the combination which works beads in addition. Get the best you can afford, but even smallest works well.
(O) Router, metal adjustable.
(T) Moulding planes. Obtain only as required.

Chisels and Gouges (Fig. 2)
(A) Firmer chisels, 1 in., *$\frac{1}{2}$ in., *$\frac{1}{4}$ in., $\frac{1}{8}$ in.
(B) Bevelled-edge chisels, 1$\frac{1}{4}$ in., *$\frac{3}{4}$ in.
(C) Sash mortise chisels, $\frac{1}{4}$ in., *$\frac{5}{16}$ in., $\frac{3}{8}$ in.
(F) Drawer lock chisel.
(D) Firmer gouges, $\frac{1}{2}$ in.
(E) Scribing gouges
} Obtain only as needed.

Brace and Bits, etc. (Fig. 2)
*(G) Ratchet brace, 8 in. or 10 in. sweep.
(O) Twist bits, *$\frac{1}{4}$ in., *$\frac{3}{8}$ in., $\frac{1}{2}$ in., $\frac{3}{4}$ in.
*(J, K) Shell bits or drill bits, $\frac{1}{8}$ in. to $\frac{1}{4}$ in. (Used mainly for screw holes.)
Alternatively, engineer's drills can be used.
(H, I) Countersinks, *snail and rose.
(M) Centre bits, $\frac{1}{2}$ in., *$\frac{3}{4}$ in., 1 in.
(L) Turnscrew bit.
(N) Expansion bit.
*(P) Bradawls. Birdcage maker's (square in section is preferable). Get two of varying sizes.

Marking-out Tools (Fig. 2)
*(W) Try square, 12 in., preferably engineer's type with sliding blade.
(Q) Try square, 24 in., wood, home-made.
(X) Mitre square, 12 in.
(Y) Adjustable or sliding bevel, 10 in.
(Z) Straight-edges, 18 in. and 3 ft. wood, home-made.
*(T) Rule, 2 ft. or 3 ft., folding.
*(R) Gauge, cutting.
(R) Gauge, marking.
(S) Gauge, mortise.
(U) Dividers, 6 in. with fine screw adjustment.
(V) Parallel strips.

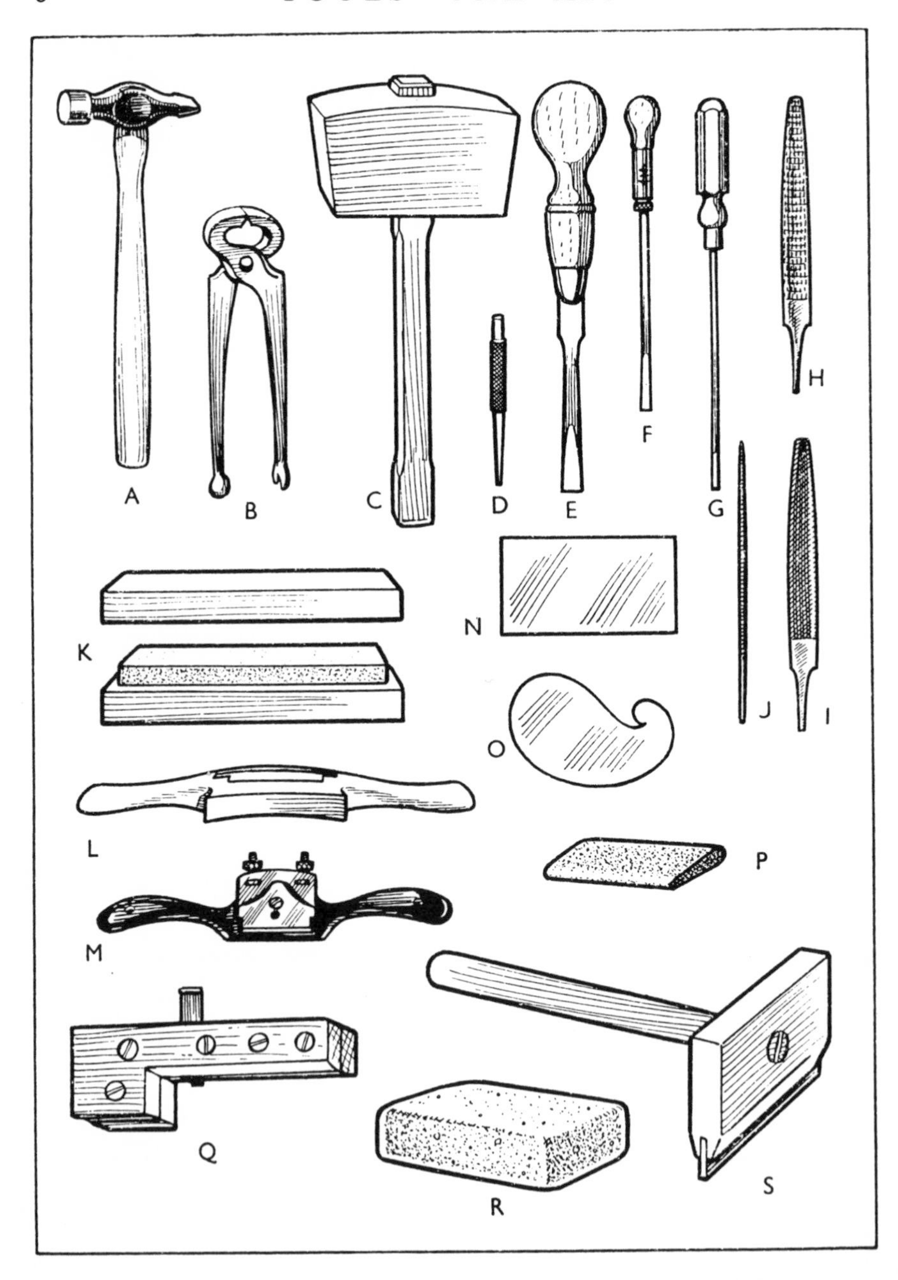

FIG. 3. RANGE OF TOOLS, SOME OF THEM HOME-MADE

You do not need the full range straightway if you are a beginner. Select those marked with an asterisk, and obtain the others as the need for them is felt.

General Tools (Fig. 3)

*(A) Hammer, Warrington or London pattern, about 8 oz.
Hammer, pattern maker's, about 3 oz.
*(C) Mallet, about 6 in. head.
*(B) Pincers, 8 in.
*(D) Punches, hollow point. One for small panel pins, other larger.
(E) Screwdrivers, *8 in. cabinet type.
*(F, G) 5 in. ratchet, and fine.
You need screwdrivers to enable you to put in screws ranging from about 12's to about 2's.
(I, J) Wood file, half-round, 7 in. rat tail ; 6 in.
(H) Wood rasp, half-round, 7 in.
Shaper tool.
(L) Spokeshave, *wood, about 2¼ in. cutter.
(M) Spokeshave, metal, round-face, 2 in. cutter.
(N) Scraper, *cabinet, 5 in. About $\frac{3}{64}$ in. thick.
(O) Shaped cabinet scraper.
*(K) Oilstone, medium or fine grade, or combination fine-coarse, *India*, *Carborundum*, *Unirundum*, etc., 8 in. by 2 in.
(P) Oilstone slip, having two varying rounded edges.
*(R) Cork rubber, about 4½ in.
(S) Veneering hammer, home-made.
(Q) Scratch-stock, home-made.

As soon as possible after obtaining your tools make yourself a container of some sort for them. It may be a simple box, cupboard, or be built into the bench. Remember to allow for expansion. You will undoubtedly buy more tools later, and it is as well to allow for what you envisage as your eventual kit. Try to arrange things so that edge tools do not come into contact with each other; chisels and saws in racks, planes in compartments, and so on. It will save you a lot of time in the long run in that you will avoid gashed edges, etc. It is possible to obtain a special paper known as V.P.I. (Vapour Phase Inhibitor) which prevents rust. A sheet of this in the tool box, and renewed from time to time, will save much trouble in this connection.

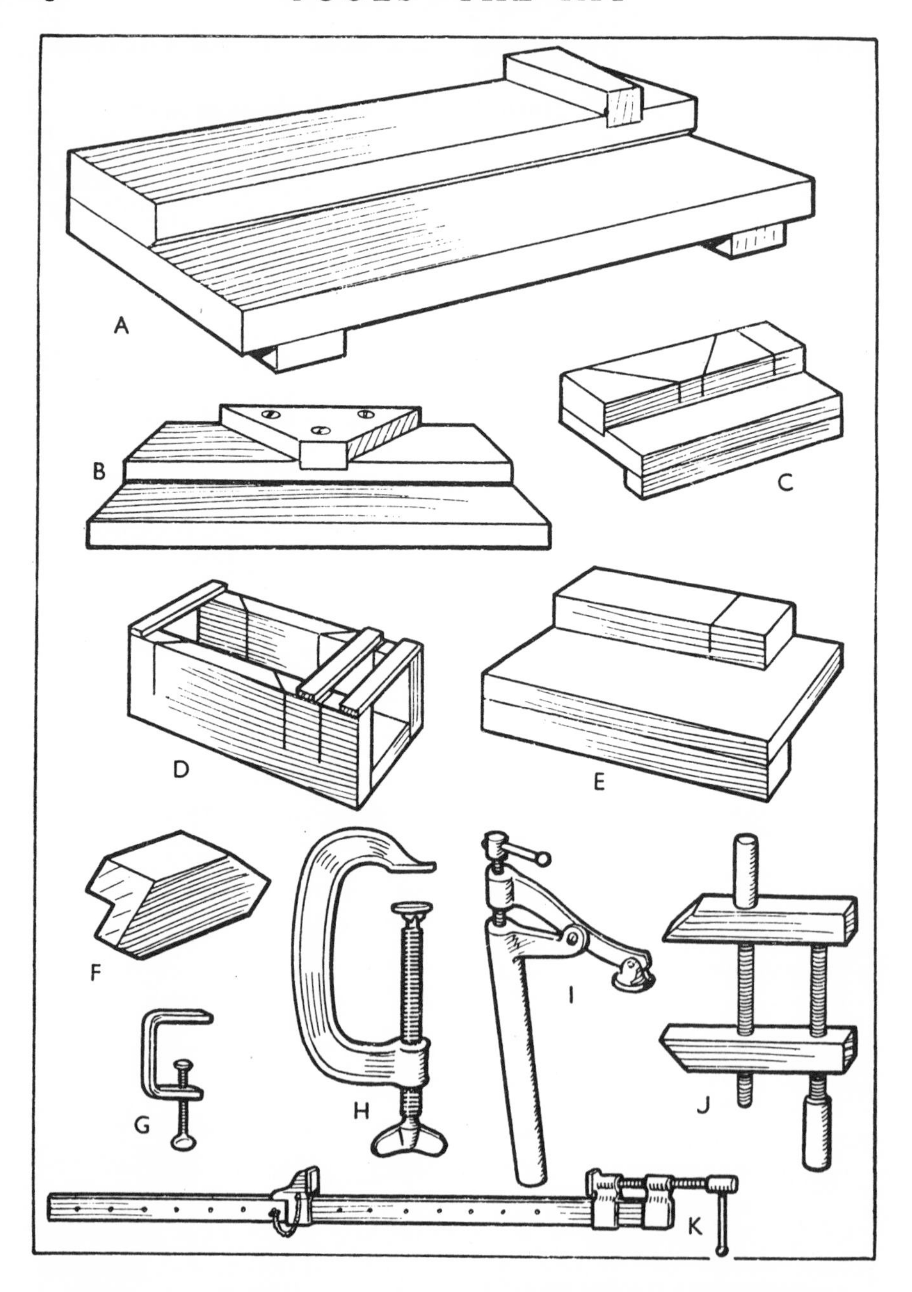

FIG. 4. TRIMMING AND CUTTING APPLIANCES, AND CRAMPS

All of the appliances could be made by the reader himself. In addition a planing board could be made. Further details of this appear on p. 40.

(Fig. 4)

(A) Shooting board, about *2 ft. and 5 ft., home-made.

(B) Mitre shooting board, about 18 in.

*(C) Mitre block, about 9 in., home-made.

(D) Mitre box, for mouldings up to 4 in., home-made.

*(E) Bench hook, about 7 in., home-made.

(F) Mitre template, home-made.

Cramps
(Fig. 4)

(K) Sash cramps, metal, pair about 2 ft., pair about 4 ft.

*(J) Handscrews, pair about 8 in. More as needed.

(H) *G* cramps. Alternatives to handscrews.

(G) Thumbscrews, 3–4 in. About 6 at least.

(I) Bench holdfast.

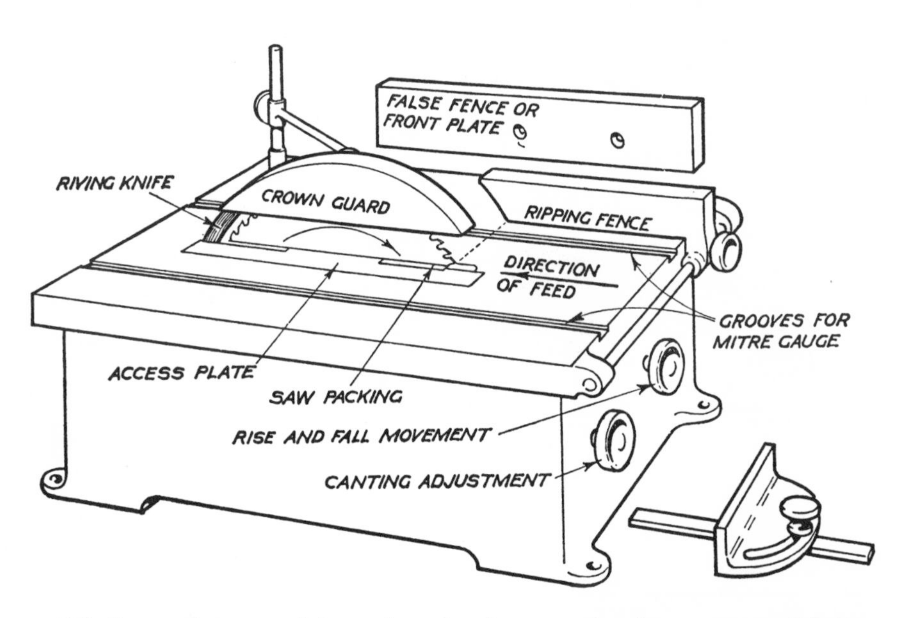

Of the various machines the circular saw is the most useful for general woodwork. It will rip, cross-cut, and mitre, and grooving and rebating can also be done on it. In some instances a moulding cutter block can be fitted. The drawing shows the essential features of the machine, though details vary in different makes.

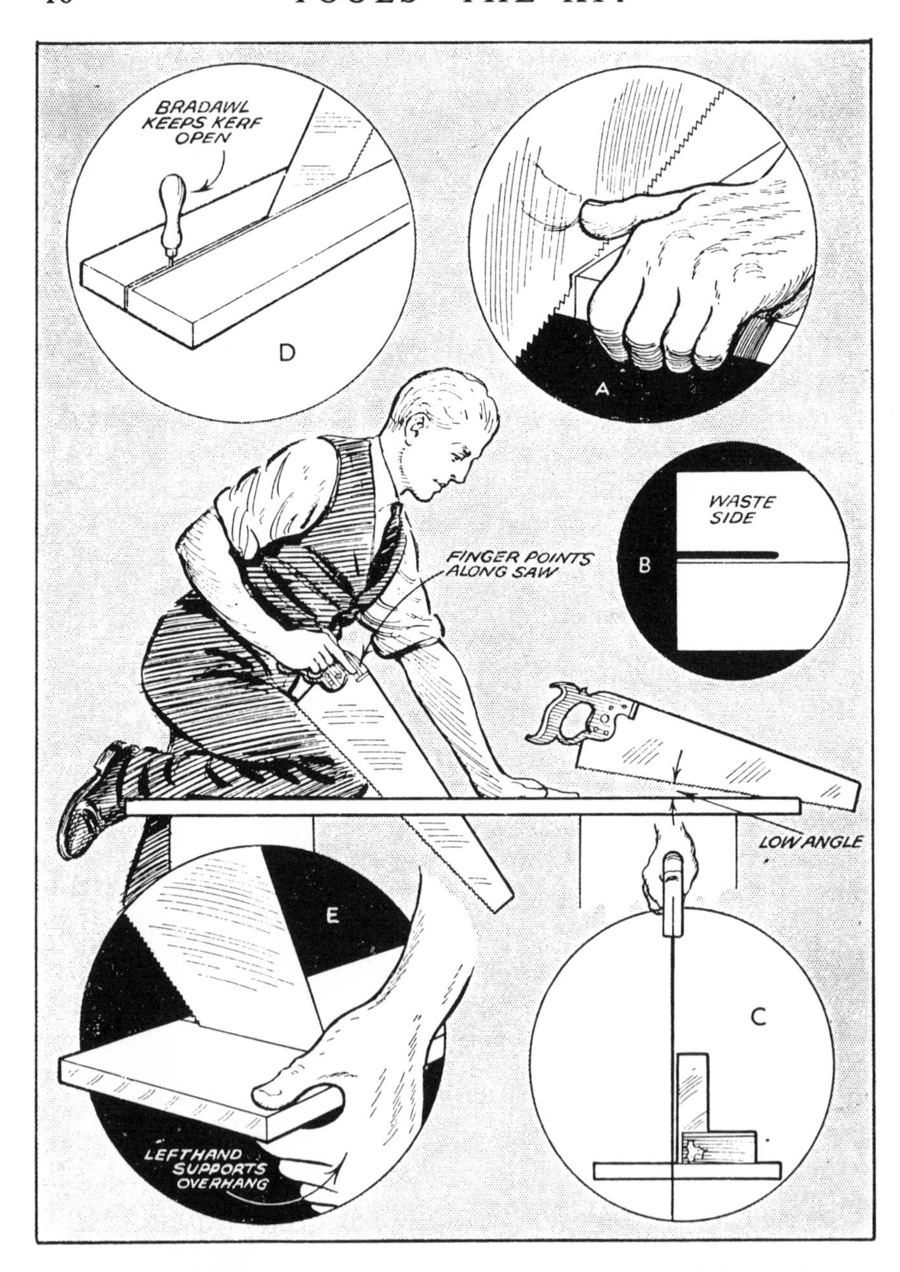

FIG. 1. POINTS TO FOLLOW WHEN USING THE HANDSAW

A. Starting the cut, the saw bearing against the left thumb. B. How saw cut is usually on waste side of line. C. Guide to holding the saw upright. D. Preventing wood from binding on saw. E. Supporting overhang on completion of cut.

CHAPTER II

HOW TO MAINTAIN AND USE TOOLS

YOU can learn the chief points to note about using tools in this chapter, but, to quote an old adage, skill to do comes of doing.

SAWS

Handsaw—This is used for cutting the larger pieces of wood. For instance, having marked out on a board the pieces you need, you cut them out with the handsaw. Choose a cross-cut saw as distinct from a rip-saw, because this can be used for cutting both with and across the grain. You can saw either with the wood laid on trestles or boxes, on the bench, or held in the vice. It is just a matter of which is the most convenient.

Fig. 1 shows the chief points to note when sawing on trestles or boxes. Start the cut with the saw held at a low angle because in this way you will be able to see whether the saw is in alignment with the line. This is most important because if you start wrong the saw will continue to go wrong, and in endeavouring to put it right you will probably err the other way. To start the cut hold the left hand over the end of the wood and raise the thumb so that the saw can bear against it as at (A) Fig. 1. This steadies the blade and enables you to start it in the exact position. Once the cut has been started an inch or so the hand can be brought back and used to help steady the wood.

Move the saw up and down a few times so that the teeth find their way into the wood, and when a reasonable start of an inch or so has been made hold the saw so that it makes an angle of about 45 deg. with the wood. It can then be worked in long, full, steady strokes. Forcing should never be necessary. If it cuts badly or slowly it needs sharpening. Apply light pressure on the down stroke to keep it up to its work. Note from Fig. 1 how the first finger of the right hand points along the blade. This is a great help in giving control.

Invariably the cut is made to one side of the line so that the plane can be used to trim the wood to the finished size. The idea is shown at (B) Fig. 1. It is a help if the line is not hidden by the saw. Thus when practicable place the wood so that the saw cuts to the right of the line. Sometimes this cannot be done, but it is an advantage to have the line visible. Remember that the saw must always be used on the waste side of the line.

It is clearly necessary to hold the saw upright. Undercutting may result in the wood being too small, and if the cut runs the other way a lot of unnecessary work in planing is involved. As a guide place a square of the wood as at (C). You will not want to keep it there all the time, but it will give you an indication of whether the saw is upright. Try to get the feel of the position when it is upright, and look at your edge after sawing to see

FIG. 2. HOW SAW IS HELD FOR THE OVERHAND RIP
To start the cut the saw is worked for a few strokes as at A.

FIG. 3. USING THE HANDSAW WITH WOOD HELD IN BENCH VICE
The wood should be held as low as possible to avoid chattering. For a long cut the wood may have to be moved several times.

whether you err one way or the other. It is worth while taking trouble early on because it will save you a great deal of work in other operations.

It sometimes happens when you have a long cut to make that the kerf will tend to close so that the wood binds on the saw. A bradawl stuck into the kerf as at (D) Fig. 1 will keep it open and prevent binding.

When cross-cutting a board never arrange the wood so that the cut is between the trestles. It will only cause the wood to bend as the cut progresses, and at best will cause the saw to bind. At worst the wood will snap off. Instead arrange the wood so that the piece to be sawn off overhangs at one end. The start of the cut is much as has already been described, but as the cut reaches its completion the left hand should be brought over so that the wood is supported (E). Otherwise it is liable to splinter off, especially when the overhanging piece is of any size.

Another method of ripping is what is known as the overhand rip shown in Fig. 2. Many consider it less back-aching. The wood is cramped down on to the bench with the line to be sawn overhanging the edge. To start the cut a few strokes are made with the saw pointed upwards as shown inset. As soon as a cut

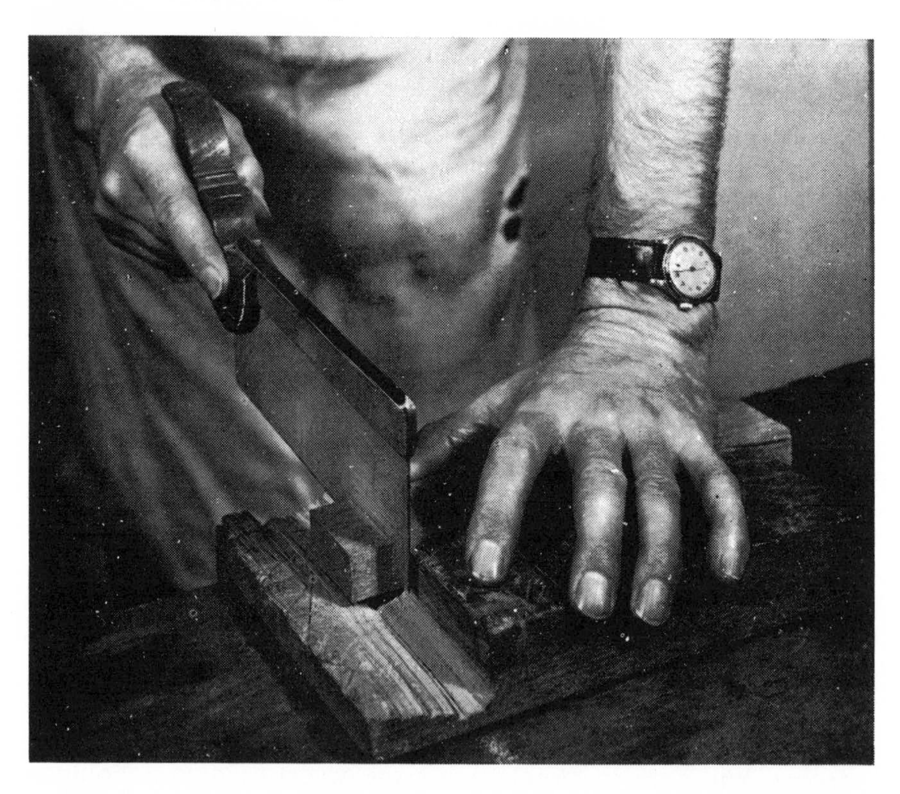

FIG. 4. USE OF BENCH HOOK TO HOLD WOOD WHEN SAWING
The left hand presses the wood hard up against the back of the hook to prevent it from moving backwards.

about $\frac{1}{2}$ in. long has been made the upright position is assumed, the saw grasped in both hands, and used for its full stroke. In some ways it is easier to tell when the saw is being held upright.

When the cut has to be along the middle of the board and it is inconvenient to fix it to the bench, you can lay the board on trestles and use the overhand rip, sitting astride the wood.

Comparatively short cuts or cuts in short wood are generally best made with the wood held in the vice as in Fig. 3. Do not give it more projection than is essential as otherwise it will chatter. To an extent it depends upon the thickness, but $\frac{7}{8}$ in. stuff, say, should project about 9 in. As the saw approaches the bench top the wood is raised in the vice. Remember to see that no tools are lying on the bench top, otherwise the saw may foul them.

The Backsaw—This is used for the general cutting up of smaller pieces, cutting joints, and so on. It is a matter for discretion whether the tenon saw or the dovetail saw is used. Sometimes it is convenient to hold the wood in the vice; sometimes the bench hook is better; occasionally it is desirable to fix the wood to the bench with a cramp.

Exact sizes are not important in a bench hook. The dimensions given at (A) Fig. 5 can be taken as a general guide. Note, however, that the lower strip which bears against the edge of the bench is held with a dowel at the end where the saw operates. This is because the saw eventually scores a rut across the wood with continual use, and a screw would be liable to be bared and so blunt the saw. Screws or nails can be used for fixing at the other end.

Fig. 4 shows the bench hook in use. Note how the ball of the left hand presses on to the edge of the wood being sawn, so keeping it up to the back of the hook. The lower edging of the bench hook prevents movement due to thrust from the saw, but unless the wood is kept up to the back it is liable to shift on the return stroke. The thumb of the left hand is used to steady the saw as the cut is started. Begin by raising the saw handle slightly so that the far corner is sawn first, and gradually lower it as the cut proceeds. For work of great accuracy, as when sawing the shoulders of a tenon, make a few strokes in this way, then start at the front corner. It is a matter of just bringing the saw level so joining the two cuts.

Learning to cut square is of great importance. A useful help in this respect is to square the line round on to all four surfaces of a thick block. Cut down about $\frac{1}{8}$ in. on one surface, turn the wood once towards you so that this cut faces you and make a second cut also about $\frac{1}{8}$ in. deep on the surface now on top. Repeat this until you have sawn all four surfaces, then gradually deepen each cut in turn. In this way the saw tends to run into the cuts already made.

When an end must be sawn perfectly square as when dowelling, or when sawing shoulders, it is a great help if the line is squared across with the chisel. By making a sloping cut against the line on the waste side a channel is formed in which the saw can run. In all these sawing operations note the pointed index finger of the right hand.

When the cut is being made with the wood held in the vice, make sure that the wood is level. Otherwise it will be awkward to saw to the line. On this score, when a cut has to be at an angle it is a help to position the wood so that the cut is vertical. In this way it is only necessary to hold the saw upright. This idea is often useful when sawing dovetails, the wood being fixed at a slight angle so that the saw is used upright.

Never try to use the saw without supporting the wood in one of the ways mentioned. Wood which is not firmly held will shift about, making the sawing difficult, and may result in a buckled saw blade. If you turn to Fig. 5 (B) you will see that a pivoted end support to the bench is suggested. This is excellent for holding wood whilst being sawn. Another and still simpler plan is to bore a ½ in. hole through the bench top near the tail, and knock a length of dowel rod into it as at (C). It can be tapped down flush when not required in use. At all events avoid the bad practice of holding wood against the bench stop when cutting right through. Eventually the saw scores a deep furrow, and when the stop is used for planing the wood is liable to tilt into the gash (see F).

For general sawing the bench hook is perfectly satisfactory, but when it is essential that the wood is held more rigidly you can use either the holdfast at (D) or the handscrew or cramp at (E). The former is extremely handy, but needs a fairly thick top to be effective as it relies upon the angularity of the post in the hole in the bench top to obtain its grip. If the top is thin you will have to thickness it on the underside locally. Of course, there must be clear space beneath.

Saws for Curves—The most generally useful tool for this is the bow saw (see page 2). Its blade is held in tension by a torniquet arrangement, and with its handles can be turned to cut in any direction. The advantage of the latter is that it enables a shape to be cut which is more or less parallel with an edge. It

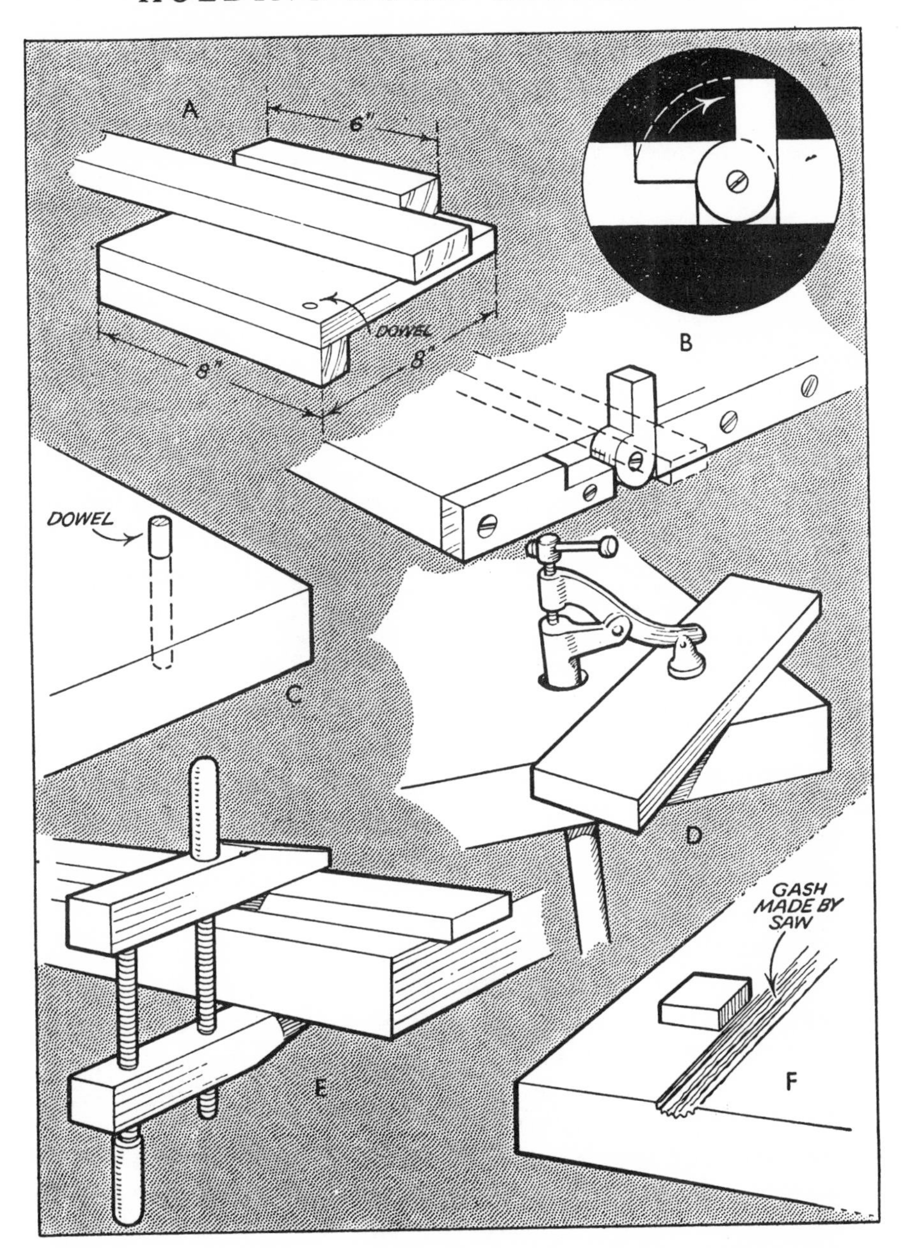

FIG. 5. METHODS OF HOLDING WOOD STILL WHILST BEING SAWN

A. Bench hook. B. Pivoting device at end of bench. C. Dowel at bench end. D. Bench holdfast. E. Handscrew. F. How bench top deteriorates if stop is used for sawing against.

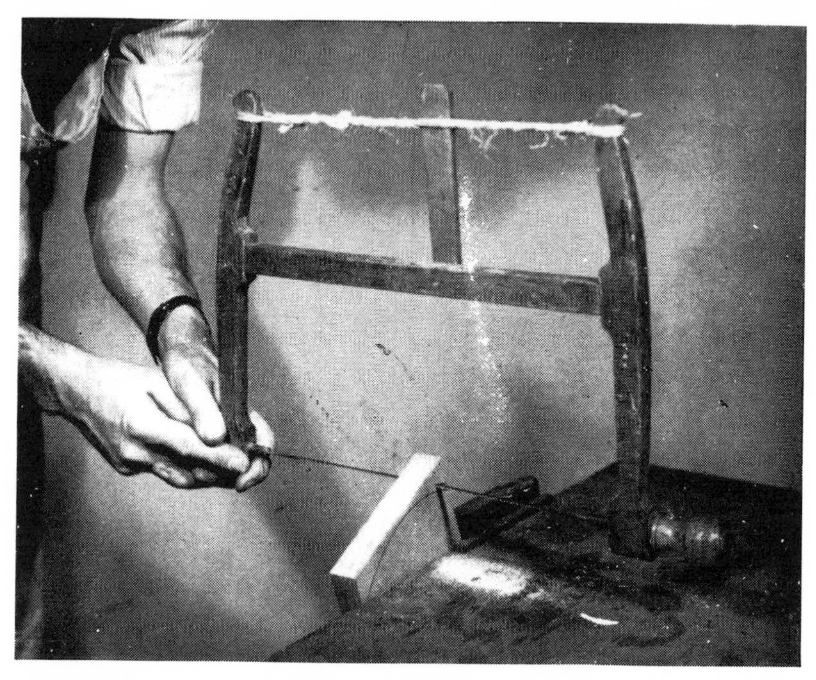

FIG. 6. HOW BOW SAW IS HANDLED, WOOD HELD IN VICE
The wood should be given the minimum projection so that it does not chatter.

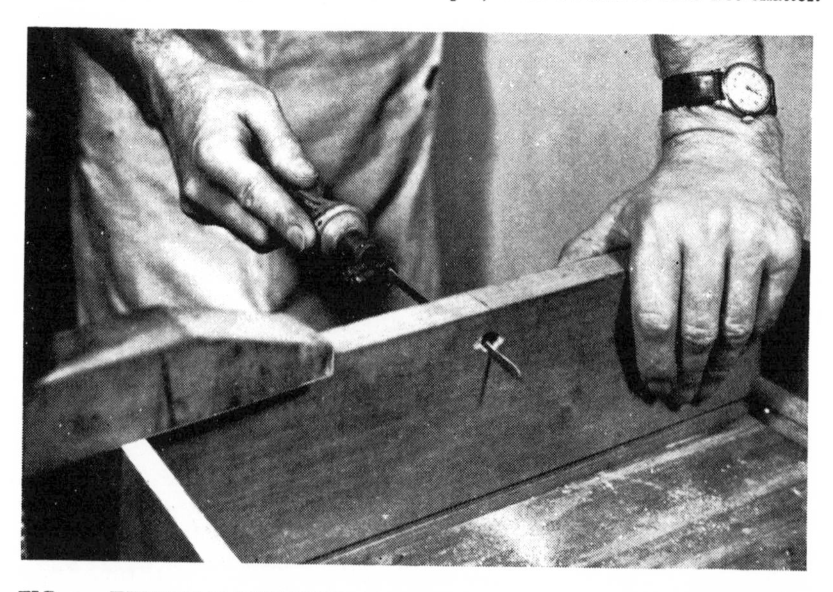

FIG. 7. KEYHOLE SAW USED TO CUT STRAIGHT PART OF KEYHOLE
Usually two hands are used. One only is shown to avoid hiding the tool.

will be realized that when set square the saw can only cut in from an edge a distance equal to that of the blade from the cross bar. By turning the handles, however, the saw can cut along the wood parallel with the edge. It is important that the blade is not twisted.

Square sawing is clearly important, as otherwise a great deal of unnecessary cleaning up is involved—in fact it may easily happen that the wood is spoilt by being undercut. It is purely a matter of judgment and practice. The best plan is to test your work as you saw it, note whether you are tending to cut one way or the other, and endeavour to correct it in future cutting. You can tell within a little whether the blade is square with the work. Fig. 6 shows the bow saw in use.

When a cut is to be made internally in the wood, that is, not emerging at the edge, it is necessary to bore a hole in the wood big enough to allow the saw blade to be passed through. This is bored on the waste side of the line, of course. The blade is held by a rivet which is easily punched out.

Generally the wood is held in the vice and it is advisable to keep it as low as possible to avoid vibration. This may necessitate raising the wood once or twice, but it makes the sawing much easier. Grasp the handle with both hands and work in long strokes, gradually turning the saw so that it follows the curve.

Another saw which has similar uses but is for smaller work is the coping saw (p. 2). In this case the wood is generally horizontal, and is fixed so that it overhangs the bench top. Avoid too great an overhang as this will cause chatter. Here upright cutting is essential. For a start you can hold a small square near the blade as a guide, but soon you should be able to do without it. Tension in this case is secured by turning the handle. Really thin wood is cut with the fretsaw, and a special table with a V cut at the projecting end is used.

Sometimes an internal cut has to be made at a distance from the edge too far for the bow saw to reach. You then have to use the keyhole saw. It is not a very efficient tool, however, as the blade has to rely upon its stiffness to keep it from buckling. The rule then is to give the blade the minimum projection consistent with a reasonable stroke. Fortunately not many cuts of this kind occur in woodwork, and the chief use of the saw is in sawing the sides of keyholes when fitting locks. The idea is shown in Fig. 7.

You could, of course, use a bow saw if necessary, but it would involve taking out the rivet and threading the blade through the hole to make two cuts of about ¼ in. in length.

Generally it is not advisable for the beginner to sharpen his own saws, as he will probably file the teeth unevenly, and a professional saw sharpener would charge more to put right the damage than the money saved. If you do decide to make the attempt, start on the saw with the largest teeth.

You will realize that, in addition to filing, the teeth have to be set—that is bent outwards alternately right and left. This is an essential feature of a saw in that it makes a kerf slightly wider than the thickness of its blade. Without it the saw would bind in the wood. The sharpener will give just the amount which experience has shown to be necessary. Excessive set is to be avoided since it means that you are removing wood unnecessarily (and so working harder than you need with no advantage).

CHISELS AND GOUGES

Apart from special chisels made for out-of-the-way jobs, there are three general kinds : firmer, bevelled-edge, and mortise. Of these the first (A, Fig. 2, p. 4) is the bench tool used for general purposes. It is robustly made so that it will stand up to the work involved in chopping dovetails and other joints, yet can if necessary be used for finer work such as paring. The latter, however, is better done with a lighter chisel kept specially for the job, the bevelled-edge chisel shown at (B, Fig. 2, p. 4). Mortising, which calls for heavy blows with the mallet, and for a certain amount of levering over, needs the specially made chisel (C, Fig. 2, p. 4). Two kinds are available, the heavy mortise chisel, and the lighter sash mortise which is strong enough for most work without being so cumbersome.

Paring—A typical operation, that of paring a groove is shown in Fig. 8. The left hand can either be held as shown, or the fingers can be brought over the top leaving the thumb below. In all cases, no matter what the operation, both hands are behind the cutting edge. In a job of this kind the sides of the groove are sawn first, and one or two intermediate shallower saw cuts made to break up the grain. The chisel is then taken in at a slight angle as in Fig. 9, the handle being struck either with the palm of the hand or the mallet. The waste is removed down to about the diagonal. Then, reversing the wood, work from the other side

FIG. 8. PARING GROOVE WITH CHISEL
To finish the groove the chisel should be worked with a slicing action. It is often an advantage to pass the fingers of the left hand over the chisel and rest the hand or arm on the vice to steady it.

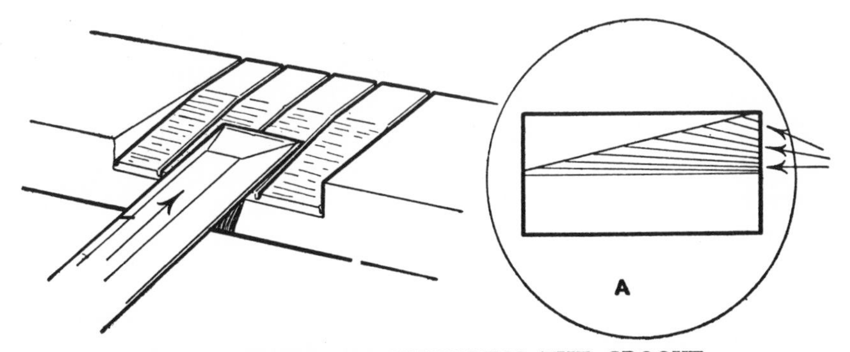

FIG. 9. STAGES IN CHISELLING THE GROOVE

as at A. To finish off work as in Fig. 8, using the chisel with a slicing action if possible. This not only eases the cut, but shows more clearly the high parts which need reducing.

Fig. 10 shows another typical paring operation. Note that the

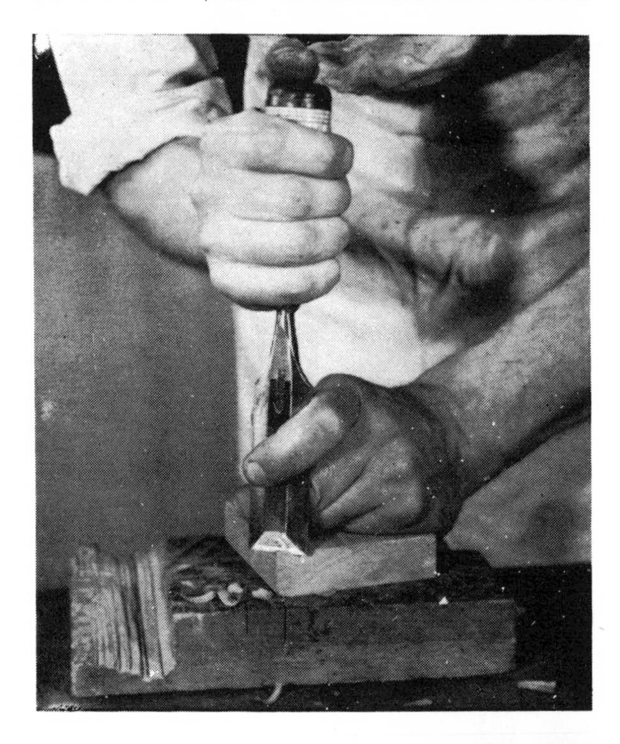

FIG. 10. CUTTING DOWN CORNER OF WOOD WITH CHISEL

The left hand presses down on the wood and steadies it, and the fingers guide the blade.

FIG. 11. CHOPPING A MORTISE

It is advisable to stand at the end of the wood so that any slope to right or left is detected.

wood must be held on a flat surface, as any unevenness may cause the lower edge to split out.

Mortising—Fig. 11 shows a door rail being mortised, and there are several points to note. Firstly the worker stands at the end of the wood, because it is then obvious whether the chisel leans to the right or left (it is clearly important that the mortise is upright). Secondly the wood is cramped down over a solid part of the bench, generally over a leg. Also a thumbscrew is put on at the end to prevent any tendency for the wood to split. It is usual to leave about an inch of wood beyond the mortise to minimize this risk, but even so the thumbscrew is advisable. When several stiles are being mortised they can be cramped

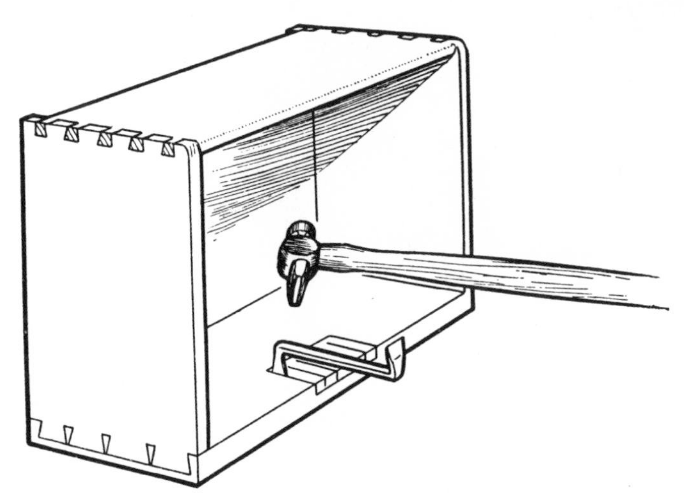

FIG. 12. HOW DRAWER LOCK CHISEL IS USED
This illustrates its use in a confined space.

together side by side. To lighten the work much of the waste can be removed by boring a series of holes with a twist bit slightly narrower than the mortise width.

The first cut is made at about the centre of the mortise and is shallow only. The next, about $\frac{1}{8}$ in. from the first, is deeper, and so on until within about $\frac{1}{16}$ in. of the end when much of the waste can be levered away. A slightly narrower chisel is useful for this. Work up to the other end in the same way, levering away the waste as you proceed. The depth, of course, has already been decided, and it is useful to stick a piece of paper to the chisel as a depth guide. When the mortise has been cleared in this way the final cuts can be taken on the lines at each end. This cleans up the dubbed-over ends caused by the levering.

Drawer Lock Chisel—This, shown at (F, Fig. 2, p. 4), is intended for use in the restricted space of a drawer. It is also useful when chopping the recess into which the bolt shoots in

FIG. 13. SHARPENING THE CHISEL ON THE OILSTONE
The chisel is ground at an angle of about 25 deg. When finishing on the oilstone the angle is in the region of 30 deg.

the drawer rail. Fig. 12 shows how it can be struck with the side of the hammer. It will be realized that it would be practically impossible to chop down with the ordinary chisel.

Sharpening the Chisel—This procedure is much the same as when sharpening a plane iron. The usual grinding angle is about 25 deg., whilst sharpening on the oilstone is in the region of 30 deg., except in the case of mortise chisels and those reserved for chopping which are better sharpened at nearer 35 deg. as this gives a stronger edge. Fig. 13 shows the sharpening operation. The burr is turned back on the stone (again as in the plane cutter), and it is vital that it is held flat as otherwise it will be impossible to pare with it properly. The burr is got rid of finally by stropping.

Gouges—These are not widely used, but are required sometimes for forming a hollow or recess. Carving tools are dealt with more fully in the chapter on carving. The firmer gouge has the bevel at the outside, and is for general work. To sharpen it hold it at right angles with the stone with the bevel flat. Raise the handle a trifle so that just the edge touches, and work back and forth with a rocking movement until a burr is turned up at the inside. To turn this back use the oilstone slip at the inside, keeping it flat. The curvature of the slip should be slightly quicker than that of the gouge.

Scribing gouges are bevelled inside, and must be sharpened with the slip. To turn back the burr hold the outside of the gouge flat on the stone and half revolve it, keeping it flat.

TOOLS FOR BORING

The Brace—You can obtain either the simple brace or the ratchet brace. The latter is well worth its extra cost, partly because it enables you to work in a corner where a full revolution of the brace is impossible, and partly because it is an advantage to have the hand in a certain position when boring a large hole as it gives more purchase. For average purposes an 8 in. sweep is about right.

It is fairly easy to tell when the brace leans to right or left, but more difficult to detect whether it bears away from or towards you. You can often make use of this fact when the verticality of a hole is more important in one direction than in another. For instance when boring dowel holes in a rail it would clearly be fatal if the holes were to lean sideways. Consequently it is advisable to stand at the end of the wood as shown in Fig. 14.

Using the Brace—Various aids can be had as a guide, one being the square placed alongside the bit. In the case of a hole being bored in the end of a post two straight strips can be cramped temporarily to the post on adjacent faces as a guide as in Fig. 15. Another plan is to ask an assistant to stand alongside to indicate whether the brace is vertical.

Generally it is advisable to hold the head on the left hand when boring, as it helps both in steadying the brace and in increasing the pressure. Sometimes it is more convenient to hold the wood

FIG. 14. BORING HOLES IN STILE PREPARATORY TO MORTISING
Note how the worker stands at the end of the bench so that any slope to right or left is detected. See also how the head is used to steady the brace.

in the vice, and then pressure is increased by pressing with the body behind the left hand. For holes, the accuracy of which is important, the method is not recommended as it is difficult to tell whether the brace is square with the wood.

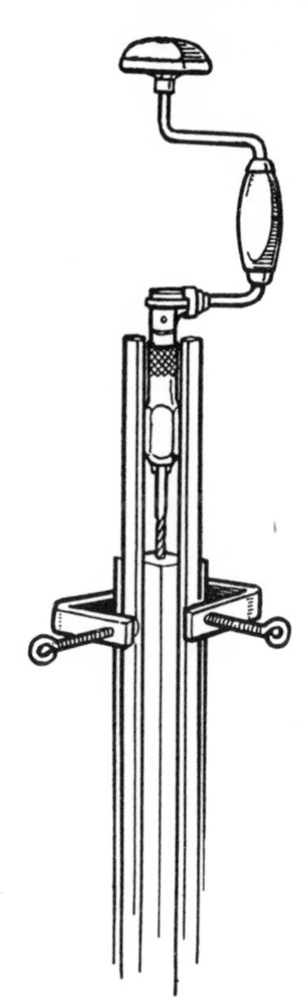

FIG. 15. AID TO VERTICAL BORING

The brace is held in line with the two rods cramped to the wood.

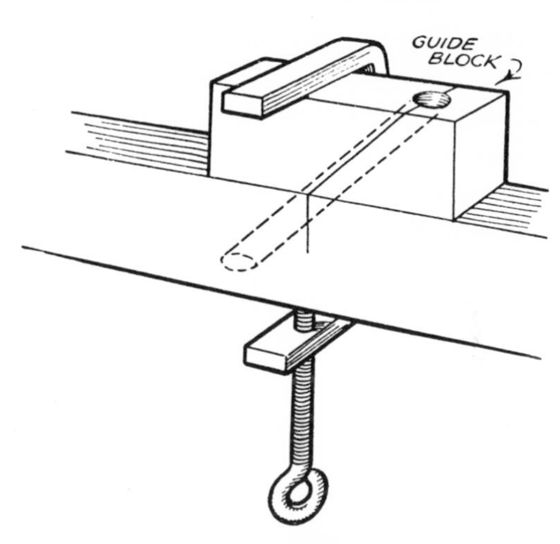

FIG. 16. HOW TO ENSURE BORING AT CORRECT ANGLE

Apart from giving the right angle this ensures that the bit starts in the correct position.

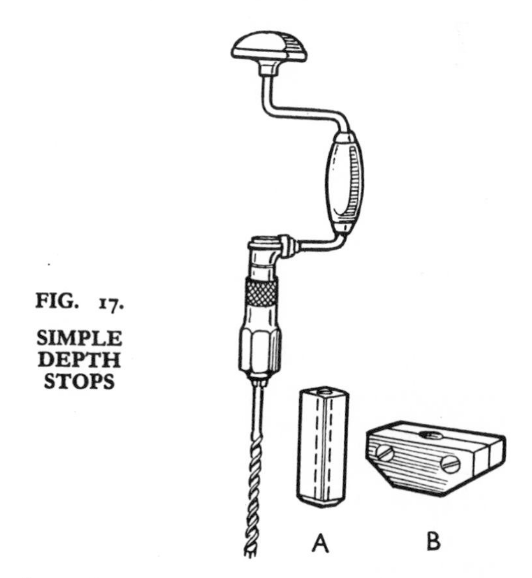

FIG. 17. SIMPLE DEPTH STOPS

When a hole has to be bored accurately at an angle a guide should be made as in Fig. 16. This is cramped to the wood and the bit passed through the hole.

Bits—For dowelling the twist bit is invariably used. Owing to its straight spiral shank it is not liable to wander with the grain if properly started, and it cuts cleanly. Furthermore its screw point draws it into the wood without undue labour. It is rather delicate, however, both its thread and cutters being easily damaged if contact is made with a hidden nail. For dowel work an extra short bit is available.

For boring to a definite depth a stop is used. An adjustable metal type is available, but it is liable to mark the surface, and is

FIG. 18. FORSTNER BIT AND HOLES IT BORES

This can work close up to the edge as shown.

specially awkward when the hole is being bored into an edge owing to the liability of the bearing surfaces to foul the edges of the wood. The simple devices in Fig. 17 are effective and make no mark that a single shaving will not remove. That at (A) is made specially for the particular job in hand, whilst (B) is adjustable to any position along the spiral of the bit.

For shallow holes, or holes right through thin wood the centre bit is used. For the latter purpose the hole should be taken in from one side until the point just emerges beneath, when the hole is completed from the other side. The centre bit with thread point has an advantage in that it pulls itself into the wood and saves the necessity for pressure. The expansion bit (N), Fig. 2,

p. 4, is useful for larger holes. It saves having to keep a wide range of centre bits.

Screw holes are generally bored with the shell or spoon bit, (K, Fig. 2, p. 4). Two or three sizes are kept to suit the general sizes of screws being used. There is a tendency, however, for the morse drill as used by engineers to replace the shell bit, and it has the advantage of being available in a wide range of sizes and of cutting easily. These drills can be obtained with square shank to fit the brace, though generally the plain round drill is held sufficiently tightly. Many men keep a small hand drill in which to use the smaller sizes of drills.

Half-twist bits with gimlet points are quick borers, and are useful for tough hardwoods. They should never be used on softwoods or near the edge, however, as they are liable to split the grain.

For screw work, the snail countersink at (H, Fig. 2, p. 4), gives a clean finish. Sometimes it is necessary to enlarge the countersinking in a brass fitting, and the rose countersink (I) is used for this. For the rapid driving of screws and when considerable purchase is needed the turnscrew bit is useful. It is essential that a strong downward pressure is maintained.

As mentioned above, the spoon bit or morse drill is used for the shank hole for screws. For the thread hole a convenient tool for small screws is the bradawl. When the normal round type is used the cutting edge should be at right angles with the grain. A most useful type, however, is the bird-cage maker's or square awl. It cuts well and is not liable to split the grain even when used near an edge. Furthermore it has a point rather than a square end.

For the screw holes of small fittings the reciprocating drill with spiral stem is useful. When the hole has to be extra small a needle can be ground to a cutting edge and used, the eye being broken off.

Forstner Bit—This (Fig. 18) is a clean-cutting bit which can be used for some jobs which would be impossible with other bits. Although it has a slightly projecting centre, it is guided by its circular rim. It is specially useful when a hole has to be bored deeply without penetrating right through. This would be impossible with a centre or twist bit since the centre point would project at the other side. To bore a hole in an exact position calls for care in that the centre point has the minimum projection and is concealed by the rim. When starting it is often an advantage to give it a couple of backward turns first so that its rim cuts the circle before the cutters begin to scoop out the waste.

Sharpening Bits—The centre bit has three chief parts, and they should project in the following order : centre point, nicker, and cutter as shown in Fig. 19. Use a fine file to sharpen as in Fig. 20. Stick the point of the bit into a block of wood to steady

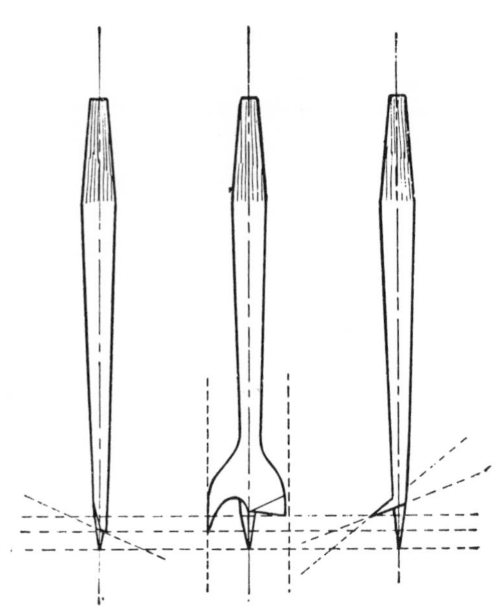

FIG. 19. DETAILS OF THE CENTRE BIT
This shows order of projection of working parts.

it, and sharpen at the angle shown in Fig. 20. Note that the nicker edge runs at an angle (Fig. 19) so that it cuts rather than scratches. This is sharpened on the inside. It is important that the outside is not burred over. The cutter is sharpened on top whilst the edges of the centre point may need a slight rub. The latter is generally triangular in section.

Twist bits are sharpened similarly, but the screw point must not be touched. If possible use a small file with a safe edge. Sharpen the nickers on the inside only, and the cutters on the side farthest from the screw point. If a burr is set up on the outside of the nickers the bit can be rubbed *flat* on the oilstone.

Occasionally the countersink calls for a rub up with a small rat-tail and flat file. For the Forstner bit grind a small three-cornered file until the serrations are removed, and use this as a three-cornered scraper on the inside only.

A book dealing exhaustively with hand tools is *Tools for Woodwork*, by C. H. Hayward, published by Evans Brothers Ltd.

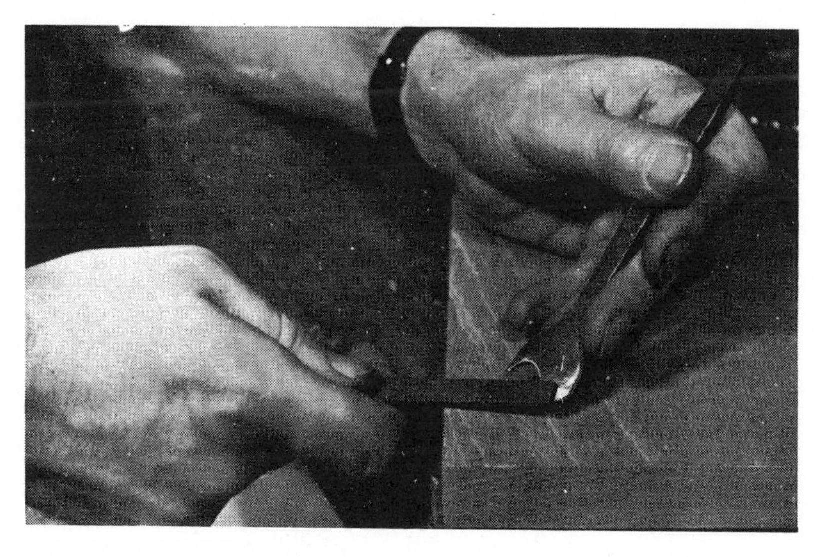

FIG. 20. HOW THE CENTRE BIT IS SHARPENED WITH THE FILE

The point is stuck into a block of wood to steady it, and the file used on the upper side of the cutter. The nicker is rubbed up on the inside only.

CHAPTER III

HOW TO MAINTAIN AND USE TOOLS *(Continued)*

PLANING

YOU plane wood for two reasons ; to make it straight, flat, and square ; and to make it smooth. For the former purpose the plane should be as long as possible in relation to the wood. A short plane would dip into the hollows too much, whereas a long plane is prevented from doing so by its own length. In the woodworking trades the craftsman uses either the fore plane or the trying plane to make an edge straight or to make a joint. For the preliminary planing to remove saw marks or other roughness he uses the Jack plane. This is long enough not to dip into the surface, and, by setting it fairly coarse, it removes the roughness quickly. In this way the trying plane is reserved for accurate work, and thus keeps its edge longer and can always be set fine.

This is the ideal arrangement, but if you have not yet been able to get a trying or fore plane, you will have to use the Jack plane for jointing as well as for the rougher operations. Should this be the case you will find that your best plan when you have a number of similar pieces to prepare will be to set the plane slightly coarse and remove the roughness from them all. You can then re-set the plane (sharpening it if necessary) and make them all true.

The truing of wood enables all marking out to be done, and joints to be cut. It does not follow, however, that because wood is true that it is necessarily smooth. The grain of wood is liable to tear out if not planed in the right way, and a plane as set for truing is not adapted to deal with this. Consequently you have the smoothing plane which is of handy size for the work, and which is specially set to prevent the grain from tearing out. We shall see more about this under the heading of setting a plane.

Sharpening the Plane—When you first buy a plane the cutter (or iron as it is generally termed) has been ground on a grindstone, but is useless until it has been given a really fine edge on an

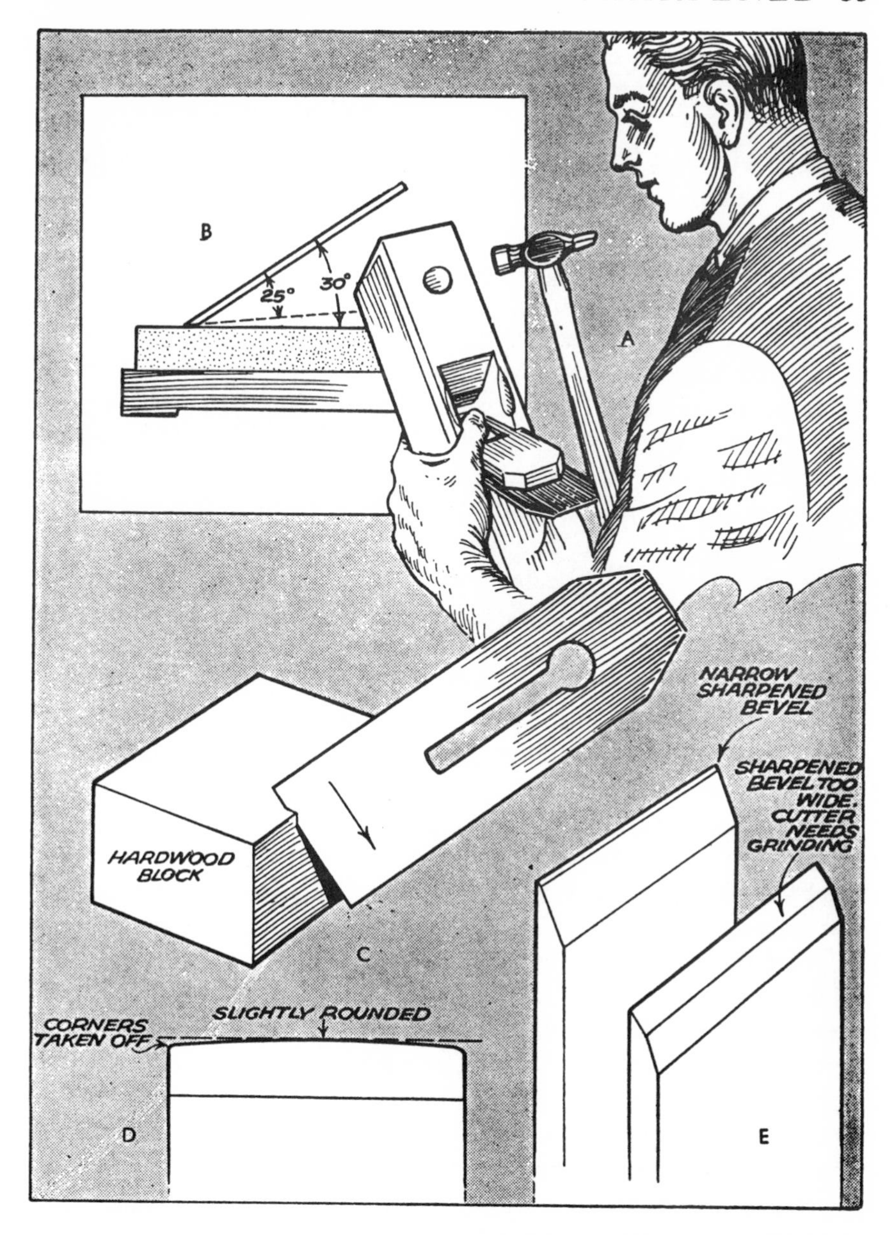

FIG. 1. POINTS TO KNOW ABOUT THE PLANE CUTTER

A. How wood plane cutter is removed, striking button being hit. B. Grinding and sharpening angles. C. Removing burr on wood block. D. Shape of cutter edge. Curve is exaggerated. E. How sharpening creates narrow bevel. Continued sharpening makes this too wide.

FIG. 2. PLANE CUTTER BEING SHARPENED ON OILSTONE
The cutter can be worked with a straight or elliptical movement.

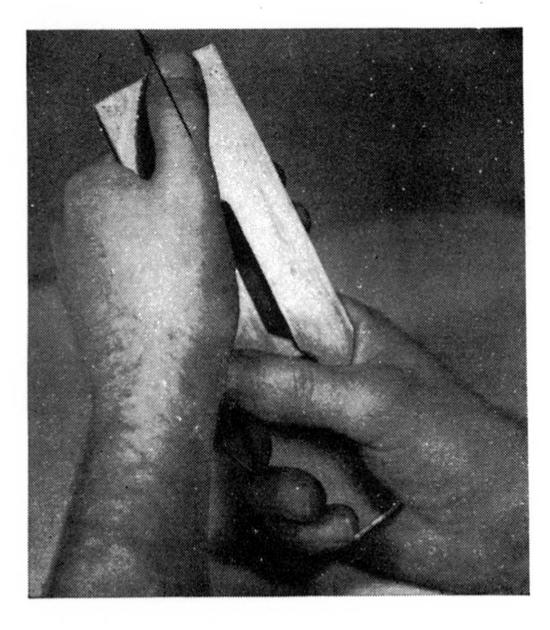

FIG. 3. TESTING WHETHER BURR HAS BEEN TURNED UP BY SHARPENING
The thumb is moved across the edge. A burr should be detected.

oilstone. To save unnecessary work the grinding is done at a lower angle than that used on the oilstone. In this way only the extreme edge has to be rubbed. The idea is shown at (B), Fig. 1.

To remove the cutter from a wood plane, hold the latter with the left hand so that the thumb passes into the escapement and bears on the back iron as in Fig. 1, (A). Strike the front of the plane (on the striking button if it has one) as shown, and the wedge and cutter will slip out, but are prevented from dropping by the thumb. A wood smoothing plane is struck at the rear.

You will find that a back or cap iron is held to the cutter with a bolt. Holding the two on the bench and gripping the cutter at the unsharpened end release the bolt until it can slide along the groove in the cutter and out at the hole. There is no need to completely remove the bolt—in fact it is better not to do so as otherwise it may be lost in sawdust or shavings. Pour a few drops of oil on to the oilstone and place the cutter on it so that the ground bevel lies flat. Raise the hands a trifle so that only the extreme edge touches the stone, and you have the right angle. The latter is not critical, but if you aim at 30 deg. you will be about right. The grinding angle is 25 deg. (see (B), Fig. 1).

Fig. 2 shows the sharpening operation. Hold the cutter so that it is skewed at a slight angle, and work it back and forth either straight or with an oval movement. Some prefer one, some the other. After a few rubs draw the thumb *across* the back as shown in Fig. 3. If it has been sharpened you will be able to detect a burr or roughness since the sharpening turns back the edge. When this appears reverse the cutter *flat* on the stone and rub it back and forth a few times to bend back the burr as shown in Fig. 4.

You need to get rid of this burr as otherwise it may be forced back on to the edge and blunt it. Draw the edge once or twice across a hardwood block as at (C), Fig. 1. This will take it off but leaves the edge rather rough. Put this right by giving a few rubs as in Fig. 2, and once again reverse flat as in Fig. 4. Finally strop it alternately on the bevel and on the back on a piece of leather dressed with oil and fine emery powder.

As you complete the sharpening look at the edge in the light. A keen edge cannot be seen, whereas a blunt one will reflect a thin line of light. In the same way any gashes will show as flecks of light. When you get used to it you will be able to tell by the appearance when the edge is keen. The burr is an indication that the edge has been turned, but does not reveal gashes.

For the trying plane and smoothing plane the edge should be slightly rounded as shown in exaggeration at (D), Fig. 1, with the corners taken off. As the Jack plane has generally to take a heavier shaving the curvature can be slightly increased. After being sharpened several times the sharpened bevel will become

FIG. 4. TURNING BACK BURR ON OILSTONE
The cutter must be held flat. To get rid of the burr it is turned back and forth by stropping.

wide as at (E), and it is then time to have the cutter ground so that there is not so much metal to remove.

Setting—To set the plane place the back iron in position and turn the bolt until finger tight. The distance of the back iron from the edge depends upon the work to be done. For the Jack plane which takes coarse shavings it might be about $\frac{1}{16}$ in. or more; for the trying plane which takes fine shavings rather less as at (A), Fig. 5; whilst for the smoothing plane when set for cleaning up difficult wood with twisted grain it should be as close as it is possible to get it. When correct tighten the bolt right home.

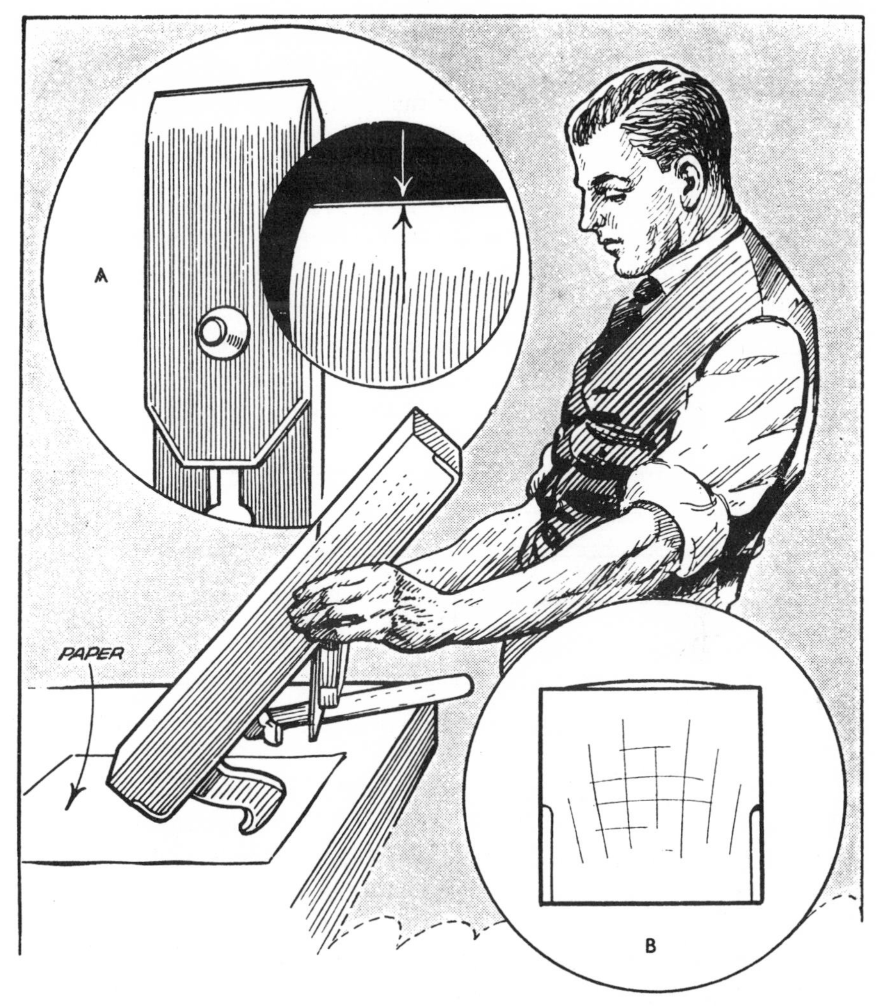

FIG. 5. HOW PLANE IS HELD WHEN SETTING
The back iron is set back as at A, the distance depending upon the work to be done. When sighting the plane the cutter should appear as a black line (B).

Place the cutter and back iron in the escapement, back iron uppermost, and hold in position with the thumb of the left hand. Look along the sole as in Fig. 5, with a piece of white paper or light coloured wood beneath. The cutter should appear as a thin black line tapering to nothing at the sides. You can adjust the cutter until correct. Place the wedge in position and lightly tap with the hammer. Take another look along the face, and if there is insufficient projection tap the cutter out. If one corner sticks out strike the rear of the cutter at the side. When the cutter projects too much tap the striking button lightly. When all is in order knock the wedge home. There is no need to hammer it home really hard—you may distort the plane if you do so.

Metal planes of the adjustable kind are never struck with the hammer. All adjusting is done by the screw or lever, and the cutter is held in position by the lever cap. Apart from this the sharpening and setting are the same, though some men never have the cutter ground (unless it is badly gashed) since it is quite thin.

Incidentally the soles of all planes should be lubricated to assist working. With metal planes it is essential. A good plan is to

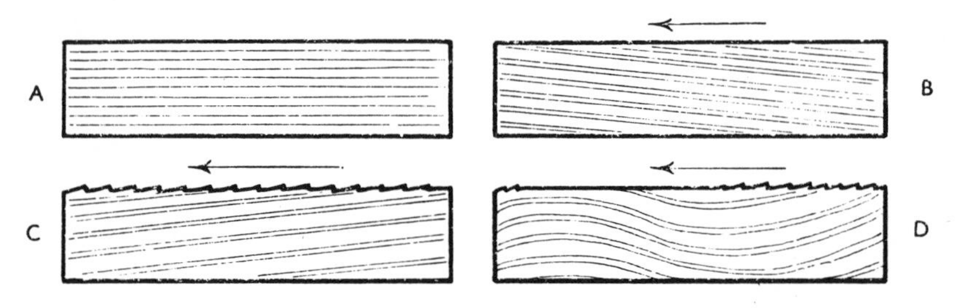

FIG. 6. HOW GRAIN AFFECTS DIRECTION OF PLANING

keep a wad of cotton wool lightly soaked in linseed oil on a piece of wood and draw the plane across this occasionally. Another plan is to rub a piece of candlegrease across the sole.

Use of the Back Iron—At this point perhaps we had better consider the purpose of the back iron. It is needed solely because of the tendency of some woods to tear out owing to the undulating grain, leaving little depressions in the surface which look unsightly. If the grain of the wood were always straight and parallel with the edge as at (A), Fig. 6 there would be no tendency for the grain to tear out. As, however, a tree is never perfectly straight it is inevitable that the saw which cuts the boards will run across the grain in parts, and you get grain which either slopes or undulates. At (B), for example, the grain runs at an angle. If planed in the direction shown by the arrow it still would not tear out, but if turned the other way as at (C) it would inevitably tear as the plane was taken across it. First a split would start. It would run in the direction of the grain, that is downwards, but the raised shaving would be caught up by the cutter edge, wrenched up, and broken, and the same thing repeated over and over again until the end of the wood was reached. The trouble, you will observe, is that the cutter is not actually cutting most of the time because the split runs in front of it. It is only when the cutter edge catches up the split that it cuts and then the shaving is more or less wrenched up. If therefore you could break the shaving immediately it is raised it would lose its strength and the split would not develop. That is the purpose of the back iron, to break the shaving as soon as possible after it is raised.

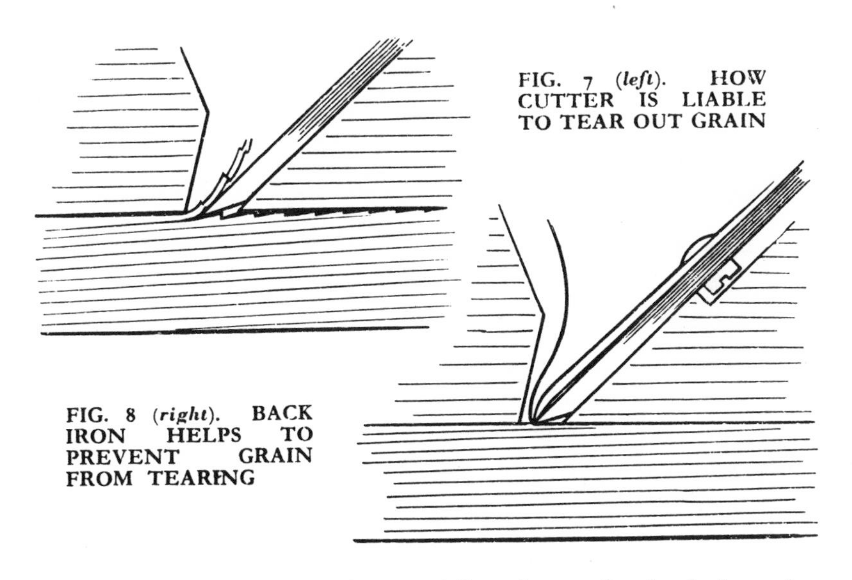

FIG. 7 (*left*). HOW CUTTER IS LIABLE TO TEAR OUT GRAIN

FIG. 8 (*right*). BACK IRON HELPS TO PREVENT GRAIN FROM TEARING

The idea is shown in Fig. 8. The closer the back iron is to the cutting edge the sooner the shaving is broken, and the less liable it is to tear out the grain. Matters are helped, too, by having a small mouth to the plane. Fig. 7 shows how this restricts the lift of the shaving even when there is no back iron, causing it to break earlier than it would if the mouth were excessively wide. The fact that the smoothing plane is used only for thin shavings also helps in that the thin shaving is not so strong as a thick one and breaks earlier or just bends away.

It will be realized, however, that the close-set back iron has a disadvantage in that the resistance to the movement of the plane is increased. It is therefore a matter for compromise, the back iron being set farther back for medium or coarse shavings at cost of slightly increased liability to tear out.

In the case of the wood at (C), Fig. 6, the simplest plan would be to turn it the other way round as at (B), and it is always worth while looking at the edge of the wood before planing to see the direction of the grain. Sometimes it makes little difference as in the example at (D), which would tear out in parts whichever way

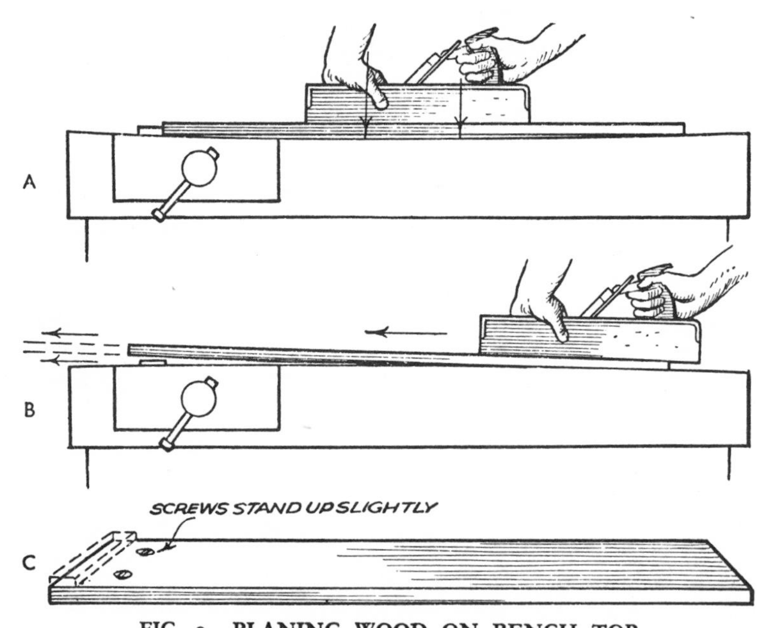

FIG. 9. PLANING WOOD ON BENCH TOP
A. Hollow bench top makes centre difficult to reach. B. Round top causes wood to lift at front. C. Planing board.

the plane were taken. Another difficult case is when the grain runs in streaks side by side as in some varieties of mahogany. Alternate streaks will be smooth whilst the others tear out. If planed the other way the reverse happens.

Using the Plane—When the surface of wood is planed the wood is generally laid on the bench and the bench stop knocked up to prevent it from moving. There is one precaution to take, however. Bench tops are frequently not flat, and the weight of the plane and the pressure used will cause the wood to bend. This may not matter a lot when it is merely being smoothed, but it may upset the accuracy when it is being trued. In Fig. 9 at (A), for instance, owing to the hollowness of the top, the wood is bent down under the pressure, and in all probability the plane would cease to cut when in the middle of the wood. At (B) the bench top is round, and consequently the far end of the wood is raised when the plane is started, and the whole thing is shot forward. These two illustrations are exaggerated, but they show the idea.

Generally the best plan is to use a planing board which is perfectly flat, and put the wood on this. This board is any plain, true piece of wood which is rather longer than the wood to be planed. A couple of screws driven half-way in at the far end serve as a stop. They can be given the projection to suit the work in

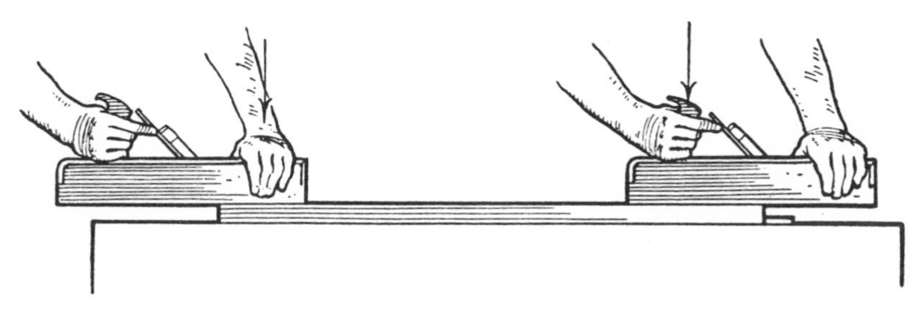

FIG. 10. WHERE TO PRESS DOWN WHEN PLANING A BOARD

hand. When these are undesirable in that they might mark the wood, they are withdrawn and replaced by a crosspiece screwed on as shown by the dotted lines at (C), Fig. 9. Even when the planing board is used or when the bench top is true, it is usually a help to put a shaving beneath the middle of the wood, especially when narrow stuff is being dealt with. Incidentally if a large piece of wood is liable to shift about on the bench top whilst being planed you can help to steady it by chalking the bench top, or sprinkling it with plaster of paris.

The usual trouble the beginner finds is that he is inclined to make the surface round, especially at the ends. To avoid this adopt the plan shown in Fig. 10. At the start of the stroke press well down at the front of the plane, and as the far end is reached transfer the pressure to the rear. After a while you will find that the process will be practically automatic. Note how the left hand grasps the front of the plane.

Testing for Wind—Nowadays most timber is bought ready planed, and requires little more than a skim to finish it after cutting to size, jointing, etc. When it is rough, however, it needs testing for truth, and this means that it must be straight in length, flat in

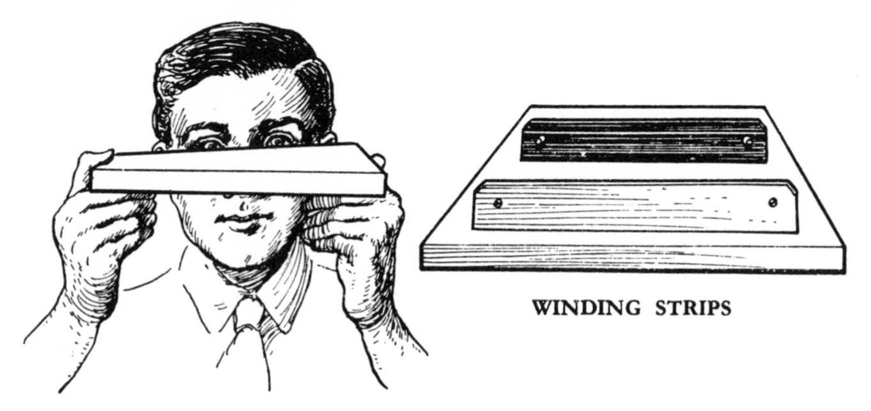

FIG. 11. DETECTING WHETHER WOOD IS IN WINDING

width, and free of wind (pronounced as when you *wind* a clock). The straight-edge is used to test straightness, but the winding strips are necessary to test for winding. However, a quick test is to look across the surface as in Fig. 11. Any serious winding will be at once obvious. For a closer test use the winding strips. If

FIG. 12. WHERE TO PLANE WOOD IN WINDING

the wood is true the top edge of the near strip will appear parallel with the inlaid line in the back one.

To correct a surface which winds work the plane diagonally from one high corner to the other as shown in Fig. 12. The plane itself is handy to use as a straight-edge. Laid at an angle across the wood it gives a quick indication of truth.

Edge Planing—When an edge is being planed the plane is held as in Fig. 15, (A). Note how the fingers of the left hand pass beneath the sole and bear against the side of the wood. They thus act as a sort of fence, so that the plane projects the same distance from the edge throughout the cut. This is important

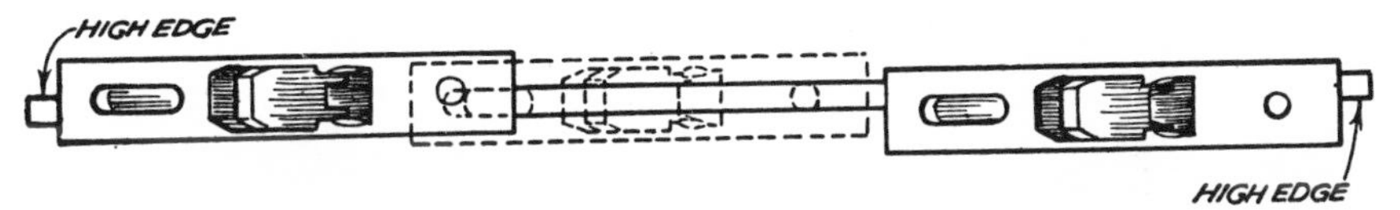

FIG. 13. CORRECTING EDGE OUT OF SQUARE AT ONE OR BOTH ENDS

because correct manipulation enables an edge which is not square to be put right. The idea is shown in Fig. 15, (B). If the plane is held central on the wood the shaving will be thicker towards the middle of the plane than towards the side owing to the slight curvature of the cutting edge. When therefore an edge is out of square the plane is held so that it projects more on the high side as at (C). The sole is held flat on the edge, of course. Never

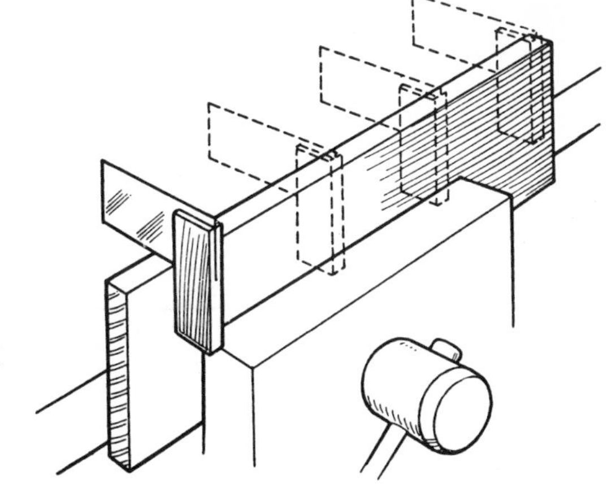

FIG. 14. TESTING EDGE FOR SQUARENESS

The square is used in several positions along the length.

attempt to rock the plane to correct an edge which is out of truth.

Sometimes an edge is square at one end and out of truth at the other; or out of truth at both ends but in opposite directions. Start the stroke with the plane towards the high side, and gradually shift the position of the fingers of the left hand on the sole so that the plane shifts to the other side as the ends of the stroke is reached as shown in Fig. 13. Fig. 14 shows how the edge is tested at various positions along the wood.

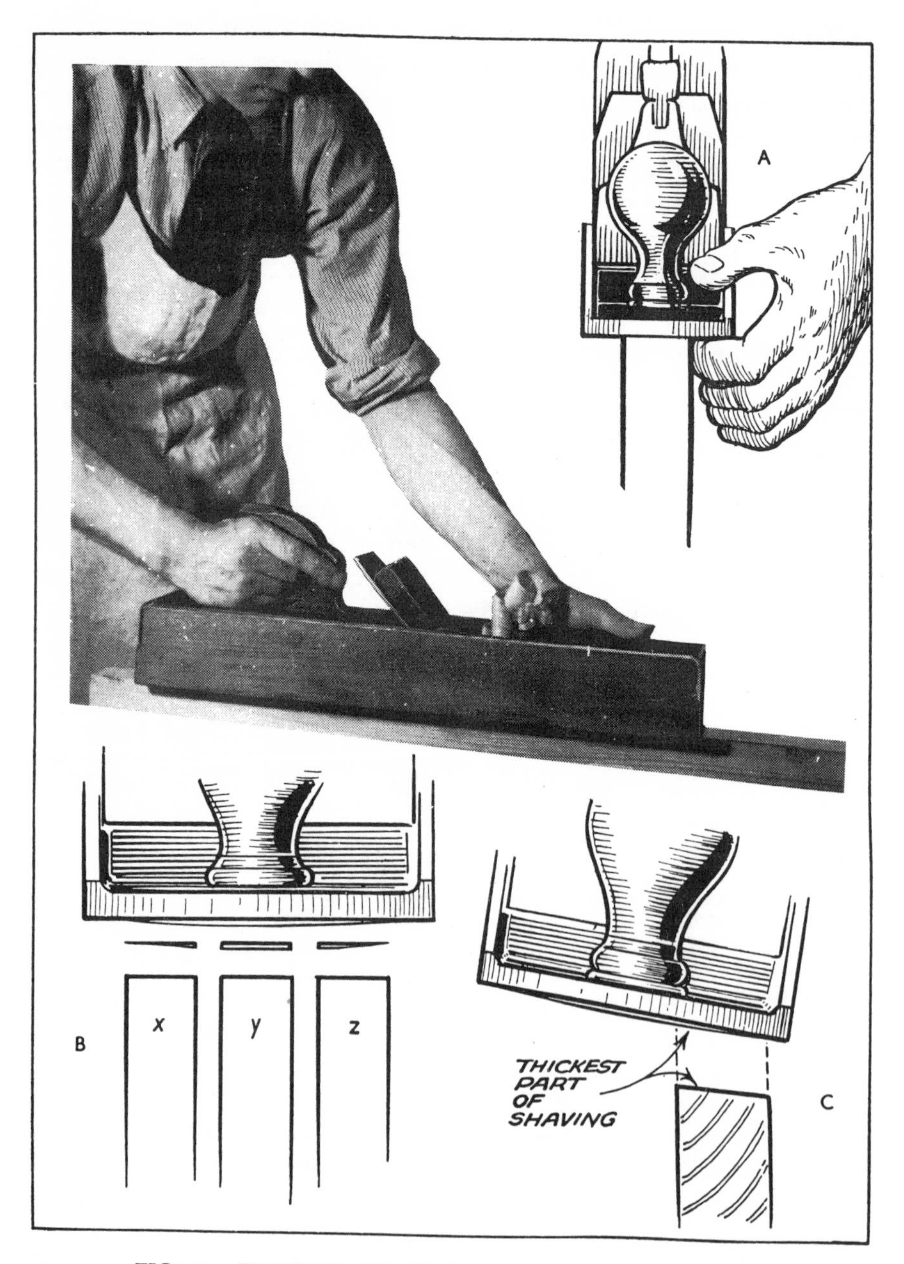

FIG. 15. PLANING AN EDGE. HOW PLANE IS HELD
A. Fingers of left hand act as a fence. B. How thickness of shaving varies across the width. C. How untrue edge is corrected.

To test whether an edge is straight use a straight-edge. This, of course, is unnecessary when a joint is being planed because the two parts are tried together. A good working method of straightening an edge is to use the trying plane and remove shavings from the middle until the plane ceases to cut. Follow with a shaving right through. A plane which has a true sole will plane an edge considerably longer than itself reasonably straight by this method.

The edges of wood about ½ in. or so thick and over can be

FIG. 16. PLANING AN EDGE TRUE ON THE SHOOTING BOARD
The wood overhangs slightly, and the plane trues the wood by virtue of the truth of its own sole.

planed in the vice in this way. On thinner wood the plane would be liable to rock, and it is advisable to use the shooting board.

Shooting Board—This is shown in Fig. 16 and is being used to plane an edge straight. The wood lies on the upper platform, and the plane rests on its side and is moved along the lower platform. The side of the plane must, of course, be square with sole if it is to plane the wood square. Since the plane makes the edge straight by virtue of the accuracy of its own sole, the wood is held so that it overhangs the upper platform by about ⅛ in. or ¼ in. Shavings are removed from the middle of the wood until the plane ceases to cut, after which a couple of shavings are taken right through. In the case of a butt joint, the one piece is planed with the face side uppermost, and the other reversed. Then if the plane is slightly out of square the two angles cancel each other out.

The method of using the shooting board is rather different when the end of a piece of wood is being trimmed. In this case the plane is kept up to the edge of the upper platform, and the wood held against the stop with sufficient inward pressure to keep it up to the sole of the plane as in Fig. 17.

Sequence in Planing—In all planing operations there is a

FIG. 17. TRIMMING END GRAIN ON SHOOTING BOARD
The plane is worked close up to the upper platform, and the wood pressed towards it.

sequence to be followed. One side is made true first and one edge made square with it. These are known as the face side and face edge respectively. They are marked with pencil as in Fig. 18, and all subsequent marking made from one or other of them. For instance the try square has its butt resting against one of them, or the gauge is used with its fence bearing against one of them. There are exceptions to this rule, but it applies in most instances. When wood has been obtained machine planed it will already have been brought to an even thickness ; otherwise the gauge will have to be set to the thickness required and both edges gauged from the face side. When the wood is wide the ends are gauged as well. The width will have to be gauged in any case as in Fig. 18.

When the edges of a panel, table top, or whatever it may be are to be planed they should be done in the order given in Fig. 19. This enables the rear corners to be taken off at an angle to prevent the grain from splitting out. The final trim at (4) takes out the chiselled corners.

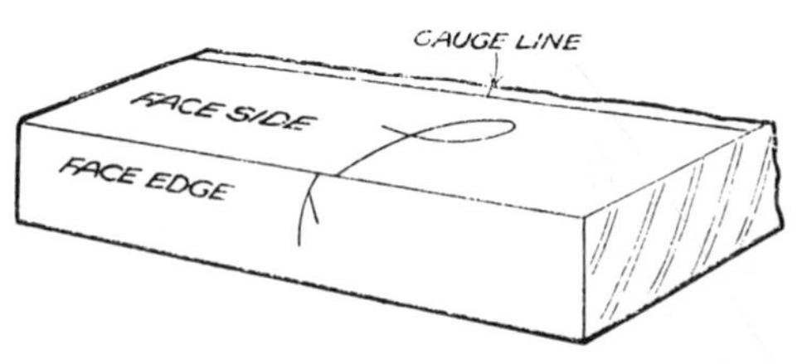

FIG. 18. IDENTIFICATION MARKS OF FACE SIDE AND EDGE

This method of taking off the corner to prevent splitting is shown in Fig. 20. (A) shows how the plain corner is liable to splinter out, whilst (B) shows the corner taken off. When the wood is not wide enough to permit this chiselling a block can be

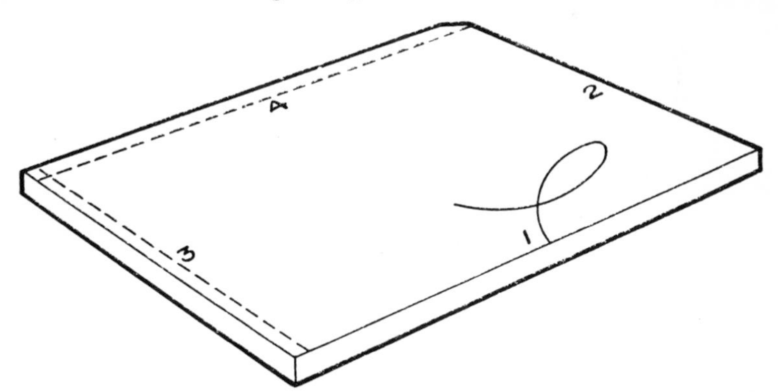

FIG. 19. ORDER IN WHICH EDGES OF PANEL ARE PLANED

cramped on at the rear as at (C). Another plan is to plane half-way in from each side as at (D). This applies equally when the wood is being trimmed on the shooting board.

Cleaning Up—It will be seen that the Jack plane is used for the preliminary planing of rough timber, and the trying plane or its smaller counterpart, the panel plane, for truing it. At this stage all marking out, joint cutting, and so on are carried out. Before the work can be assembled, however, certain parts require to be cleaned up finally, and the smoothing plane is used for this. The same plane is used for the cleaning up of table tops and similar parts, framed doors, and so on. Nowadays the adjustable metal plane is generally used. It is an extremely handy tool for bench work generally. Fig. 22 shows one of the older pattern metal smoothing planes in use cleaning up a surface.

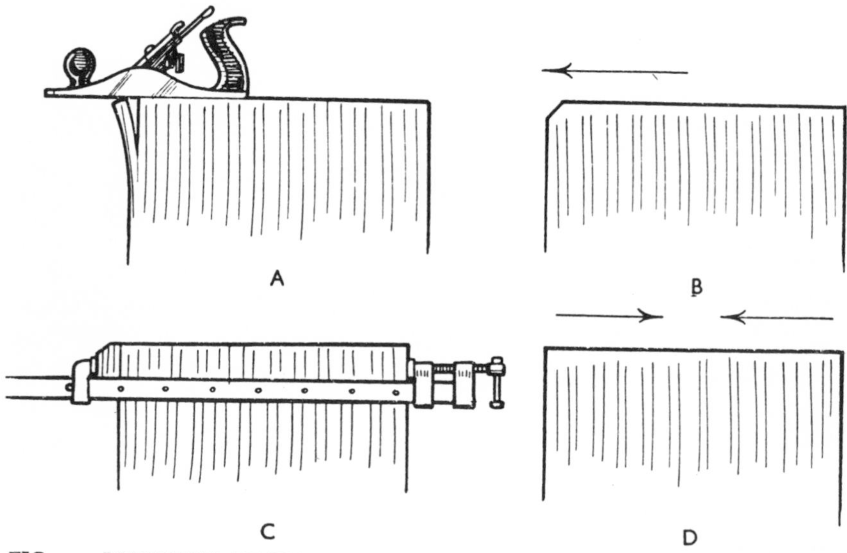

FIG. 20. LIABILITY OF END GRAIN TO SPLIT, AND HOW TO PREVENT IT

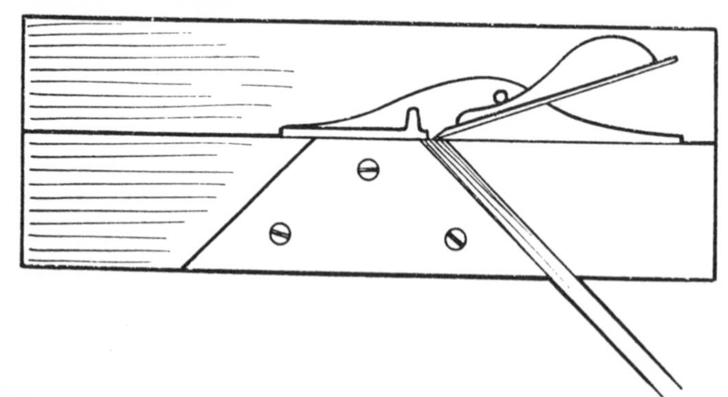

FIG. 21. SECTIONAL VIEW OF BLOCK PLANE ON MITRE SHOOTING BOARD

One other small plane which is extremely handy for trimming small parts is the block plane shown in Fig. 21. It is particularly handy for trimming the mitres of small mouldings and similar parts because of the smallness of its mouth. The larger bench planes have the bevel of the cutter downwards so that, although the mouth itself may be small, there is an aperture behind it, and the end of a narrow piece may drop into this making accurate work impossible. The block plane has its bevel uppermost which necessarily reduces the aperture as shown in Fig. 21.

FIG. 22. CLEANING UP WITH THE METAL SMOOTHING PLANE
For this work the back iron is set close to the cutting edge, and the cutter set fine.

PLANES FOR SPECIAL PURPOSES

Rebate Plane—The most generally useful kind is the adjustable metal type which has a moving fence. It thus acts as a fillister plane. Once set, any number of rebates can be planed to the same size. A depth stop ensures that the plane ceases to cut when the required depth is reached. A spur is fitted to the right hand side, but this is used only when the plane is used across the grain. Its purpose is to cut across the grain so that it does not tear out. It is necessary to draw the plane backwards with fair pressure a couple of times before using it in the normal manner. Otherwise the grain will not be cut through sufficiently. As the spur cuts quite deeply it is necessary to stop the rebate about $\frac{1}{32}$ in. short

FIG. 23. WORKING A REBATE USING THE METAL FILLISTER PLANE
The fence is set to give the required rebate width and is worked close up to the wood. The depth stop is omitted to reveal the spur used for cross-grain working.

of the finished depth, and finish off with the spur taken out or reversed into a neutral position.

The wood rebate plane is preferred by some. It has no fence, and to start the plane the fingers of the left hand are curled beneath the sole to enable it to be kept equidistant from the edge. Sometimes it is more convenient to fix a straight-edge to the wood to act as a guide. As no spurs are fitted it is essential that a saw cut is made first when cross grain is being worked. Otherwise the grain will inevitably tear out.

Fig. 23 shows a rebate being worked with the metal plane. Start at the far end of the wood and remove one or two short shavings. Then at each successive stroke bring the plane a little farther back until it takes a shaving along the whole length. In this way it is not so liable to drift from the edge. In any case, however, it is essential that a firm inward pressure is maintained. The cutter should stand a trifle proud at the side of the plane facing the wood —not more than the thickness of a piece of stout paper. Unless this is done the plane is liable to shift outwards a trifle at each stroke so resulting in a rebate which is not square.

Shoulder Plane—Although this is a special form of rebate plane, it is used for trimming rather than for working a rebate. It is of special value for end grain. Thus wide shoulders can be trimmed with it, hence the name. The cutter has its bevel uppermost, and this means that it has close support practically up to the cutting edge. It is always set fine since its purpose is solely that of trimming. It is important that the edge of the cutter is sharpened square, because, although it is generally possible to knock the back of the cutter over slightly if not true, it causes the side of the cutter to protrude unevenly so that the plane does not bed down properly on its side. Fig. 24 shows a typical operation.

Bullnose Plane—This again is another form of rebate plane, but the cutting edge is near the front of the plane so that it will

FIG. 24. FINISHING REBATE WITH SHOULDER PLANE.

It is more generally used for end grain trimming.

work close up into a corner. Apart from this, however, it is an invaluable little tool for general work, and can often be used more conveniently than the shoulder plane. Fig. 25 shows it in use. A quite narrow type is also available.

Compass Plane—The metal type with flexible sole is shown in Fig. 26. It can be used for both concave and convex curves. Although provided with back iron, the plane should be used *with* the grain as far as possible. Only curves which are struck from a circle can be planed. To set it hold the plane over the sawn wood and turn the adjusting screw till the sole takes up approxi-

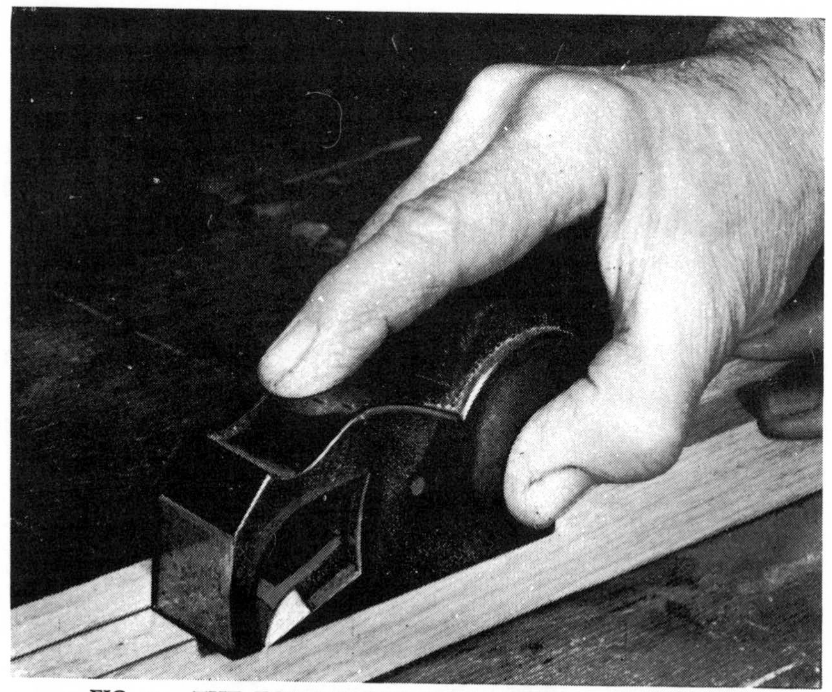

FIG. 25. THE INVALUABLE BULL-NOSE PLANE IN USE
The nearness of the cutting edge to the front enables the plane to work close up to a corner.

mately to the shape. For concave shapes the sole should be of slightly quicker curvature, and rather flatter for convex shapes.

Grooving Plane or Plough—There are a great many varieties of this, both in wood and metal. The wood type shown in use in Fig. 27 generally has a set of eight cutters of varying widths. When setting it is important that the fence is parallel with the metal sole. It may have screw adjustment as in the example shown, or may have wedge fixing and need a tap with the hammer.

Metal grooving planes are of many forms from the simple small plane with three sizes of cutters up to $\frac{1}{4}$ in., to the multi-plane of *Record* (405) or *Stanley* (45) make. These last named will work grooves up to any practical width, though for extra wide ones it is usual to use it twice, resetting the fence for the extra width. This is specially true when hardwood is being planed.

In addition to grooving this multi-plane can be used for rebating, beading, and for working almost any section which finishes at the

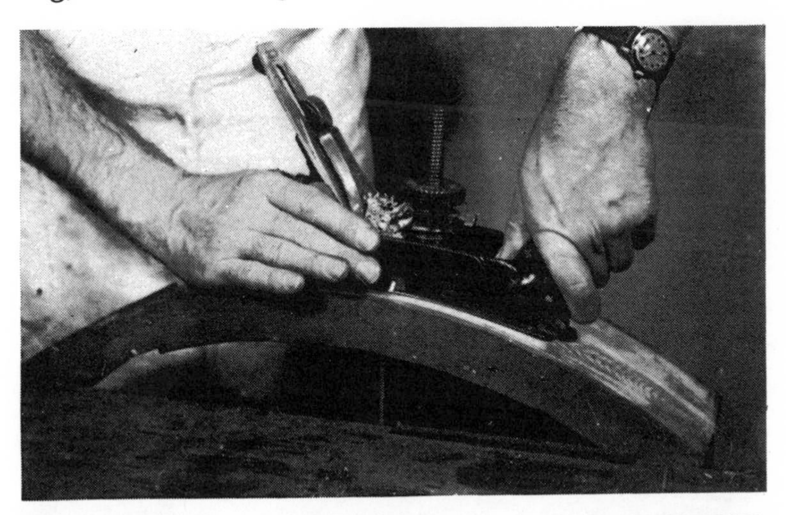

FIG. 26. PLANING A CURVED SURFACE WITH THE COMPASS PLANE

The flexible sole can be bent to either a concave or a convex shape.

same level at both sides. When a moulding is required which is lower at one edge than at the other, the *Stanley* 55 plane is required. This has a sliding section which is adjustable vertically as well as laterally. This is necessary to enable it to align with the members of the cutting edge. When used as a plough, however, it is much the same as other grooving planes. The cutter being set, the fence is fixed at the required distance from the edge, and the depth stop set so that the plane ceases to cut when the depth is reached

Whichever type of plane is used, it should be started at the far end of the wood and one or two short cuts taken. Then at each successive stroke it is brought a little farther back until it can run right through. In this way the plough runs into a groove it has already worked, and any liability to drift from the edge is avoided. In any case a steady inward pressure must be maintained.

Moulding Planes—These have only a limited use nowadays since most mouldings are machined. A small round plane is handy for working hollows, however. This has no fence and the angle at which it is held is a matter for judgment. To work a hollow at an edge a plain chamfer should be worked with the bench plane first. The fingers of the left hand pass beneath the sole and act as a sort of fence. Other types of moulding planes to work

FIG. 27. GROOVING WITH THE WOOD PLOUGH PLANE
A fully adjustable metal type is also available.

special mouldings have a fence, and this is held hard up against the edge of the wood. Many planes require to be held at an angle. You can tell this by the fence member which must be upright when the plane is in use.

Toothing Plane—This, shown at (Q), Fig. 1, p. 2, is used to roughen the surface before veneering and on certain wide joints. Its cutter, which is practically vertical, has a series of grooves at the back which produce a saw-like cutting edge. Apart from giving a suitable key for the glue, it takes out inequalities left by the ordinary plane.

CHAPTER IV

HOW TO MAINTAIN AND USE TOOLS *(Continued)*

GENERAL TOOLS

Hammer—The most useful type for general indoor woodwork furniture making, etc., is the Warrington or London pattern (see A, p. 6). It has the cross pene at the back which is handy for starting nails, and also for rubbing down inlay strings, etc. A useful weight (including the handle) is about 11 oz. For extra small nails the pattern maker's type of about 6 oz. weight is invaluable. The claw hammer is of little value for furniture making. It is used mostly by carpenters for whom the claw for withdrawing nails is useful. An inclusive weight of 1 lb. 11 oz. is a good size.

Hold the hammer by the end of the shaft and so take advantage of the leverage it gives. Always look at the point of the actual object you are striking. Thus, when using a punch, look at the head of the punch, not the nail which it is driving.

Punches—Sometimes known as nail sets, these are required to drive nails beneath the surface of the wood. The most generally useful type is the hollow point which is not so liable to start from the nail head, though for flooring brads and other cut nails a square punch is mostly used. Pincers are a necessity, and a fairly large pair is desirable. When using them always place a spare block of wood or a scraper beneath to avoid damaging the surface.

Mallet—An all-round useful size is the 7-in. head which weighs in the region of 2½ lb. Make sure that it has the tapered handle which fits the head with a wedge fit, so preventing it from flying.

Screwdrivers—At least two are required, preferably three. The large one should be capable of driving 12 to 16 gauge screws, and be 10–12 in. long ((E), p. 6). For screws around the 8 gauge size a smaller driver is needed. The large one would not fit the slot, and would project at the sides.

The small screwdriver is needed for the screws you would use

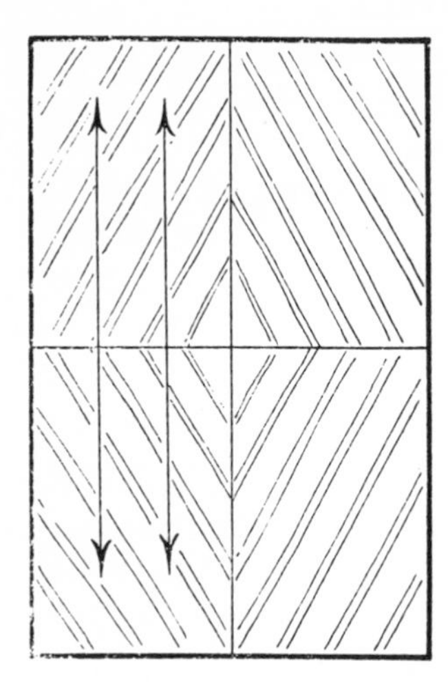

FIG. 1. DIRECTION IN WHICH GLASS-PAPER IS USED FOR A QUARTERED PANEL

It is impossible to follow the direction of the grain, and the block is worked in straight lines, generally along the length of the panel.

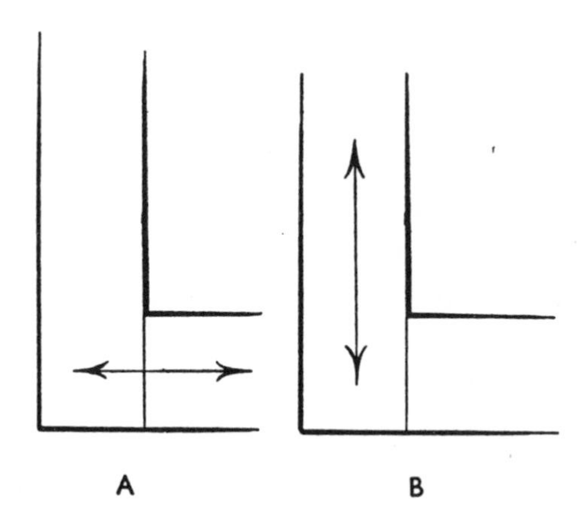

FIG. 2. GLASSPAPERING OVER JOINT

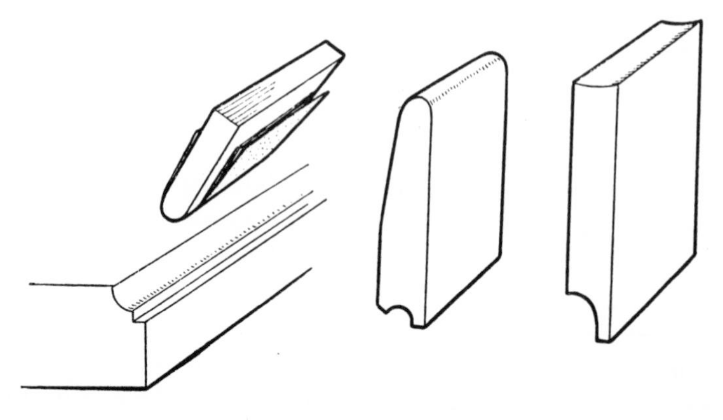

FIG. 3. GLASSPAPER RUBBERS USED FOR CLEANING MOULDINGS

for small hinges, etc., say 4–6 gauge. An excellent type is the ratchet ((G), p. 4) which can be used with one hand whilst the other supports the door, or whatever it may be. It is only necessary to turn the hand back and forth without altering its position. The finger grip is also a great convenience since the first turn or two can be made with thumb and finger, the rest of the hand remaining still and just exerting pressure. For the smallest screws the long thin electrician's screwdriver ((G), p. 6) is invaluable.

Veneer Hammer—This is invariably made at home. It is used to force out glue from beneath the veneer. It consists of a main stock with handle let into it at right angles (see (S), p. 6). A strip of brass fits in a slot in the stock, the edge of this being straight and rounded over in section. Exact sizes are not important. The brass strip might be about 6–7 in. long.

Cork Rubber—Always use this when cleaning up a flat surface. Its use prevents corners and edges from being dubbed over. Use it always in the direction of the grain in a straight line. Working across the grain or in a circular path causes scratches to show badly, and results in stain taking unevenly in patches. Sometimes it cannot be avoided. In a quartered panel, for instance, it is impossible to follow the grain, and the only way is to avoid coarse paper and work along the length of the panel as in Fig. 1.

Another occasion calling for compromise is when a door framework is being cleaned up. First the rubber is taken right across the shoulder as at (A) Fig. 2, when it will inevitably work across the grain. If, however, the rubber is afterwards taken parallel with shoulder, it will take out the scratches previously made.

To clean up mouldings it is necessary to make small wood rubbers shaped to a reverse of the section as in Fig. 3. Unless this is done the edges will be dubbed over. In any case it is the only way of exerting any degree of pressure.

Spokeshaves—Both wood and metal shaves are available. The latter is similar to a plane in both the setting and sharpening. As the cutter is rather short to handle it is a good plan to make a holder having a slot cut in it. It can then be handled much like a plane cutter. To sharpen the wood type the simplest plan is to hold the cutter in the jaws of a handscrew as in Fig. 4, or in the bench vice, and work an oilstone slip on the bevel. As a rule the tool works better if no attempt is made to remove the burr.

The cutter is held purely by the friction of the tangs, and these are tapped one way or the other to give the required setting. After prolonged use the tangs tend to become loose and liable to drop out. Round-head screws with the points nipped off can be driven in as in Fig. 5.

Two chief points need to be watched when using the spokeshave; to work in the direction of the grain, and to keep the edge square. The former point is obvious from Fig. 6. Squareness of edge,

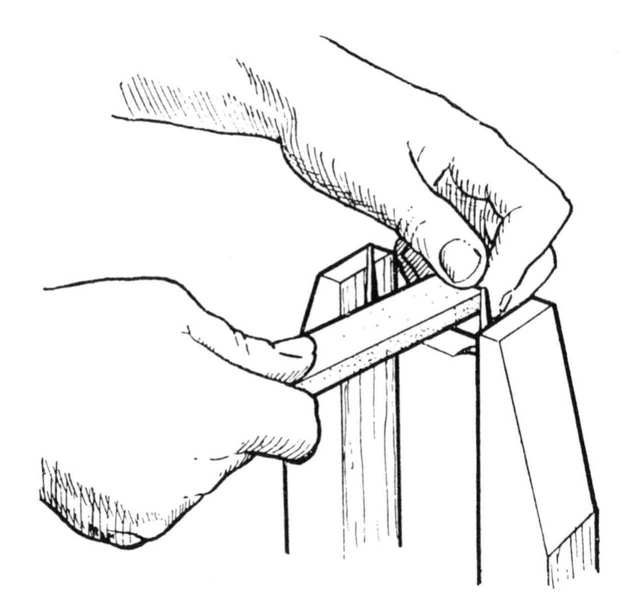

FIG. 4. SHARPENING WOOD SPOKESHAVE CUTTER

The latter is held in the jaws of a handscrew and the latter placed in the bench vice.

however, comes only with practice, and the only plan is to test the work with the square frequently and at various points.

Clearly the spokeshave cannot reach into the extreme corners, noted at (X) Fig. 6, and such parts need rubbing with the file following by the scraper, and finally glasspaper. In the same way a concave curve of small radius could not be reached with the spokeshave (Y). For this either a small half-round file or a rattail file would be needed.

File and Rasp—The file is used with a sort of compound movement as shown in Fig. 7. As it is pushed forward it is partly revolved. In this way it takes out lumps and removes saw marks. In its turn it leaves file marks, of course, and these are removed by the scraper. When a lot of wood has to be removed it is quicker to begin with the rasp, the coarse face of which takes out inequalities quickly. It is followed by the file. The file used should be of rather quicker curvature than the curve being cleaned. The shaper tool is also invaluable for the quick removal of waste. One of its virtues is that it never clogs.

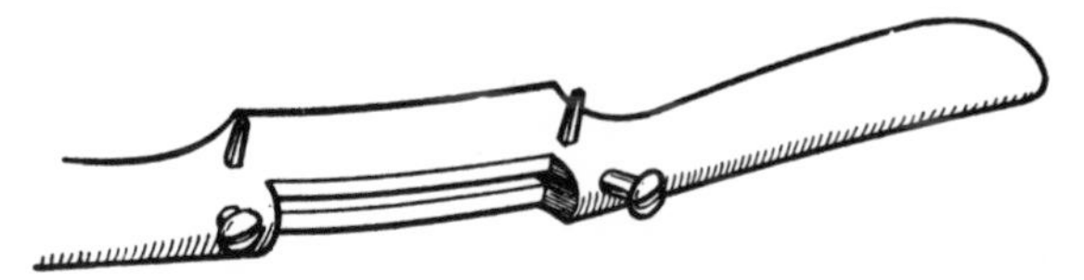

FIG. 5. LOOSE CUTTER HELD WITH SCREWS

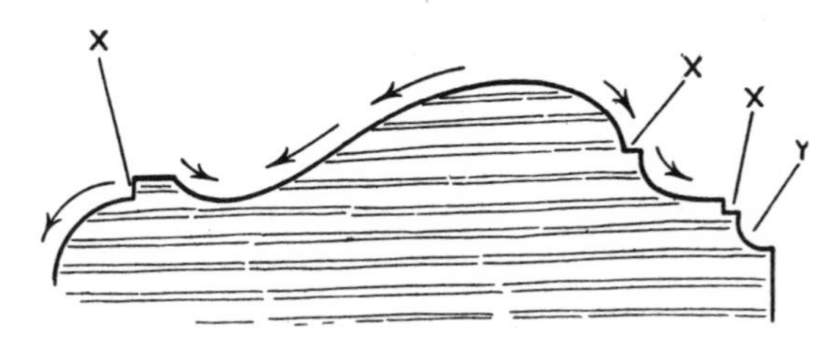

FIG. 6. DIRECTION IN WHICH SPOKESHAVE IS USED

Scraper—No matter how carefully a surface is planed, the plane is bound to leave some marks. Furthermore some woods tear up in parts no matter in which direction the plane is taken. The only way of taking out such blemishes is to use the scraper. A handy size is about 5 in., the thickness being about $\frac{3}{64}$ in. A thin scraper heats up quickly and becomes painful to use. A thick one is difficult to bend and is therefore tiring to use.

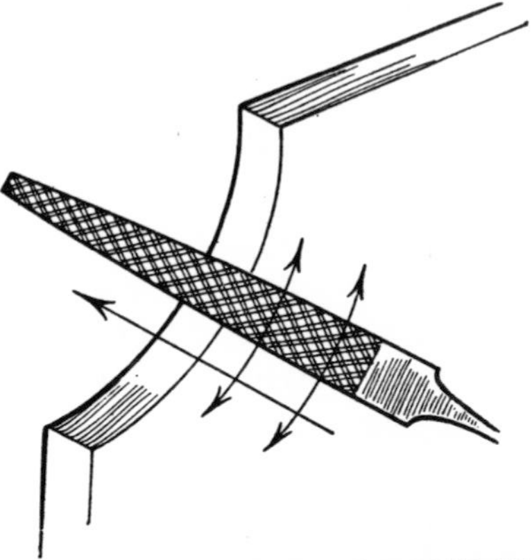

FIG. 7. COMPOUND ACTION OF THE RASP OR FILE OVER A SHAPE

Fig. 8 shows it in use. It is pushed forward by the thumbs, the fingers at the ends bending it back slightly. In this way the edge is slightly curved, the centre part touching the wood. Note that it leans forward at an angle, the exact slope depending upon the way it is sharpened. Trial shows the most effective slope. Fine shavings should be removed, not mere dust.

The most awkward part of scraping is the start at the near edge, and the best way is to hold the scraper at a slight angle as in the plan view, Fig. 10. In this way part of the scraper is already lying on the wood, and there is no difficulty about starting the cut.

Sharpening the Scraper—To sharpen the scraper hold it in the vice and with a fine flat file make the edge straight and square, taking out any rounding-over that may have occurred at the edges

FIG. 8. HOW SCRAPER IS HELD, THUMBS BEARING AGAINST BACK
The angle at which it is held can be found by trial. It depends upon the angle at which it has been sharpened.

(see (A), Fig. 9). To remove the file marks hold the scraper in a pad and work it on the oilstone as at (B), changing the direction of the movement so that wear on the stone is equalized. A slight burr will be set up at the edges, and this is removed by laying each side of the scraper on the stone and rubbing flat as at (C).

The edge is now ready to be turned. Hold the scraper flat on the bench about ¼ in. from the edge and draw a hard steel tool such as a gouge along it once or twice as at (D). Take care not to catch the fingers with the gouge. Bring the scraper forwards so that it overhangs the edge of the bench by about ¼ in. as at (E). Wet the side of the gouge in the mouth and, holding it at a slight angle, draw it along the scraper, first in one direction, then the

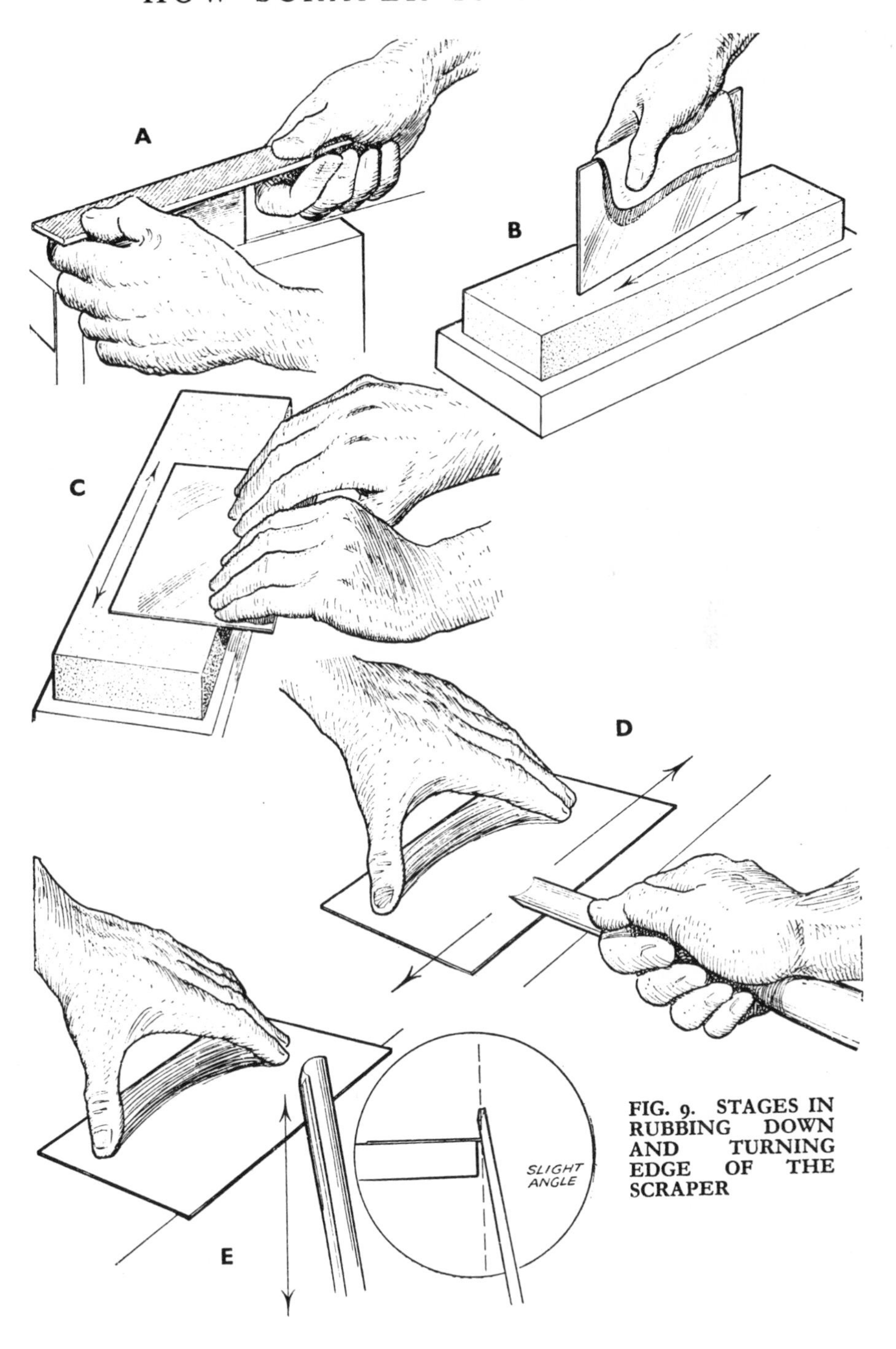

FIG. 9. STAGES IN RUBBING DOWN AND TURNING EDGE OF THE SCRAPER

other, using strong pressure. This should turn up a strong edge. Some prefer to hold the scraper upright, and draw the gouge upwards.

After being in use for a while the edges will become dull. They can be restored a few times by turning back as at (D) and re-turning as at (E). Eventually, however, this will fail to turn up a satisfactory edge, and it is necessary to use file and oilstone again.

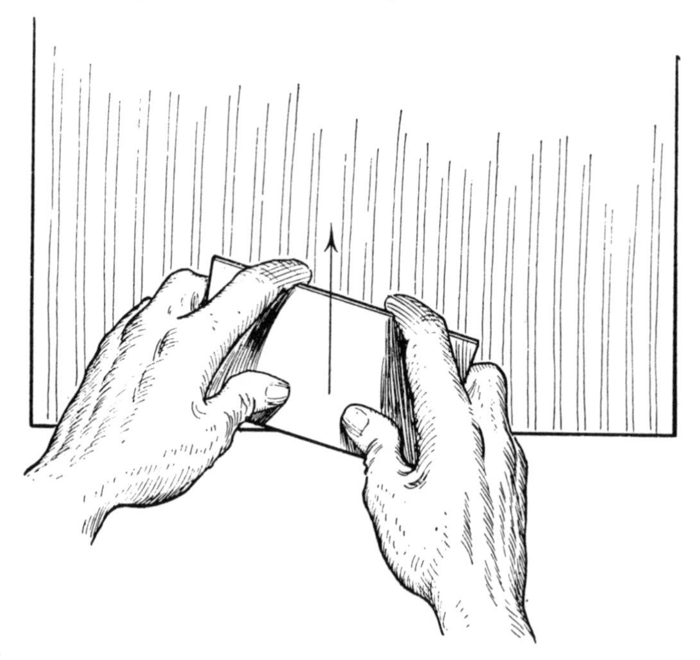

FIG. 10. HOW SCRAPER IS STARTED AT END OF WOOD
By holding it askew part of the scraper already bears on the wood.

Oilstone and Oilstone Slips—Nowadays the manufactured stones such as the *India*, *Carborundum*, and *Unirundum* are widely used in preference to the natural stones, because of their consistent quality combined with rapid cutting. They can be obtained in three grades, coarse, medium, and fine; also in combination form. For cabinet work the fine grade is recommended. Use a thin lubricating oil, and wipe clean after use. Make a container for it immediately as it is easily broken.

One or two oilstone slips are needed, and it is advisable to choose those of tapered section, as these give rounded edges of varying curvature.

CHAPTER V

HOW TO MAINTAIN AND USE TOOLS (*Continued*)

RULE, GAUGES, DIVIDERS, SQUARE, BEVEL, PARALLEL STRIPS, APPLIANCES, CRAMPS

THESE include a wide range of tools, and are most important because accurate work is impossible unless the wood is set out correctly.

Rule—For general bench work the 2 ft. or 3 ft. folding rule is convenient, though there is a tendency to replace it with the flexible metal type, which has the advantage of opening up to 6 ft., yet taking up little space when closed.

Always hold the rule so that the calibrations actually touch the wood. Thus in Fig. 1 the rule is on the edge and there is no doubt of the measurement as there might be if the rule were held flat.

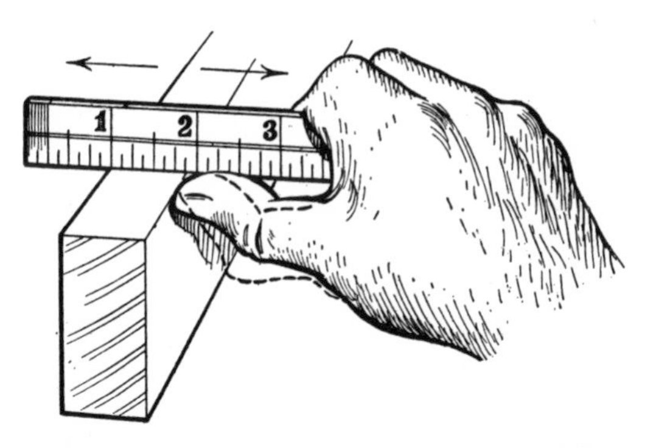

FIG. 1. CORRECT WAY TO MEASURE THICKNESS (OR WIDTH) OF WOOD

In the latter case the measurement would appear to vary according to whether the wood were seen from the right or left. This illustration is also of value in that it shows how the thickness (or width) of a piece of wood is measured. Note that measurement is not taken from the end of the rule, but from one of the calibrations. It is far easier to judge when a mark is level with the edge of the wood rather than the end of the rule. By rocking the thumb over one way or the other the rule can be made to slide the most minute distance, and the exact measurement can be noted with ease. In any case the thumb acts as a bearing in keeping the rule steady.

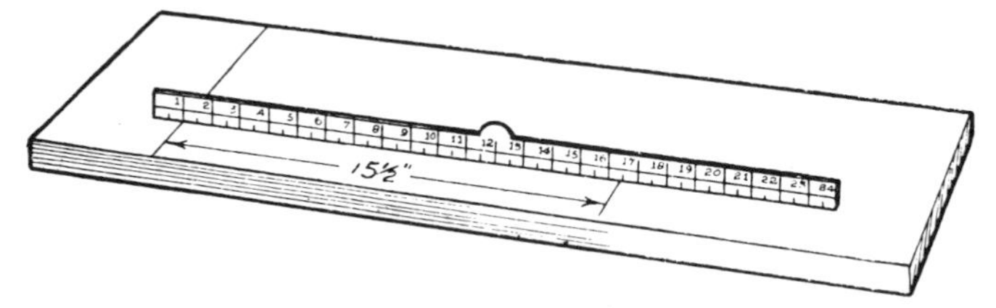

FIG. 2. MEASURING AN EXACT DISTANCE ALONG A BOARD

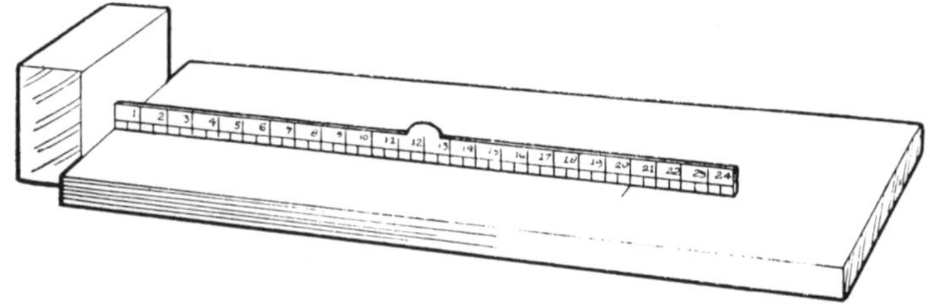

FIG 3. ALTERNATIVE METHOD OF TAKING A CLOSE MEASUREMENT

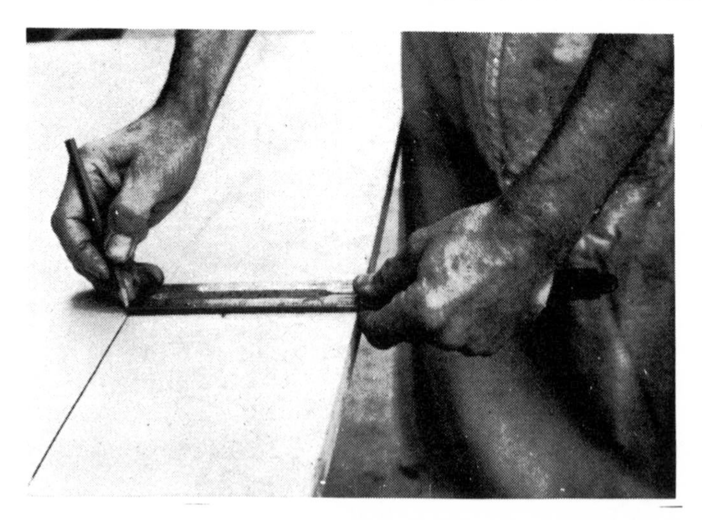

FIG. 4. DRAWING A PENCIL LINE PARALLEL WITH AN EDGE

The same idea is followed in Fig. 2 when an exact distance is being marked. Instead of the end of the rule being placed on the mark, the first 1 in. calibration is used. Then in measuring the distance 1 in. is added. Thus, suppose the distance to be noted is $15\frac{1}{2}$ in., the mark is made opposite the $16\frac{1}{2}$ calibration on the rule. Another way is to place a block of wood exactly at the mark and put the end of the rule against this. The same idea can be followed when the distance has to be taken from the end of the wood as in Fig. 3. All these methods are used for close work. They are unnecessary for approximate measurements.

The rule can often be used for drawing a pencil line parallel with an edge as in Fig. 4. Whilst it does not give the close accuracy of a gauge line, it is quite suitable for, say, the marking of a board for ripping out.

One other occasional use for a rule is in marking a board of odd width into approximately equal parts. Thus, suppose a board say $13\frac{7}{8}$ in. wide has to be divided into five equal parts. Take the first figure above the width into which five will go. Clearly it is 15. Set one end of the rule at one edge of the board, and 15 at the other, the rule sloping at an angle. Mark the wood at 3, 6, 9, and 12 as shown in Fig. 5.

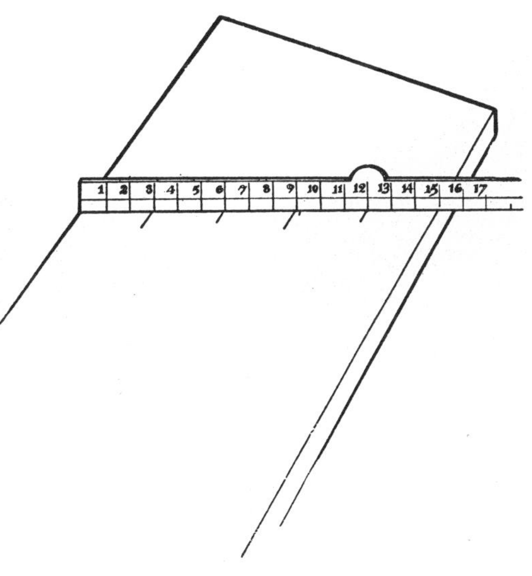

FIG. 5. DIVIDING AN ODD MEASUREMENT INTO EQUAL PARTS

Gauges—The three chief kinds are, marking, cutting, and mortise. In addition there is the panel gauge which is similar to the marking gauge but is much bigger and has a pencil in place of a steel marker. It is used for marking wide boards such as panels.

Fig. 6 shows how the marking or cutting gauge is held. The first finger bears down on top of the gauge, whilst the root of the same finger and the thumb push forward. The remaining three fingers press inwards towards the edge. This last is of great importance in that it is vital that the gauge does not drift outwards. This may easily happen, especially if the grain tends to run in that direction. Only marks *with* the grain or at *end* grain should be made with the marking gauge.

For *cross* grain the cutting gauge is necessary; the other would merely scratch. This tool has a knife rather than a marker. It is used in the same way but it is advisable to set the cutter at a

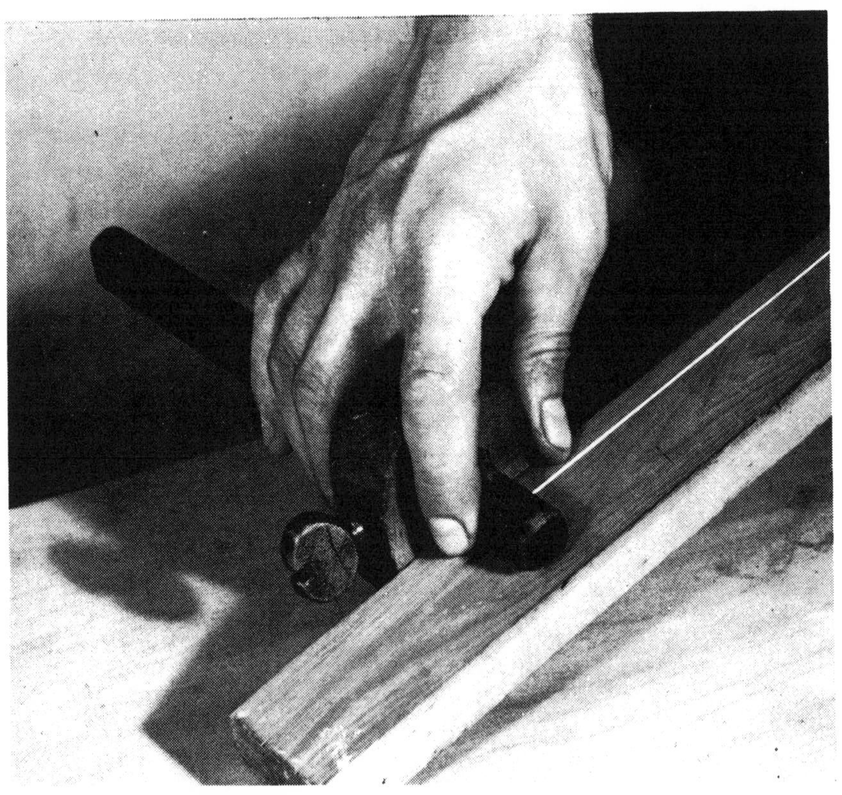

FIG. 6. HOW CUTTING OR MARKING GAUGE IS HANDLED
The fence is pressed close to the wood to prevent it from drifting.

slight angle as in Fig. 7 so that it tends to run *into* the wood. The fence, of course, prevents it from actually doing so; the great thing is to stop any tendency for it to run outwards.

In addition to marking, the cutting gauge is used to cut right through thin wood. The cutter is given a fair projection, and a deep cut made from each side. Softer varieties of wood can be cut up to about ¼ in. thick in this way.

The gauge can either be set with the rule, or to the item for which it is needed. In the former case the end of the rule is held against the fence of the gauge and the latter adjusted until the cutter or marker is level with the required measurement. Final fine adjustment is made by tapping one end or the other of the stem on the bench. When a fitting such as a lock or hinge is being fitted the gauge is set to the fitting itself, the latter being placed on the fence and the marker set to the pin or whatever it may be. When dovetailing the gauge is held to the wood itself so that it can be set to its thickness.

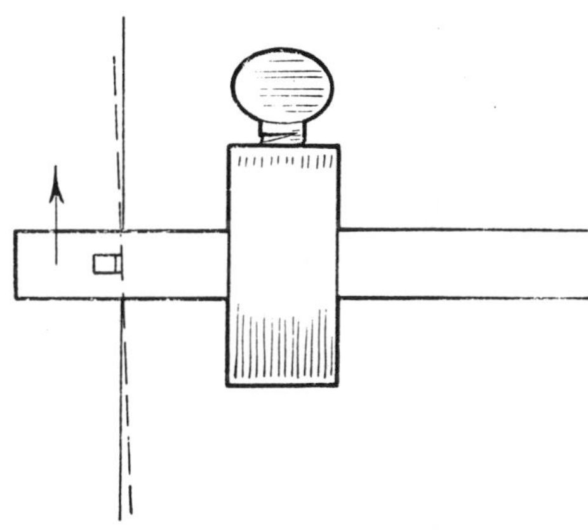

FIG. 7. SETTING OF CUTTING GAUGE
The cutter inclines at a *slight* angle so that it tends to draw the gauge inwards.

The mortise gauge has two markers, one fixed and the other adjustable. The distance between them is regulated to the width of the chisel to be used in mortising, the latter being held to the gauge. The fence is set afterwards to whatever position is required. In the case of a mortise and tenon joint to fit flush, the gauge is used from the face side of both pieces.

Dividers—These have various uses, from scribing a circle to

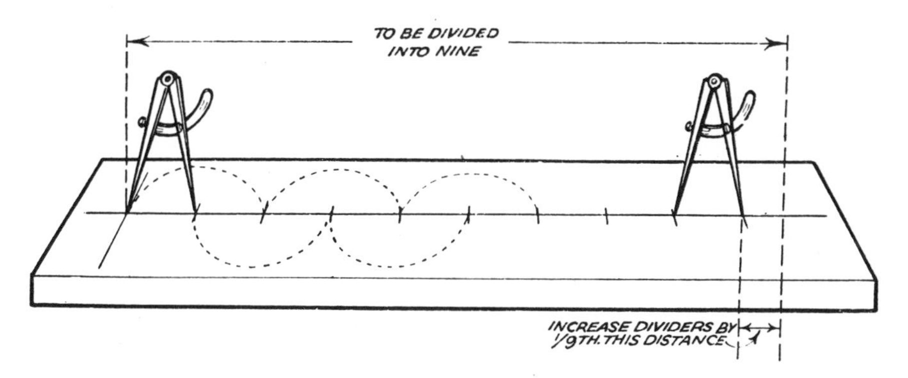

FIG. 8. DIVIDING DISTANCE INTO ODD NUMBER OF PARTS, USING DIVIDERS

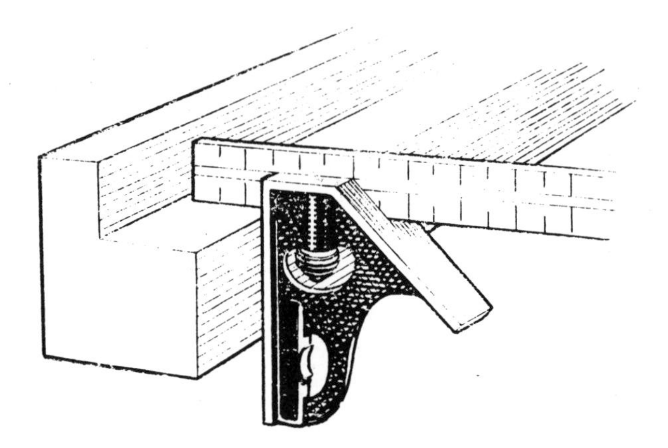

FIG. 9. TESTING SQUARENESS OF REBATE
As the rule or blade portion slides it can be given a short projection so that it can be used in the rebate.

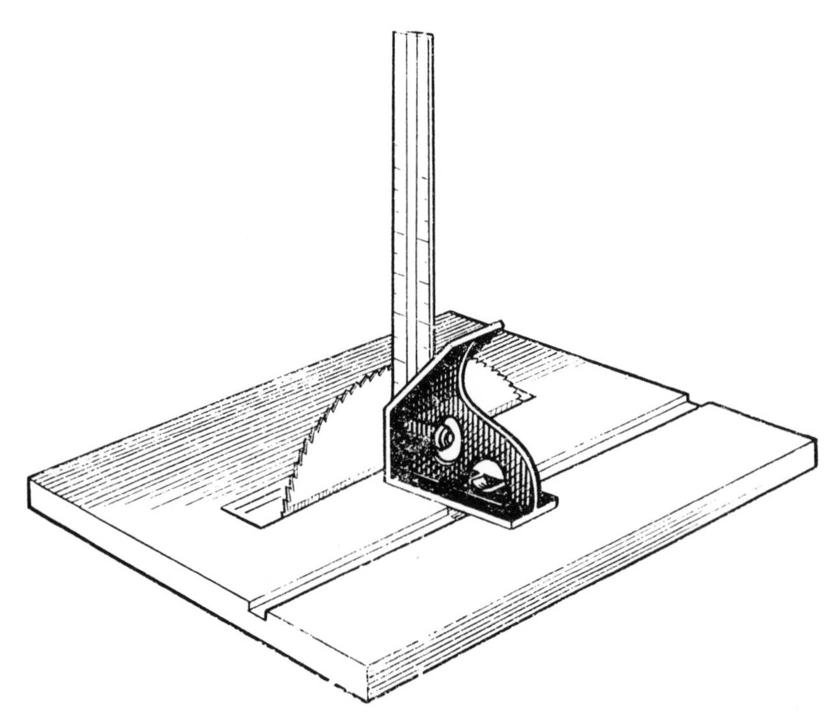

FIG. 10. TESTING SQUARENESS OF CIRCULAR SAW OR ANY OTHER ITEM

The wood-metal square is seldom true at the outside. By sliding the blade as here a true reading is bound to be given. The blade should stand just inside the face of the stock.

dividing a distance into an odd number of parts. Fig. 8 shows how the latter is done. It is assumed that the distance has to be divided into nine equal parts. Set the dividers to what you think is one ninth, and step along as to the left. If badly out re-set until approximately right—a little trial and error is inevitable. If nine steps are short increase the setting by what you estimate one ninth of the remaining distance, and step out again. This will bring the setting much nearer, and a second adjustment will put it right. If on stepping out the nine moves takes the point beyond the mark, the setting is decreased by one ninth of the distance over-run.

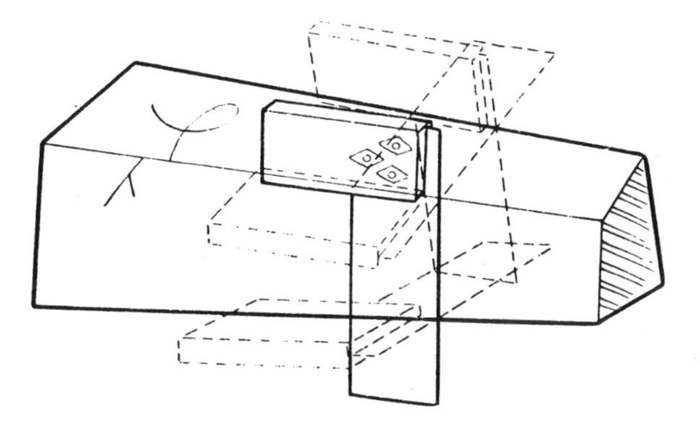

FIG. 11. USE OF SQUARE FROM FACE SIDE AND EDGE

The irregularity of the wood is purposely exaggerated.

Square—The adjustable type of engineer's square shown at (W), p. 4, has many advantages. Apart from normal use in marking and testing, it can be used for rebate work as in Fig. 9, and as a set square as in Fig. 10. The ordinary wood-metal square could not be used for either purpose. In any case this latter type of square is notoriously inaccurate. The 12-in. square is a handy all-round size.

A rule to keep in mind is that the square should be used from either face side or face edge whenever possible. There are exceptions, but since these two have been made true and square with each other the desirability of working to them is obvious. Fig. 11 is an exaggerated example of the application of the rule. Lines such as might be required for the shoulders of a joint are to be marked round all four sides of a piece of wood. This particular piece is intentionally inaccurate, but if the butt of the square rests always against either face side or face edge the marks should meet.

When two or more pieces have to be marked alike it is an advantage to cramp them together and square the marks across all. They can then be separated and the mark squared round each independently. A typical example is in the rails or stiles of a door.

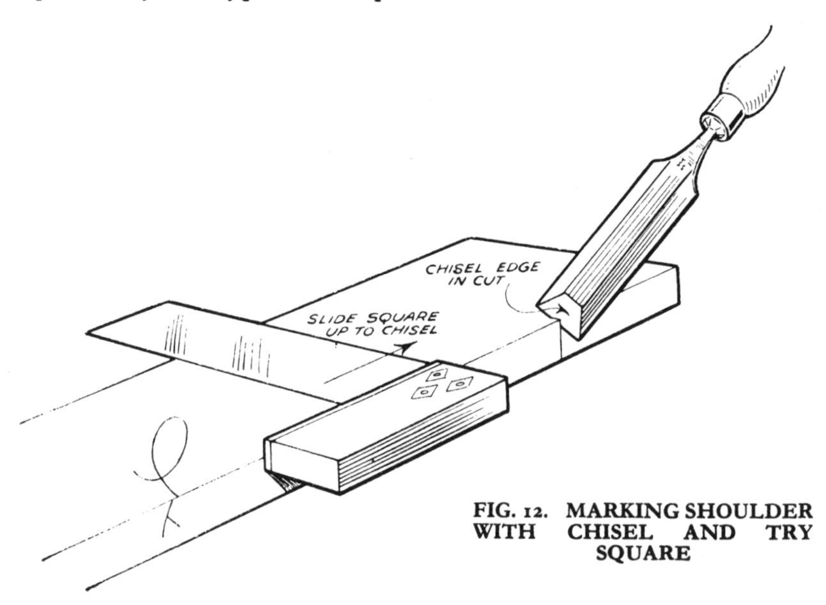

FIG. 12. MARKING SHOULDER WITH CHISEL AND TRY SQUARE

For close accuracy always make a knife or chisel cut rather than a pencil line. The latter is for approximate or rough working only, or when the knife marks might appear as a blemish.

As a typical example of marking with the square, take the rails of a door, the shoulders of which have to be marked. Cramp the rails together flush and, using the rule, make marks with a sharp pencil at the shoulder positions. Placing the knife or chisel on each mark in turn, square lines right across both rails. Separate the rails, and square the marks around each independently. To do this place the knife at the corner of the wood, its edge resting in the slight cut already made as in Fig. 12, and slide the square up to it. In this way the position is bound to be correct. Note that the chisel or knife should bear over to the right so that bevel is about square with the edge. Otherwise the bevel may prevent the blade of the square from sliding to the correct position. This sliding up of the square to the knife is invariably more accurate than trying to position the square by eye only. For large work the wood square shown at (Q), p. 4, is necessary. It is usual for the craftsman to make his own.

Mitre Square—This is needed for marking and testing the usual 45 deg. mitres. There is no special point in its use,

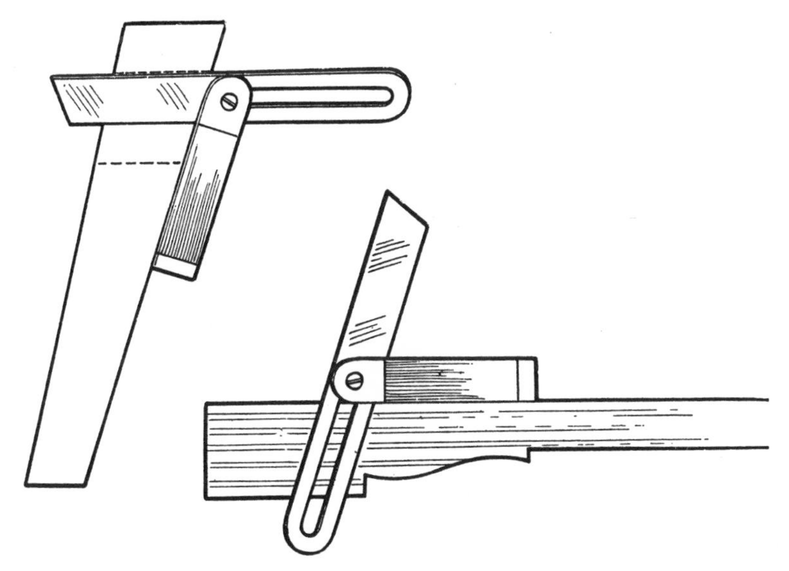

FIG. 13. MARKING STAND WITH SPLAY LEGS, USING SLIDING BEVEL

except that when mitre lines have to be squared on to all four surfaces, care has to be taken to position the square exactly, otherwise the lines may not meet owing to the angle.

Sliding Bevel—This is used mainly for odd angles—for instance the rail shoulders of a stand with legs set at an angle. The angle can be set by a protractor or by a drawing. For some work it is an advantage to have the blade set centrally in the stock as this gives both the acute angle and its complementary obtuse one. Fig. 13 shows it in use when marking the joint of a stand with leg set at an angle. In the leg the bevel must be worked from inside the leg owing to the taper, whilst the rail, owing to its shaped edge, needs to be marked from above. On the other hand, in Fig. 14, which shows the table of a circular saw being set at an angle, the blade projects at one side only.

Straight-edge and Parallel Strips—Both of these are usually made by the worker himself. The former should be in well-seasoned straight-grained hardwood. A test for the working accuracy of the edge is to place it on a flat board and draw a line along the edge with a keen pencil. When reversed on to the other side it will align with the pencil line if true. It has many uses for marking out and testing generally, and can be of any

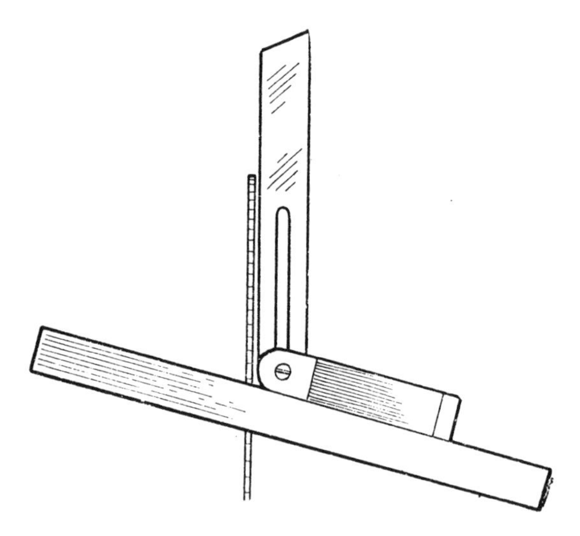

FIG. 14. TESTING ANGLE OF SAW TABLE, USING BEVEL

convenient size. Many workers keep two; about 18 in. and 4 ft. respectively.

Parallel strips are used mostly to test whether a surface is free from winding. The strip to the rear has a line inlaid on it, and this will appear parallel with the edge of the front one if the board is free from winding. Another use is in testing whether the four legs of a cabinet will stand square on the floor. If the strips are not long enough to reach across the legs they are placed on longer strips of wood, the edges of which are parallel.

Diagonal Strip—When a large carcase has been assembled it may be misleading to test with the square since any slight curvature in the wood would give a false reading. It is therefore advisable to use the diagonal strip shown in Fig. 15. Placed across the job the diagonal length is noted with the pencil. When reversed into the opposite corners it will show the same length if true.

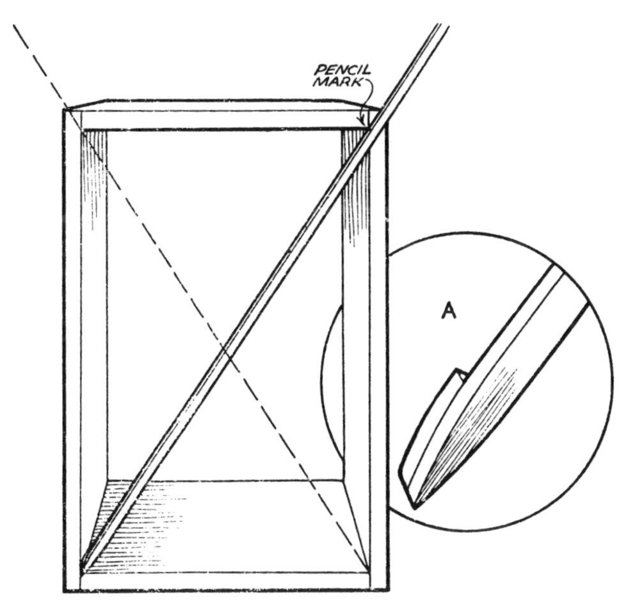

FIG. 15. DIAGONAL STRIP USED TO TEST SQUARENESS OF CARCASE

APPLIANCES

All of these can be made by the craftsman himself.

Shooting Board—There are various ways of making this. The simplest is shown in Fig. 17. Exact sizes are not important, but those given can be taken as a general guide. Two are handy; a short one, say 2 ft. or 2 ft. 6 in., for general trimming and short joints; and one from 4 to 6 ft. for long joints in thin wood. Note the chamfered lower corner of the upper platform which forms a dust trap and avoids false working. The effective edge of the stop is at 90 deg. Its wedge formation ensures a tight fit. It can always be tapped in in the event of its becoming loose, and the projecting end levelled. If possible use quarter-cut wood throughout as this is not liable to warp.

FIG. 16. AVOIDING SPLINTERED CORNER WHEN TRIMMING END GRAIN

The far corner of the waste block can be chiselled off.

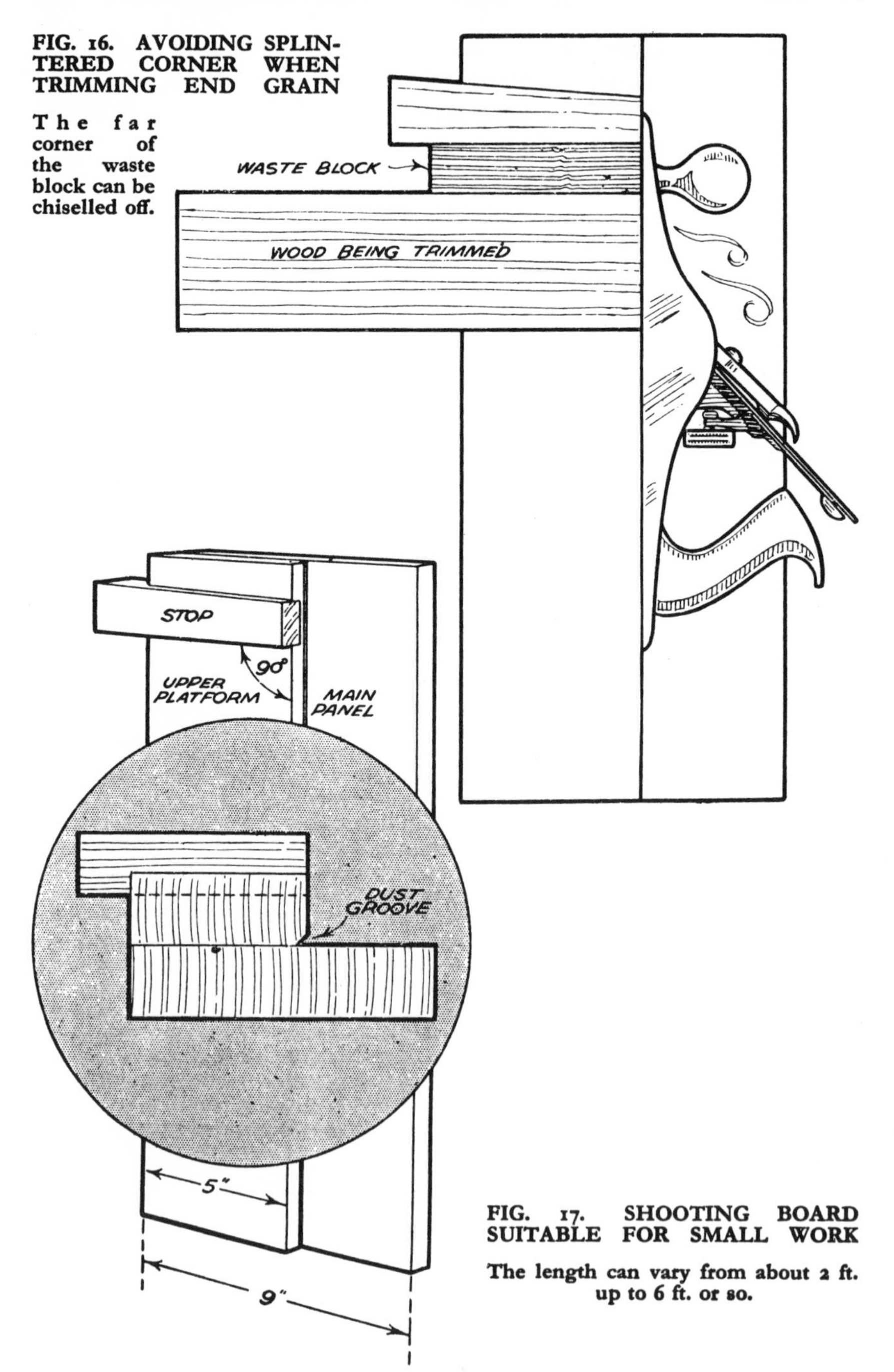

FIG. 17. SHOOTING BOARD SUITABLE FOR SMALL WORK

The length can vary from about 2 ft. up to 6 ft. or so.

The shooting board is used in two distinct ways. The first is in planing joints in thin wood, or in planing an edge straight and square. Its advantage for thin wood is that there is no liability for the plane to wobble. The operation is shown in Fig. 18. Note that the wood overhangs the upper platform by about $\frac{1}{4}$ in., and that the plane makes the edge true by virtue of the truth of its own sole. It does not run along the edge of the upper platform.

FIG. 18. TRUING THE EDGE OF A BOARD ON THE SHOOTING BOARD

The wood should overhang slightly so that the plane trues the edge by the accuracy of its own sole.

The usual plan is to remove shavings from the middle until the plane ceases to cut, then take a couple of shavings right through. Generally this will automatically make the edge straight, though in the case of a joint the parts are tried together, or the edge tested with a straight-edge in the case of a single edge.

Theoretically the edge should be square, assuming the sole of the plane to be square with its side. In the case of a joint, however, it is always advisable to plane one piece with the face side uppermost, and the other with it downward. In this way any angularity in the one is cancelled by that in the other, and the parts go together in alignment.

The second use of the shooting board is in trimming the ends of wood square. In this case the wood is held tight up against the stop, and the plane is worked along the edge of the upper platform. The wood is pressed towards the plane and in this way is fed steadily out as planing proceeds. As the far corner is liable to splinter out, it is advisable to chisel it off. If this is impracticable owing to there being insufficient width the plane will either have to be taken halfway in from each edge, or a spare piece of wood with parallel edges placed behind it as in Fig. 16.

Mitre Shooting Board—This has similar uses to the normal shooting board but is for trimming mitres. It is shown on p. 8 at (B). The direction of the plane is reversed when the wood has to be placed on the far side of the stop.

Bench Hook—Used chiefly to hold the wood steady when being sawn, this is an important item (see (E), p. 8). An important point about it is that the strip which bears against the edge of the bench should be dowelled on, not screwed or nailed—at any rate at the end over which the saw is used. The reason for this is that with continual use the wood is worn away by the saw, and any fixing screws or nails may ultimately become bared and foul the saw. Fig. 4, p. 14, shows how it is used, the wood being held firmly against the back of the bench hook.

FIG. 19. PITCHED CORNICE MOULDING BEING MITRED

Mitre Block and Box—These are needed for sawing mitres, the former for small mouldings. The only special point about the mitre block is that the wood must be kept firmly up against the stop, and whenever possible the saw should cut *into* the section not out of it. In other words the back of the moulding should be against the stop of the mitre block, so that any rag created by the saw occurs at the back where it does not matter.

The same thing applies to the mitre box. Thus when cutting, say, a large cornice moulding it is advisable to place it upside down and saw towards the moulding as in Fig. 19. In this way the teeth cut into the section in both a horizontal and vertical direction. This illustration is also interesting in that it shows the way to deal with a pitched cornice moulding which has no backing. To form a true mitre the top and back faces of the moulding which are at right angles with each other must bear against the back and bottom of the mitre box, and, to ensure this, a packing piece is planed so that it fits exactly between the edge of the moulding and the side of the box. This makes the position definite. It does not matter if the saw cuts right through it.

Mitre Template—Fig. 20 shows the use of this in cutting the mitre needed in a door frame having a moulding worked in the solid. It is placed over the moulding and its sloping end (at 45 deg.) used as a guide for the chisel. For small mouldings it can be held in position with the hand. On larger ones a thumbscrew can be tightened over it.

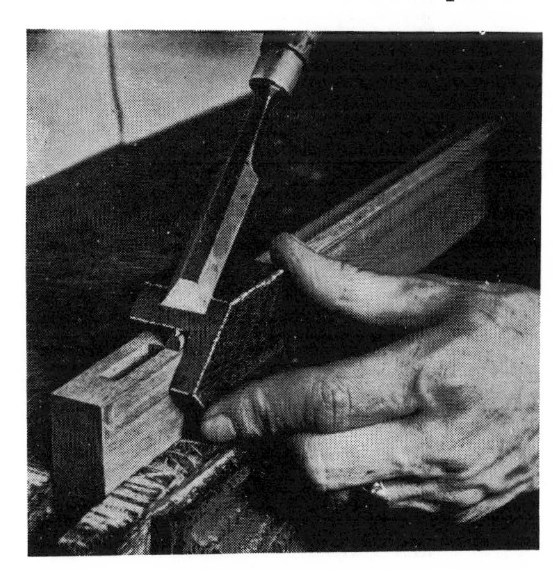

FIG. 20. TRIMMING MOULDING, USING MITRE TEMPLATE

The left thumb is normally placed on the chisel to steady it. To avoid hiding the blade it is here shown at the side.

CRAMPS

These are used to pull the parts of joints together and to hold them whilst the glue sets, and also to hold wood to the bench whilst being worked.

Sash Cramps—For assembling a door frame or a butt joint these are a necessity. Length ranges from 2 ft. upwards, and size should be selected to suit the average work done. Blocks should be placed beneath the cramp shoes to prevent damage to the surface.

Tests for both squareness and freedom from winding should be made as soon as possible after tightening the cramps. If the square reveals an inaccuracy as in Fig. 21 the position of the shoes

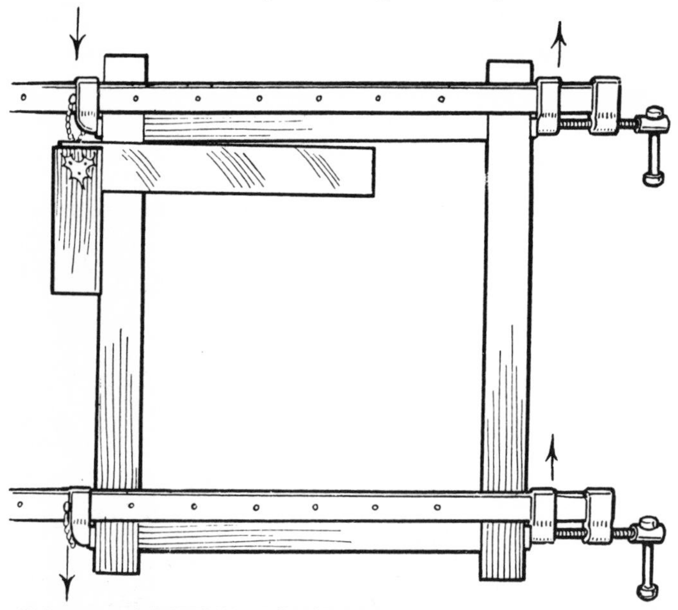

FIG. 21. TESTING SQUARENESS OF FRAME WHEN CRAMPING
The arrows show the direction in which cramps should be moved to correct inaccuracy.

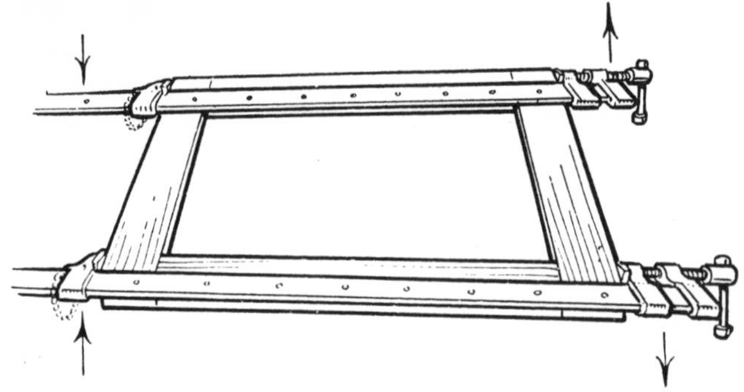

FIG. 22. CRAMPED FRAMEWORK IN WINDING
Cramps should be shifted as shown by the arrows.

should be shifted in the direction shown by the arrows. A winding test is made by looking across the work. Both near and far rails should appear parallel. If out as shown in exaggeration in Fig. 22. the cramps should again be adjusted in the direction of the arrows,

A point to remember is that cramps are necessarily heavy and may pull a framework out of truth by their weight and so give a false reading. They may also cause a framework to appear true when the weight of the cramps is pulling it down. The frame may spring into winding again after the cramps are removed.

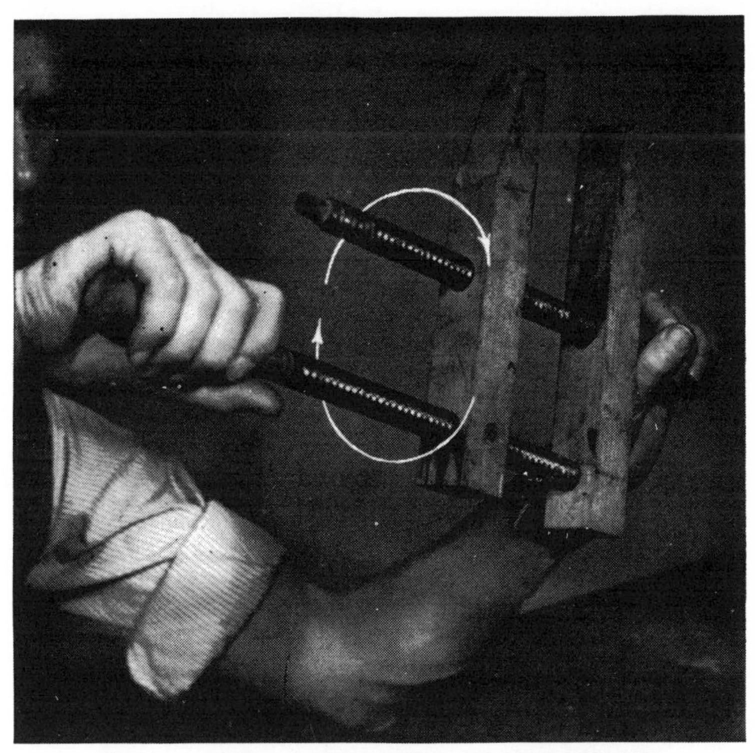

FIG. 23. QUICK ADJUSTMENT OF HANDSCREW
Revolving one handle about the other shifts the jaws.

When an extra large framework has to be assembled and the available cramps are not long enough, two can be held together by nuts and bolts passed through them. In this way the length can be adjusted to suit the job in hand. The two shoes are removed, enabling the screws to be tightened from either end.

G Cramps, Handscrews, and Thumbscrews—These are used chiefly when wood is joined in its thickness. Their application is fairly obvious. The handscrew is particularly useful. To use it open the jaws to the approximate size by grasping a handle in each hand and revolving the one about the other as in

Fig. 23. Rapid adjustment can be made in this way. The inner screw is then tightened (1) Fig. 24 (see arrow), and lastly the outer screw, again in the direction of the arrow. This has the effect of levering over the jaw on to the wood. When finally tightened the jaws should be approximately parallel.

The thumbscrew is just a small edition of the *G* cramp and is used for small work.

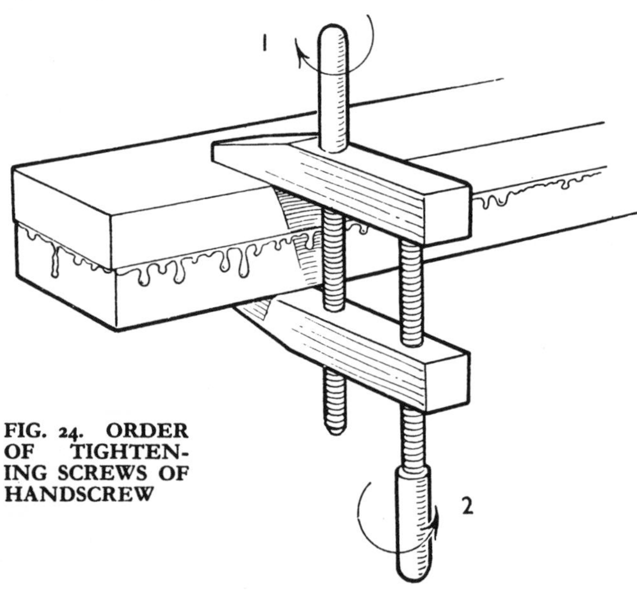

FIG. 24. ORDER OF TIGHTENING SCREWS OF HANDSCREW

Bench Holdfast—This (1, p. 8) is used to hold wood still on the bench whilst being worked. Its stem passes through a hole in the bench and it exerts its power by being levered over sideways. It is therefore effective only on a thick bench top. If the latter is thin it is necessary to thickness it locally. When a hole is bored through the bench to receive it it is clearly necessary to avoid doing so over a drawer or cupboard.

Improvised Cramps—These can always be made from lengths of wood with stops screwed on at the ends to act as shoes. Pairs of folding wedges are knocked in at one end to give the necessary pressure. For the light cramping of odd shapes springs can be used. These are simply old upholstery springs cut down and partly straightened out in the form of a *C*. They are specially useful in repair work in which moderate pressure only is required over surfaces of awkward shape.

CHAPTER VI

LIGHT MACHINES FOR WOODWORK

ALTHOUGH most home woodworkers follow hand methods in woodwork, there is an increasing tendency to install a machine of one kind or another to cut out some of the more

FIG. 1. UNIVERSAL MACHINE WHICH IS SUITABLE FOR THE SMALL WORKSHOP

The attachments for this machine include a circular saw, bandsaw, planer, disc sander, polishing head, and bowl-turning face plate. The machine is also available with long bed when it becomes a wood turning lathe dealing with work 30 in. between centres. (By courtesy The Myford Engineering Co. Ltd.)

tedious and back-aching operations. The most obvious choice in this connection is a small saw since sawing is probably the most laborious task connected with woodwork. It is as well to point out at the outset, however, that there is a great advantage in having a basic machine to which various machine attachments can be added. This basic machine usually takes the form of a wood-turning lathe, for which circular saw, bandsaw, planer, sander, and mortising attachments are available. Various makes are on the market as can be seen from the illustrations in this book. There is also the small universal machine which may include circular saw, planer, and borer, but is not a lathe.

FIG. 2. LATHE WITH ATTACHMENTS CONVERTING IT INTO A UNIVERSAL MACHINE

Apart from normal turning operations, this machine has the following attachments: Circular saw, bandsaw, planer, mortiser, belt sander, and flexible drive with chuck. The head can be pivoted, enabling work to be passed along the length of the machine. (By courtesy The Coronet Tool Co.)

As a general rule a machine which is designed for a single purpose is more satisfactory than one which has to be adapted to various uses, but taking into account the limitations of workshop space and the fact that it costs less, the single adaptable machine is generally the better proposition for the home craftsman than several separate machines. Typical machines are shown in Figs. 1 and 2, and the various attachments are detailed below the illustrations. The use of the individual machines is much the same whatever the type or make, though slight variation in method of use or of sharpening may be needed in accordance with the particular type. The following general principles apply. Those who seek fuller information should refer to *Light Machines for Woodwork*.

CIRCULAR SAW

For general woodwork this is the most useful type of saw to have because not only can ripping, cross-cutting, and mitreing be done on it, but rebating and grooving are also possible. An essential feature is a table which can be raised or lowered so that the depth of rebates and grooves can be adjusted. Preferably too it should be adjustable at an angle up to 45 deg. to enable wood to be cut at angles other than a right angle. In some machines the saw is adjustable rather than the table, and this is just as effective.

A fence is an obvious requirement so that wood can be ripped to width; also a grooved bench top so that the mitre gauge can be used for cross-cutting at right angles or any other angle. A riving knife is a necessity so that the wood does not tend to bind on the saw itself in the event of the kerf closing. Lastly an efficient guard should be fitted both above and below (though in many machines the lower casing acts as a guard beneath the top).

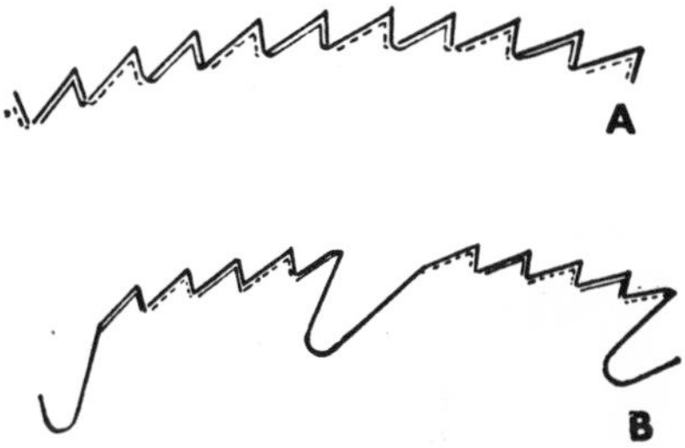

A

B

FIG. 3. TYPES OF SAW TEETH
A. Radial cross-cut teeth. B. Combination teeth.

For general use either the combination saw (B), Fig. 3, or that with radial cross-cut teeth (A) should be fitted, as either can be used for both ripping and cross-cutting. Here a word of warning is necessary: *keep the saw sharp*. A dull saw will burn the wood, and an endeavour to force the wood may result in inaccurate work and possibly cause an accident.

Ripping—When the timber already has a straight edge it is only necessary to set the fence to the required distance from the saw (the latter cutting on the waste side), and push the wood through, keeping the edge close up against it. For long boards it is a help to have someone at the back to take off, pulling and supporting the boards as the cut nears completion. If this is not possible the wood can be cut half-way from one end, reversed, and the cut completed from the other end. In all cases avoid putting the fingers near the revolving saw and never have them between

FIG. 4. PUSHER STICK IN USE ON CIRCULAR SAW
This is of special value when cutting small pieces.

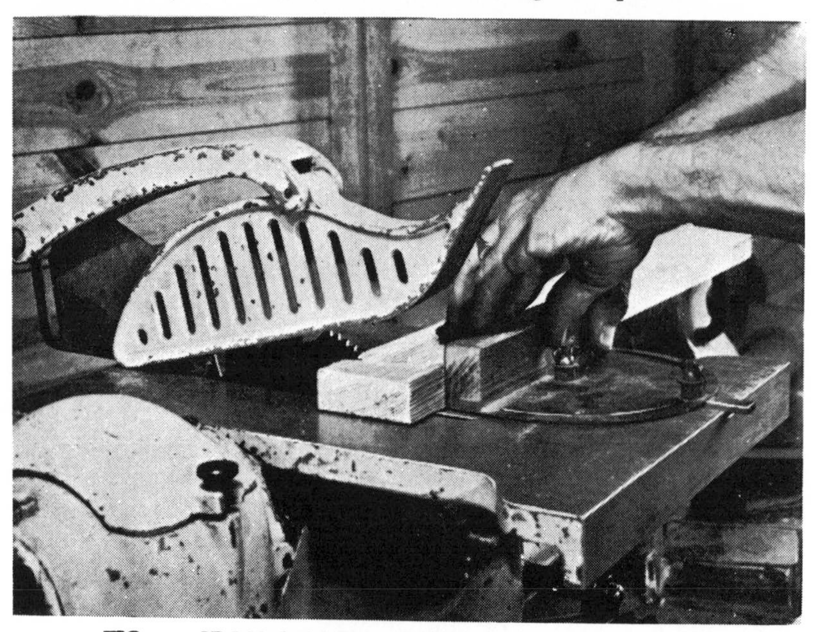

FIG. 5. CROSS-CUTTING USING THE MITRE GAUGE
The gauge slides along the groove. It can be set to cut at any angle.

the saw and the fence where they might be trapped. The pusher stick shown in Fig. 4 should always be used to push the wood at the end of the cut.

If there is no straight edge to start off with, you can either plane it straight first (by machine or hand) and work from this, or you can draw in a pencil line with the straight-edge, and, standing behind the wood, pass the wood through without using the fence. All subsequent cuts can be made from this, using the fence as a guide.

Cross Cutting—Fig. 5 shows a typical operation. Note that both hands are kept to the side of the saw. When several pieces have to be cut all to the same length the method shown in Fig. 6 can be followed. A block of wood to act as a stop is fixed to near the front of the saw table with a *G* cramp. Its position is adjusted so that its distance from the saw equals the length of the pieces to be sawn. The wood is held against the mitre gauge and pressed up to the stop. The gauge is pushed up to the saw, and the process repeated until the required number of pieces has been sawn. Mitreing is done similarly to square cross-cutting, and in the case of compound cuts the table is also tilted.

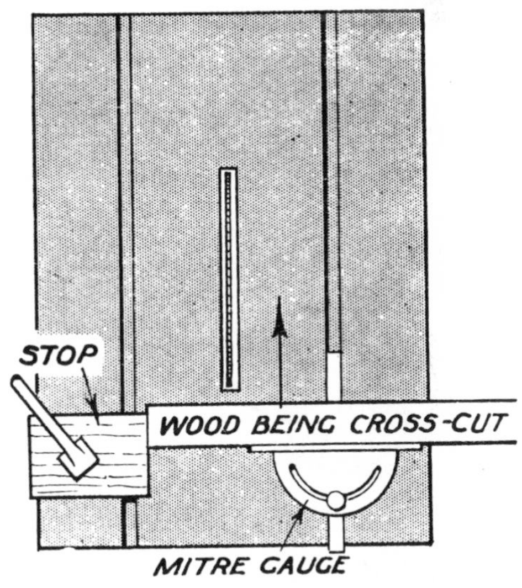

FIG. 6. CROSS CUTTING TO LENGTH

Any number of pieces can be cut to the same length.

Grooving—Frequently on light machines it is necessary to pass the wood over the saw for as many times as may be needed to give the required width of groove. If a drunken saw is available this can be set to the width, though the bottom of the groove is not flat, but slightly curved. For most work, however, the curve is so slight as not to matter. Some saws can be fitted with a dado head which will cut grooves up to any reasonable size in onesixteenths. Light machines, however, are frequently not made to take these, partly because there is insufficient spindle room, and also because the cut would be too heavy.

The table is first adjusted so that the saw projects by an amount equal to the required groove depth. The fence is positioned so that the cut is level with one side of the groove to be cut. If the fence reaches only to the saw, a lengthening piece must be screwed on so that the wood can bear against it until it is past the saw. After a trial cut all the parts are run through. The fence is shifted to cut to the other side of the groove, and again all the parts cut. For narrow grooves this second cut will probably give the required width, but third or even fourth runs may be needed.

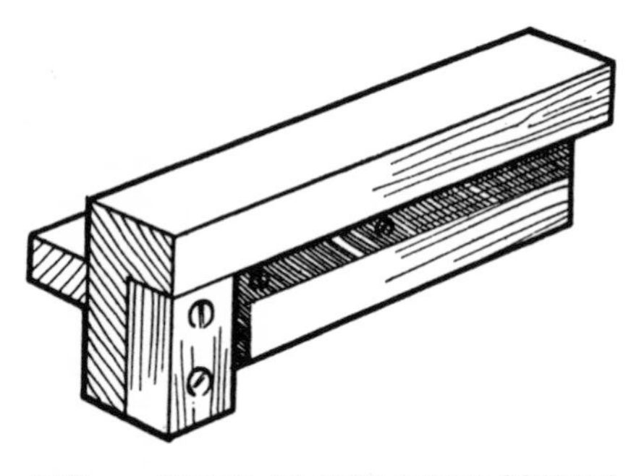

FIG. 7. PUSH BLOCK USED WHEN REBATING

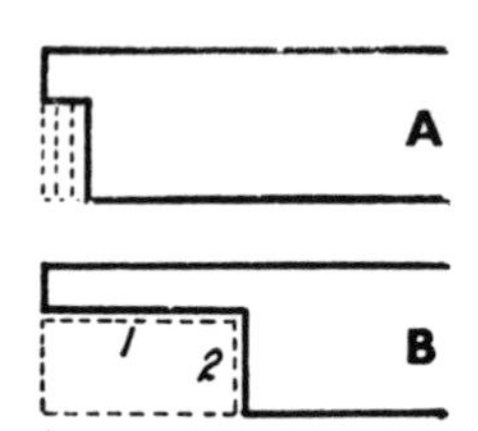

FIG. 8. ALTERNATIVE METHODS OF REBATING

Remember in every case to keep the face side of the wood to the fence.

The pusher stick is needed for completing the cut, though the push block is an advantage for larger pieces, as shown in Fig. 7. It enables downward as well as inward pressure to be maintained.

Rebating—Narrow rebates can be worked by taking parallel cuts side by side as at (A), Fig. 8, the wood being passed through as many times as may be needed to give the rebate width. For a rebate of any size, however, two cuts at right angles are the simpler method as at (B). Other things being equal cut No. 1 should be made first because, at the completion of the second cut the waste piece drops away, and it is desirable to have the broad surface of the wood bedding on the saw table where it is not liable to tilt over. Once again the pusher stick is used towards the completion of the cut. This is specially desirable since the riving knife cannot be used, and quite possibly the guard (this depends upon the size of the wood being rebated).

Tenoning.—It would not be economical in time to set up the saw to cut a single tenon or pair of tenons, but considerable saving in time occurs when a whole series is required. The simplest plan is to make the special device shown in Fig. 9. The parts are glued and screwed together. Exact sizes are not important, but the length might be about 6 in., height 7 in., and width 4 in. In use the wood to be tenoned is held against the vertical guide with a thumb-screw, the latter being either passed through the cramp hole or fixed at the side according to the width of the wood being tenoned. The far edge bears against the ripping fence, the latter being positioned so that the saw cuts to the side of the gauge line. A lengthening piece must be screwed to the fence so that the device is supported throughout its cut. The height of table or saw is arranged so that the shoulder line is just reached. One cut is made at each tenon, the saw readjusted, and the other side of all the tenons cut. It is usual to cut the shoulders by hand.

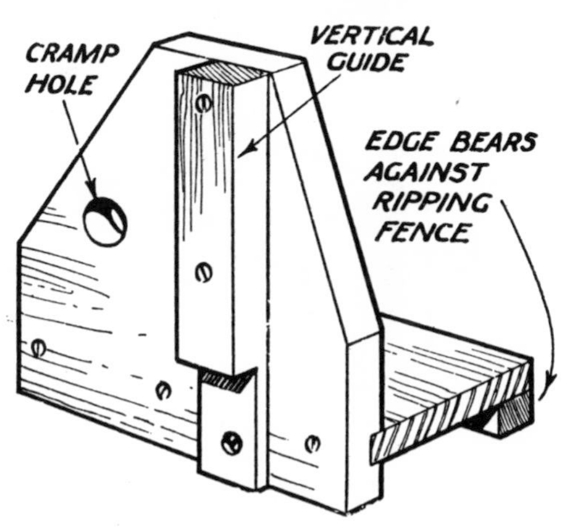

FIG. 9. JIG USED WHEN TENONING

It will be realized that the over-all length of all tenons must be alike, otherwise the saw will over-cut some tenons, and under-cut others. This means that a different system must be followed as compared with that usually used for hand work. Exact over-all length including tenons must be fixed beforehand. Apart from actual cutting there is a further saving in time in that only one piece need be marked with the cutting gauge.

Speed—The theoretical optimum speed of an 8-in. circular saw is in the region of 4,500 r.p.m., but few small saws are designed for so high a rate. The more usual speed ranges from 1,500 to

2,500 r.p.m., and the saw should cut perfectly well if kept sharp. As a guide to the power required, the following are average.

FIG. 10. CUTTING TENON ON CIRCULAR SAW
This is worked along the ripping fence, the latter being re-set for the second cut.

Saw diam.	H.P. motor
7 in.	$\frac{1}{3}$–$\frac{1}{2}$
8 in.	$\frac{1}{2}$–$\frac{3}{4}$
9 in.	$\frac{1}{2}$–1

BANDSAW

Next to the circular saw this is the most useful machine saw to have. It can be used for straight cuts much as the circular saw is used, and also for curves for which the latter is useless. On the other hand, it will neither rebate nor groove, though tenons can be cut on it.

FIG. 11. THE SMALL BANDSAW IN USE

Whenever possible avoid backing out from the saw. If unavoidable move the wood carefully in line with the saw.

Adjustment—There are several adjustments to be attended to on the bandsaw. First the table is usually made to tilt, and the correct angle should be tested with try square or protractor. The top wheel has a tensioning screw which is slackened off when the saw is not in use. When a new saw has to be fitted the locking device has usually to be unscrewed at the front of the table to enable the saw to be passed through the slot. The purpose of the device is to hold the table rigid.

Tracking is the first adjustment of the saw itself, and is accomplished by tilting the top wheel one way or the other. It should be carried out without guides or thrust wheel. Turn the wheel by hand and note whether the saw tends to keep central on the wheels or run to front or rear. If it is inclined to run towards the rear

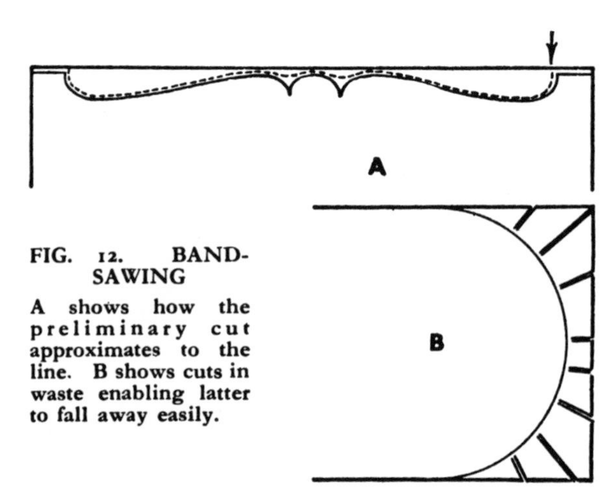

FIG. 12. BAND-SAWING

A shows how the preliminary cut approximates to the line. B shows cuts in waste enabling latter to fall away easily.

tilt the top of the wheel slightly forward at the top. Continue to adjust until it runs in the required position. It is advisable to vary this from time to time so that wear on the tyres can be equalized.

When satisfactory bring forward the thrust wheel so that it barely touches the back of the saw—it should turn only when the saw is being pressed against it in use. The guides may be blocks of metal or hardwood, and they are adjustable horizontally. They should just touch the sides of the saw—not the teeth, of course. As a rule the upper guides form a complete unit with the thrust wheel, the whole being movable vertically. In use it should be set to clear the wood being sawn with just sufficient space above to enable the line to be followed.

Practical Sawing—When possible avoid backing the wood from the saw. Sometimes it cannot be helped, when it should be done carefully and the path of the kerf followed. When a line is fairly intricate follow the main sweep first, ignoring the smaller detail. For instance, in Fig. 12 (A) the first cut would be as shown by the dotted line. This would clear away the bulk of the waste without backing, and enable the acute corners to be cut afterwards. Note that the cut is made to the waste side of the line, allowing for later cleaning up. In the case of Fig. 12 (B), the preliminary cuts enable the waste to fall away when the acute curve is being sawn.

Some items call for sawing on two surfaces. For example, the

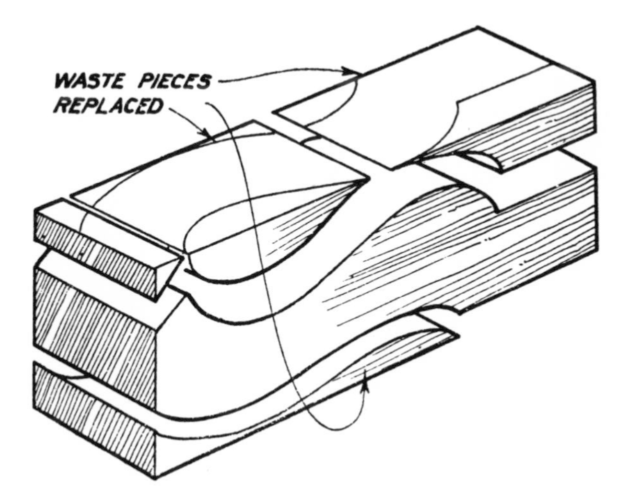

FIG. 13. STAGES IN BANDSAWING A CABRIOLE LEG

shape of a cabriole leg is marked out on two adjacent faces, and saw cuts made at right angles, producing a square section ready for rounding. The shapes on one side having been cut, the waste parts are replaced as in Fig. 13 enabling the remaining cuts to be made. In some cases the lower waste is also replaced to act as a sort of supporting cradle. It is scarcely necessary in the present case because the back curve reaches practically to the bottom and there is no tendency for it to be unsteady.

When the saw is used for ripping straight cuts a fence is used. This may be a special adjustable item made for the table, or simply a straight piece of wood cramped to the table as in Fig. 14. Make sure that it is fixed parallel with the edge so that the saw is in alignment with the cut.

Sometimes it is useful to use the bandsaw for resawing—that is cutting a board in its thickness. It is a great help if preliminary saw cuts can be made on the circular saw as it lessens the work the bandsaw has to do. The operation is shown in Fig. 15, which shows the tall fence used to ensure that the wood is upright.

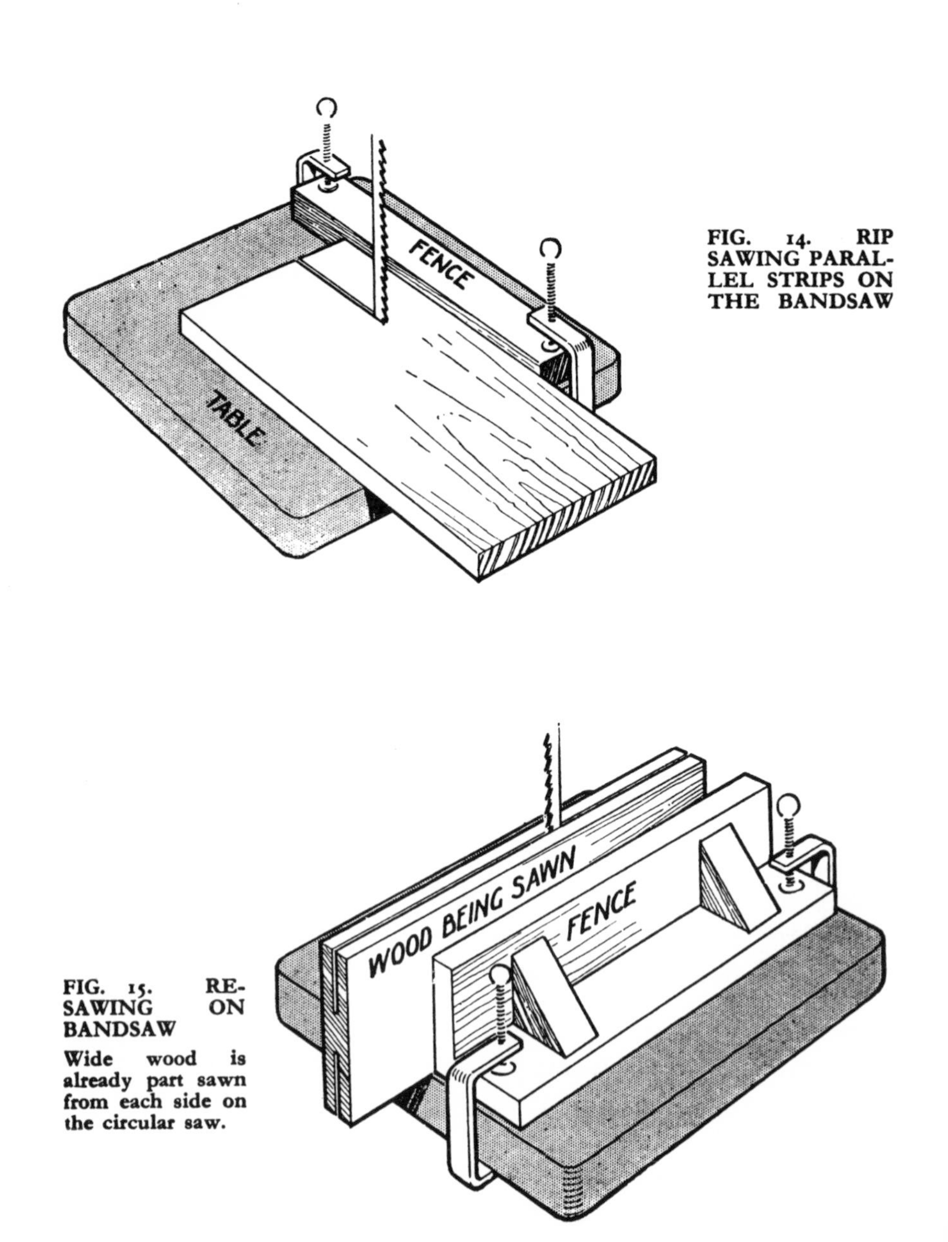

FIG. 14. RIP SAWING PARALLEL STRIPS ON THE BANDSAW

FIG. 15. RE-SAWING ON BANDSAW

Wide wood is already part sawn from each side on the circular saw.

PLANER

Two kinds of machines come under this heading; the surface planer and the thicknesser. The latter, as the name suggests, is used to bring timber to an even thickness, but is not much used in the small home workshop because it is expensive. It is, however, possible to obtain a thicknessing attachment for most planers.

Parts of the Surface Planer—The diagram in Fig. 16 shows the chief parts of the machine. There is the main body in the centre of which the cutter block revolves. This block may have either

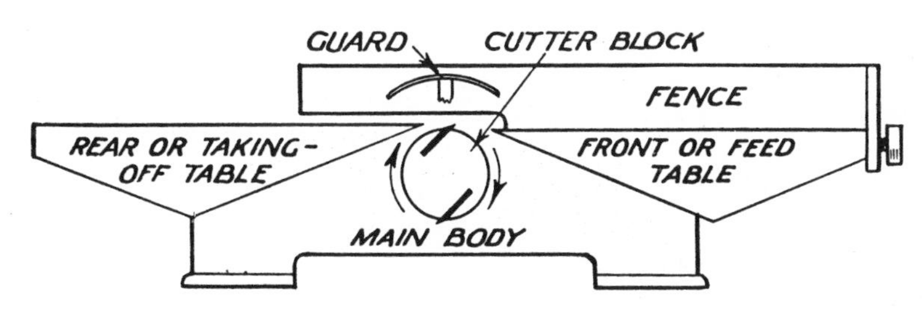

FIG. 16. DIAGRAM SHOWING CHIEF PARTS OF THE PLANER

two or three cutters. In front and to the rear of the cutter block are two tables which are adjustable along two inclined beds. Their height in relation to the cutter is thus adjustable. A fence is fitted to the front table, this being adjustable to any position and also free to cant to any angle. On many machines a rebating table (which is really a side extension of the front table) is fitted. Invariably, too, there is a guard which should be capable of extending right across the cutter block, and also be variable in height.

Sharpening and Setting—Although ground, the cutters of a new machine require to be honed on an oilstone to give a fine edge. A simple jig is shown in Fig. 17, and variations can be worked out to suit the individual cutters. The

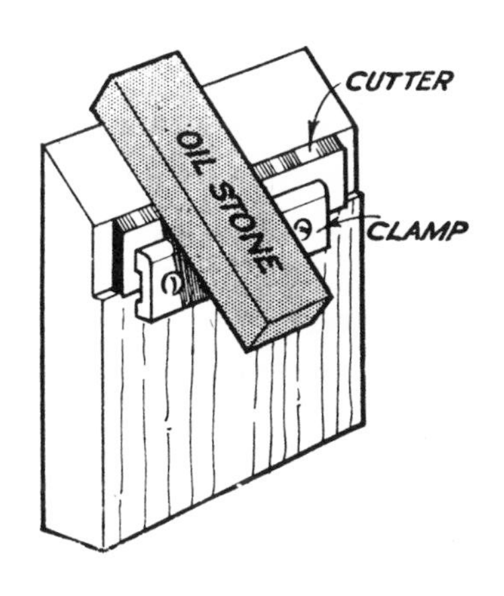

FIG. 17. WOOD JIG FOR SHARPENING PLANER CUTTERS

device enables the correct angle to be maintained. When regrinding is needed it is necessary to mount the cutters upon a special carrier which runs back and forth across the face of the grinding wheel, thus ensuring even grinding.

The cutters are held in the block in various ways, some with wedge pieces held by bolts, or by a separate cap again bolted. As a rule there is some means of adjustment for height—either an adjustment screw at each end or a hole at the rear which enables the cutter to be tapped. Turn the bolts finger tight only when

FIG. 18. SETTING PLANER CUTTERS USING WOOD WITH STRAIGHT EDGE

Both cutters should just touch the wood and no more. The cutters should be tested at both sides of the table.

placing the cutters in the block and carry out all adjustment before finally tightening.

In use the rear table must be exactly level with the tips of the cutters when in the highest position, and once set is never moved for normal planing until sharpening is required again. Deal with one cutter at a time. Place a piece of wood having a straight edge on the rear table, as in Fig. 18, towards one side and turn the block by hand, adjusting the height of the rear table until the cutter just barely catches the wood. When one side is correct bring the wood to the other edge and test this side of the cutter. The latter will probably need raising or lowering, and this should be done until both sides just touch the wood, no more. From this point on the rear table must not be moved (the front table is set well down below the level).

Now deal with the second cutter, adjusting this until both sides of this also just touch the wood. When all is in order tighten the fixing bolts and make a second test. The thickness of cut is fixed by the height of the front table. To ascertain this hold the straight wood on the back table as before. The thickness of cut will be equal to the gap between the wood and the front table. Some machines have a scale showing thickness of cut, but this requires adjustment after each sharpening. To do this set a gauge to exactly $\frac{1}{8}$ in. and mark along the edge of a straight piece of wood.

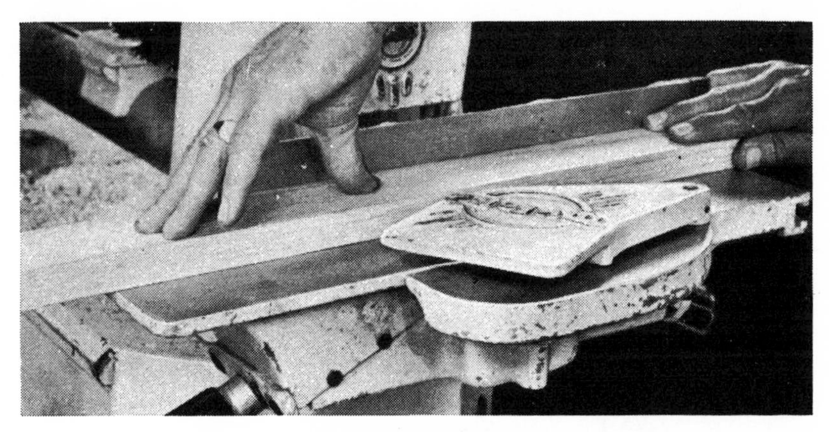

FIG. 19. SURFACING ON THE PLANER

The guard here is pivoted. Some guards extend across the table, and should just clear the wood.

Set the front table to what is obviously less than $\frac{1}{8}$ in., and, setting the machine in action, pass the wood part way over the block. Lower the front table until the gauge line is just reached and set the pointer to the $\frac{1}{8}$ in. mark. All thicknesses will then be correct to this.

Surfacing—Set the fence to slightly more than the width of the wood, and the guard so that the wood will pass beneath with comfortable clearance. The front table is also adjusted to the required thickness of cut. Push the wood forward with the right hand and press steadily down with the left on the front table. As the wood passes over the block withdraw the left hand so that it does not approach near to the block. When a reasonable length has passed beyond the block take the left hand over to the wood on the rear table and again press down. As the end of the wood approaches the block take also the right hand over to the rear table where it assists in both pressing down and moving the wood. Done in this way neither hand is ever immediately over the revolving block. Figs. 19 and 20 show the idea.

When a short piece has to be planed it is advisable to use a

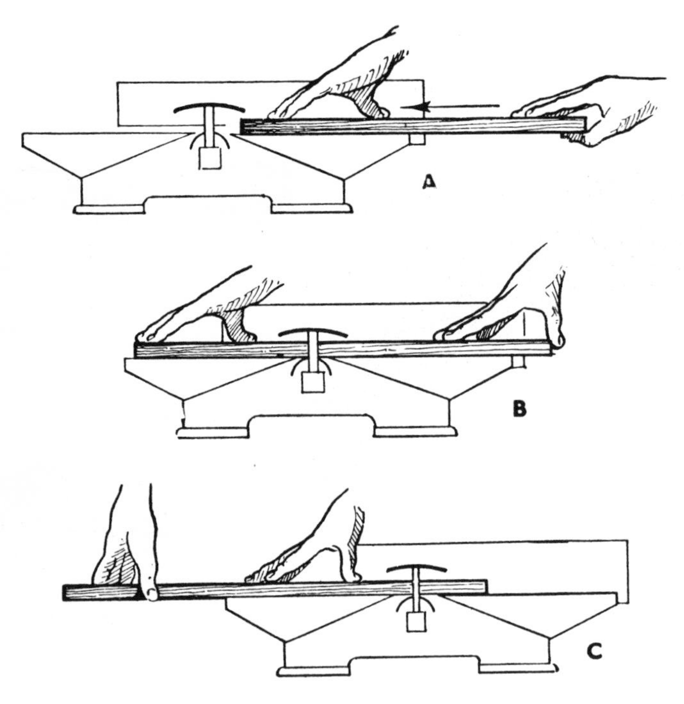

FIG. 20. POSITION OF THE HANDS WHEN SURFACING

Note that neither hand is ever over the cutters.

pusher block as given in Fig. 21. At the start of the cut the wood is fed with the hands in the usual way, but once the rear end is fairly on the table the pusher block is used. When practicable put the hollow side of the wood down on to the table as it is easier to get it straight. If this cannot be done it is necessary to take shavings from the middle first before passing the wood right across.

Edging—This is a similar operation, but the wood must be held firmly up against the fence so that the edge is planed square. If the guard is of telescopic form it is usual to set it low over the block and leave just sufficient gap between its end and the fence for the wood to pass through. In the case of extra wide wood it is as well to increase the height of the fence by screwing a wood face to it. This gives an increased bearing surface against which the wood can bear. As quite a lot of pressure is required in all planing operations it is as well to wipe over the surface of the tables and the fence with a lightly oiled rag. One last word. Examine the wood and pass it through in the direction in which it is less likely to tear out the grain.

FIG. 21. USE OF PUSHER BLOCK WHEN SURFACING
This enables pressure to be maintained at completion of operation.

Rebating—Many machines are provided with a rebating table which is a lateral extension of the front table. This supports the wood as it passes through. The rear table is unaltered; that is, it remains level with the top of the cutters. The front table is lowered to the rebate depth, and the fence is brought over so that it leaves exposed a length of cutter equal to the rebate width. Normally the wood can be passed through in a single operation, but if the rebate is large or the wood extra hard it is as well to set it to half depth first and pass the work through twice. At the start of the cut feed the work slowly; otherwise the cutters may snatch the wood and jolt it backwards. Fig. 22 shows the rebating process.

Bevelling and Chamfering—When these run right through the procedure is much as in normal edging except that the fence is set over at the required angle. If the chamfer is small it can usually be completed in one operation, the front table being set down to the chamfer depth.

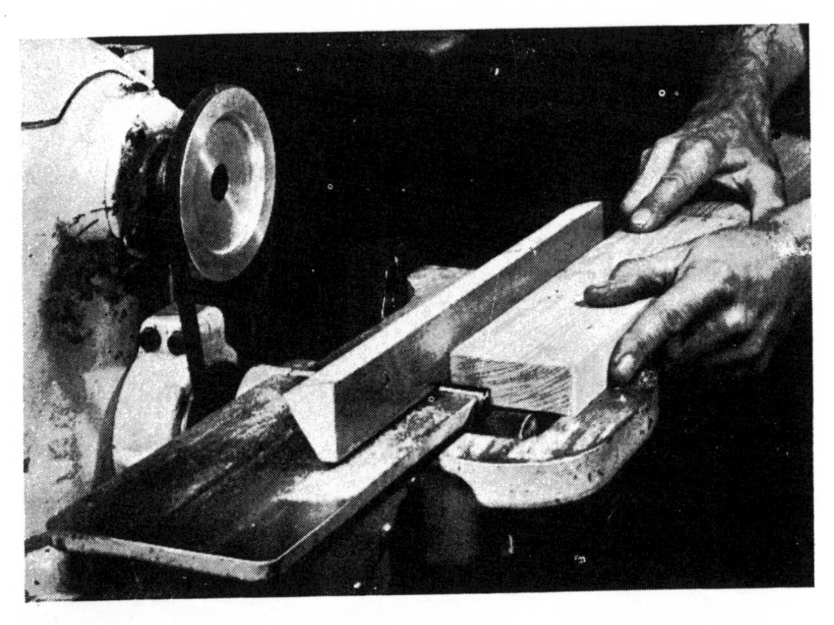

FIG. 22. REBATING ON THE PLANER

Note how the work rests on the rebating table. The belt guard is omitted to show connection to the drive. In practice the belt would be covered.

Stopped chamfers are different, and it is necessary for both tables to be exactly level with each other, the cutter block standing up by an amount equal to the chamfer depth. A wood facing is fixed to the metal fence, and stop blocks are screwed to this so that the chamfer begins and ends in the required positions. The wood is held firmly against the near stop and the far end slowly lowered on to the revolving block. The cutters tend to grab as this happens, but the rear block prevents it from being knocked back, and once it lies on the table all grab ceases. The wood is then fed forward until the front stop is reached when it is lifted clear of the machine. Fig. 23 shows the piece of wood being stop-chamfered.

Tapering—The rear table is level with the top of the cutters as in normal planing, and the front one lowered by an amount equal to the wood to be removed at the thin end. A stop is fixed either to the table or to the fence so that the cutters begin to operate just short of the required point as at (A), Fig. 24. The near end

FIG. 23. STOPPED CHAMFER BEING WORKED ON PLANER

For this operation the guard cannot be used, but it is advisable to bring the fence well over the table so that only a minimum of cutter is exposed.

of the wood rests against the stop, and as the far end is lowered a slight grab will be noticed. The stop prevents it from kicking, however. The wood is pushed forward as at (B), the pusher stick being used, at any rate towards the completion of the cut. It can either be taken right through or be stopped at any particular point to form a spade foot. In the latter case a pencil mark is made on the fence so that all sides can be stopped in the same position.

If the *entire* length of the wood is to be tapered, the cut will have to be started short of the end because it is essential that the end of the wood drops on to the lip of the rear table. The length

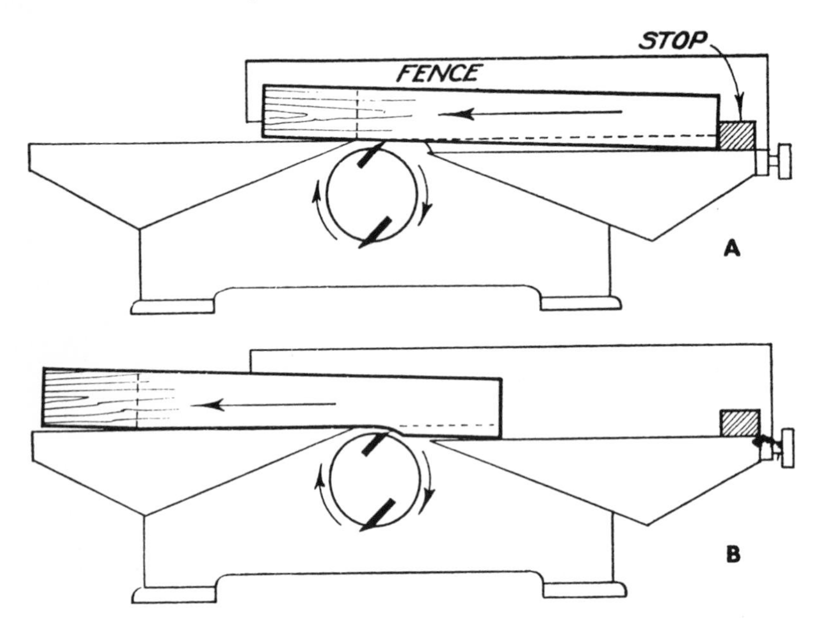

FIG. 24. WORKING TAPERED LEGS ON THE PLANER

of the wood should be noted and the stop fixed so that there is at least $\frac{1}{4}$ in. of wood resting on the lip. Without this it would fall right down on to the revolving cutters and there would be a heavy throw back.

SANDERS

There are two chief kinds of sanders used in the home workshop ; disc and belt. The former of these is shown in Fig. 25, its chief use being to trim wood rather than to smooth it. For instance it is invaluable for trimming mitres after sawing, or for cleaning up the squared ends of wood. Another use is in cleaning the shaped edges of wood when the curvature is convex. Clearly the table must be at right angles with the disc, and the groove along its surface must be parallel with it. The mitre gauge is used as a guide for the wood, and this is slid back and forth so that wear on the abrasive is equalized. Only the down-coming side of the disc is used, as otherwise the wood is liable to be lifted.

Perhaps the chief way in which the disc sander saves time is when a number of pieces have to be trimmed all to the same length.

FIG. 25. TRIMMING WOOD ON THE DISC SANDER
The mitre template is shifted back and forth so that wear is equalized.

One end of all the pieces is first made square by holding it against the mitre gauge. A jig is then made as shown in Fig. 26. A notch is cut in it, and its length is such that when pressed against the end of the work it touches the edge of the table when the far end of the work is hard up against the sanding disc. In use the jig is held against the end of the work and the jig pressed forward until it touches the table and the sander thus ceases to cut. For large pieces it is advisable to hold the jig to the work with a cramp.

Mitreing is done in much the same way as square trimming, but with the mitre gauge set to the required angle. If necessary a jig similar to that in Fig. 26 can be made, but with its notch cut to accommodate the mitre cut. In all cases the face of the moulding should be uppermost so that the inevitable rag is formed on the underside where it will not show. Compound mitres which slope in both thickness and width can be trimmed readily on the sander.

Renew the abrasive paper as soon as it ceases to cut, otherwise it will merely burn the wood. One of the cold tube glues such as *Seccotine* gives good adhesion. Place over a flat board, if necessary

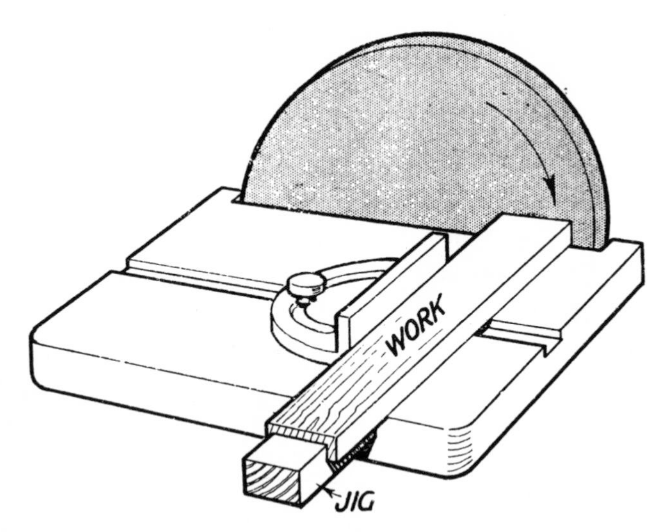

FIG. 26. JIG FOR TRIMMING SEVERAL PIECES TO SAME LENGTH

with a weight above, so that the paper is in close contact with the disc. One of the special sanding discs sold for the purpose can be used, or garnet paper can be stuck down. Avoid allowing it to become damp.

Belt Sander—This type can be used for trimming much as the disc sander is used, but it has two advantages ; the movement is in a straight line so that it can be used for cleaning up polished work for which the disc sander would be quite unsuitable ; and the drums around which it passes enable concave shapes to be smoothed. Fig. 27 shows a belt sander.

Nearly all belt sanders are provided with a stop of some sort, and in the better models an adjustable table is fitted. When this is not provided it is usual to build up one, the details being adapted to suit the individual machine. It should include a table

FIG. 27. BELT SANDER WITH ADJUSTABLE FENCE
Flat work can be sanded on top, and concave work on the drum.

which can be set to varying angles so that mitres, etc., can be trimmed. A tracking device is invariably included which ensures that the glasspaper remains on the drums.

POWERED HAND TOOLS

Just as the lathe is the basis of a series of attachments for sawing, planing, sanding, etc., so the electric drill gun is the basic powered tool for which saw, sanding disc, and grindstone can be obtained.

The drill gun itself will generally take drills up to $\frac{1}{4}$ in. (larger and heavier drills go up to $\frac{1}{2}$ in., but their use in woodwork is limited). The usual metal-worker's morse drills can, of course, be used, but it is necessary to pop all holes with a centre punch, as morse drills have no centre point, but an edge. Special twist bits with round shanks can be obtained, but if there is any difficulty the square end can always be sawn from the ordinary twist bit intended for use in the brace. Many of these twist bits have a screw centre, and, owing to the speed of the drill are inclined to grab into the wood, and, when the hole is large, the machine may stall. It will generally be more satisfactory if the screw is filed into the form of a square pyramid, as the drill can then be fed into the wood at whatever speed is required. For holes which must be dead upright it is advisable to use a drill stand which enables the drill to be lowered into the wood. There are two advantages ; the hole is perfectly square or at whatever angle is desired, and the

FIG. 28. CIRCULAR SAW ATTACHMENT FOR THE ELECTRIC DRILL
The tool is guided by the fence. For grooving the face plate is adjusted to give the required depth of cut.

holes can be stopped at any depth without the necessity of individual testing.

A small circular saw attachment is shown in Fig. 28. It has a fence for parallel cuts and the depth can be regulated as required. Either square or cuts at an angle can be made as shown. A retractable guard is provided. Its great advantage (like its elder brother, the hand electric saw) is in work in which it is impossible to take the wood to the machine.

Reciprocating Saw Attachment—This is used for cutting curves and has the advantage that it can be used for interior cuts. It is shown in use in Fig. 29. It is at its best for wood ½ in. thick and under, but can be used for the occasional cutting of thicker stuff. It can be used in one of two ways, the choice depending upon the job. For a large panel the saw can be taken to the wood, but small items are best done in reverse. The saw is fixed on to the bench or in the vice, and the wood passed across it. It is, of course, necessary to bore a preliminary hole for interior cuts.

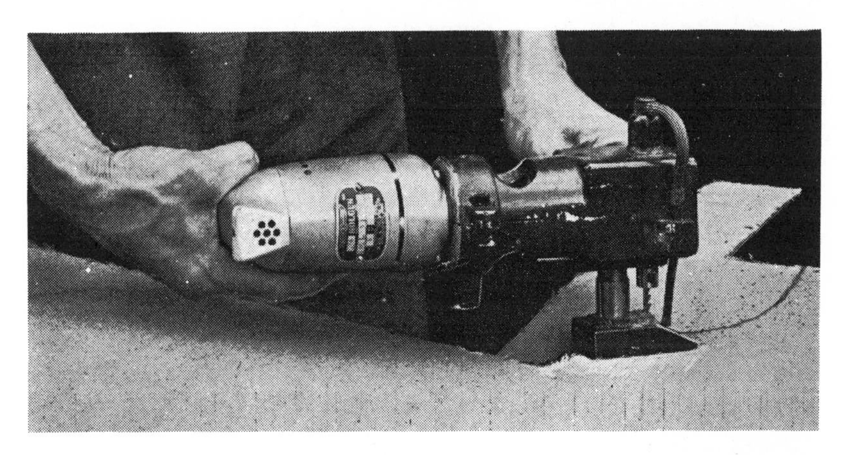

FIG. 29. JIG SAW ATTACHMENT FOR THE ELECTRIC DRILL
Alternatively for small work the machine can be held in the vice upside down and the wood passed across it.

Sander—This takes the form of a rubber disc over which a sanding disc is held. The side of disc is in action on the wood, the path of the abrasive being more or less straight. Alternatively a polishing mop can be used, this being specially useful for wax polishing, or the cleaning up of old metal fittings, etc.

Router Bits.—These can be used with an electric drill if the speed is great enough. The usual method is to rig up a table on which the work can move laterally. An arrangement of fences or a jig is required. It is chiefly useful for recessing and for stopped grooves, etc.

Those interested in machining should see *Light Machines for Woodwork*, by C. H. Hayward, published by Evans Brothers Ltd.

CHAPTER VII

CONSTRUCTION—CARCASES, DOORS, WINDOW FRAMES, DRAWERS

THE way things are put together in solid wood may be conveniently divided into three main groups : the frame, the box, and the stool. Some items do not fall exactly into any, and some are a combination of two or even three ; but the division is useful as nearly all methods are founded upon one or other of them. All have been evolved with strength in view, but, equally important, with allowance for shrinkage. The latter is a fundamental characteristic of timber ; it shrinks as it dries out, and swells again if it becomes damp. This inevitable movement has to be taken into consideration, no matter what the item to be made may be. It is true that modern materials such as plywood, lamin board, and so on are free from this feature, and a great many things can be done with these materials which could not be done with solid wood. These are noted in the methods of construction outlined below.

The three methods are shown in Fig. 1 which gives a typical cabinet on modern lines. The doors are two frames with either grooved-in or rebated-in panels. The main carcase is virtually a box without lid standing on end, and the drawer is another. Lastly the stand is a sort of stool without a top. If the back is panelled it becomes a frame. Details vary according to the particular job, of course, but basically all are much the same.

CABINET DOORS AND FRAMES

These are of two chief kinds ; panelled and flush. The former consists of a main framework put together with mortise and tenon joints, and one or more panels fitted either into a groove or rebate. The idea is that the framework provides the strength, the panel being simply a filling-in piece, free to move in its groove or rebate as shrinkage or swelling occurs.

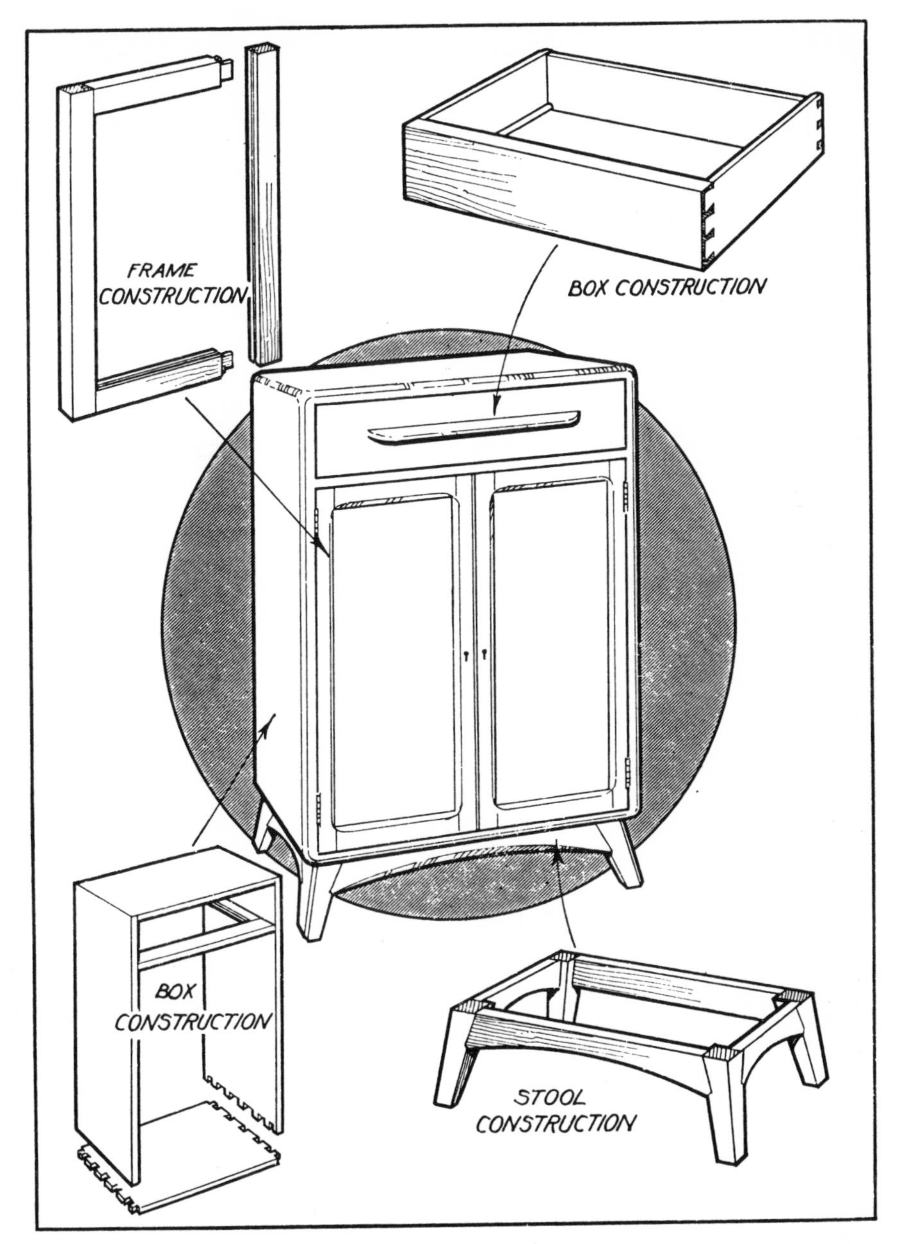

FIG. 1. EXAMPLES OF THE THREE MAIN BASIC FORMS OF CONSTRUCTION

Nearly all pieces of woodwork are made on the lines of one of these forms of construction. Some are a combination of them.

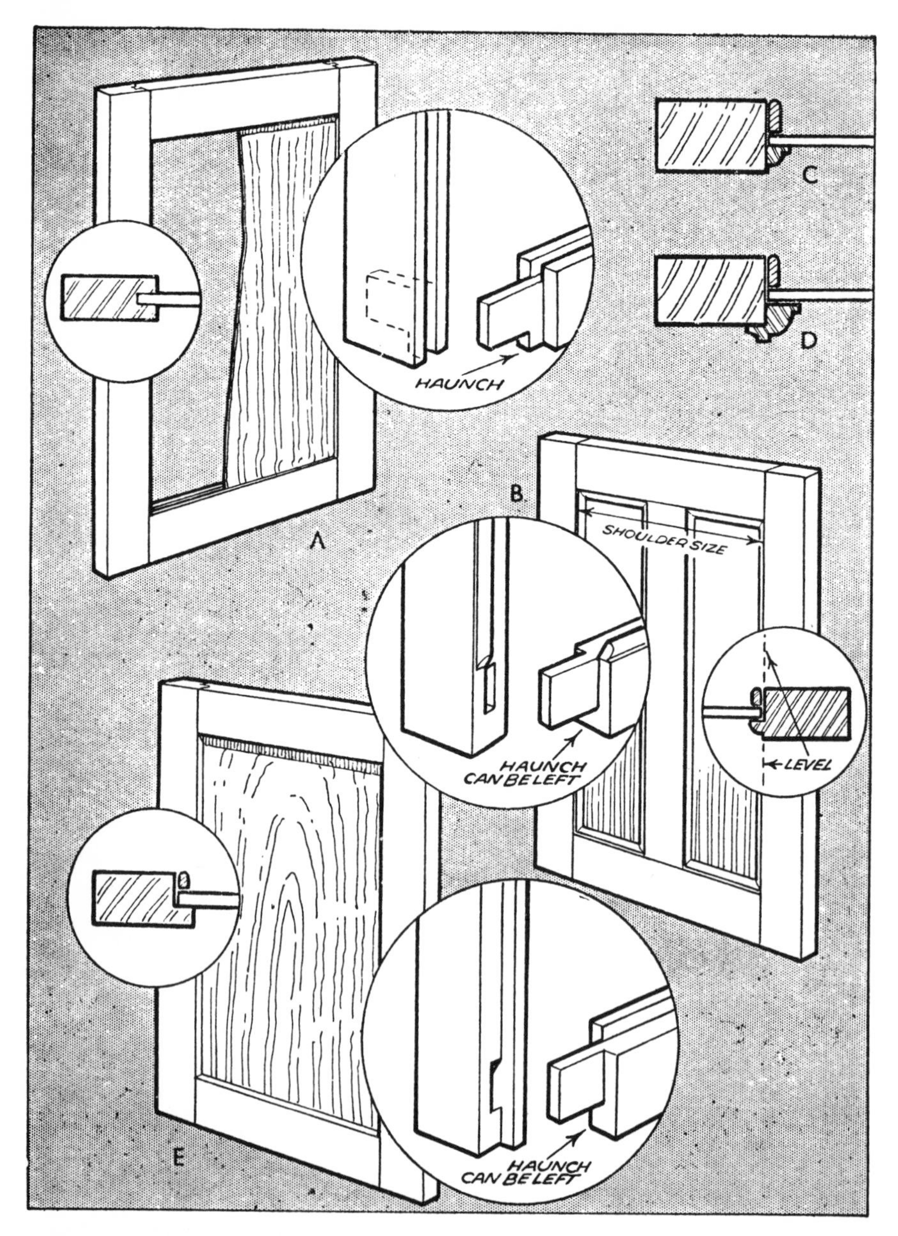

FIG. 2. EXAMPLES OF FRAMED DOORS WITH VARIOUS METHODS OF FITTING THE PANEL

A. Grooved-in panel. Note how haunch fills in end of groove. B. Door with moulded and rebated framework. C. Planted-on moulding. D. Bolection moulding. E. Rebated-in panel.

Grooved-in Panel—The grooved-in type is shown at (A), Fig. 2. It is used chiefly for painted doors in which there is no difficulty about the application of the finish since the brush is used. It is undesirable for a polished finish in that it is difficult to work the rubber into the internal edges and corners. In the case of stained work, such as cabinet backs, the panels (when in solid wood) should be stained at the edges before assembling. Then in the event of their pulling out of the grooves owing to shrinkage there is no danger of white, unstained wood showing.

Note that the grooving automatically cuts away the tenon at the inside ; consequently the mortise must be set in at the inside correspondingly. Another point is that a haunch is left at the outside of the tenon to fill in the groove which necessarily runs right through in the upright.

Moulded and Rebated Door—For cabinet work with polished finish this is widely used since the panel can be polished separately and fitted afterwards. The front edges are moulded in the solid in the best work (as distinct from an applied moulding), and an essential feature is that the bottom of the moulding is level with the rebate as shown at (B), Fig. 2. This is because the moulding is cut away locally opposite the joint, and this produces a flat surface for the shoulders of the tenon.

When setting out note that the shoulder length is taken up to the rebate, not to the edge of the stiles (see inset). This seems obvious enough after moulding and rebate have been worked, but is not so clear beforehand when the wood is still square-edged. It makes a stronger job if a haunch is cut at the bottom as suggested inset.

For cheaper work the moulding is applied separately (C), Fig. 2, being mitred round. It is quicker to make because only a plain square-edged frame is needed, and the moulding can be obtained ready-made. A more legitimate use is when a bolection moulding is required as at (D). This could not easily be worked in the solid.

Rebated Panel—When the panel is to be rebated in and there is no moulding, the joint at (E) is used. This calls for long- and short-shoulders to the tenon, the back shoulder being longer than the front one by the rebate depth. Here again a haunch can be allowed with advantage. In all these examples the joints are marked out and cut first. This is followed by the rebating or groov-

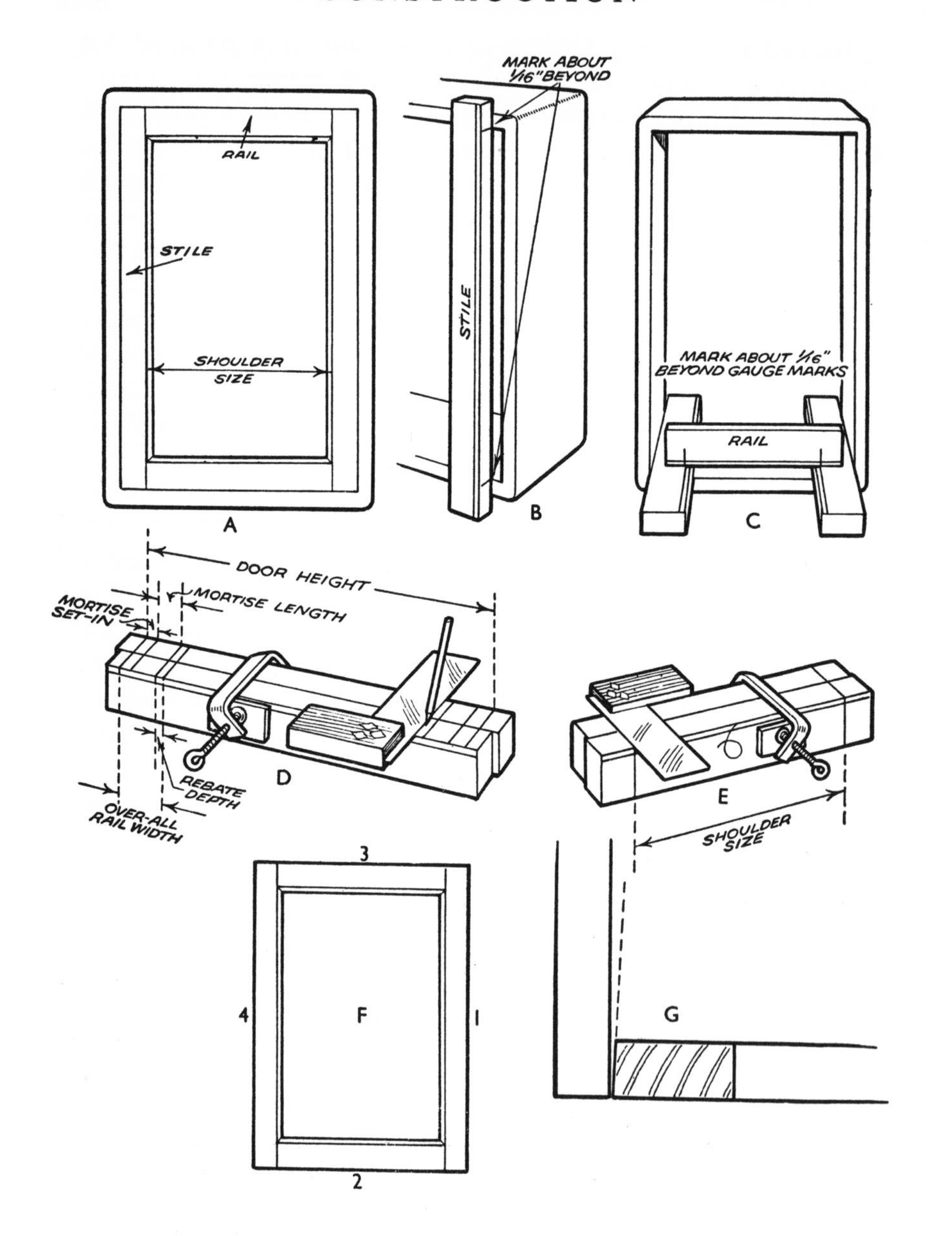

FIG. 3. DOOR MAKING: HOW PARTS ARE MARKED OUT

A. Where shoulder size is taken from in moulded and rebated frame. B. Marking stile size. C. Shoulder length of rail. D. Marking mortise positions on stiles. E. Shoulders being squared. F. Order in which door edges are trimmed. G. How closing edge slopes.

ing, the moulding being worked last. Any mitreing (as in (B)) is the final process and is carried out during the fitting.

Making a Framed Door—Fig. 3 shows the general procedure. Details would be adapted in accordance with the particular kind of door being made. In the example given at (A) the framework is moulded and rebated, and the joint used would be that shown on p. 108, at (B). Having planed stiles and rails true mark out the rebate and moulding depth with the gauge (the two are equal). Holding a stile against the cupboard carcase (B) mark with pencil the door height, adding about $\frac{1}{16}$ in. to allow for trimming and fitting. To mark the shoulder size of the rails place the two stiles at the bottom of the carcase and lay the rail on them as at (C). Transfer the *line of the rebate*, again adding about $\frac{1}{16}$ in.

To ensure both stiles being alike they should be cramped together temporarily as at (D) and the marks squared across both. Note that in addition to the over-all rail width it is necessary to square in the rebate depth and the mortise set-in at the end. The two latter lines give the mortise length. All marks should be put in with pencil.

A similar procedure is followed for the rails, but the marking knife or chisel is used (E). Afterwards the parts are separated and the marks squared all round each rail independently. The butt of the square should be against face side or face edge in every case.

Cutting the joints follows, after which the rebate is worked, and lastly the moulding. The shoulders should not be sawn until the last two processes have been completed. The mitreing of the moulding is described on p. 77. During fitting test for winding.

After assembling level the joints and fit the door in the order shown at (F). If after planing the No. 1 edge to fit the cupboard the door is appreciably too wide, plane the surplus equally from both edges. Otherwise they will not balance. The same thing applies to the top and bottom edges.

FLUSH DOORS

These are more in accordance with modern ideas of design, and have become practicable largely owing to the introduction of

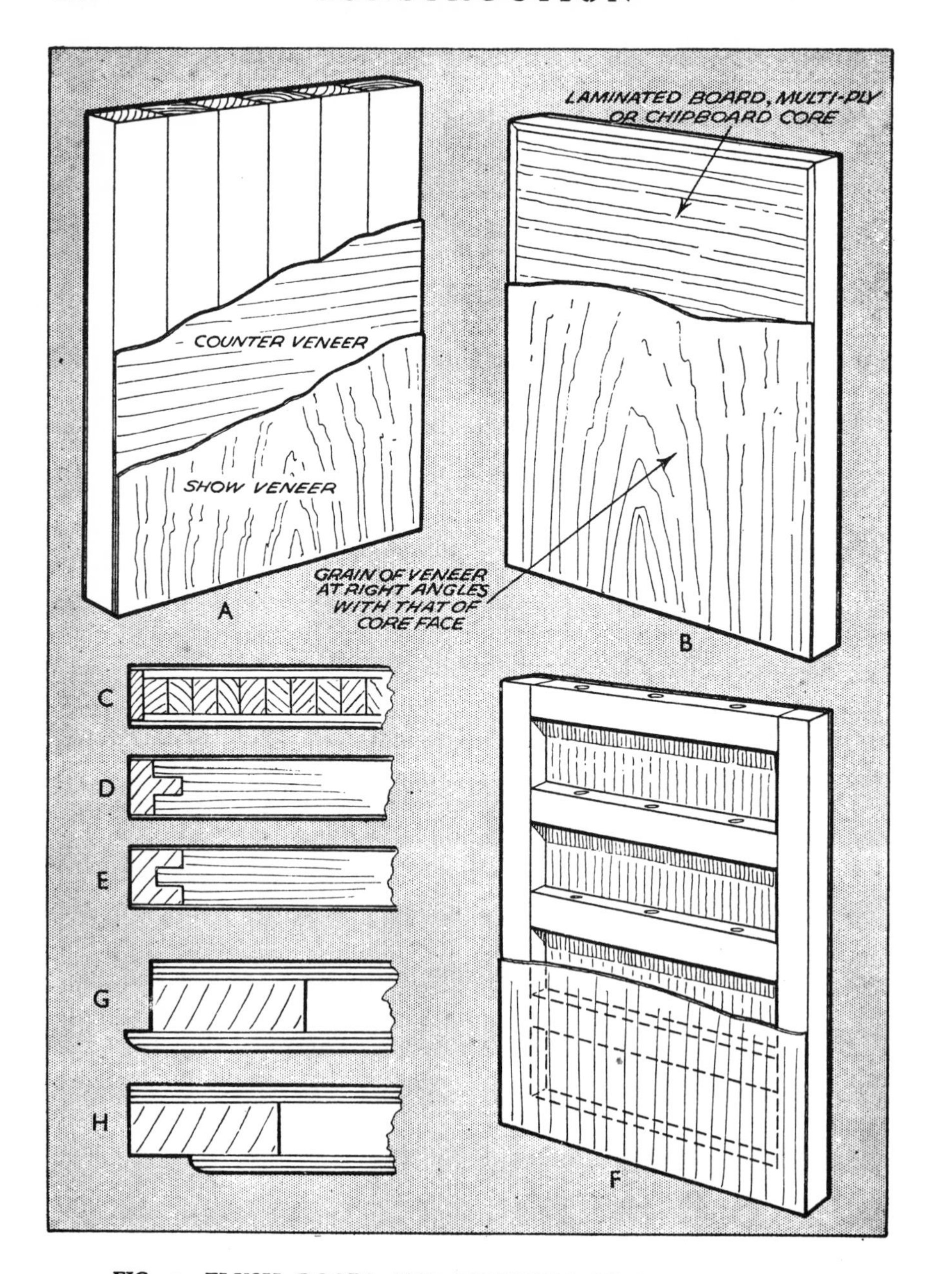

FIG. 4. FLUSH DOORS AND METHODS OF CONSTRUCTION

A. Strips glued together side by side and veneered. B. Laminated or plywood door, edged and veneered. C–H. Examples of edge treatments. F. Framed door with glued-on panels.

materials such as plywood and laminated board which are available in extreme widths and are free from shrinkage.

Jointed and Veneered Door—In smaller sizes the method at (A), Fig. 4 can be followed, this being the original way of making such doors, and still used to an extent. Straight-grained, dry, reliable wood is used, strips of about 2 in. width being glued together with the heart side alternately front and back. Both sides are levelled and laid with a plain veneer, the grain of which runs crosswise. Over these counter veneers the face show veneers are laid. It is important that veneers of equal thickness are laid on both sides. Sometimes the counter veneer is omitted, but the result is not so reliable.

Lamin Board or Multi-ply—This is shown at (B), Fig. 4. Whichever substance is used, the veneers should have their grain at right angles with that of the outer surface. In the best way counter veneers are used as at (A), but frequently this is omitted. Both sides should have the same treatment. To conceal the layers at the edges a lipping is needed, and in most cases this is added before veneering as this gives an unbroken effect at both front and back. If, however, the panel is liable to be subjected to much wear at the edges it is better to veneer first. The edging then affords protection, and it is so narrow that it does not show up badly.

Methods of arranging the edging are shown at (C), (D), and (E). The simplest, that at (C), is about $\frac{3}{16}$ in. or $\frac{1}{4}$ in. thick and is glued round, the corners being mitred. The veneer is taken right over it. A stronger method is that at (D) and is widely used in the trade. As, however, the edging section is rather awkward to make by hand methods owing to the two rebates having to be of exactly the same depth, the edging at (E) may be preferred. Here only a groove is needed, and the rebates on the ply which form the tongue are more easily worked because there is a much larger area to grip. The rebates could be marked out with cutting gauge and worked independently from each side.

Framed and Covered Door—The method at (F) is frequently used, especially for painted work. In the best way both sides are covered with ply, though the back one is often omitted. Intermediate cross-rails are desirable to stop any tendency for the panels to sink in locally. When both sides are covered complications are sometimes caused owing to the air necessarily trapped

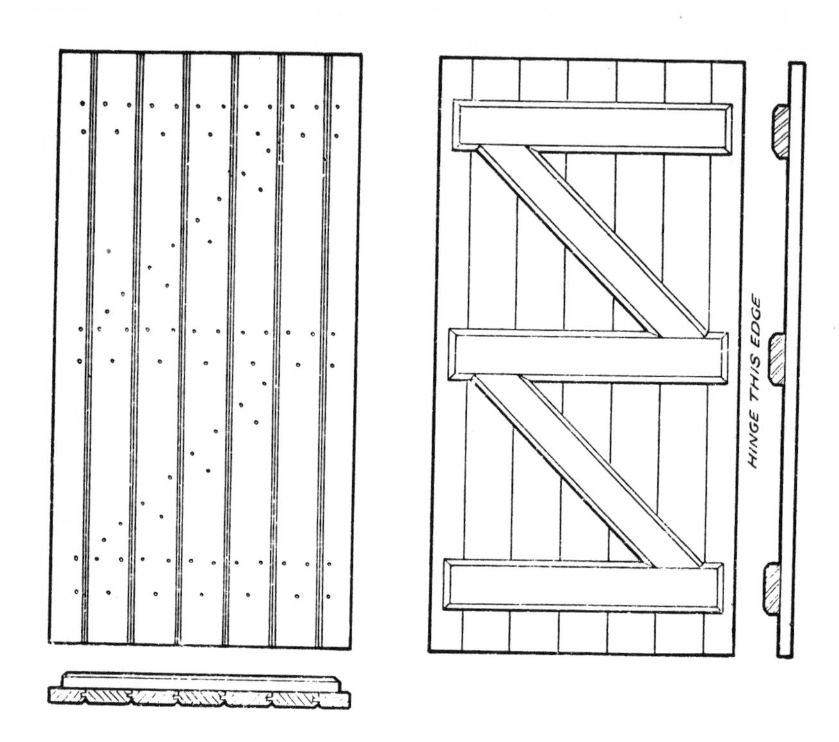

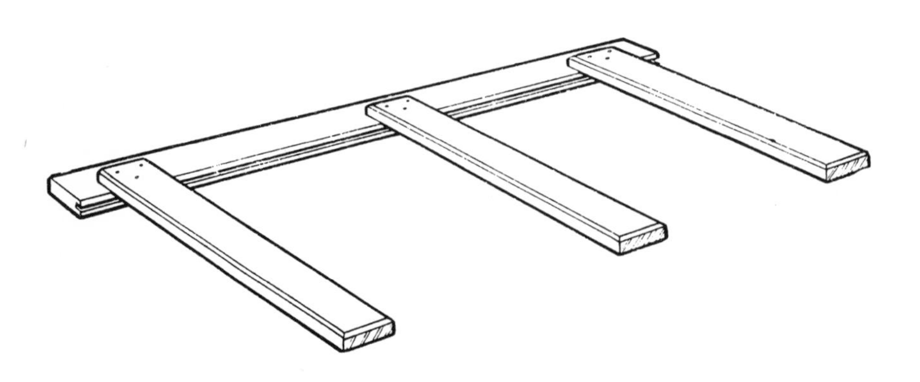

FIG. 5. LEDGED AND BRACED DOOR AND FIRST STAGE IN MAKING IT

Tongued and grooved boards are used. If an exact number does not go into the width the two outer boards should be cut down so that the effect is balanced.

between the panels not being equalized with that of the surrounding atmosphere. To get over this a series of holes can be drilled through all rails as shown.

The front ply can either finish flush with the framing at the edges, or it can be made to project as at (G). The latter is useful in that it forms a rebate and helps to keep out dust. Alternatively the set-in panel at (H) can be used.

LARGE DOORS

Ledged and Braced Door—The simplest form of door is the kind one might make for a shed. It consists of tongued and grooved boards, usually $\frac{7}{8}$ in. or less for a light door, with ledges or cross pieces of heavier stuff—say $1\frac{1}{4}$ in.—nailed across. To prevent sagging diagonal braces are added as in Fig. 5, these fitting into notches cut in the ledges. It is unlikely that the width can be made up by an exact number of boards and, the procedure is to go beyond the width and reduce the two outer boards so that the effect is balanced. Remember that the outer tongue and groove have to be removed from these outer boards in any case. It may occasionally happen that very narrow strips are left at the outside, and it is then advisable to reduce the width of all the boards, re-grooving them where necessary ; or, better still, choose a width of board which is more convenient.

Prepare the ledges, remembering to set them in where necessary to clear the door jamb. Bevel or chamfer the edges as shown. Ledges are usually inside, but for outside work the lower edges should be left square and a drip groove worked. It is convenient to cut the notches to receive the braces before fixing as it is merely a matter of sawing across the grain and chiselling the sloping notches. Nail all three ledges to one stile, test for squareness, and turn the whole over. With straight-edge and pencil mark the positions, and nail the boards, punching in the heads. In this way the nails pass through the thinner wood into the thicker.

Once again reverse the door and cut the braces to make a close fit in their grooves. Nail on finally from the other side, pencil lines being drawn in as a guide. In all cases stagger the nails when possible to avoid splitting.

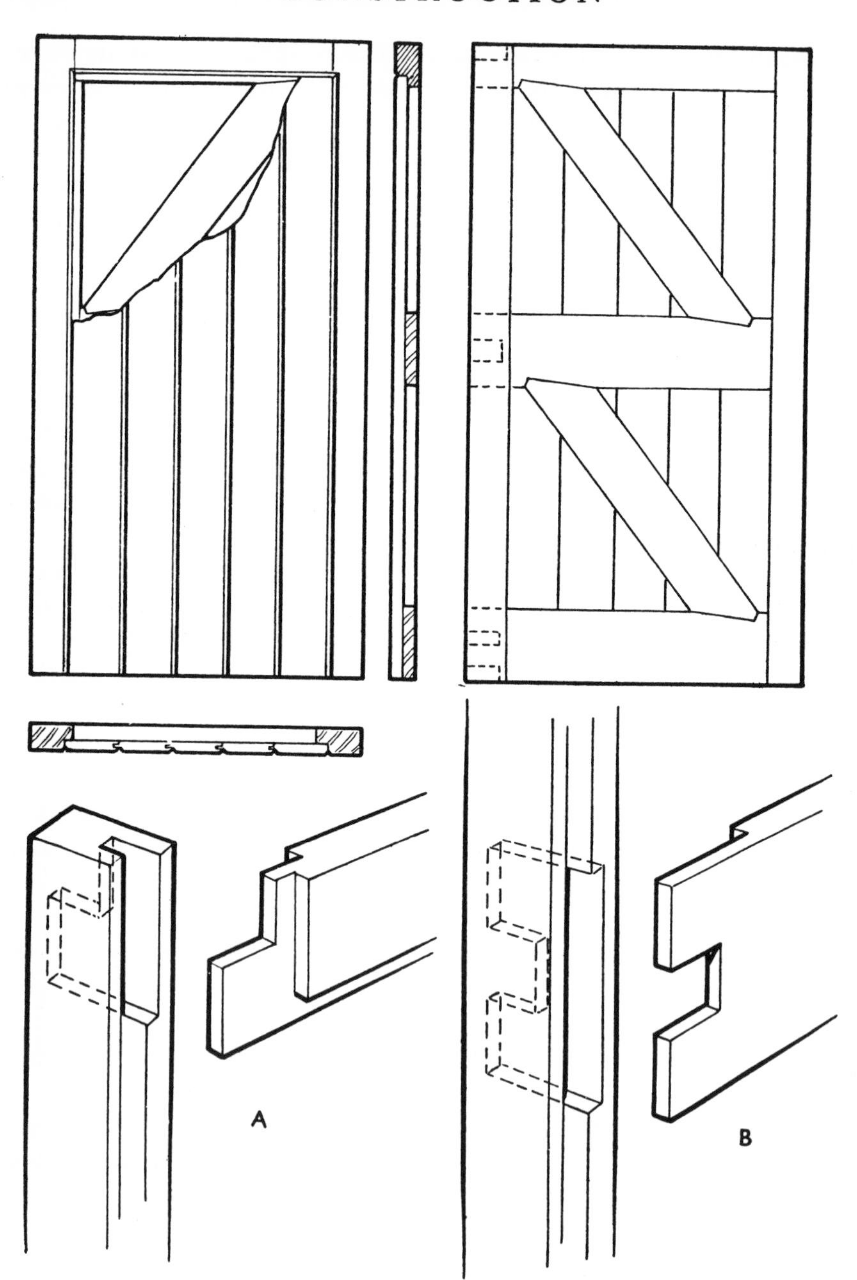

FIG. 6. FRAMED, LEDGED AND BRACED DOOR AND ITS CONSTRUCTION

A. Mortise and tenon joint at top. B. Bare-faced tenon of mid rail.

Framed, Ledged and Braced Door—This is used in better class work. A framework is put together with mortise and tenon joints, and braces fitted to prevent sagging. Tongued and grooved boards are nailed on to one side as in Fig. 6.

Top rail and stiles are rebated to receive the *T* and *G* boards, but the mid and bottom rails are thinner by the thickness of the boards and have bare-faced tenons. (A) shows the top rail joints. Note the long- and short-shoulders, the front one reaching down to the rebate. The bare-faced tenons of mid and bottom rails are given at (B). All are taken through and wedged from outside.

Assuming that the boarding has a *V* joint at the tongue, the main frame should be chamfered to agree before assembling. That of the top rail runs right through, but that of the stiles should run out short of the joint and be finished with a mason's mitre cut in the solid after gluing up. Cut in the braces, and fix with a nail at each end driven through the edge.

The *T* and *G* boarding should be even as far as possible. Any reduction that may be needed should be taken equally from the outside boards. Nail in position, and punch in all heads.

Flush Door—These are of many kinds. An attractive pattern with or without glass panel is shown in Fig. 7. A main framework is put together with mortise and tenon joints and a veneered plywood panel glued on at each side. To prevent sinking between the rails a number of slats are inserted. Also a lock piece is set in to enable a mortise lock to be cut in, and uprights to enable the circular window to be cut. Tongued edges are added finally, partly to give a neat finish, and also to protect the veneer edges.

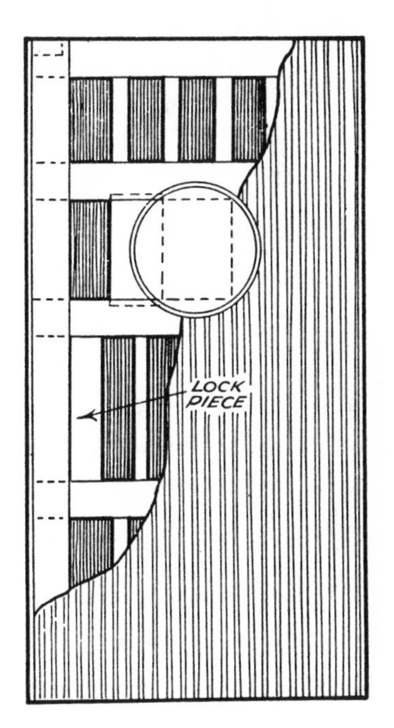

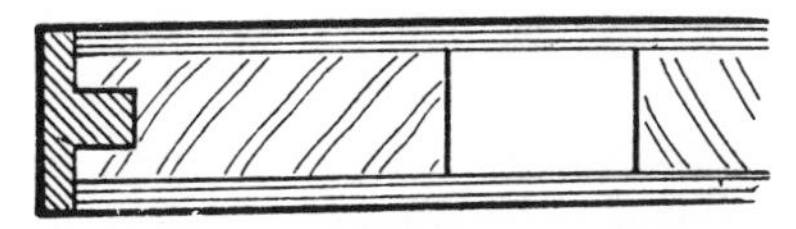

FIG. 7. BUILT-UP FLUSH DOOR

It is essential that the door frame is entirely free from winding; also that the whole is kept completely flat when the panels are being pressed. Otherwise any winding will be perpetuated.

SLIDING DOORS

There are many ways of arranging these.

Solid Wood Doors—A simple method for wood doors is given in Fig. 8. There is a rebate wide enough to take both doors with a separating bead between. It is successful up to a point, but the bearing surfaces are wide, and there is consequently considerable friction. Furthermore the wear takes place on the surface and edge of the door itself, and an unsightly wear mark is eventually formed. The use of candlegrease as a lubricant is a help in reducing friction, but it is still considerable, especially in a heavy door.

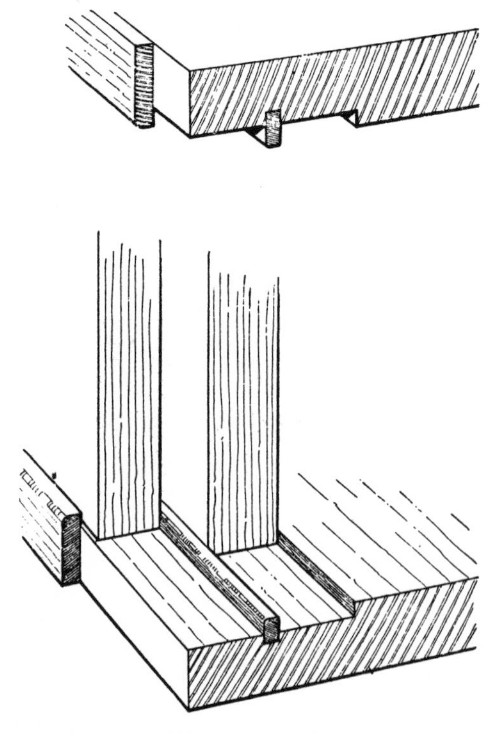

FIG. 8. SIMPLE SLIDING DOOR

The separating bead is inserted when the doors are being put in position. Make it a tight fit and use only one or two dabs of glue so that removal is not unduly difficult. If preferred the top bead can be glued in permanently beforehand. The lower one can be in two lengths with a short spliced joint. One piece only is glued in permanently. This allows the door to be passed in and slid along, after which the remaining piece is tapped in with two dabs of glue to hold it.

Another scheme is that in Fig. 9 in which brass strips are let into the top and bottom. The doors are grooved to make a free fit over the brass, and a short brass or copper piece screwed into the lower groove at each end. These metal pieces are let in, but stand a trifle proud in the grooves so that they only rest on the strip. These strips should be in two separate lengths as previously described to allow insertion of the doors.

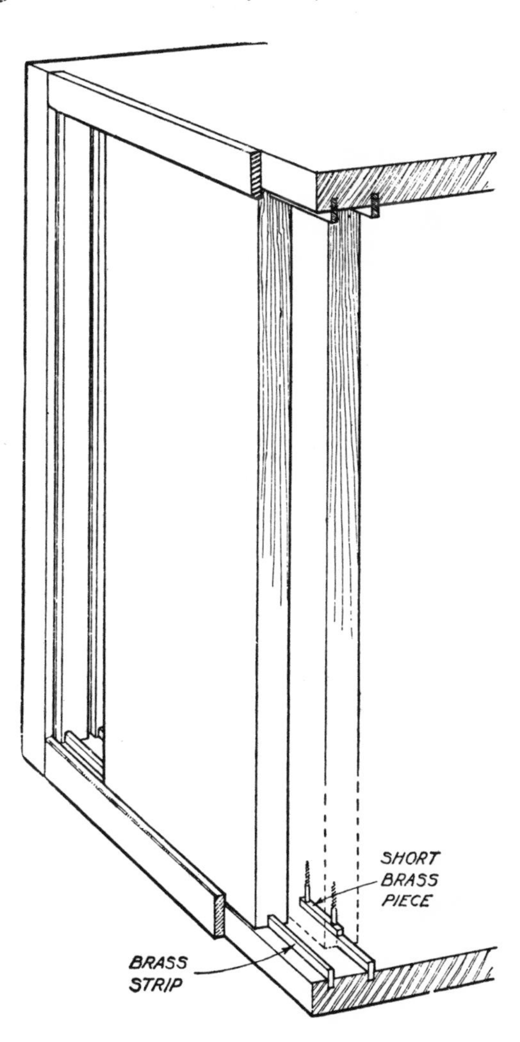

FIG. 9. ALTERNATIVE METHOD WITH BRASS RUNNERS

Figs. 10 and 11 give a third method with wood beads at top and small brass pieces let in at the back at the bottom. Note that the door itself does not touch at the bottom. The weight and wear are taken by the brass pieces. Note that the brass channelling in which they fit is not vertically below the top grooves. It will generally be found that the doors can be passed into position without difficulty by putting the top in first and screwing the brass pieces at the bottom afterwards. Front facing beads are added lastly.

An alternative is the scheme in Fig. 12, often used for multi-ply doors. The top tongues are slipped in first and the bottom beads again arranged in separate lengths.

Special Tracks and Runners—For heavy doors the ball-bearing runner and track in Fig. 13 is often used. The runners are let into the underside of the door, and the track is screwed to the cupboard bottom. When a facing-fillet can be fixed the arrangement as shown is satisfactory. Otherwise it is necessary to groove the underside of the door so that it fits right over the track. At the top are simple wood beads.

A specially successful fitting is the fibre track and gliders in Fig. 14. The fibre track is let into grooves worked in the cupboard

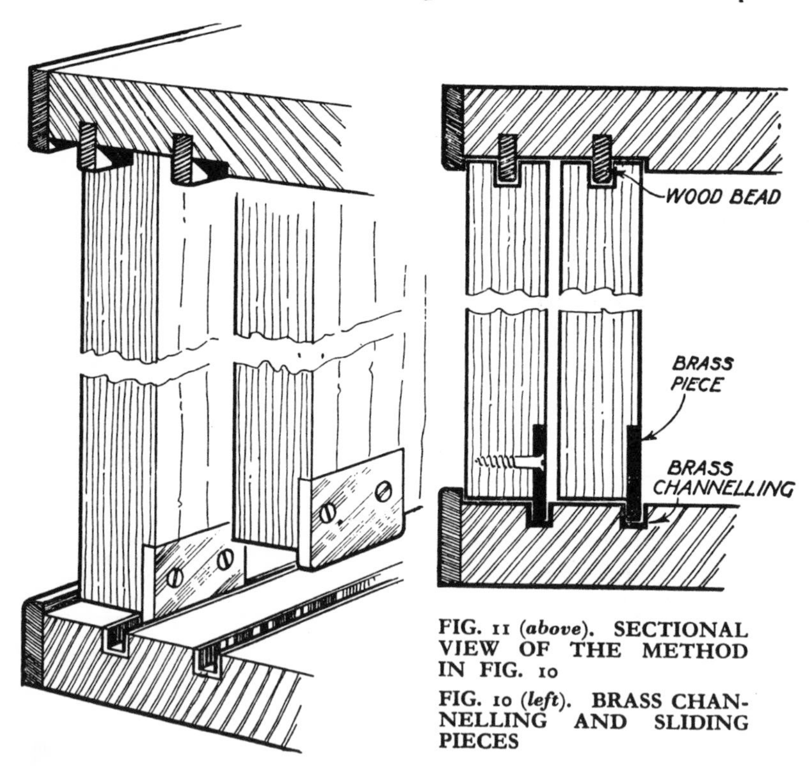

FIG. 11 (*above*). SECTIONAL VIEW OF THE METHOD IN FIG. 10

FIG. 10 (*left*). BRASS CHANNELLING AND SLIDING PIECES

bottom, and when a covering bead can be used the gliders are merely recessed into the underside of the door. A better method, however, is to work grooves in the door so that the latter fits closely down to the cupboard bottom as in Fig. 15.

Glass Doors—A simple method is given in Fig. 16 in which grooves to give a free fit are worked in top and bottom. It will be noted that the top grooves are extra deep to allow the doors to be lifted up and dropped into the bottom ones. This allows for the removal of the doors at any time. Rather sweeter running is obtained by placing strips of fibre in the bottom grooves as

FIG. 12 (*right*). SLIDING DOORS TONGUED AT TOP AND GROOVED AT BOTTOM

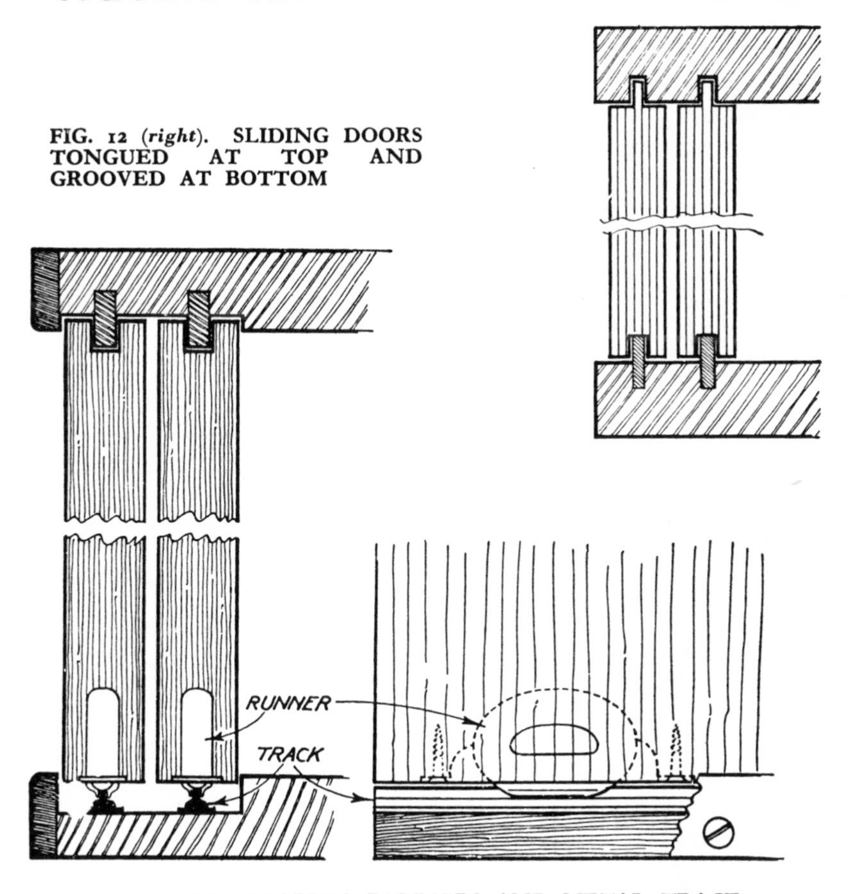

FIG. 13. BALL-BEARING RUNNERS AND METAL TRACK

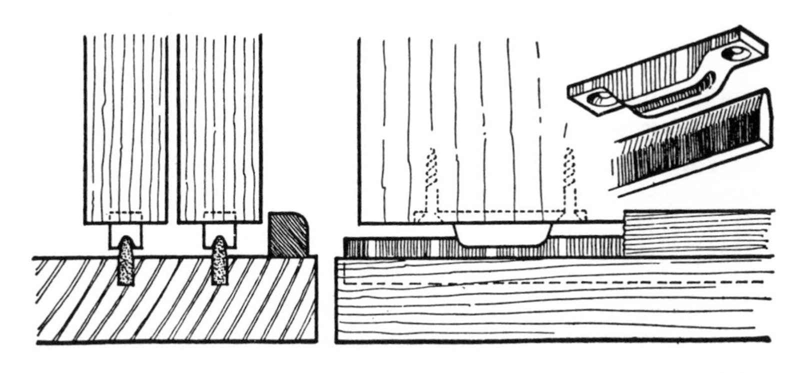

FIG. 14. SILENT RUNNING FIBRE TRACK AND GLIDERS

shown to the left. *Tempered Masonite* does very well for the purpose. An alternative is to glue strips of felt along the grooves, though this does not wear so well.

Special metal and fibre channelling is also available as in Fig. 17. In both of these a large groove is worked in top and bottom to receive the channelling as a whole.

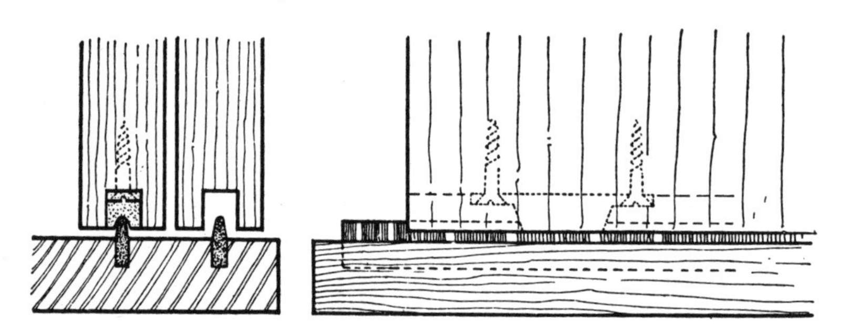

FIG. 15. ALTERNATIVE FITTING OF FIBRE TRACK AND GLIDERS

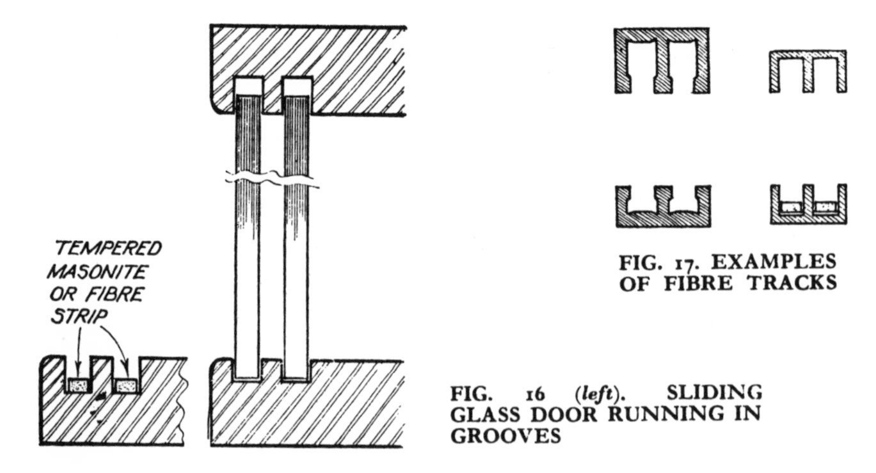

FIG. 17. EXAMPLES OF FIBRE TRACKS

FIG. 16 (*left*). SLIDING GLASS DOOR RUNNING IN GROOVES

One last word with regard to any scheme which has projecting beads at the bottom is that it is a good plan to stop both beads about 2 in. short at one end so that the bottom can be dusted out easily.

TAMBOURS

A tambour consists of a series of narrow strips of wood glued down on to a canvas backing. The ends fit in grooves worked in the cabinet, and it can thus travel around any curve of reasonable radius. Generally only convex curves can be negotiated (the canvas fitting on the inner side) because the joints can open as the tambour passes around the bend. Some tambours, particularly those fitted to the older type of writing desk, have wires passing through them to hold them together in place of canvas. This makes it simple to use a tambour which can bend either way since

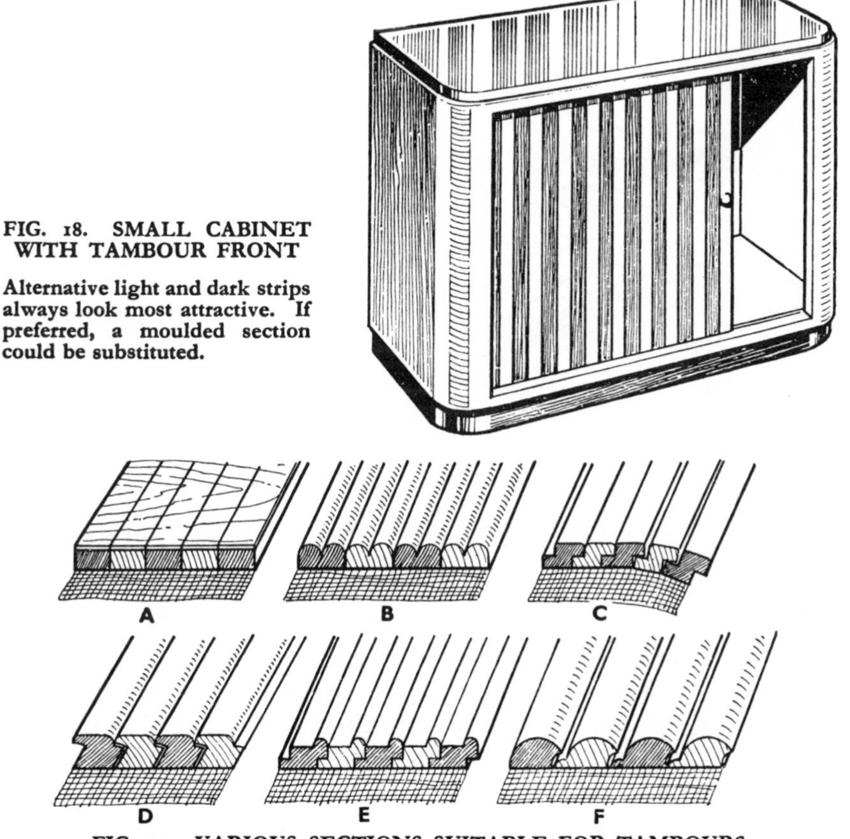

FIG. 18. SMALL CABINET WITH TAMBOUR FRONT

Alternative light and dark strips always look most attractive. If preferred, a moulded section could be substituted.

FIG. 19. VARIOUS SECTIONS SUITABLE FOR TAMBOURS

the pivoting point is in the middle of the wood in line with the wire.

Various Sections—Some sections of tambours are given in Fig. 19. The simplest is that at (A). In this particular case the surface is veneered, but solid strips could be used. For the latter a common practice is to use alternate strips of light and dark wood.

When veneer is used as at (A), the grain is often taken crosswise, and a single sheet of veneer is used so that the grain is continuous. In making such a tambour the work is prepared in a width sufficient for all the strips to be cut, two or more pieces being jointed together. It is then veneered, and the whole cut into strips afterwards, each being numbered so that it can be replaced in the same order and so preserve the continuity of grain.

When a bead section is required the strips can be prepared to

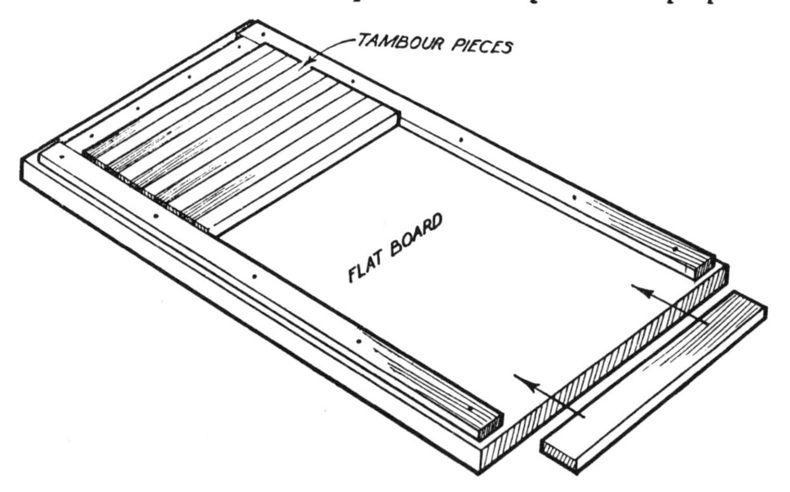

FIG 20. ASSEMBLY BOARD USED WHEN LAYING CANVAS

form single beads each, unless they are extra narrow, in which case they can be formed in two to each strip as at (B). It will be realized that in both this section and that at (A) the joints necessarily open as the tambour passes around a curve. As a rule this does not matter because it is generally concealed around the curve. Where this cannot be arranged an overlapping section is advisable as shown at (C).

A rather neater section is that at (D), in which the small curved portion is struck from a centre in line with the canvas backing. The two parts thus fit neatly within each other. (E) is simply a variation of (C), whilst (F) has the advantage that it can bend in either direction.

Assembling a Tambour—It is necessary to make an assembly board on which the parts can be put together as shown in Fig. 20. This has edging pieces nailed down ou three sides, the thickness of the strips being rather less than that of the tambour pieces. The last named must be all of exactly the same thickness, and the edges should be planed perfectly straight and square. Before placing in position rub a piece of candlegrease along the edges to prevent any glue which may penetrate from adhering. They are assembled side by side and the fourth edging piece passed on at the end. This should be lightly tightened with a cramp then nailed, thus bringing all the pieces close together. To prevent

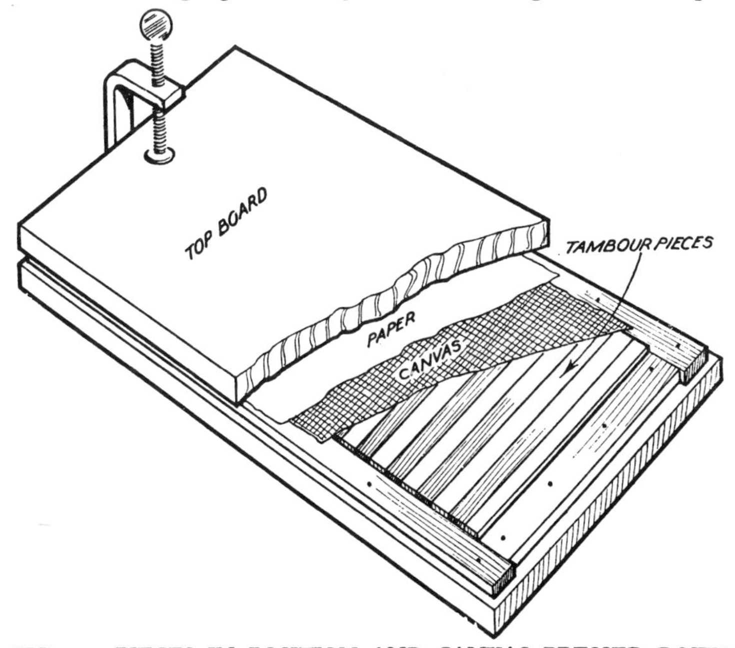

FIG. 21. PIECES IN POSITION AND CANVAS PRESSED DOWN

any tendency for the pieces to be lifted up by the pressure hold a batten across the face of the tambour pieces until the nails have been driven into the edging piece. In any case only light pressure is needed.

For the backing use a good quality piece of fine canvas. Stretch it as far as possible by drawing it back and forth over the rounded edge of a straight bar of wood. Fix it to one end of the board with a few tacks, and fold it back clear. Glue the tambour pieces, draw the canvas right across to the far end, and fix down with one or two tacks. Smooth out any creases in the canvas, and fix down a top board with cramps (Fig. 21). A sheet of paper prevents any glue which may have squeezed through from sticking to the board. Often it is not necessary to use the top board, the canvas being just smoothed down by hand. Make sure that all creases are got rid of.

Fitting—Allow ample time for the glue to set and try the movement, making sure that every joint opens. The ends are then trimmed so that they enter the groove. Sometimes the groove is narrower than the thickness of the tambour pieces, a rebate being

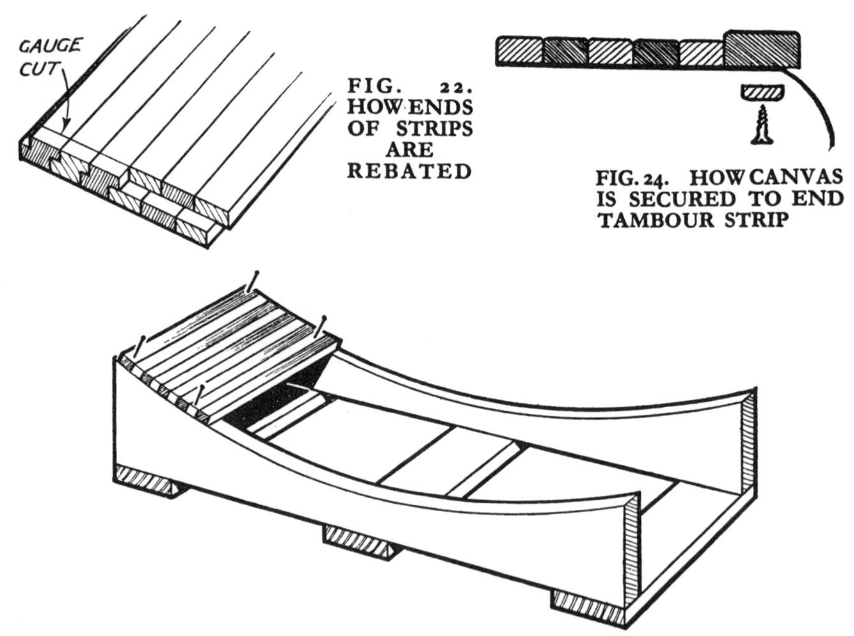

FIG. 22. HOW ENDS OF STRIPS ARE REBATED

FIG. 24. HOW CANVAS IS SECURED TO END TAMBOUR STRIP

FIG. 23. CRADLE FOR ASSEMBLING STRIPS FOR CURVE

worked at the front of the tambour as in Fig. 22 to form a shoulder. The advantage is that the groove is entirely hidden by the shoulder even after considerable wear. It is specially useful for moulded tambour pieces as otherwise the groove would be visible in the recesses. To work the rebate cut the face of the tambour with the cutting gauge and use the shoulder or bullnose plane.

When the tambour is fitted to a bow shape which is visible it is usual to have the members in the form of beads and to glue up flat. The slight opening at the curve scarcely shows. If, however, the flat section ((A), Fig. 19) is required it is desirable to fit on a cradle which has the same curvature as the job as shown in Fig. 23. The pieces are cut about 1½ in. over length and are placed face downwards on the cradle. When the joints are shot the shooting board should be arranged so that the edge is a trifle out of square thus ensuring a close joint when the parts are in the curve. The first strip has a couple of nails driven half way in, about half a dozen strips laid in and pushed tightly home, and another piece nailed. You can turn the cradle upside down to see that there are close joints on the face side.

As a rule the end member is made extra large as this enables a handle to be fixed to it. The canvas is glued about half way across it and 2 or 3 in. free end left as in Fig. 24. This is taken around a fillet or bead and the latter screwed at the back so locking the canvas.

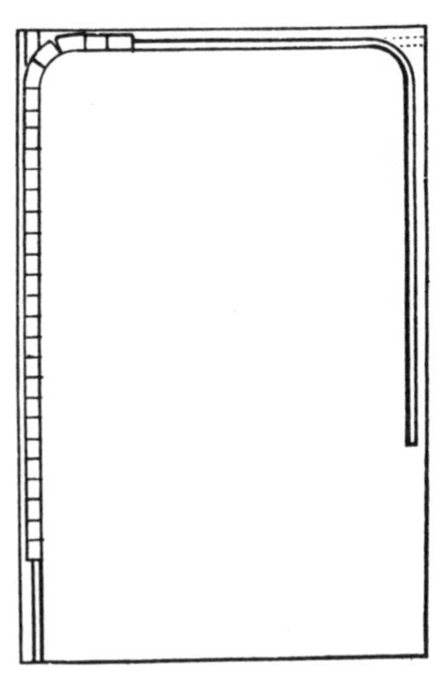

FIG. 25. GROOVE IN WHICH TAMBOUR RUNS

Tambour Grooves—The groove in which the tambour works has usually to be cut in with the chisel. The router can be used to finish off to even depth, and for the straight portions a fence can be fixed to enable it to be used as a plough. Do not have the curves too sharp. As a rule it is necessary to cut the groove rather fuller at the curves to enable the tambour to pass easily. There must, of course, be a place (generally at the rear) where the tambour can be started (see Fig. 25). This can be blocked up after the tambour is in position or a stop can be fitted. Sometimes it is practicable to make a separate lining for the cabinet in which the grooves can be worked.

The tambour should not be finally fitted until both it and the cabinet have been polished because it would be impossible to polish cleanly. In fact, in the case of a moulded tambour the individual members should be polished—or at least bodied up before the canvas backing is glued on. Otherwise it would be impossible to reach the quirks with the rubber. When the whole thing has been fitted and the working tried, the ends of the tambour should be lubricated with candlegrease. This will both ease the running and make it silent.

DRAWER MAKING

In the best way drawers are dovetailed, and the joints are still cut by hand in good cabinet work. Fig. 26 shows the setting out for the usual form of drawer at (A). The lapped dovetails at the front have the pins running almost to a point, this giving a very neat appearance. Note that, since the bottom fits in a groove worked in the front it is necessary for this groove to be contained within the bottom dovetail (see dotted lines). Otherwise a gap would appear at the sides. The sides are not grooved since an applied grooved moulding is used (see sections (B) and (C)). At the back the bottom fits beneath the square lower edge of the back.

In the case of a small shallow drawer in which the utmost interior depth is required, the bottom fits flush with the lower edges of the sides and rests in rebates. This necessitates the small square member being cut at the bottom as at (D), Fig. 26. Sometimes the drawer sides have to be set in from the ends, in which case the slotted dovetail at (F) is used. This is stopped at the top.

Making a Drawer—Plane the drawer front to make a close fit in the opening ((A), Fig. 27). It helps to make it *slightly* tapered

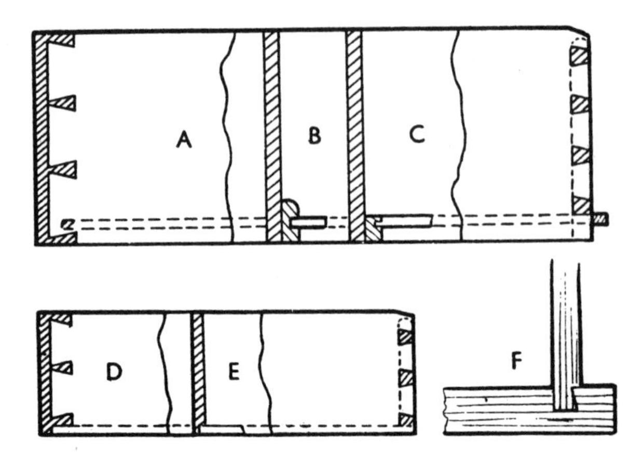

FIG. 26. SETTING OUT OF DOVETAILED DRAWERS

—no more than the thickness of a thin shaving. Plane the bottom edge first, and trim one end to align with the opening. Mark the length, trim to fit, and plane the top edge lastly. The back is

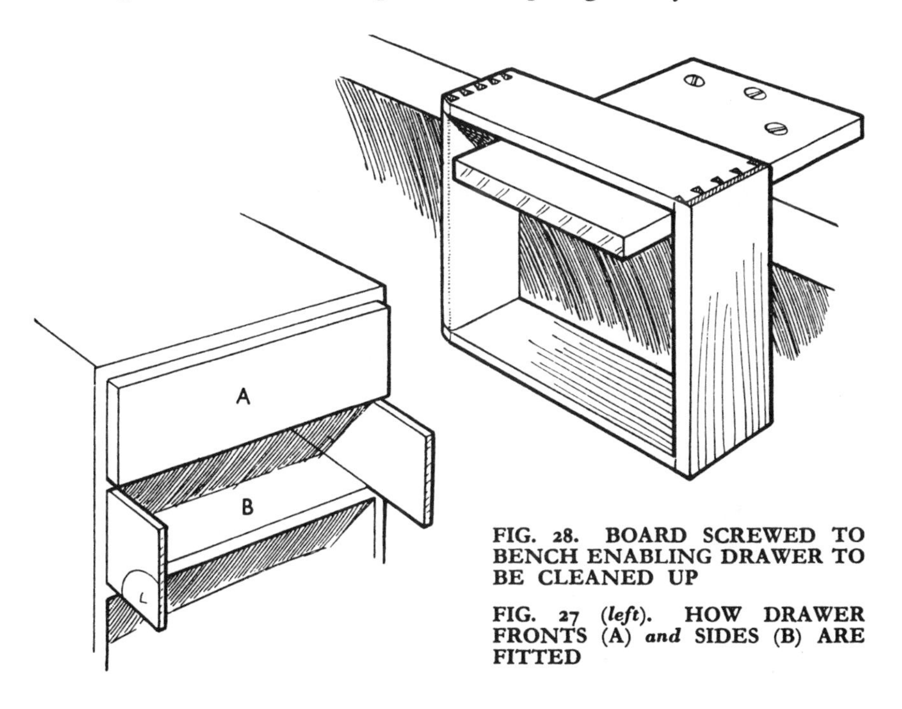

FIG. 28. BOARD SCREWED TO BENCH ENABLING DRAWER TO BE CLEANED UP

FIG. 27 (*left*). HOW DRAWER FRONTS (A) *and* SIDES (B) ARE FITTED

treated similarly but the width is less owing to its resting on the drawer bottom, and the set-down from the top. Trim the bottom edges of the sides, plane the ends square, making both alike, and plane the top edge till a fairly tight fit is secured (B), Fig. 27. Dovetailing follows (see p. 143), and, after assembling, the drawer is fitted before the bottom is added. A convenient way

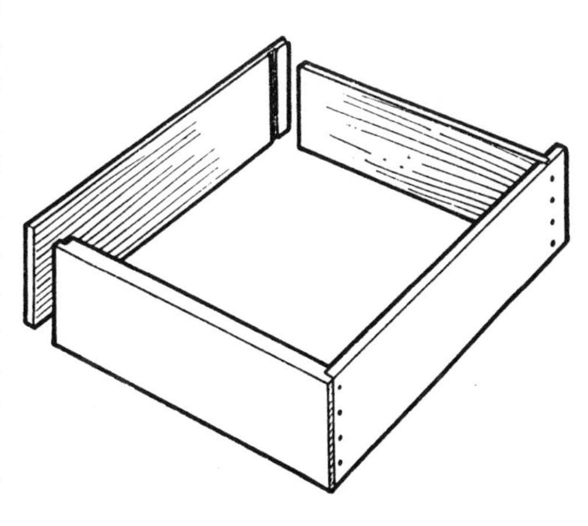

FIG. 29. SIMPLE DRAWER CONSTRUCTION

of planing without danger of racking is shown in Fig. 28. Candlegrease rubbed cold over the bearing surfaces is a good lubricant, but should not be used until after polishing.

For a quick and cheap alternative the construction in Fig. 29 can be followed. A lapped joint is cut at the front, and a simple groove at the rear. The whole is assembled with glue and nails, the last named being driven in askew so that they slope towards each other dovetail fashion.

WINDOW FRAMES

It is seldom that the home craftsman needs to make a house window, but he often requires one for a garden shed or garage. A typical double frame casement window is given in Fig. 30.

Frame—This is made as shown at (B), Fig. 31. Uprights and top have a simple rebated joint. At the bottom the uprights fit into a sill which is planed at its top outer surface to give a slope. Under the front edge is a drip groove. A simple checking is cut to receive the upright, and it is advisable to do this before working the chamfer because this enables the router to be used.

Casements—A standard section is used for this. The joint shown at (A), Fig. 31 is used, and it will be noticed that in place of the cabinet maker's haunch is a franking. The mortise width is made equal to the width of the centre square. Wedged through-tenons are used, and the moulding is scribed rather than mitred. Note how the moulding is cut away locally opposite the mortises, enabling equal shoulders to be used on the tenon.

The centre closing mould should fit in a rebate as in Fig. 30, and this necessitates each frame being rebated. It is necessary to bevel the bottom edges to align with the sloping sill.

FIG. 30. CASEMENT WINDOWS AND THEIR FRAME

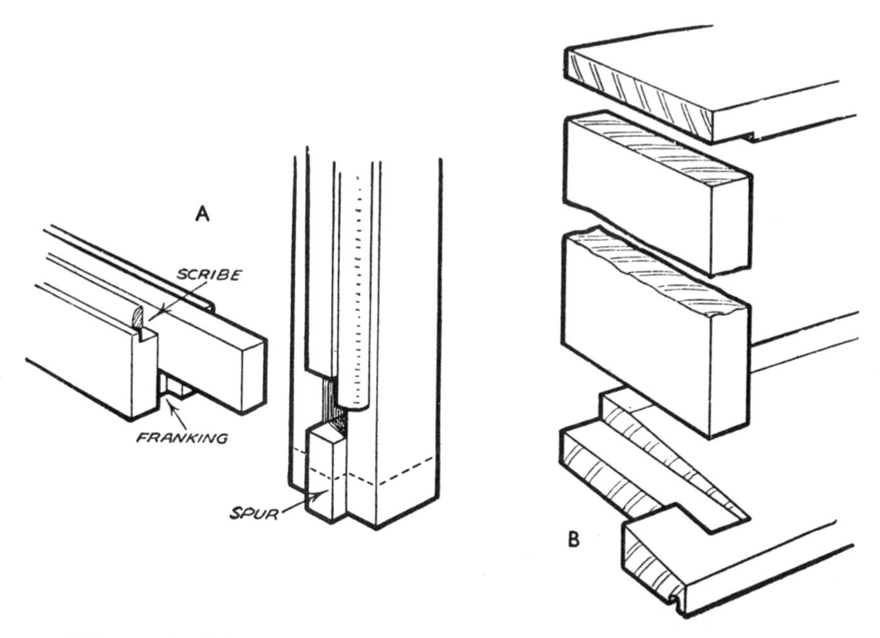

FIG. 31. A. JOINT FOR CASEMENTS. B. HOW FRAME IS MADE

CHAPTER VIII

JOINTS

THE number of joints used in woodwork is little short of staggering when their variations in detail and size are taken into account. One need only bother with the relatively few basic joints, however, and we give these on the following pages. Their application will be found in the designs for things to make.

Mortise and Tenon Joints—The chief kinds are shown in Figs. 3 and 4. Generally the tenon is as near as possible one third the thickness of the wood, and it is a case of selecting a chisel for mortising which is the nearest to this size. Thus for $\frac{3}{4}$ in. stuff a $\frac{1}{4}$ in. chisel is used; for $\frac{7}{8}$ in. and 1 in. wood a $\frac{5}{16}$ in. size is suitable.

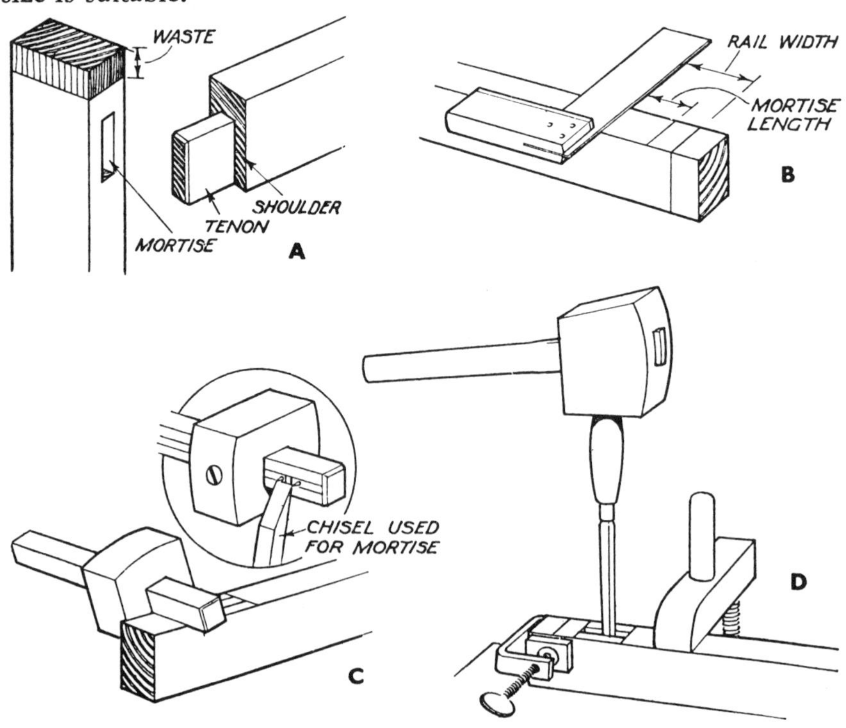

FIG. 1. MORTISE AND TENON. MARKING AND CHOPPING MORTISE
A. Completed joint. B. Marking out. C. Setting mortise gauge. D. Chopping mortise. In best work the tenon has a haunch as at (C), Fig. 3.

A simple stub-tenon joint and the method of cutting is given in Figs. 1 and 2. At the outset it should be realized that when several corresponding joints are to be cut, as in, say, a door, all tenons would be marked out at the same time, the shoulder marks being squared across all. This is explained more fully on p. 111, where door construction is dealt with. Here, however, we give the procedure in a single joint for clearness.

Square the rail width in pencil across the edge of the stile as at (B), noting that the whole thing is invariably set in from the end of the wood as it lessens any liability for the wood to split (A). A third line is put in to give the mortise length. Now set the pins of the mortise gauge to the width of the chisel being used (C), and fix the fence so that the pins are as near as possible central on the edge of the wood (in the case of rebated frames the mortise is generally level with the corner of the rebate). Mark the wood (C) with the fence bearing against the face side of the wood.

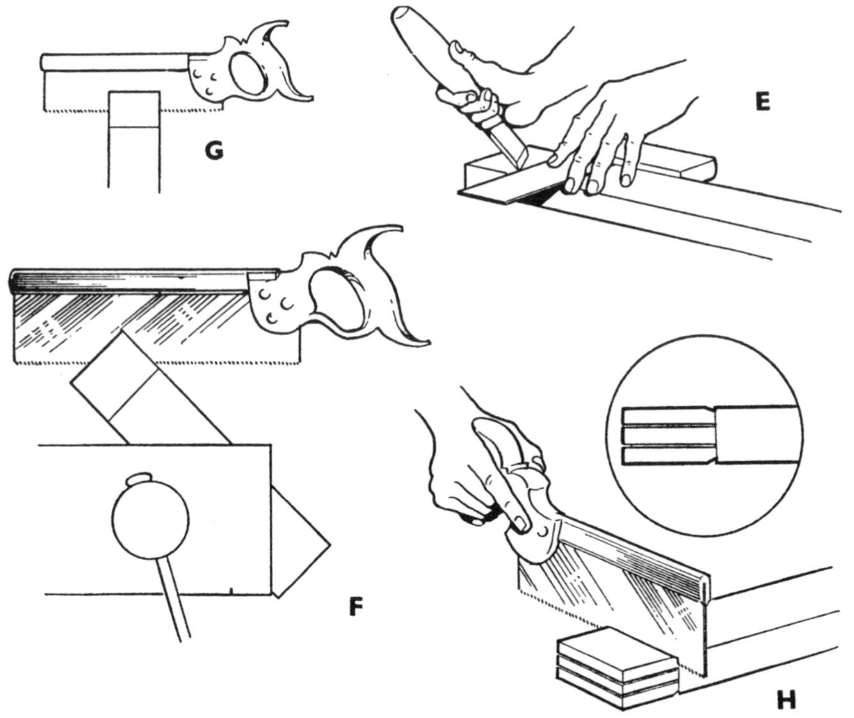

FIG. 2. MORTISE AND TENON JOINT. HOW TENON IS MARKED AND SAWN

E. Marking shoulders. F, G. Sawing tenon. H. Sawing shoulders.

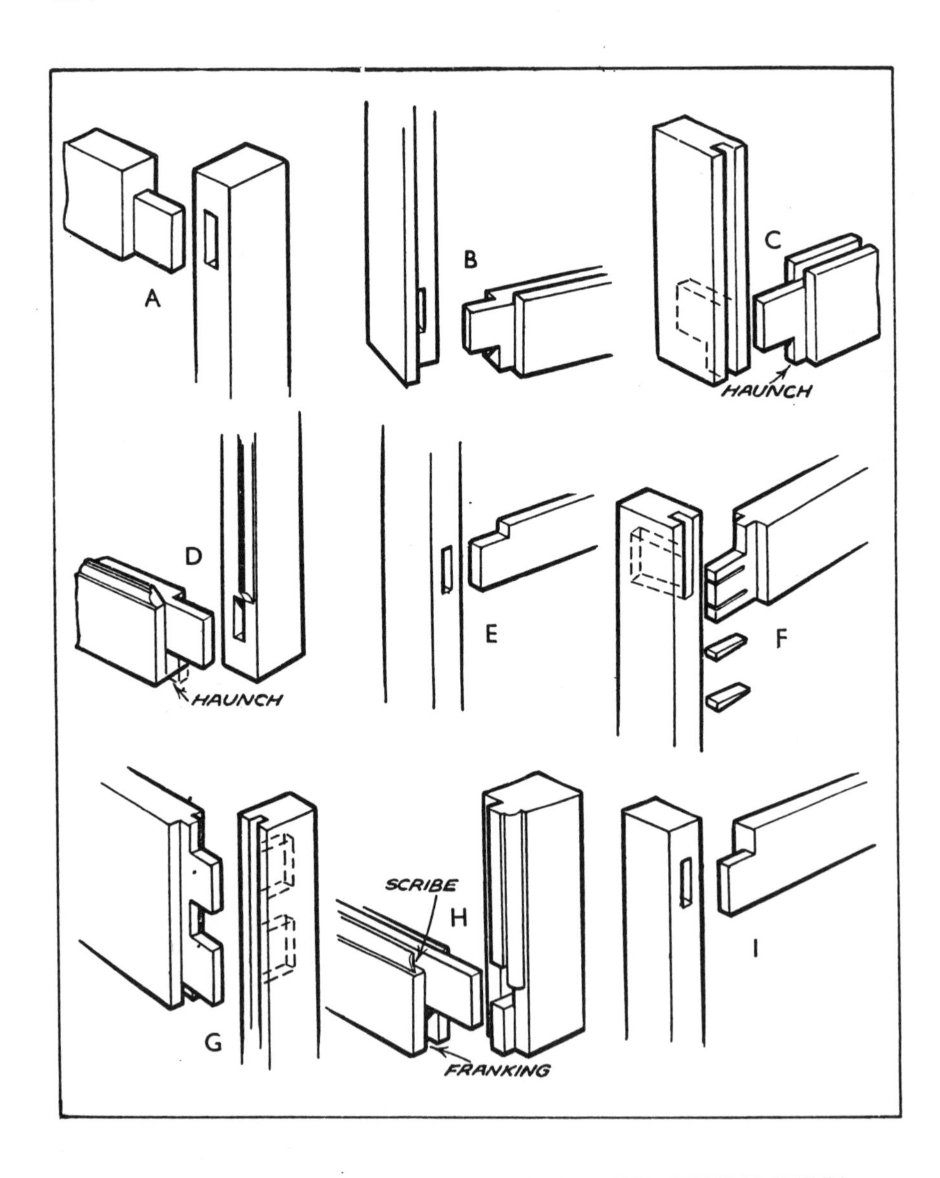

FIG. 3. VARIETIES OF THE MORTISE AND TENON JOINT

A. stub mortise and tenon. A haunch could be added (see C). B. Mortise and tenon for rebated frame. Note long and short shoulders. Haunch could be added. C. Mortise and tenon for grooved frame. D. Mortise and tenon for rebated and moulded frame. E. Bare-faced mortise and tenon. F. Wedged through-mortise and tenon. G. Double mortise and tenon. H. Mortise and tenon for window frame. I. Bare-faced mortise and tenon.

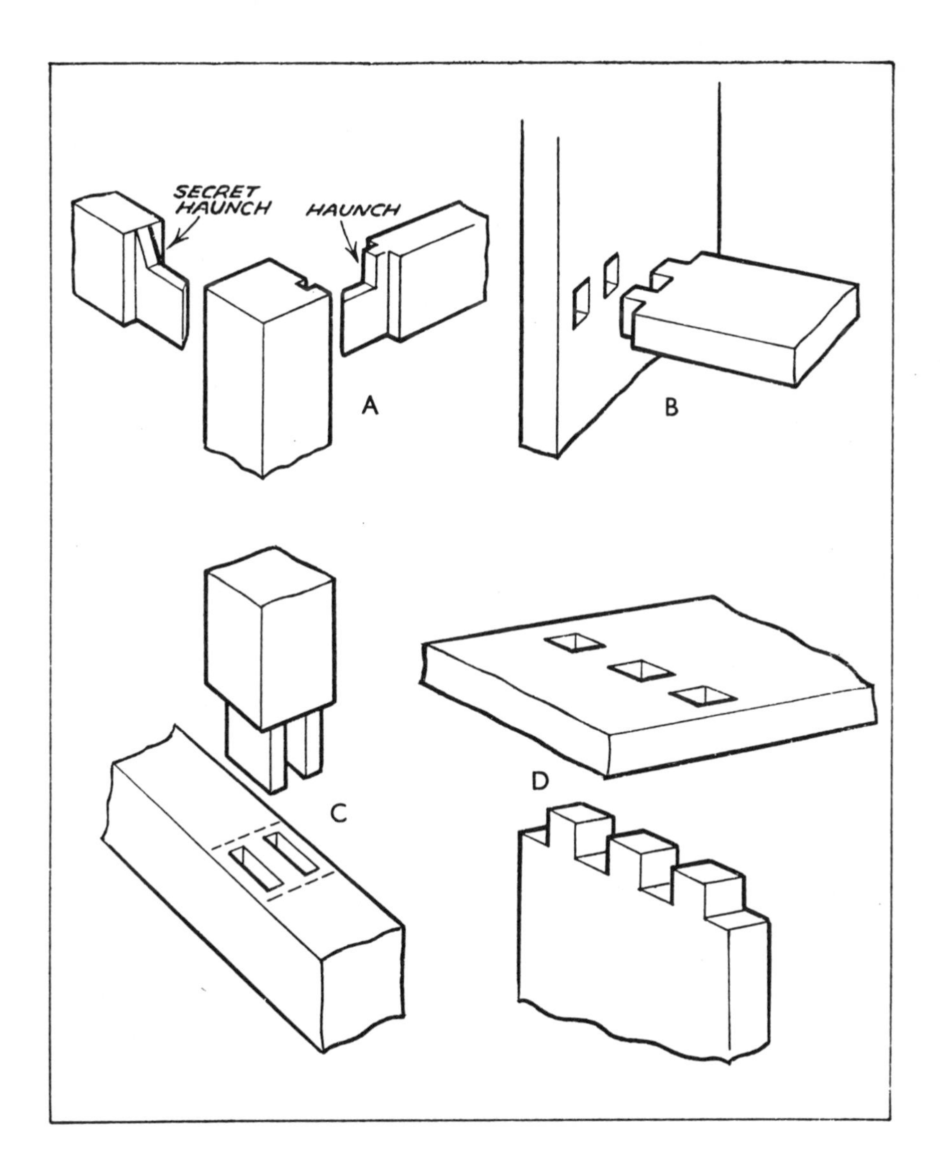

FIG. 4. FURTHER EXAMPLES OF THE MORTISE AND TENON JOINT

A. Mortise and tenon for leg and rails. Alternative haunches are given. Tenons are cut at angle at ends to meet in thickness of wood. B. Twin tenons for drawer rails. C. Twin tenons for heavy framing. D. Pinned joint for carcase partitions, etc.

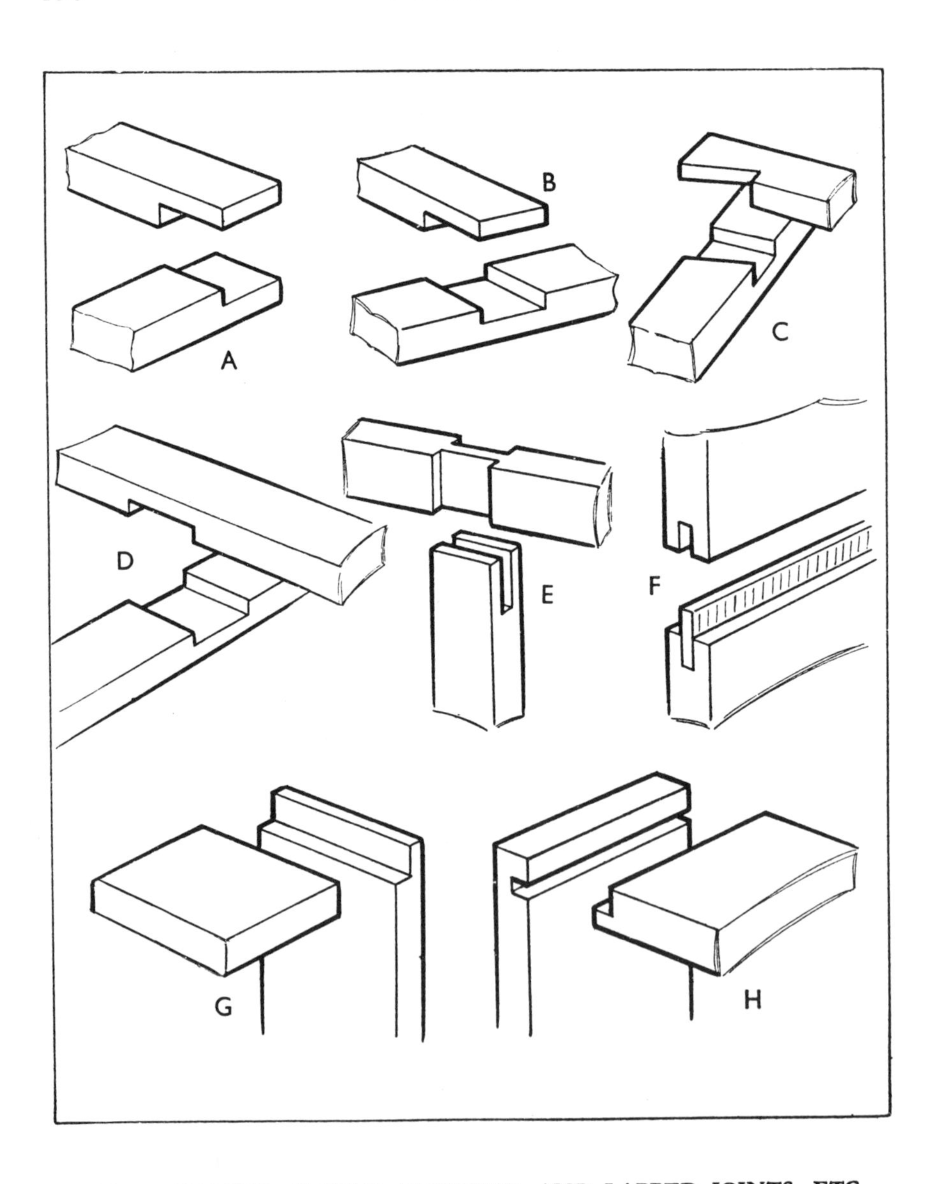

FIG. 5. HALVED, BRIDLE, TONGUED, AND LAPPED JOINTS, ETC

A. Angle halving. B. T halving. C. Dovetail halving. D. Cross halving. E. Bridle joint. F. Loose tongue and groove. G. Simple lap. H. Bare-faced tongue and groove angle joint.

Much of the waste can be removed by boring, using a bit slightly smaller than the mortise width. This is shown more clearly on p. 26. The mortising is shown at (D), Fig. 1. The wood is cramped over a solid part of the bench, and a thumbscrew put on at the end with a waste piece of wood beneath the screw. This reduces any liability for the wood to split. Make the first cut at about the middle, and cut in a little way only. Shift the chisel a little way along and chop down again, this time a little deeper, and so work up to about $\frac{1}{16}$ in. of the end. Reverse the chisel and repeat the process in the other direction. Levering over the chisel will remove the centre waste. Finally cut down on the pencil lines, keeping the chisel upright. These final cuts take out the dubbed-over ends caused by the levering-over with the chisel.

The tenon shoulders should be squared round with the chisel or a knife as at (E). Hold the butt of the square always against either the face side or face edge of the wood. Mark the tenon with the mortise gauge again used from the face side. End and both edges should be marked. Hold the wood at an angle in the vice as shown at (F) when sawing, and place the saw to the waste side of the gauge line. To complete the cut reverse the wood as at (G), this time upright. A properly cut tenon should fit as it is with no further attention.

To enable the shoulders to be sawn make a sloping cut with the chisel on the waste side as shown inset at (H). This provides a channel in which the saw can run. Lastly mark the amount to be cut away at the side of the tenon and cut. It is advisable to put a thumbscrew on the wood at the mortise end to prevent splitting when the joint is being fitted. In some cases a haunch is left on the tenon as in Fig. 3.

Halved Joints—These are used in the construction of frames, etc., often as a simple substitute for the mortise and tenon. Their chief value is when the material is too thin for the mortise and tenon to be cut. The positions in which the joints are used are obvious from Fig. 5 (A, B, C, and D). A centre line is marked with the gauge from the face side in every case, and a saw cut made immediately to the waste side of the line. The shoulder line is squared across with chisel or knife, and a sloping groove cut similar to that of the tenon, (H) Fig. 2. When the joint has to withstand any strain (as in the loose seat of a chair, for instance),

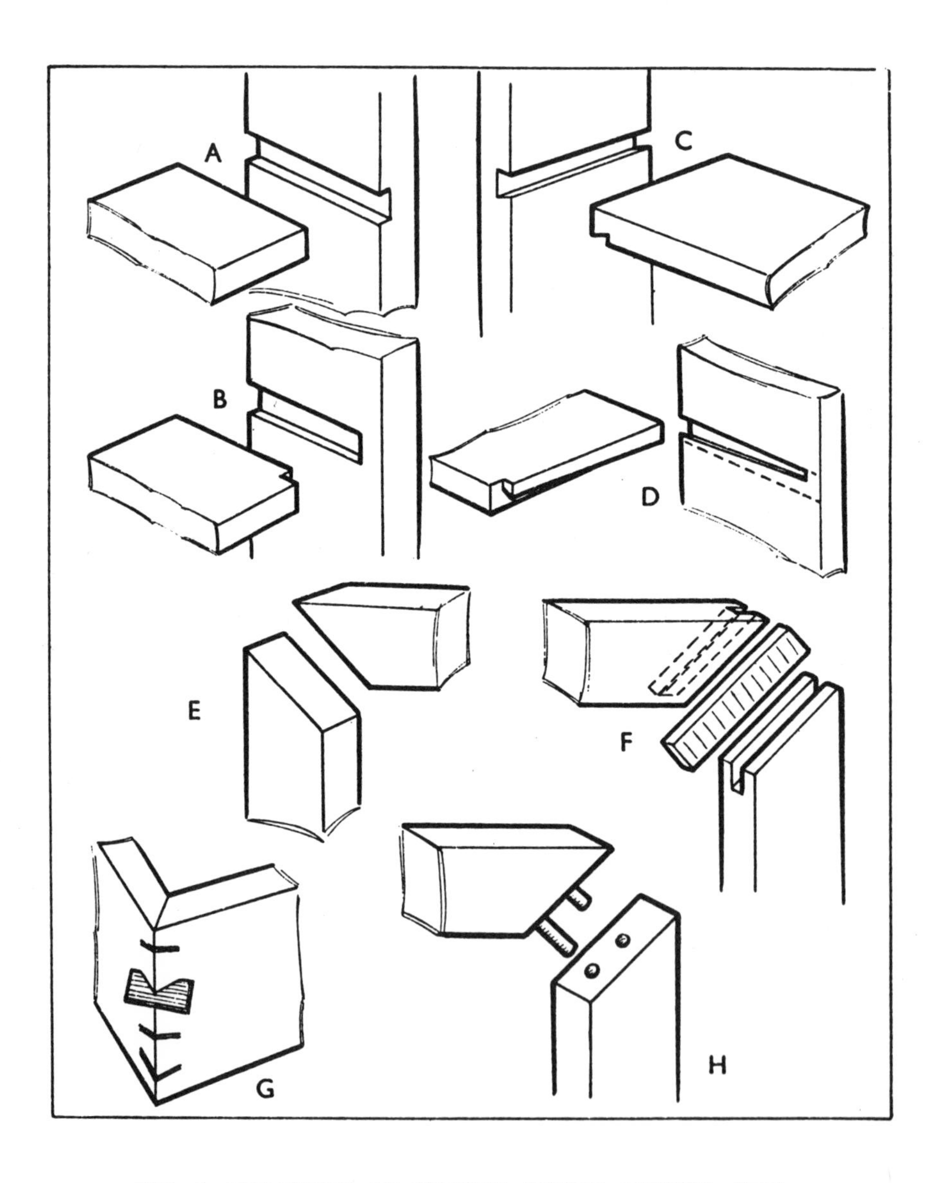

FIG. 6. EXAMPLES OF HOUSED JOINTS, MITRES, ETC.

A. Common housing. B. Stopped housing. C. Dovetail housing. D. Tapered dovetail housing. E. Simple mitre. F. Tongued mitre. G. Veneer keyed mitre. H. Dowelled mitre.

it should be screwed as well as glued. In the case of the cross-halving (D) the parts should be just hand tight. Too tight a fit may cause distortion.

The bridle joint (E) is handy when a sideboard, table, or similar piece has three legs at the front. The top rail can be in a single length and the centre leg bridled into it.

(F) shows the grooved joint with loose tongue used for strong joints required when boards are glued side by side—table tops, carcase ends, etc. The lapped joint (G) is often used as a simple

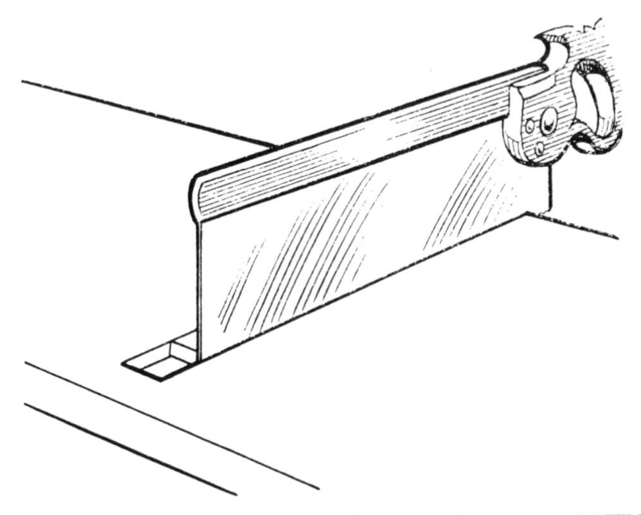

FIG. 7. HOW SIDES OF STOPPED GROOVE ARE SAWN

alternative to the lapped dovetail. It requires to be both glued and nailed. (H) is used similarly, but is not very satisfactory owing to the short grain at the end which is liable to split away.

Housed Joints—The simple housing (A), Fig. 6, is used chiefly for shelves, partitions, etc. When its front appearance is an objection the joint is stopped as at (B). In the case of (A) the groove is simple to cut. Two lines are squared across the wood with knife or chisel, sloping grooves chiselled on the waste side, and the tenon saw worked in these. The bulk of the waste is chiselled away, and the depth made even with the router.

It is not quite so simple with the stopped groove. The method is to chop a recess immediately against the stop as in Fig 7. This enables the saw to be worked back and forth in short strokes until the depth is reached. The removal of the waste is with chisel and router as before.

For a stronger joint the dovetail housing at (C) can be used. This can be cut right through as shown, or it can be stopped similarly to (B). As a guide to holding the saw at the correct angle a block of wood can be fixed to the side of the line as in Fig. 8, being either cramped or nailed down.

Just as easy to cut and certainly simpler to fit is the tapered and shouldered dovetail housing at (D). Its advantage is that the joint

FIG. 8. GUIDE FOR SAWING DOVETAIL GROOVE

is quite slack until pushed right home. This makes it much easier to tell just where the joint may need easing.

Mitred Joints—The simple mitre is given at (E) Fig. 6. It is cut on the mitre block or box according to its size. Small mitres can often be glued up straightway from the saw, but larger ones need trimming on the mitre shooting board (A), p. 8. Various ways of strengthening mitres are given at (F, G, and H). The first and last are used chiefly for frames, whilst (G) is handy for strengthening a small mitred box to be veneered. Saw cuts are made across the mitre, and slips of veneer glued in, these being levelled after the glue has set.

Dovetails—These make the strongest joint for such structures as boxes, etc. When the appearance of the dovetails does not

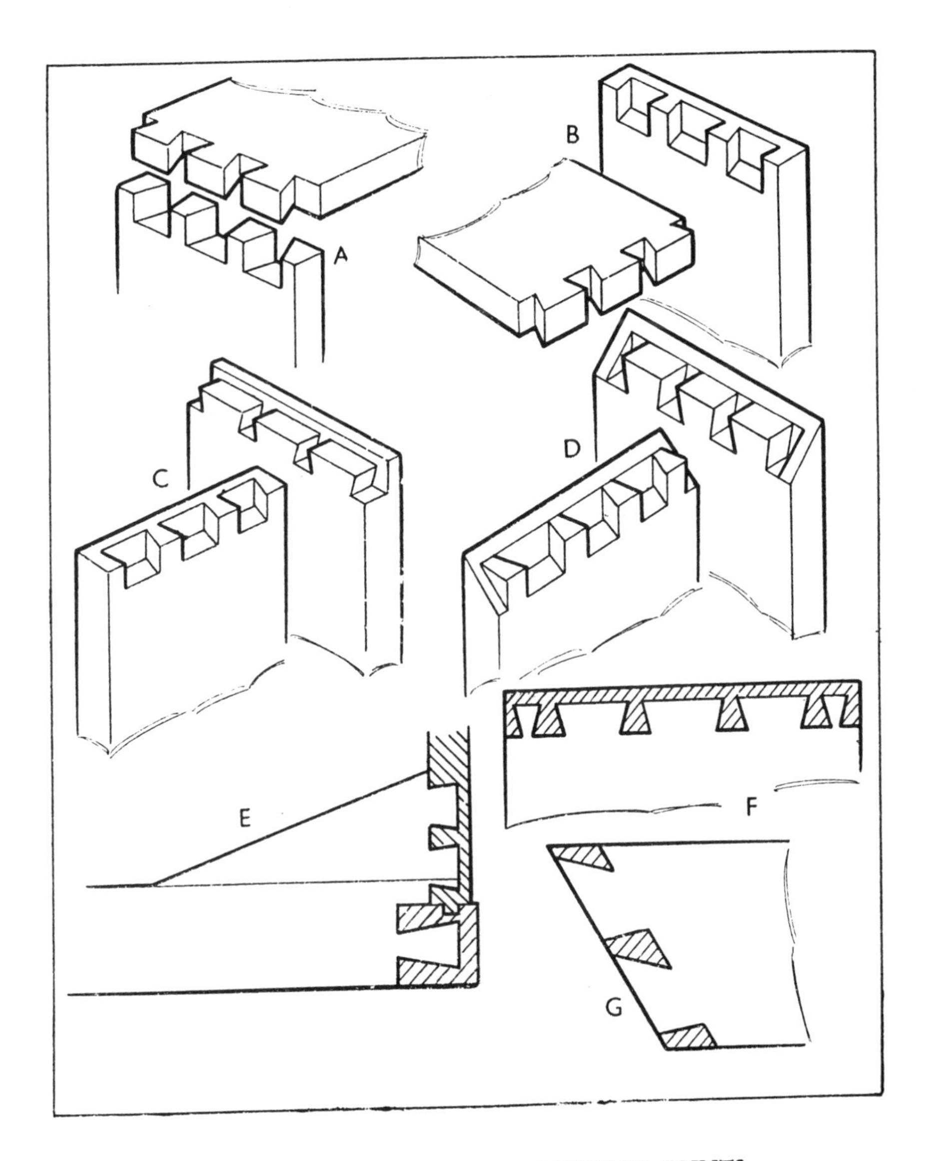

FIG. 9. VARIOUS TYPES OF DOVETAIL JOINTS

A. Through dovetail. B. Lapped dovetail. C. Double-lapped dovetail. D. Mitre secret dovetail. E. Lapped dovetail for carcase frame. F. Lapped dovetail for carcase. Note narrow end dovetails to prevent corners from curling away. G. Angle dovetails.

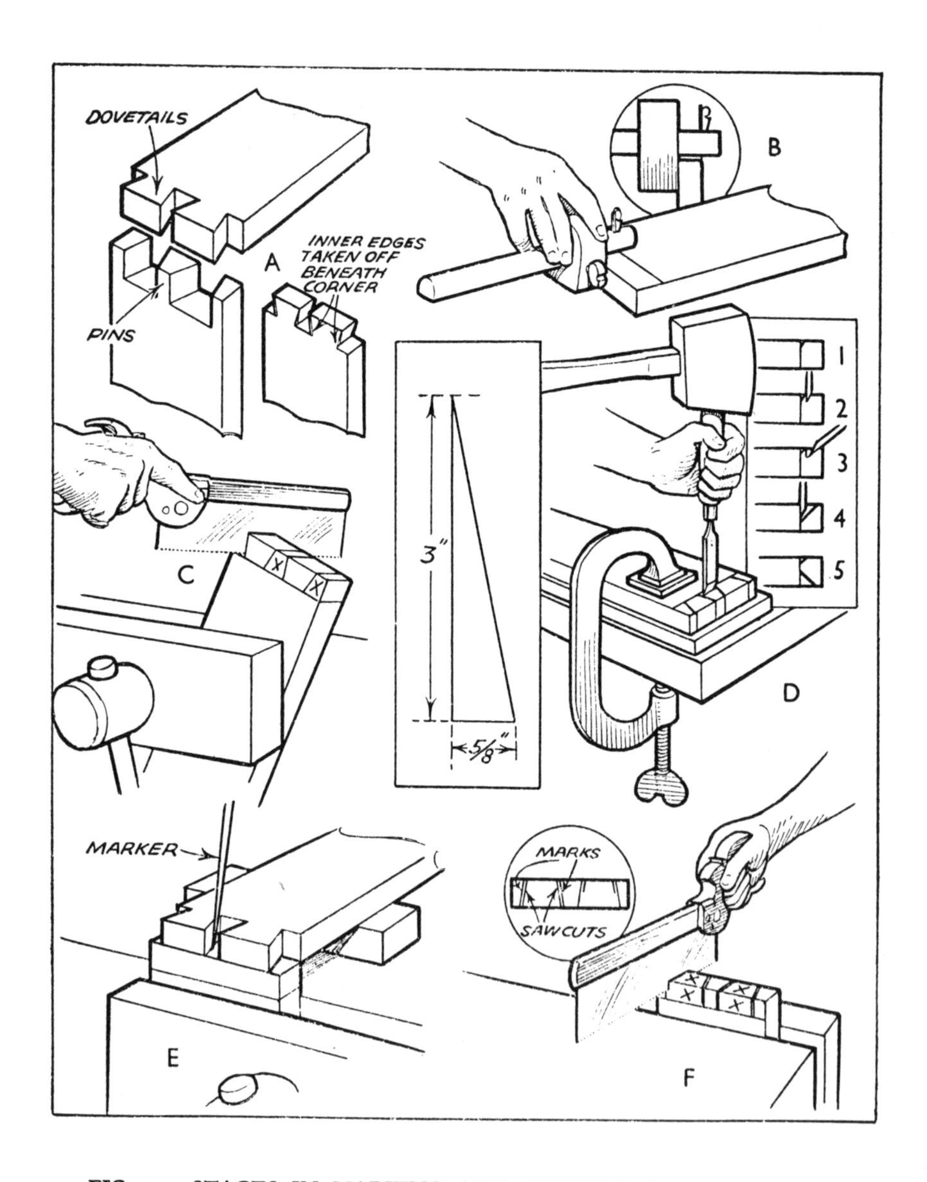

FIG. 10. STAGES IN MARKING AND CUTTING DOVETAIL JOINT

A. Completed through-dovetail. B. Marking with cutting gauge. C. Sawing dovetails. Note angle of wood to give upright cut. D. Chopping dovetails. Inset stages are shown. E. Marking pins from dovetails. F. Sawing pins. Saw is held on waste side of mark.

matter the through dovetail (A), Fig. 9, is the simplest and strongest. The lapped dovetail (B) is used when one side must be plain, as in carcase sides, drawer fronts, etc. At (C) the joint is concealed on both sides except for a thin line of end grain formed by the lap. At (D) it is entirely hidden.

The application of the lapped dovetail to the joining of a top rail to a cabinet side with corner post is shown at (E). (F) is for a wide carcase where the narrow end dovetails prevent any tendency for the wood to curl away at the corners. When one piece slopes at an angle the arrangement at (G) is followed.

The method of cutting the through dovetail is given in Fig. 10. The thickness of the wood is gauged across as at (B). When the thickness of the two varies, the thickness of the one is gauged on to the other. Do not cut in deeply as the mark has later to be planed away. Pencil in the dovetail positions. In an important position they are measured and marked with a template. The slope is $\frac{5}{8}$ in. in 3 in. as shown in Fig. 10. Place the wood in the vice at an angle so that the saw can be held upright and cut down as at (C). Put crosses on the waste pieces.

Chop away the waste as at (D). Make a sloping cut up to the gauge line (1), and chop down about $\frac{1}{16}$ in. from the line (2). Make a sloping cut as at (3) so that the actual corner is not removed. Repeat the process right on the gauge line (4), and finally turn over and work from the other side (5).

Place the part with the pins in the vice, and lay the dovetailed piece on it in position as at (E). A waste piece at the back will support it in the correct position. Run a marker around the dovetails as shown, and cut as at (F). The saw should be held just to the waste side of the mark, this giving a comfortable hand-tight fit. Note the crosses which denote the waste pieces. It makes it obvious which parts are to be removed. The chopping is much the same as for the dovetails. Before assembling the inner edges of the dovetails are lightly chiselled away as at (A) so that they start together easily.

The lapped dovetail is cut similarly, but the pins can only be chopped from the one side. In the mitre dovetail the pins must be cut first as otherwise it is impossible to mark the one from the other.

Those who seek fuller information on cutting joints should see *Woodwork Joints*, a WOODWORKER handbook.

CHAPTER IX

METAL FITTINGS, ETC.

LOCKS

THERE are many kinds of locks made for special purposes. Fig. 1 shows those most commonly used. A, B, C, and D, are furniture locks; E, F, and G are for house doors.

Kinds of Locks—(A) is the straight cupboard lock which is screwed to the inside of the door and is not let in. Mostly these locks shoot both right and left, and can so be used for doors opening right or left. The cut lock at (B) is much neater, but requires recessing into the wood. As the bolt shoots in one direction only the lock must be ordered R. or L. To tell which you need, face the door from outside. If the lock is on the left you need a L.H. lock. Thus the lock shown is L.H.

Similar in form is the drawer lock at (C). This has to be let into the drawer front. The box lock (D) is also let into the wood, but in addition is a plate which needs recessing into and screwing to the lid.

Of locks for house doors the simplest and cheapest is the rim lock at (E). It is simply screwed on, though there is sometimes a projecting plate which needs to be recessed into the edge. (F) shows the Yale pattern latch in which the cutting-in is reduced to a minimum. The mortise lock at (G) requires to be set right into the edge of the door.

Fixing a Cut Door Lock—This is widely used on furniture. The stages of fixing are given in Fig. 2. Square on the surface and edge of the door a centre line. Set the gauge to the distance of the pin from the outer plate as at (A), and mark across the pencil line. This gives the keyhole position, and a bit is selected which will give a close fit to the rounded portion of the escutcheon. A hole is bored right through the door and the escutcheon laid in position as at (B). A slight tap with the hammer will give

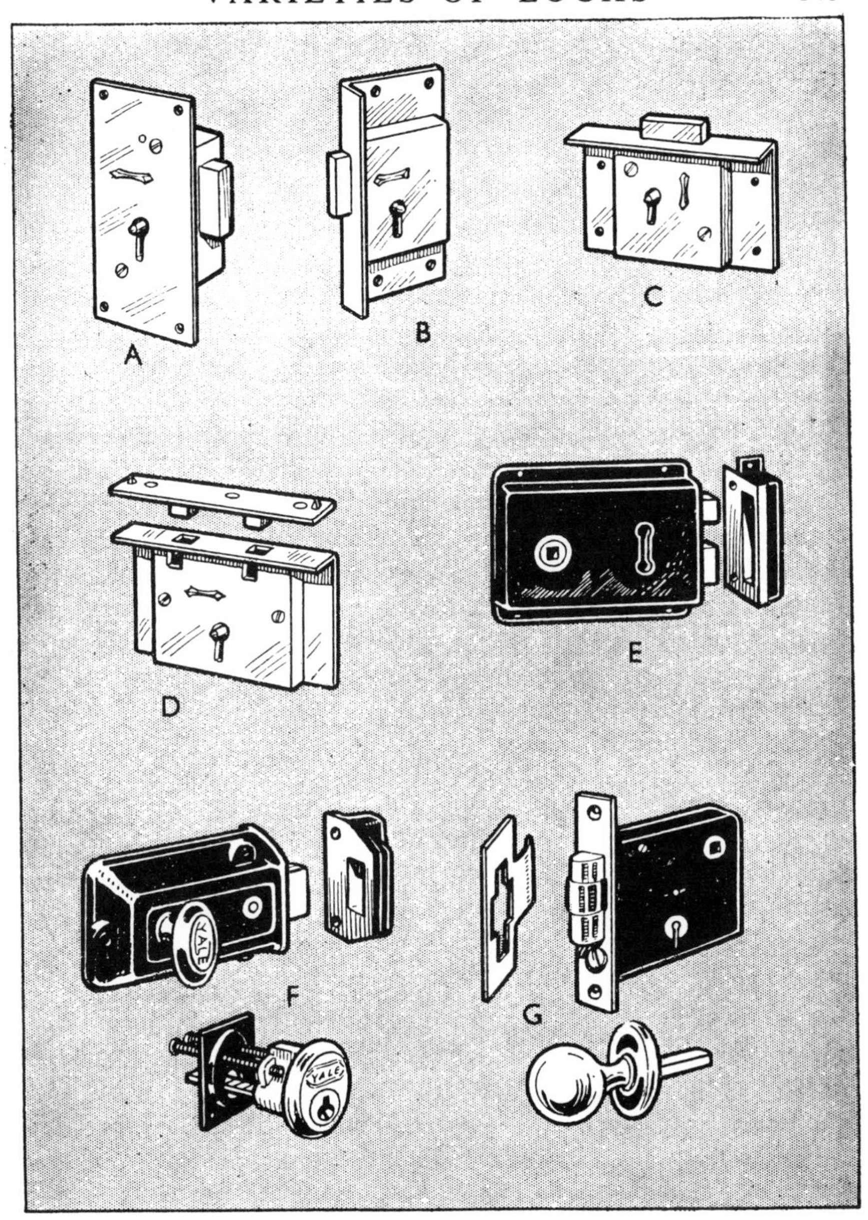

FIG. 1. EXAMPLES OF LOCKS USED IN FURNITURE AND HOUSE DOORS

A. Straight screw-on lock. B. Cut cabinet lock. C. Cut drawer lock. D. Cash box lock. E. House door rim lock. F. Yale type latch. G. House door mortise lock.

an indentation of the shape, the sides of which can be sawn with the keyhole saw. A narrow chisel will remove the waste.

Place the lock with the pin level with the pencil line, and mark the door in line with the body of the lock as at (C). Set a gauge to the thickness of the body including the plate, and mark the edge from the inside. Re-set the gauge to the width of the body including the top plate, and mark the back of the door. This gives the position and extent of wood to be cut away. Make a series of saw cuts across the grain down to as far as they can be taken as at (D). The door should be held down on to the bench with hand screws. Remove the waste with the chisel as shown, and chop down at the ends and back. The latter needs to be done carefully to avoid splitting along the grain. Once again ease away the waste.

Place the lock in position, making sure that the pin is level with its hole, and mark round the ends of the plate with a marking knife. It is of little use marking the sides of the plate as at this stage the lock cannot be pushed right home. The simplest way of marking these sides is to use the gauge in conjunction with a waste piece of wood with parallel sides. Set the gauge as shown at (F). Then, holding the waste piece right over the lock recess (this waste piece must be longer than the lock) mark the door edge. The back plate is marked similarly.

Screw on the lock and try the action with the key. To find the position of the recess to be cut to take the bolt, shoot out the latter and smear its surface with thin paint, or say the dirty oil from the oilstone. Shoot the bolt back and close the door. Now turn the key as far as it will go. This will leave a mark on the cupboard side which can be chopped out with a small chisel.

Drawer locks are fitted similarly, but the keyhole is the other way round. It may also be necessary to use the special drawer-lock chisel (p. 4) when the space is restricted. In the case of a box lock the link plate has also to be attached. To find its position place it on the lock and turn the key. Bring down the lid and thump it. There is generally a small spike at the back of the plate which will be driven into the lid. Turn the lock, and raise the lid, the plate being lifted with it. Mark round its edge and chop the recess to receive it, finally screwing it in position.

Mortise Lock—Assuming that you are fixing the lock to a framed door, the vertical position will be decided by the main

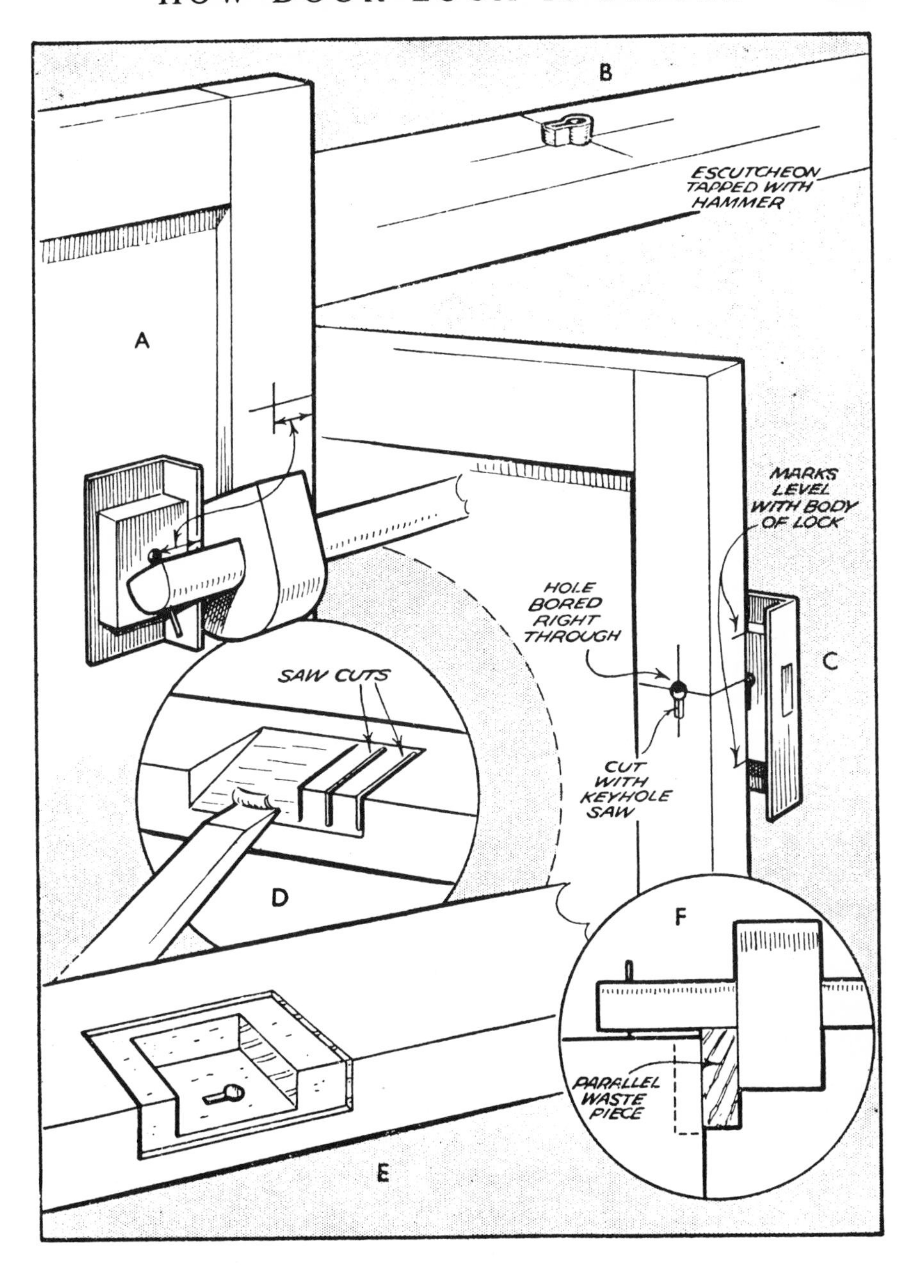

FIG. 2. STAGES IN FITTING DOOR LOCK

A. Gauging the keyhole position. B. Marking escutcheon position. C. Position of body of lock being marked. D. Cutting the recess. E. Completed recess. F. Gauging plate position.

centre horizontal rail. The tenons of this rail run right through and there is a fair distance between them. The lock should be let in here. If it cuts a trifle into the tenons it will not matter a lot.

Marking the Position—Wedge open the door and, holding the lock in the position shown in Fig. 4, mark lines across the edge level with the top and bottom of the body of the lock. The lock should extend equally into both tenons. Now turn the lock into the position it will occupy, and, keeping the body level with the marks just made at the edge, mark the position of the spindle hole and keyhole, using a pointed scriber (Fig. 5). Mark all round the holes. Work from the inside of the door because the edge is frequently planed at a slight angle to allow it to clear easily. The holes cannot be bored directly over these marks because they do not allow for the face plate. The bit must therefore be started farther in by a distance equal to the thickness of this plate (see Fig. 6). The usual sizes are $\frac{3}{8}$ in. for the keyhole and $\frac{5}{8}$ in. for the spindle. When the point of the bit just emerges finish the hole by boring from the reverse side.

The Mortise—Turning now to the edge again, draw in a pencil line exactly down the centre (see Fig. 5), using the rule and finger as a gauge. With a twist bit of the same size as the thickness of the body of the lock bore a hole on the centre line so that it is just inside the top horizontal line. A lath of wood cramped to the door as in Fig. 6 will enable you to judge whether the bit is being held square. A series of holes is bored right along the mortise, and it is desirable to bore them as close together as possible so that the subsequent chopping out is minimized. To enable this to be done, knock a plug of wood into the first hole before you bore the second. Remove it and put it into the second before boring the third, and so on. This will enable you to start each hole right up against the previous one without danger of the wood crumbling away and making the bit run out of truth. A piece of paper stuck to the bit will mark the depth to which each hole should be taken.

Chop out the mortise with the chisel. The professional carpenter has a swan-necked chisel for finishing, this enabling the cross grain of the tenons to be cut in the corners, but it is not essential. You can now finish the keyhole with pad saw or with the chisel. A waste block in the mortise will prevent the wood from splitting.

FIG. 3. THE LOCK AND ITS PARTS

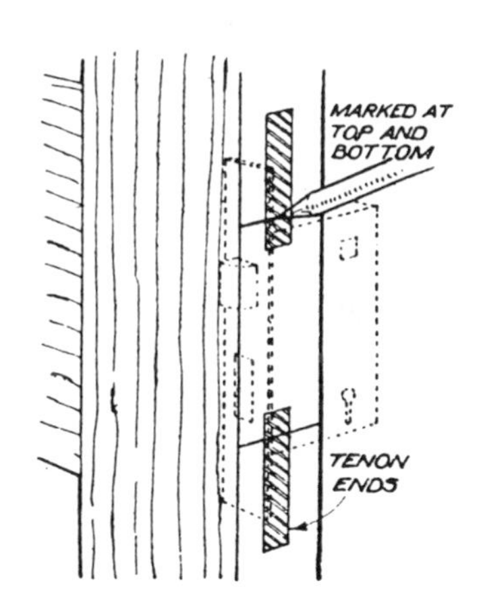

FIG. 4. PRELIMINARY MARKING

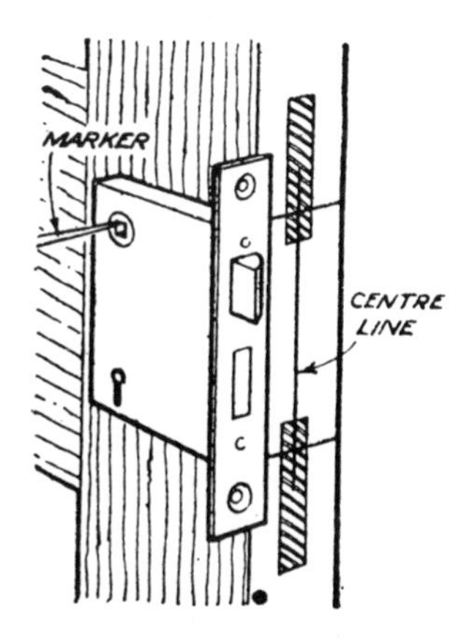

FIG. 5. KEYHOLE AND SPINDLE BEING MARKED OUT

FIG. 6. BORING HOLES TRUE

The Face Plate—The face plate has now to be fitted. The lock is put in position and a line scribed round. As it may be awkward to withdraw the lock when it is pushed right home a useful hint is to put a couple of screws in the plate the reverse way round as in Fig. 6A. These give you something to grip when you want to withdraw the lock. Test to see that the spindle hole and keyhole coincide with those bored, and screw up. Incidentally, some locks have two face plates, the outer one being held with metal screws. This should always be removed during re-painting.

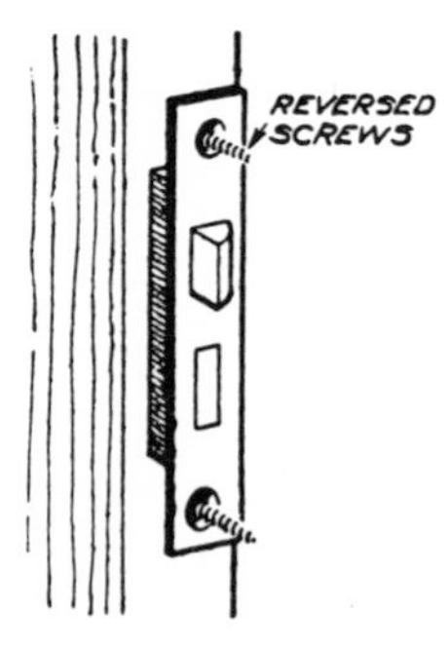

FIG. 6A. HINT WHEN FITTING FACE PLATE

Fitting the Striking Plate—To fix the striking plate, nearly close the door and scribe a line where both bolts occur. Square this across the door rebate. Now open the door, shoot out the bolts and put a film of the dirty black oil from the oil stone on the faces. Shoot in the bolts, close the door tightly, and open the bolts as far as they will go so that they leave a mark on the jamb. This gives the position for the striking plate which can now be placed level with the top of the marks and a line scribed round. Always work to the top, because this allows for subsequent dropping of the door. Screw on the plate and mortise the holes. You will probably find that part of the plate projects at the front. This should be bent over, partly to enable the latch to close more easily, and also because a projecting corner is liable to catch the clothing of anyone passing.

HINGES

Kinds of Hinges—Some of the more generally used hinges are shown in Fig. 7. Of these the butt (A) is the kind mostly used in furniture making, windows, and internal doors, etc. It is intended to be recessed into the wood, and its comparatively narrow shape makes it suitable for the edges of doors. The back flap (B) is let in similarly but is wider, and is used for bureau falls, flap table tops, etc., where there is plenty of width. For the special kind of flap table having what is known as the rule joint, the fixed edge rounded and the flap edge hollowed, the table top hinge (C) is used. Note that the screw holes are countersunk on the side opposite to the knuckle, and that one flap is longer than the other to bridge across the hollow.

(D) is the centre hinge fitted at top and bottom edges, and generally used when the pivoting points of butts would not be

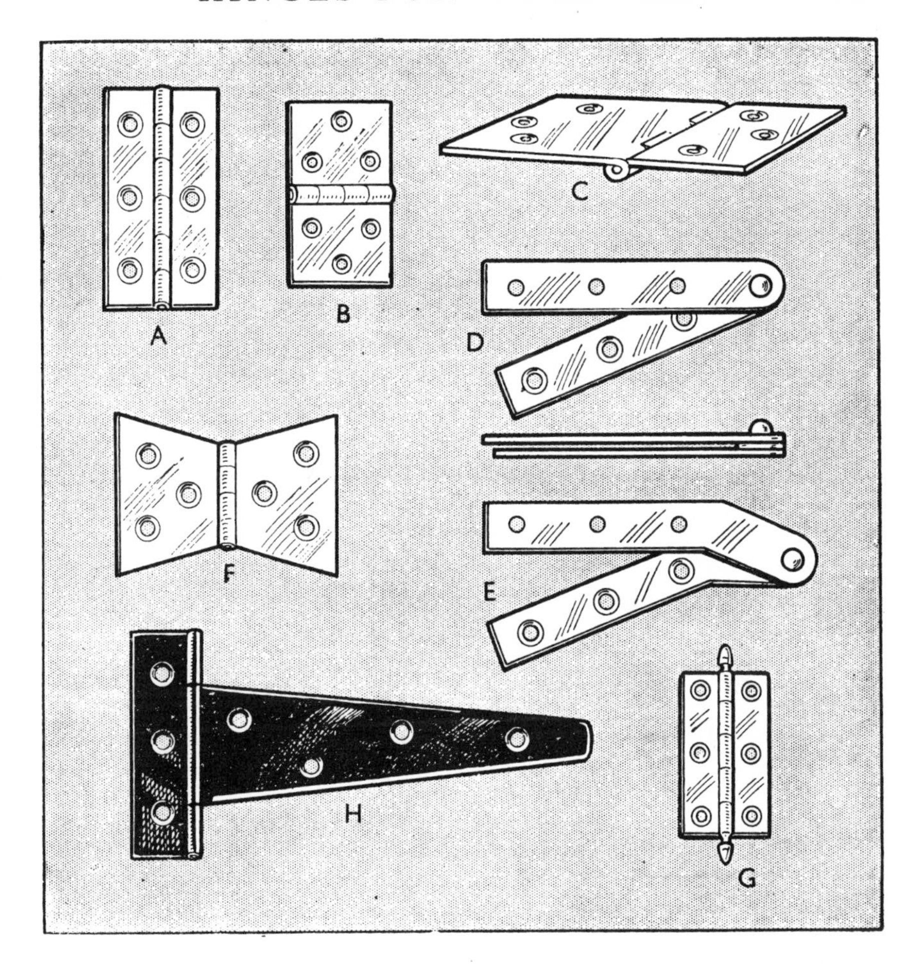

FIG. 7. COMMON TYPES OF HINGES FOR VARIOUS PURPOSES

A. Plain butt hinge. B. Back flap hinge. C. Table top hinge. D. Centre hinge. E. Cranked centre hinge. F. Butterfly hinge. G. Acorn hinge. H. Cross-garnet hinge.

practicable. The cranked type (E) brings the centre to yet another position. Ornamental hinges sometimes known as butterfly hinges are shown at (F). They are not recessed but are screwed straight on to the face. When for any reason the centre of the hinge has to project well from the face of the work it is usual to use the acorn hinge at (G) as its appearance is neater. (H) shows the cross-garnet hinge used for large external doors of the ledged and braced type. The strap portion extends well across the face and obtains a good hold.

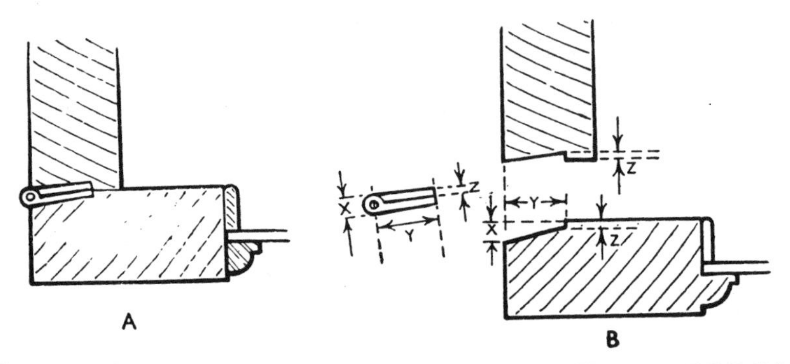

FIG. 8. DOOR CLOSING OVER ENDS, KNUCKLES LET WHOLLY INTO DOOR

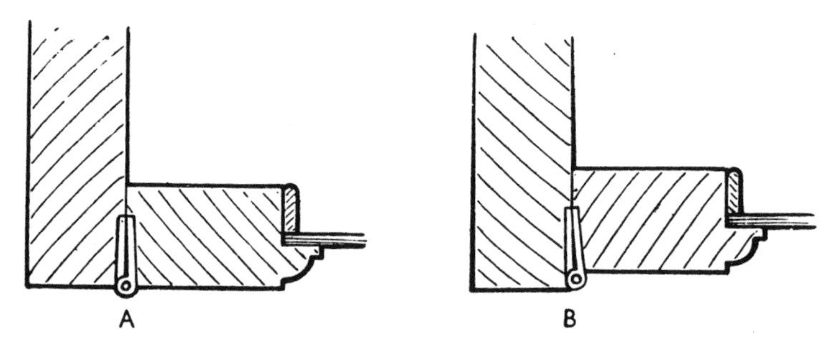

FIG. 9. DOOR CLOSING BETWEEN ENDS. A. HINGE LET EQUALLY INTO DOOR AND END. B. KNUCKLE LET WHOLLY INTO DOOR

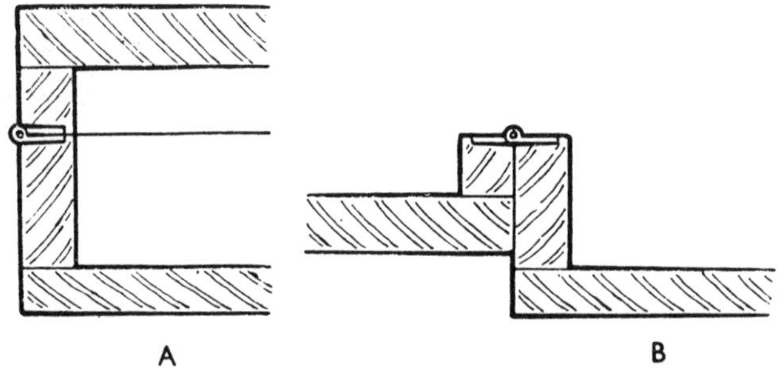

FIG. 10. HINGEING OF BOX LID. HINGE LET INTO BOTH LID AND BOX

Position of Butt Hinges—These can be fitted in various ways according to the position and detail of the door. At (A), Fig. 8, the door closes over the face of the cupboard. If preferred the hinge could be let equally into door and cupboard. Usually, however, the method shown at (A) is followed because a bead is generally worked along the edge of the door to give a neat finish, and the knuckle of the hinge lines up with this. The knuckle is let into the door in its entirety, but to make the appearance as neat as possible and relieve the screws of the entire strain it is usual to cut sloping recesses in the cupboard edge. Note that only the opening edge is let in; at the knuckle side the wood is uncut. (B) shows how the sizes taken from the hinge are marked on door and cupboard.

When a door is contained between the sides of the cupboard either of the methods in Fig. 9 can be used. At (A) the door is flush at the front with the cupboard ends, and the butt is let equally into door and cupboard. At (B) the door is recessed and the butt knuckle is let entirely into the door, though sloping recesses for the flange only are cut in the cupboard. To enable this door to swing through 180 deg., the centre of the knuckle is brought forward so that it is midway between the surface of the door face and the outer edge of the cupboard.

Boxes are hinged similarly to doors, but as a rule the butts are let equally in lid and box as shown in Fig. 10, which shows the opening movement.

Rising Butts—These are used for room doors, their function being to raise the door clear of a centre carpet. They are made in sizes corresponding with ordinary butts, and can therefore be used to replace ordinary butts. One point to note is that they are right- and left-hand and the correct hand must be ordered. To ascertain which you need, stand outside the door. If hinges are to your right you need right-hand hinges.

A framework intended for rising butts has its top rebate at an angle to allow for the slope. When the rebate is square as when simple butts are used it is invariably necessary to take off the corner of the door when rising butts are fitted. This does not show when the door is closed because the rebate hides the corner. The hinges should be oiled periodically to give easy movement.

Hingeing a Door—Decide on the position of the hinges and square in across the edge as at (A), Fig. 11. There is no rule about this but its own distance from the end is a general guide. To

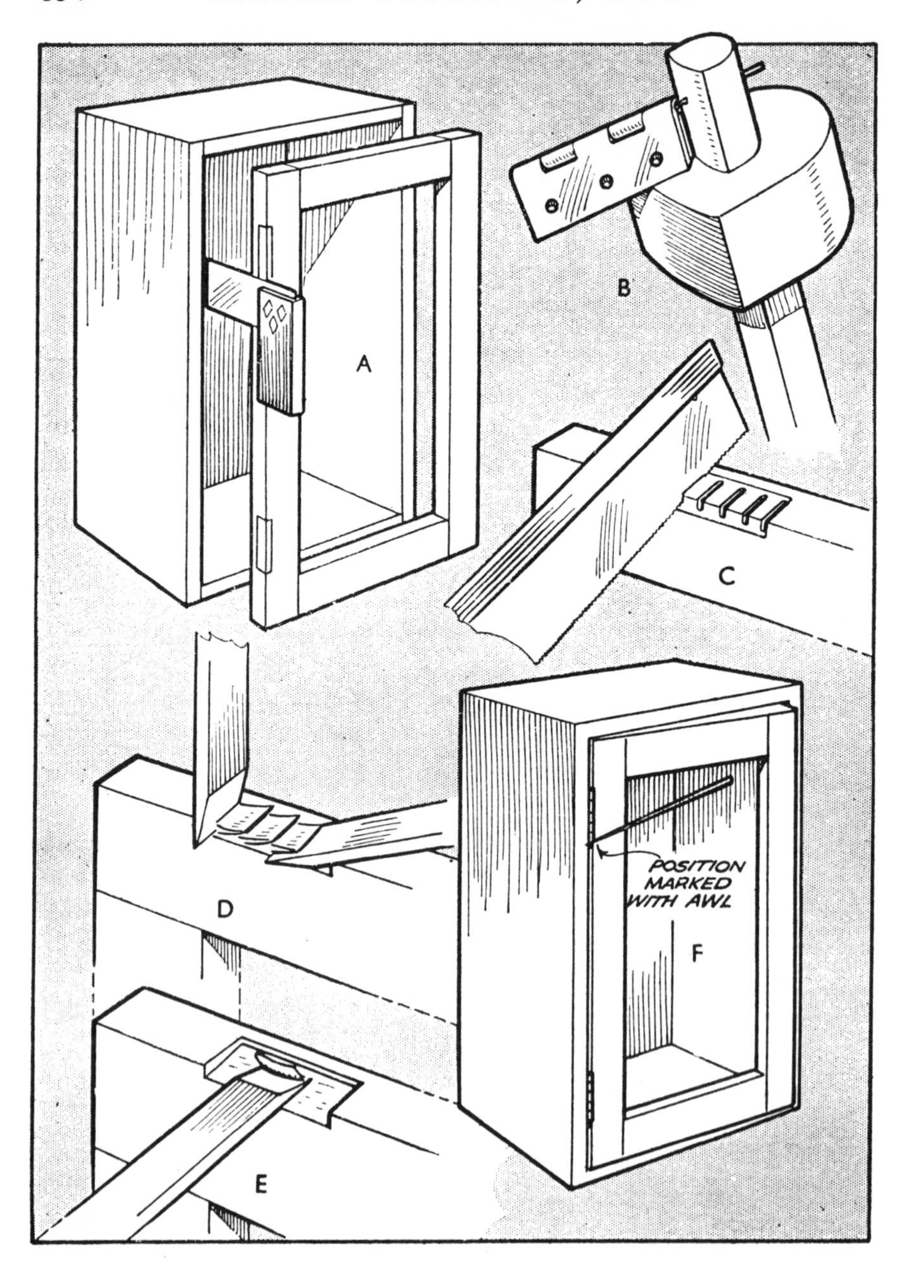

FIG. 11. STAGES IN HINGEING DOOR TO CUPBOARD

A. Marking position on edge of door. B. Setting gauge to knuckle. C. Preliminary sawing of recess. D. First chiselling. E. Completing chiselling. F. Transferring positions to cupboard.

mark the width and depth set the gauge to the hinge itself as at (B). Do not over-run past the pencil lines. Saw across down to just short of the diagonal as at (C), the intermediate cuts serving to break up the grain thus preventing a split from developing. With a keen chisel cut in the ends (D), and waste away the wood to be removed. Finally pare the recess flat as at (E). Fix the butts with two screws each only.

Placing the door in position, transfer the butt positions to the cupboard, and mark and cut the recesses similarly. Fix with a single screw to each hinge, and try the movement. Carry out any adjustment before adding the remaining screws. The closing edge of the door needs to be taken off at a slight angle at the inside, otherwise it will tend to bind as it is opened.

Reversible Screen Hinges—These enable a screen to open in both directions. They have knuckles at both edges, and it is important that the thickness of the wood equals the distance between the pins. If the wood is thicker than this the screen will bind as it opens. If it is thinner there will be a gap down the joint as it opens. This is the lesser evil of the two, but in the case of a draught screen it means that the screen is not wholly effective in its purpose.

NAILS AND SCREWS

Nails—Of the wide variety of nails made for special purposes, those shown in Fig. 12 are the most useful for general woodwork.

French nails (A) have a strong grip, and are used in positions where their large heads are not an objection. Sizes run from ½ in. to 6 in. Thus they are used for carpentry, etc. A similar nail having a smaller head is known as the lost head (B). Not being so strong, but having a smaller head and not so liable to split the wood is the oval wire nail (C). It is driven in with the long oval in line with the grain. Sizes are as for french nails. Panel pins (E) from ⅜ in. to 2 in. are the general nails for cabinet work, as they are thin and have small heads. They are thus not so unsightly, and are not liable to split the wood. A smaller variation is the veneer pin (F), a popular length of which is ½ in.

or $\frac{5}{8}$ in. Apart from its use in veneering it is handy for small mouldings, etc.

Cut nails (D) range from $\frac{1}{2}$ in. to 3 in. and are for carpentry

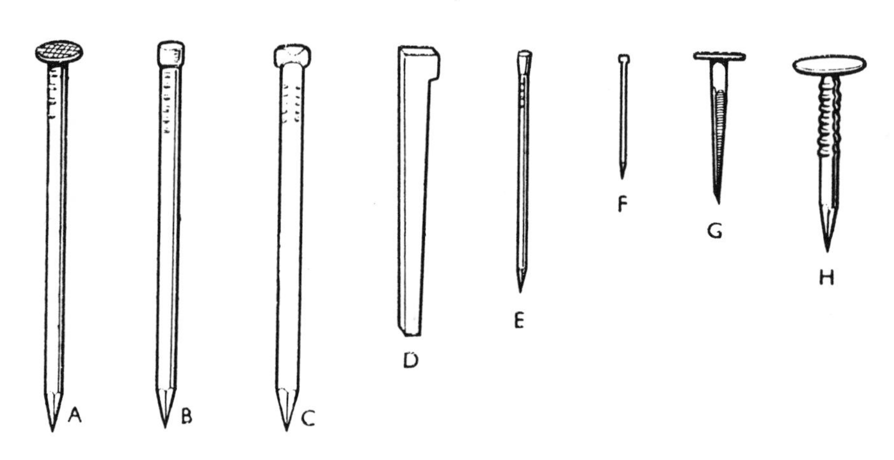

FIG. 12. TYPES OF NAILS IN EVERYDAY USE

A. French or wire nail. B. Lost head. C. Oval wire nail. D. Cut nail. E. Panel pin. F. Veneer pin. G. Tack. H. Clout nail.

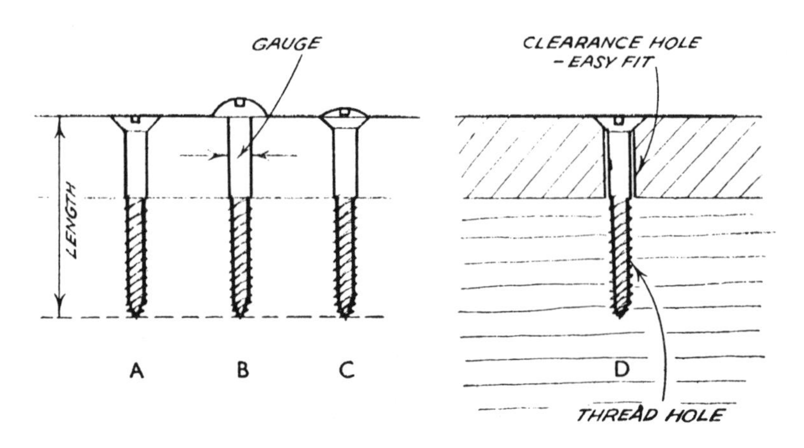

FIG. 13. THREE COMMON TYPES OF SCREWS AND WHERE SIZE IS TAKEN FROM

A. Countersunk. B. Round head. C. Raised head. D. Details of screw holes.

generally. Similar but rather heavier is the floor brad. Both kinds have the advantage of not being liable to split the grain. Tacks (G) are used generally for upholstery. The improved tack has a rather larger head. Clout nails (H) are used to a limited extent in upholstery for webbing, but are more generally used for fixing roofing felt, etc.

Whatever the nail used, always endeavour to nail from the thin wood to the thick. It is an advantage, too, to dovetail the nails; that is, drive them in askew at a slight angle in alternate directions. In the case of outdoor work use galvanized nails.

Screws—The three main types are given in Fig. 13, which also shows where the length is taken from. The gauge is the diameter of the shank and is regardless of length. Thus a No. 8 2-in. screw has the same diameter as a No. 8 3-in. screw. The clearance hole should be an easy fit as shown at (D), and the thread hole should be bored to the diameter of the central rod without the thread. It is purely the hold of the thread which gives the grip.

GLUE

The glues chiefly used in woodwork are: animal (generally known as scotch), casein, and resin.

Animal glue—A strong and reliable glue if properly prepared and used. It is free from any tendency to stain, but is neither heat nor waterproof. It must be used hot. It can be obtained in cakes or in broken-down crystal form. If the former is used it should be placed in a piece of sacking and broken up small with the hammer. The pieces are placed in a clean container (a glass jar is excellent), covered with water, and left to stand overnight. The container is placed in a saucepan and heated, the glue being stirred until it has mixed freely with the water. It should not be boiled but should be rather above the temperature than can reasonably be borne by the hand. When the brush is lifted from the pot it should run down freely without lumps, yet without breaking up into drops.

To apply glue to a piece of cold wood would cause it to chill. The wood should therefore be heated beforehand, care being taken not to blacken shoulder lines by scorching. Furthermore the gluing should be done in a warm shop, and everything made ready beforehand, cramps being opened the right amount, cramp shoe blocks prepared, and testing tools ready to hand. Any squeezed-out glue should be wiped off immediately before it sets as it is almost impossible to remove it once it has hardened. When light woods such as sycamore are being glued, a little flake white powder is added to prevent dark glue lines.

Casein glue—This is another strong glue which has the advantage of cold application. It is, however, liable to stain certain woods (oak and mahogany in particular) and precautions are therefore necessary. Squeezed-out glue should be washed off immediately. Although much of the staining can be removed by the use of oxalic acid crystals dissolved in water, it is better to avoid the glue on important show parts of wood liable to be stained.

Casein glue is in the form of a white powder, and is mixed with water for use. As the glue has no natural tackiness all joints have to be cramped. In the case of veneering the caul method is the only practicable one.

Resin glue—This has several advantages. It is free from staining, the normally available kind is used cold, and is highly water- and heat-resistant. Against this it is more expensive and sets with a cement-like hardness so that edge tools rapidly become blunt. Various kinds of glue are available. One is in the form of a fairly thick liquid which keeps for several months unused, but which eventually becomes rubbery and unusable. A water-like hardener is used with this glue. The glue itself is applied to one part of the joint, and the hardener to the other. No setting takes place until the two are brought into contact, when setting is fairly rapid, the time depending upon the particular hardener used, and the temperature. Generally three hardeners are available, fast, medium, and slow. The medium is suitable for general use. The higher the temperature the faster the setting.

In another form of resin glue the glue itself is in powder form, and will stay in good condition for a year or so if kept sealed. It requires only to be mixed with water, when it becomes just like the liquid glue and is used similarly with a hardener.

Yet another kind is in powder form and has the hardener already added. It is mixed with water to make it ready for use.

All joints should be cramped, and, in veneering, the caul should be used. In this connection note that once the glue has set it is impossible to re-liquefy it. It is therefore extremely difficult to correct any faults such as bubbles or blisters in the veneer.

Polyvinyl acetate glue—This is often used for wood nowadays, but can be used for many other purposes. It is generally reckoned to be non-staining, but the glue itself, although white when in the container, turns to a dark brown colour on setting—at any rate on some woods. It is thus liable to leave a dark glue line, and should be avoided on light woods. The glue is used cold and has fair water resistance.

Rubber based glue—This is not suitable for wood-to-wood gluing, except for some repair jobs which would be awkward to cramp. It is an impact glue, so that when the two glued parts are brought together they immediately grab. Its chief use is in bonding plastic-wood, rubber-wood, leather-wood, etc.

TIMBER AND MATERIALS

(*Continued from page* 193)

Laminated board, etc.—These are built up as shown in Fig. 1, there being an inner core with thinner outer layers, the grain at right angles. Of the three kinds shown the laminated board is the least liable to move.

Chipboard—This is largely made from machine planer chips bound with resin glue and highly compressed. It is frequently used for partitions, backs, furniture parts, but is unsuitable for outdoor use. In the best way the board is attached to a framework, but when used structurally as distinct from a filling, it should have a substantial lipping around the edges, this being tongued in. Apart from strengthening it, it provides a suitable surface in which hinge recesses, etc., can be cut. Veneering is quite successful, both sides being covered.

Wallboards—These cover a tremendously wide range, from really hard, compressed boards suitable for caravan covering, etc., to softboards intended mainly for insulation. The better and medium qualities are frequently used for backs, bottoms, and for panelling generally which is to be painted.

CHAPTER X

VENEERING

THIS is an entirely legitimate process providing that it is not used merely to cover up bad workmanship and materials. It enables certain decorative woods to be used which would be unreliable if cut in the solid, and makes possible many attractive effects such as quartering and built-up patterns which would be entirely impracticable in any other way. Furthermore it has to

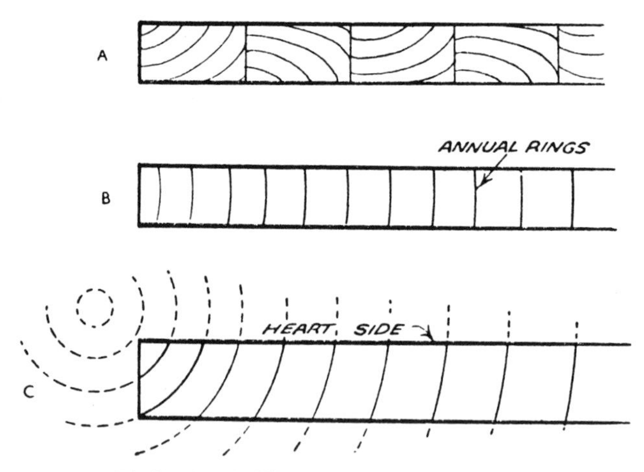

FIG. 1. DETAILS OF GROUNDWORK FOR VENEERING
A. Solid ground made from solid strips with heart side alternately up and down. B. Quarter cut board making good groundwork. C. How to tell heart side of wood.

be accepted that economy in the use of many of the fine decorative hardwoods is essential, and by cutting them into veneers there is a minimum of waste.

Groundwork—So far as the home craftsman is concerned, there are two main methods of veneering; hammer and caul, both of which are dealt with in the following pages. Whichever is used, however, the groundwork and its preparation are the same. Various materials can be used, such as:

Solid wood—Almost any straight-grained wood can be used, but it must be reliable and it should hold glue well. Mahogany is excellent but expensive. Obeche, American whitewood, Parana pine, etc., are widely used. Baltic pine, too, is used, but it must be as free of knots as possible, any small, unavoidable ones being chopped out and the holes filled in. It is also necessary to give softwood a coat of glue size after preparation before the glue proper is used. Otherwise it soaks up more than its share. Oak is sometimes used, but it is not ideal because its coarse grain is liable eventually to show through to the surface owing to the glue contracting in the pores. In any case it is not the best of woods for holding glue.

The most reliable form of solid wood groundwork is made from strips glued together side by side with the heart sides alternately up and down as at (A) Fig. 1, the reason being that any twisting tendency in one piece is countered by that in those adjoining which would tend to twist the other way. Another good solid ground is that at (B) in which the wood is quarter-cut and is not liable to twist either way.

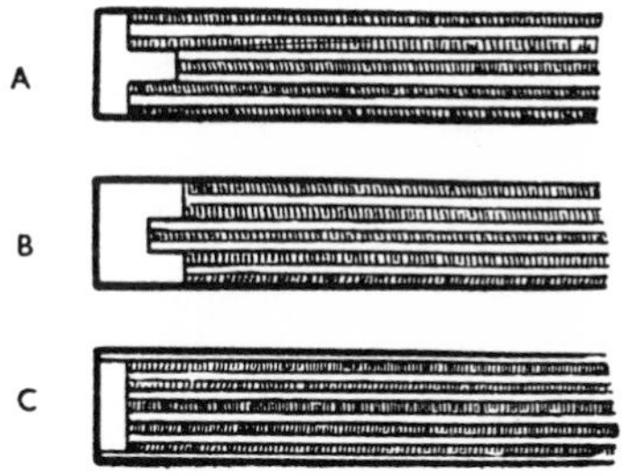

A

B

C

FIG. 2. EDGINGS FOR MULTI-PLY AND LAMINATED BOARDS

It will be realized that veneer tends to pull a panel hollow as it dries out, and for this reason it is always wise to veneer the ground-work on both sides so that the pull is equalized. By taking certain precautions this pull can be minimized or even eliminated altogether, but it is always safer to veneer both sides, especially for such parts as doors which have no stiffening framework. When single side veneering is unavoidable it is advisable to lay the veneer on the heart side of the wood, (C) Fig. 1. The reason is that the pull of the veneer is opposed to the natural twisting tendency of the wood.

Plywood—This makes a good groundwork if of reliable make; the cheap tea-chest variety is useless. Gaboon ply is specially suitable. The veneer should always be laid with its grain at right angles with that of the outer layer of the ply. The edges are sometimes a problem. Veneer does not hold really well on the end grain, and generally the only plan is to fit an edging as in

Fig. 2. That at (A) is the usual trade method, but, as the section is rather awkward to work with hand tools, that at (B) is simpler. The tongue on the ply is more easily worked as there is more wood to grip. (C) is altogether simpler, being just glued and pinned. It would not be used in first-class work.

A point to note in all these edgings is that if veneered first the edging affords considerable protection to the veneer which is always vulnerable at the edge. On the other hand the edging necessarily shows on the surface.

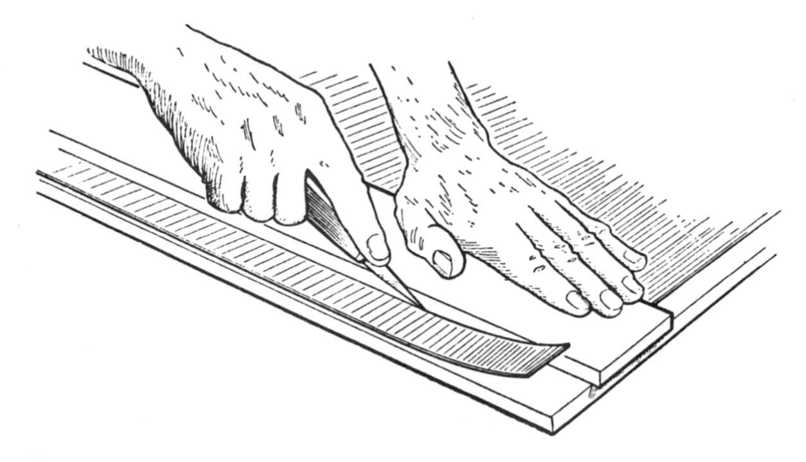

FIG. 3. CUTTING VENEER WITH KNIFE AND STRAIGHT EDGE
It is important that the veneer rests on a flat board, as otherwise pressure from the knife may split the veneer over an undulation.

Lamin board, block board—These make good, reliable grounds. The former is the better since the narrow strips used in the core are less liable to movement. The notes about the direction of the grain given about plywood apply equally. The edgings in Fig. 2 can also be used.

Chip board—This has come in for increasing use as a groundwork—much of it in fact can be obtained ready veneered. For panels and supported parts it is satisfactory, but is not recommended for flush doors which have no stiffening framework. As an edging that at (A) Fig. 2, is the most suitable, with (C) as a cheaper alternative. (B) is unsuitable.

Hardboard—There are many varieties of these, some being more suitable than others. None is as durable as the materials already mentioned, and they would only be used for cheap work or less important parts.

Preparation of Groundwork—As the veneer must be in close contact with the surface of the groundwork it is obvious that any inequality in the latter will show through the veneer. It must therefore be planed dead true. To roughen the surface so giving a key to the glue, and to take out marks left by the plane, a toothing plane (Q, p. 2) is used, this being worked in all directions, along, across, and diagonally. If the ground is softwood it should be

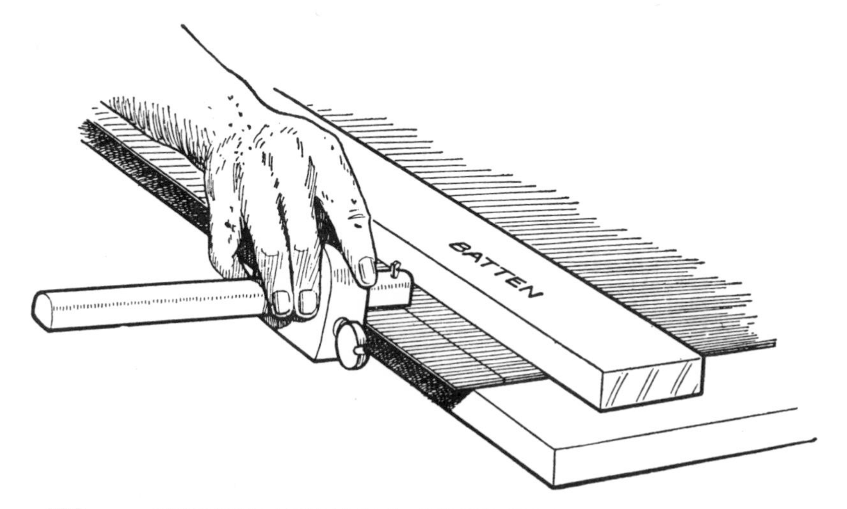

FIG. 4. CUTTING PARALLEL STRIPS WITH CUTTING GAUGE
The batten pressed down over the veneer prevents the latter from cockling. Note that the veneer rests on a flat board.

given a coat of glue size and allowed to dry out. The inevitable roughness is removed by rubbing with the coarsest glasspaper held on a rubber.

Handling Veneer—Most veneer nowadays is knife cut as it is produced with practically no waste. Occasionally saw cut veneer is found, and it is always thicker, and shows the marks of the circular saw on which it was cut. The most convenient way of cutting it is to place it on a flat board, press a batten with a straight edge on it, and cut with keen knife or chisel as in Fig. 3. The batten is essential as otherwise the veneer may cockle and split. When several strips of equal width have to be cut the cutting gauge can be used as in Fig. 4. Here again the veneer rests on a flat board, the edge overhanging about $\frac{1}{8}$ in., and a batten is pressed across it to stiffen it. A single cut will generally sever it, but thick veneer may need cutting from both sides.

Sometimes it is necessary to trim the edge of the veneer, for example, when jointing. It is done on the shooting board, the veneer overhanging the upper platform by about $\frac{1}{8}$ in., and a batten is pressed down to prevent cockling.

FIG. 5. HOW THE VENEER HAMMER IS USED
It should be used along the grain as far as possible to avoid stretching the veneer

HAMMER VENEERING

For this the special tool shown at S, p. 6, is used. It has a strip of brass about $\frac{1}{16}$ in. thick let into the edge, and it is used to press out the surplus glue. The groundwork being prepared and the veneer cut to size, both are covered with glue, and the veneer placed in position and smoothed down. Scotch glue is used, and it should be free of lumps. If a light wood is being used a little flake white powder should be added to the glue as this prevents dark glue lines from showing.

For a job of any size *lightly* damp about one half with a swab, and pass a warm flat iron across it to liquefy the glue. Use only a minimum of dampness, and do not have the iron hotter than is

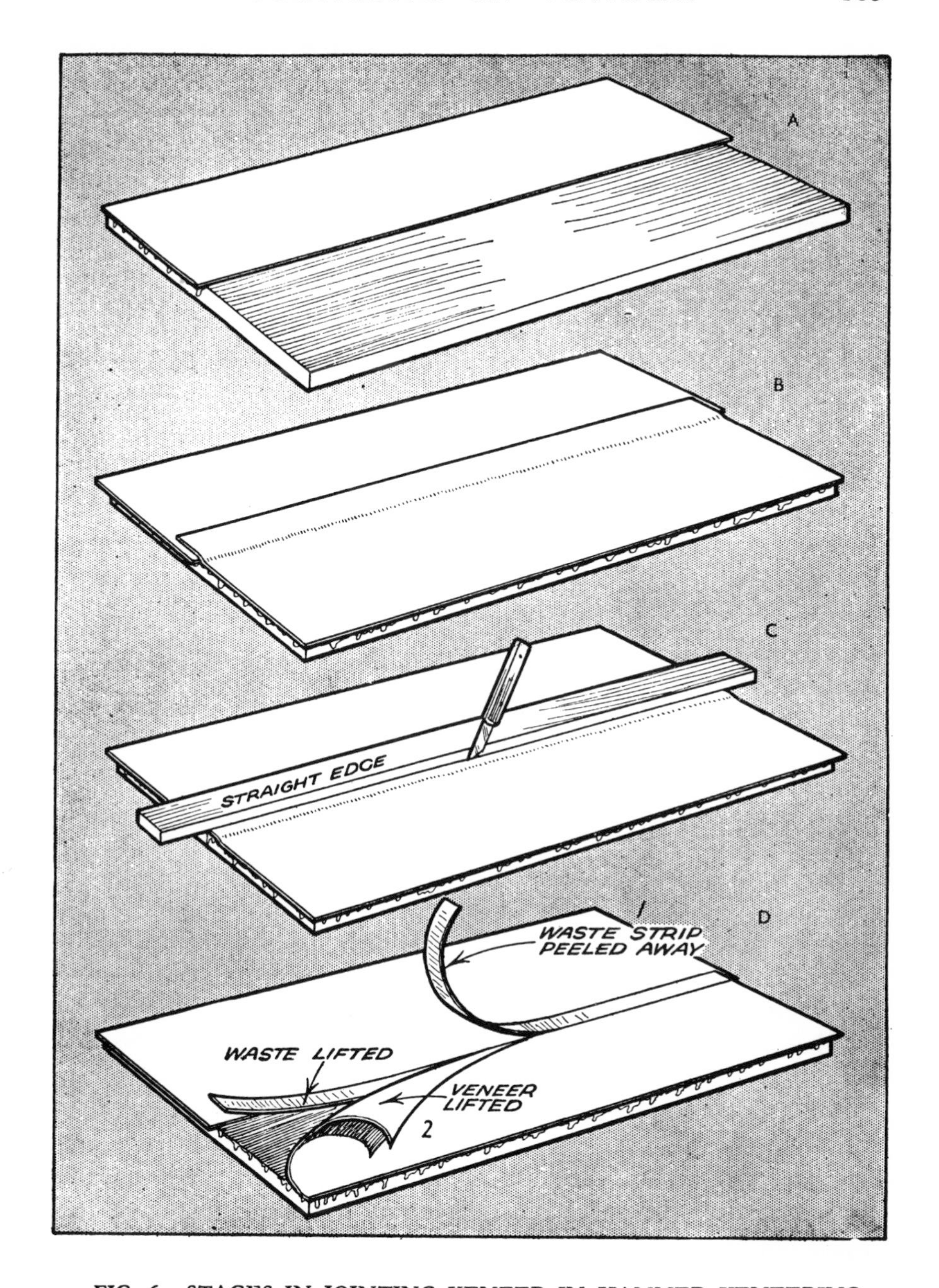

FIG. 6. STAGES IN JOINTING VENEER IN HAMMER VENEERING

A. First leaf laid. B. Second leaf laid with overlap. C. Cutting through overlap. D. Peeling away waste.

essential. Work the veneering hammer with a zig-zag movement from the centre towards the end as in Fig. 5, and try to avoid stretching the veneer in its width. Most veneers will go down easily, but woods with tricky grain may be inclined to lift, and quite a lot of patience may be needed. It is sometimes a help to place a block of metal (say an iron smoothing plane) on a part which is inclined to lift, as the cold metal will make the glue set more rapidly and hold the veneer. In extreme cases it may be necessary to cramp a wood block over the part with a piece of newspaper beneath to prevent it from adhering. To test whether

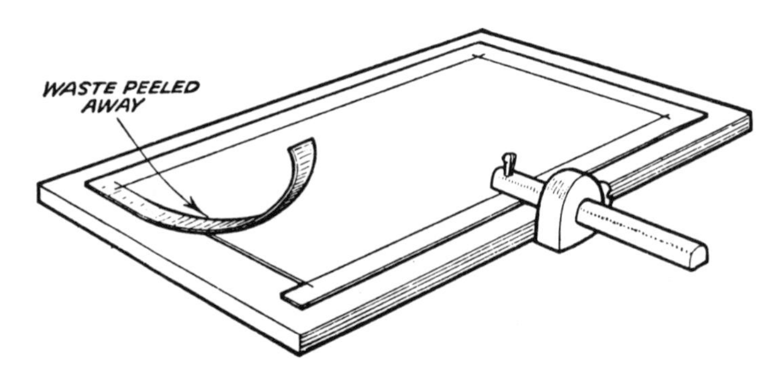

FIG. 7. REMOVING WASTE WHEN CROSS BANDING

The main sheet of veneer does not reach the edge. A cutting gauge is worked around the edges and the waste removed before the glue sets.

the veneer is down tap it with the finger nails. A bubble (as it is called) will be apparent from the hollow feeling it gives.

One half being down correctly deal with the other in the same way. Any traces of glue on the surface should be wiped off with the damp swab straightway, but use as little moisture as possible because it is chiefly this which causes the pull.

Jointing—This may be necessary simply because the veneer is not wide enough, or it may be needed in a halved panel in which two consecutive leaves of veneer are put down side by side, the grain matching. In this latter case the joint line must be drawn in pencil on the groundwork, and care taken in positioning the veneer to make sure that the grain is balanced.

One piece of veneer is laid so that it extends about $\frac{1}{2}$ in. beyond the pencil line as at (A) Fig. 6. The next is laid similarly, overlapping the first as at (B). A straight-edge is laid along the overlap (in line with the pencil mark if there is one), and a keen knife or chisel drawn along it as at (C). If the panel is large it is advisable to fix the straight-edge down with thumb screws.

The one strip of waste can be peeled away straightway. The other is removed by lifting the veneer (D), so revealing it. It is necessary to replace the veneer at once and rub it down with the hammer. A piece of gummed tape stuck over the joint will prevent it from opening as the glue dries out.

Crossbanding—A common practice in veneering is the cross-

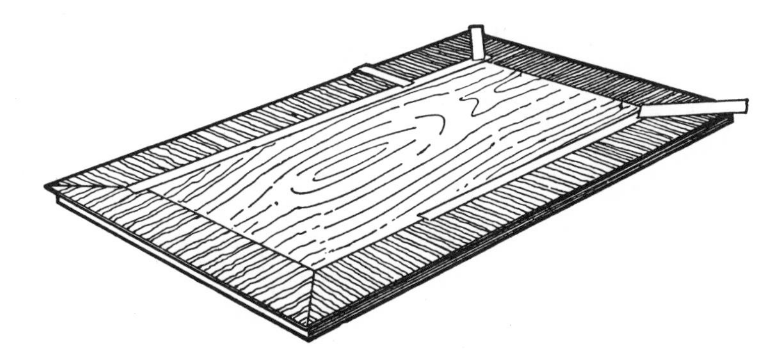

FIG. 8. HOW JOINTS IN CROSS-BANDING ARE TAPED

The tape is stuck over the joints immediately after laying. It prevents them from opening as the glue dries out.

banding of a panel. To do this the main panel is veneered normally except that the veneer is cut short all round. Immediately after laying a cutting gauge set to the banding width is run all round as in Fig. 7, and the waste peeled away.

The crossbanding is cut in cross-grain strips a trifle wider than the banding. The edge is trimmed on the shooting board and the strips cut with the cutting gauge (Fig. 4). In a panel of any great size it will be necessary to joint the strips, and this is done on the job itself, Fig. 8. Mitres are cut with a wide chisel and trimmed if necessary on the shooting board. The veneer is rubbed down with the cross-pene of the hammer, and pieces of gummed tape are stuck over the joints to prevent opening as the glue dries out.

CAUL VENEERING

In this method the veneer is pressed down with a flat board of wood known as a caul. The groundwork is prepared as before, but any jointing in the veneer is done before laying. In a simple joint the edges are planed, the parts put together on a flat board, and a piece of gummed tape stuck over the joint. A pattern, other than the simplest kind, would need a drawing on which the veneer could be assembled.

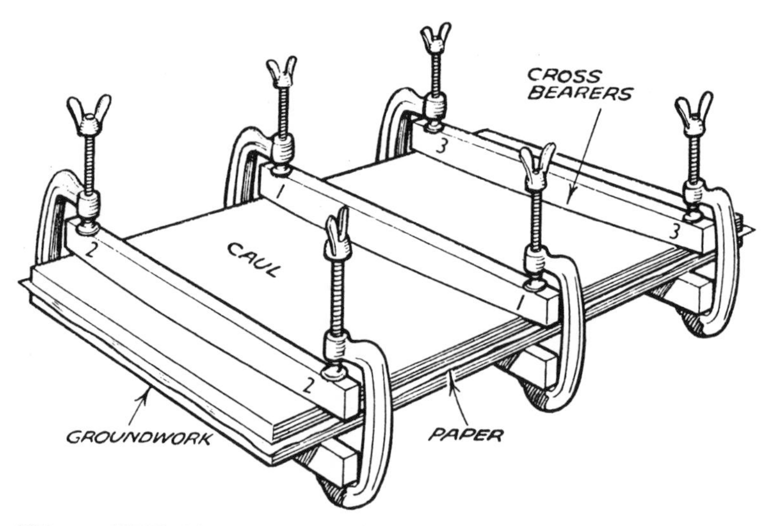

FIG. 9. HOW CAUL IS CRAMPED DOWN IN CAUL VENEERING
The cross-bearers are slightly curved in their length so that pressure is exerted in the middle first, so driving out the glue. Note too the order in which the cramps are tightened with the same object in view.

The groundwork is prepared as before, and both it and the veneer glued and allowed to half set. The veener is placed in position, and, in the case of a pattern centre lines are drawn on both it and the groundwork to enable the correct position to be found. A couple of veneer pins knocked half-way in in an unnoticeable position will prevent movement.

The caul is a flat panel of wood slightly larger than the groundwork, and it should be heated thoroughly all through, not merely surface heated. As soon as it is ready it is placed over the veneer with a sheet of newspaper above to prevent any glue from adhering, and is cramped down.

For a small panel the cramps can be applied all round, but for a larger one it is necessary to use pairs of cross bearers with slightly curved edges as in Fig. 9. The idea is to drive the glue from the centre outwards, the curve ensuring that the pressure is felt in the centre first. Since the curvature in the pairs of bearers is opposed the work remains flat. Note too the order in which the battens are applied, the centre ones again being fitted first to drive the glue outwards.

When both sides are being veneered, the operation is simultaneous, two cauls being used, one each side.

Cleaning Up—Leave the work for as long as possible before cleaning up. Any gummed tape on the surface should be lightly damped and peeled off, but avoid water as far as possible. Clean up the surface with a scraper. Often it is a help to hold the scraper at an angle so that it has a slicing cut. This is specially necessary on a crossbanded part as otherwise the grain may tear up. When satisfactory go over the whole with glasspaper wrapped around a cork rubber, first *Fine* 2, then No. 1. In the case of woods with intricate grain such as burr walnut, use only the finest glasspaper and use the rubber with a circular movement. This is necessary because the wood has no definite grain direction.

Readers seeking further information on veneering should see *Practical Veneering*, by Charles H. Hayward, published by Evans Brothers Ltd.

CHAPTER XI

WOOD CARVING

TO get good results in wood carving it is essential that the tools are really sharp and are sharpened in the right way. The method is different from that used in ordinary woodwork in

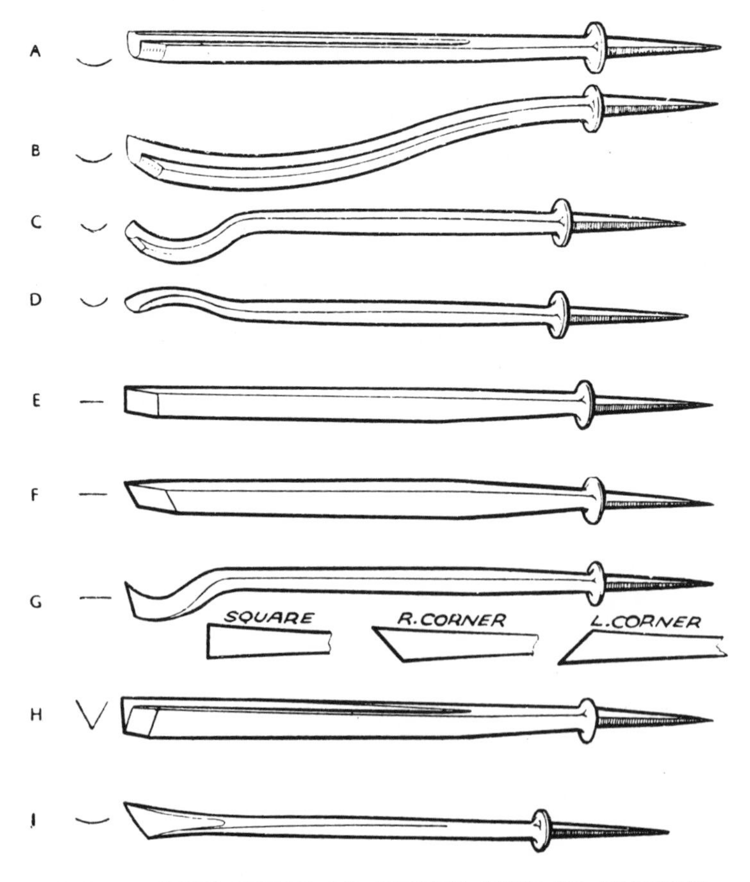

FIG. 1. CHIEF FORMS OF GOUGES USED IN CARVING

A. Straight gouge. B. Curved gouge. C. Front bent gouge. D. Back bent gouge. E. Chisel. F. Corner Chisel. G. Bent chisel (three kinds). H. *V* tool. I. Spade gouge.

which the bevel is on one side only. Carving gouges have the main bevel at the outside, but a second bevel is formed inside.

There are several reasons for the inside bevel. One is that when the tool is used with the hollow side downwards it gives it a tendency to lift as a cut is made. Without it the tool would tend to run into the wood. Another point is that the inside bevel widens the clearance of the tool so that it makes a deep cut more easily.

Range of Tools—The chief kinds of tools are shown in Fig. 1, and of these the straight gouge A is used for all general carving.

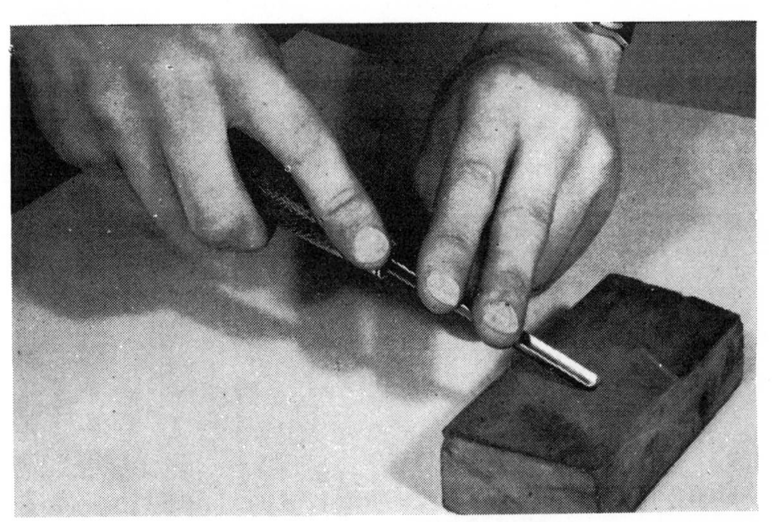

FIG. 2. SHARPENING OUTER BEVEL OF GOUGE ON OILSTONE

The others are special tools for particular purposes. For instance, the curved gouge may be needed for removing the waste when hollowing, say, a bowl. Similar in form but for much more acute hollows is the front bent gouge. The back bent gouge has not many uses, and should not be obtained until actually required.

There are two kinds of straight chisels, square and corner. They are used mostly for setting in, the corner type being useful for reaching into acute corners. For the cleaning up of recessed backgrounds the bent chisel is invaluable. In addition to the square type the *L* and *R* corners are needed for acute corners.

The *V* or parting tool is used chiefly for outlining, lettering, and sometimes for leaf detail. It can be obtained with either 90 deg. or 60 deg. angle. Spade gouges are available in almost all the above forms, but it will be seen that the tool splays out at the ends and is of lighter form. It is used chiefly for finishing off.

All the tools are obtainable in varying degrees of curvature and in several widths. It can be rather confusing, but the rule is that all tools of a certain number have the same degree of curvature in relation to their width. As an example, the No. 9 straight gouge is a half-round curve, whatever its width. Thus the $\frac{1}{4}$ in. No. 9 would be one half of a circle struck from $\frac{1}{8}$ in. radius, and a 1 in. No. 9 would be a semi-circle of $\frac{1}{2}$ in. radius.

SHARPENING THE TOOLS

Gouges—The main outer bevel is sharpened on the oilstone, the tool being held at right angles with the stone and turned with a

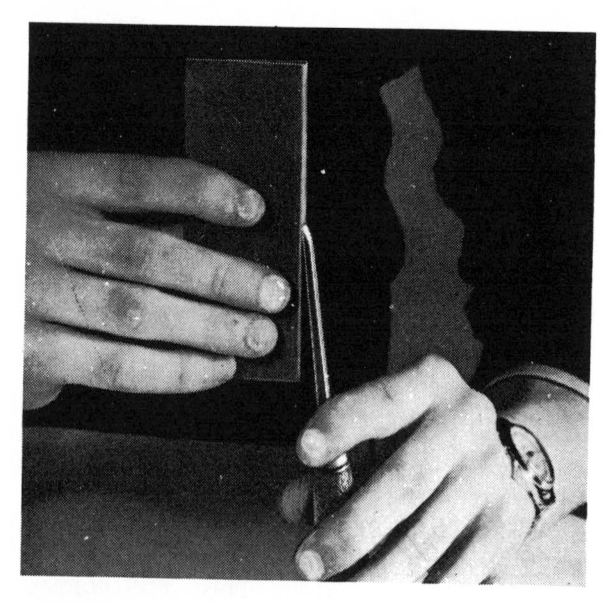

FIG. 3. HOW INSIDE OF GOUGE IS RUBBED WITH OIL-STONE SLIP

rocking movement as it is moved back and forth as in Fig. 2. Now use an oilstone slip of curvature that approximates to the inside or is a trifle quicker, and rub it along the inside at a slight angle much as in Fig. 3. It takes many sharpenings to get the gouge into first-class working order, but it helps after the initial outer rubbing to sharpen chiefly inside.

Stropping follows, and for this a piece of soft leather is dressed with a mixture of oil and the finest emery powder. The *fine* grade preparation sold for grinding in motor car valves can also be used. Place the leather on a flat board and draw the bevel of the gouge flat along it, rocking it so that every part of the edge is stropped, and drawing it back slightly so that the edge is drawn away, not into the leather. For the inside either a piece of leather can be wrapped round the finger or bent on itself, or the leather can be glued to a rounded rubber.

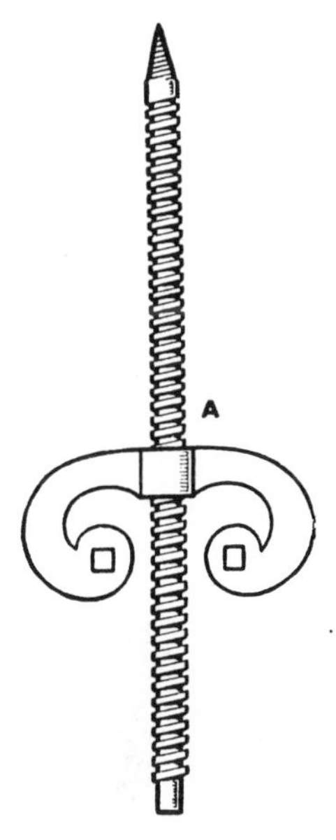

Chisels are sharpened in much the same way except that they are kept flat, not rocked. The bevels are equal on both sides. The *V* tool sometimes causes difficulty. Each outer bevel is rubbed on the stone, and a *V* shaped oilstone slip used at the inside, this being at an angle much as when the gouge is sharpened. When the slip becomes worn it frequently fails to reach into the corner, and instead of being

FIG. 3A. METHODS OF HOLDING WOOD DOWN

A. is the carver's screw. B shows clamps screwed into the bench.

sharp the angle becomes a slight hollow. This results in a point being formed, and will probably necessitate taking off the outer extreme corner.

Bench—The bench at which carving is done should be sturdy with a fairly thick top so that there is a solid feeling when the mallet is used. To hold the wood various methods can be used. Sometimes the ordinary joiners' *G* cramps are suitable, but it is always an advantage to avoid projecting parts. For this reason the carver's screw at (A) Fig. 3A is useful, especially when the wood is fairly thick and when a hole in the back does not matter. The pointed screw end is driven into the wood and tightened by using the wing nut as a spanner. The end of the screw is passed through a hole in the bench and the nut tightened from beneath. When the wood is thin the method at (B) can be followed. Round-head screws are passed through dogs or little pieces of hardwood or metal into the bench. The outer ends of the dogs rest on waste blocks of about the same thickness as the work, and so hold the work firm.

Lighting is important and should be from one direction only so that the undulations of the surface can be seen easily. An all-round light eliminates the shadows caused by the varied surfaces and so robs the carving of form. For daylight a window at the back of the bench is ideal. At night time a single electric lamp which can be raised or lowered at will is the most satisfactory. It should have a shade so that the work itself is illuminated without glare to the eyes.

USING THE TOOLS

When using the tools for the general run of work the right hand provides the forward pressure, whilst the left hand guides the tool and exercises a certain restraining effect, so preventing the tool from over-shooting. Note also that the wrist and ball of the hand rest firmly on the work or the bench so steadying the tool. We speak here of right and left hand, but in fact the good carver is ambidextrous and can vary the hands at will, this enabling awkward parts to be reached without having to shift the work.

Sometimes the mallet is used, especially for some setting-in operations, and the best type of mallet is round in form. This enables the tool to be struck with any part of it, it being unnecessary to turn the mallet to bring the right face into use.

The tools should be laid out in a row at the back of the bench, blades towards the carver. This enables the carver to grasp any tool with the hand in the position it will be held, so saving much unnecessary handling. A common practice is to have all the handles different, either in form, kind of wood, or in colour, so that the right tool is quickly recognizable. In an elaborate piece of work there may be thirty or forty tools in a row, and much time is saved if the right tool can be spotted quickly. Sometimes a carver puts a ring of colour on the handle as a help. Handles are mostly octagonal as this prevents their rolling sideways on to the floor.

Carving may be divided into three main groups:

Incised work, in which the design is cut into the wood, generally with the *V* tool. The cut-away part forms the design.

Modelled Work. Here the groundwork is recessed leaving the design standing up, and a certain amount of modelling is carried out. Thus the form of a leaf may be made to undulate, or one detail, such as a ribbon, made to appear to pass over another.

Carving in the Round. The most difficult, all sides being carved, without any background. The human form, animals, etc., are examples of this.

The same general rules apply to all carving. The whole thing is brought up to one stage before any further work is done. These stages, varied according to the job, are:

Setting In—Here the main outline is cut in, either with a gouge cut on the waste side, or by chopping down with gouges to suit the curves. Often both are used as explained later.

Bosting In—In this stage the bulk of the unwanted wood is removed, leaving main chunks where the detail will later be cut. The main undulations are worked without any attempt at detail.

Modelling—Here the detail takes shape, the complete form being worked, and the final surface chiselled.

In all carving the wood must always be *cut*, not scraped, torn, or split, or levered away. The surface, too, must be left straight from the tool. Glasspaper completely spoils it, and it is this that makes the work exacting. No attempt is made to remove the facets formed by the tool, and it is probably in this that the work of the skilled man shows most to advantage. In his work the tool marks are purposeful and crisp, and their direction helps the flow of the design.

Sometimes the background can be given a special texture by the use of a punch, but this must not be made an excuse for bad work with the gouge. Its purpose is solely to show up the design itself by giving the background an entirely different appearance. Punches can either be bought ready made, or they can be made

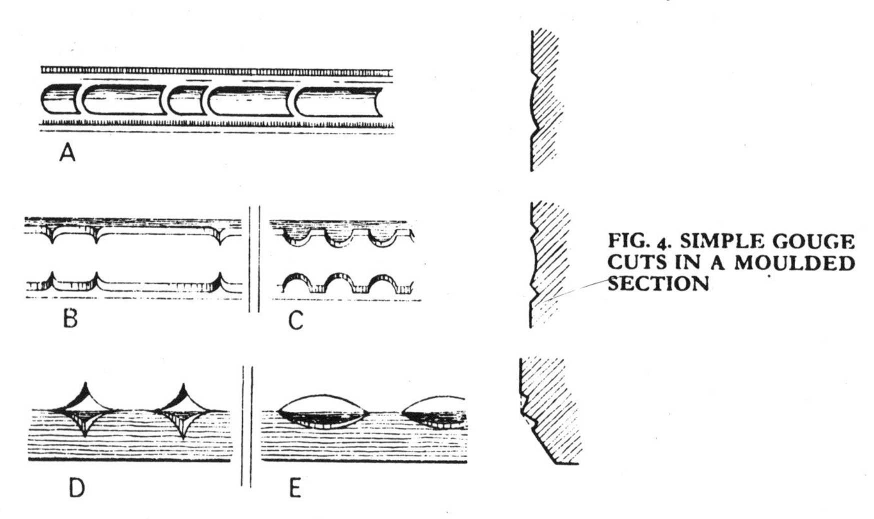

FIG. 4. SIMPLE GOUGE CUTS IN A MOULDED SECTION

from a 6 in. french nail filed off square, and with indentations filed in the end.

Gouge Cuts—The best way of describing the process is to take actual examples, and for a start the simple gouge cuts in Fig. 4

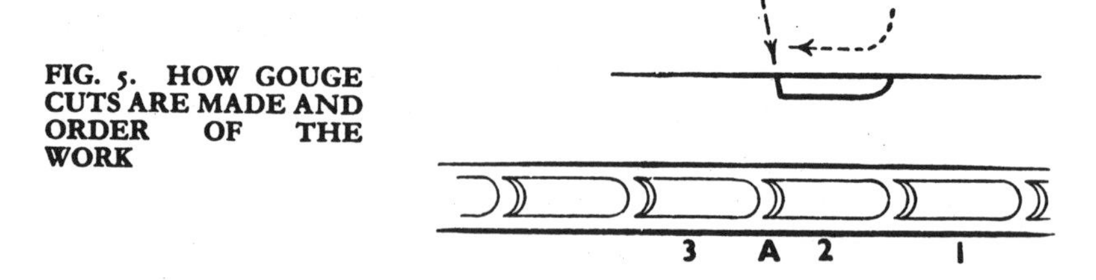

FIG. 5. HOW GOUGE CUTS ARE MADE AND ORDER OF THE WORK

are good practice. At (A) is a moulding formed with *V* cuts at each side and rounded centre. A gouge rather narrower than the rounded member is used to make a series of downward stabs at the points (A), Fig. 5. Hold the gouge at a slight angle as shown by the dotted arrow in the section, and use the mallet. There is an advantage in making all the downward cuts first. The heavy work is rather hard on the tools, and, once this is done, it enables the edge to be kept in good condition for the following process of scooping out the waste. Furthermore the downward chopping may cause the short grain occasioned by the adjoining cut to split out, though this difficulty can be avoided by making the cuts in the order shown in Fig. 5.

Note that to preserve the parallel sides of the cuts the gouge must be taken downwards and the handle rapidly lowered as shown by the dotted line, Fig. 5. As a rule a single cut is made

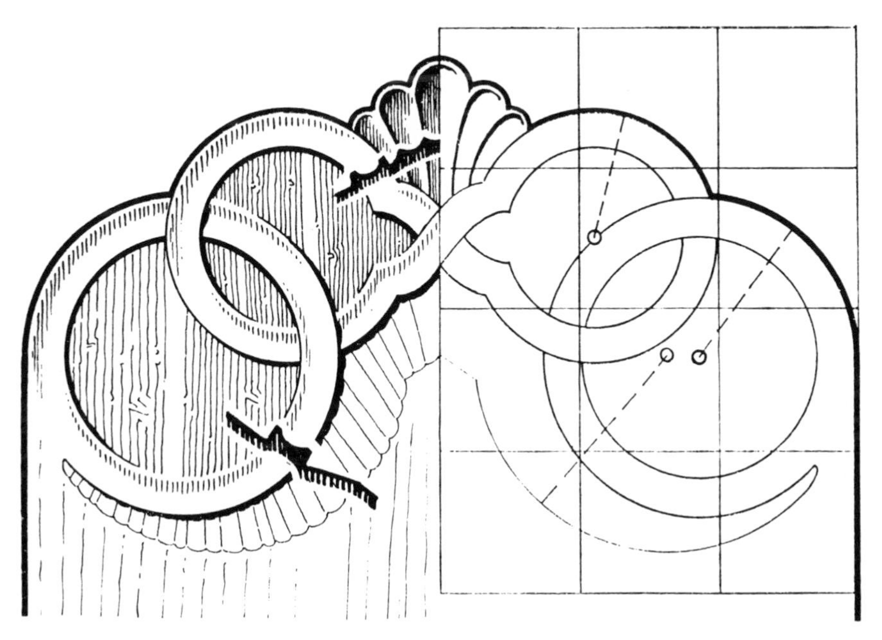

FIG. 6. DESIGN SUITABLE FOR BOOK END

This would look specially well in oak or chestnut. The design could be drawn map-fashion by the use of the grid, which represents 1 in. squares.

first to remove the bulk of the waste, and a second cut to finish cleanly to size. This work is mostly done by eye, apart from the initial stepping of the stabs, though pencil lines can be put in as a guide. They will have to be scraped out locally afterwards.

At (B), Fig. 4, a hollow section is worked first, and the position of the members either stepped in with dividers or marked from a slip of paper. A gouge is used to cut downwards each side of the indentation, this being held at an angle so that the edge finishes in line with the outer sloping side of the *V*. The cuts must meet.

A flat gouge can be used in line with the side of the *V* to cut away the small waste pieces.

A similar process is followed at (C), the gouge being used to cut the semi-circle. Again it is held at an angle so that the edge finishes in line with the outer slope of the *V*. This enables the little waste piece to be cut out cleanly with a flat gouge or chisel. Some may find a skew chisel easier to use for this.

At (D) and (E) are similar devices worked at the corner of a chamfer. In both cases downward stabs are made, and the waste eased away with a flat gouge afterwards.

Book Ends—Fig. 6 shows a simple pattern that might be used for the top of a pair of book ends. The design could be

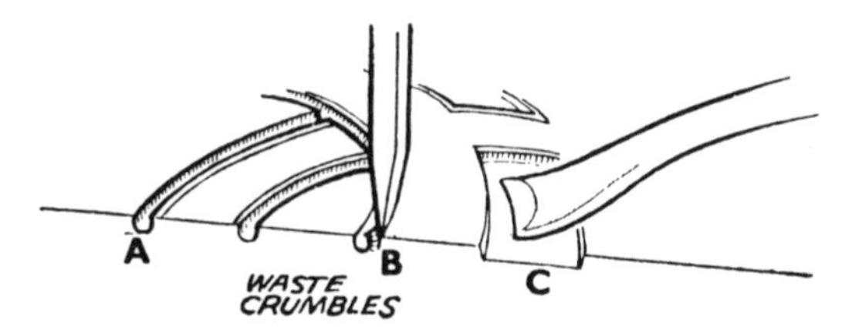

FIG. 7. HOW PRELIMINARY OUTLINING WITH GOUGE HELPS WASTE TO CRUMBLE AWAY WHEN STABBING IN AROUND DESIGN

drawn full size on the wood using the grid. The main outline is sawn out and later cleaned with gouges. As the highest part of the design is the interlacing strap, the outline to this is cut first, and the work is much simplified if a quick gouge is taken all round the outline on the waste side first as shown at (A), Fig. 7. Then when the gouge is used to cut down right on the line the waste crumbles away as at (B). Unless this is done the gouge may be forced into the design owing to the wedge shape of the tool. Furthermore it would be heavy going, especially in a really hard wood.

The waste can be partly removed with the ordinary gouge, but the cranked tool shown at (C) is extremely handy, the *R* and *L* skew tools in particular being useful for corners. In the portions entirely enclosed by the strap the background can be taken down level to a depth of about $\frac{3}{16}$ in. or $\frac{1}{4}$ in., but the part below is sloped

FIG. 8. FOUR SUGGESTIONS FOR BOOK ENDS. SIZE ABOUT $7\frac{1}{2}$ IN BY 5 IN.

Much of the detail is interchangeable.

FIG. 9. FULL SIZE DETAIL SUITABLE FOR MANY PURPOSES
Although the pattern could be traced and transferred with carbon paper, it is advisable to put in the circular parts with compasses.

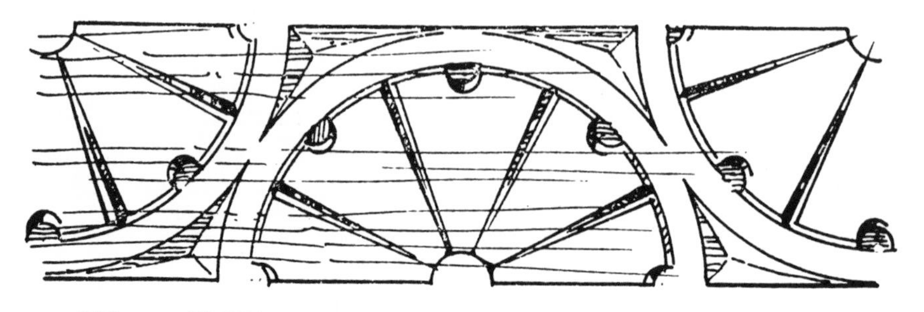

FIG. 10. SIMPLE LUNETTE DESIGN SUITABLE FOR A FRIEZE
Here again the curves should be struck with compasses.

in at an angle, the gouge being used. The cuts should approximately radiate. At the top the wood is lowered about $\frac{1}{16}$ in. only at present.

As the strap interlaces the level of the lower one should be lowered gradually so that the one appears to pass over the other in a natural way, not abruptly. Lastly, the conventional leaf can be carved by cutting a series of hollows, allowing ribs to stand

FIG. 11. EXAMPLE OF SIMPLE CHIP CARVING

up as shown. Care is needed in deciding the direction in which the tool is taken, because it will tear out at one side and be smooth at the other.

Alternative designs for book ends are given in Fig. 8. These could be enlarged up to whatever is required. Other *motifs* appear in Figs. 9 and 10. These could be adapted to many things.

Readers seeking fuller information on carving should see *Practical Wood Carving and Gilding*, by W. Wheeler, A.R.C.A. (Lond.) and C. H. Hayward, published by Evans Brothers Ltd.

CHAPTER XII

WOOD TURNING

THERE are two ways of turning; you can cut or you can scrape. Each has its uses, and the skilled operator uses both. Of the two scraping is by far the easier, but for certain work it does not give so clean a finish and it is not so quick. In scraping, the tool is presented to the work almost radially; it is held with a slight dip and the cutting edge brought level with the centre of the wood being turned. For some work it is the only practicable method, but it is almost impossible to scrape softwood, as it is crushed beneath the pressure. Furthermore the layers of hard and soft grain result in an uneven surface. On the other hand, close-grained hardwoods generally scrape well, and for finishing wide surfaces on the face plate it is the only method.

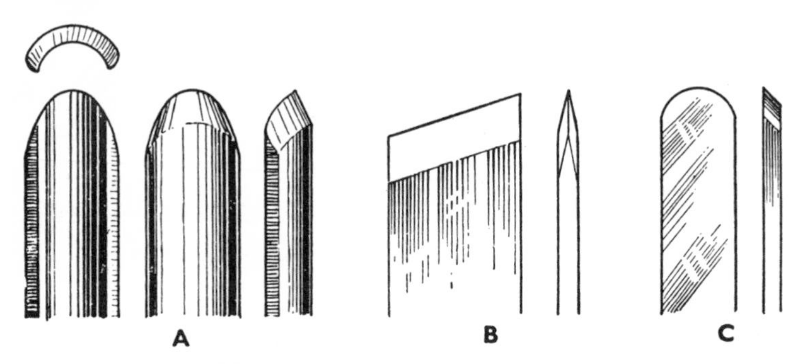

FIG. 1. CHIEF TOOLS USED IN WOOD TURNING
A. The gouge. B. Skew chisel. C. Scraping tool.

In cutting (more generally known as gouge and chisel work) the tool is inclined so that the cutting edge points towards the oncoming wood, and is frequently turned at an angle so that a slicing cut is produced. The gouge and chisel (both in various sizes) alone are used, and neither tool is ever used for a scraping action. For the preliminary roughing down of the work it is very quick, and for finishing it gives a beautifully clean finish which is burnished and needs no glasspaper. Softwoods *must* be turned with gouge and chisel.

The Tools—Keep an oilstone and slip handy by the lathe, and give the tools two or three rubs frequently. The shapes to which they should be sharpened are shown in Fig. 1. Note that the gouge (A), apart from its sectional curve, has its nose well projecting. If it were straight like a normal woodworking gouge the corners would catch in. It is sharpened at the back only, the inside being kept flat. The grinding angle for work between centres is about 35 deg. For turning the inside of bowls, the angle is about 45 deg. because the bevel must rub to prevent digging

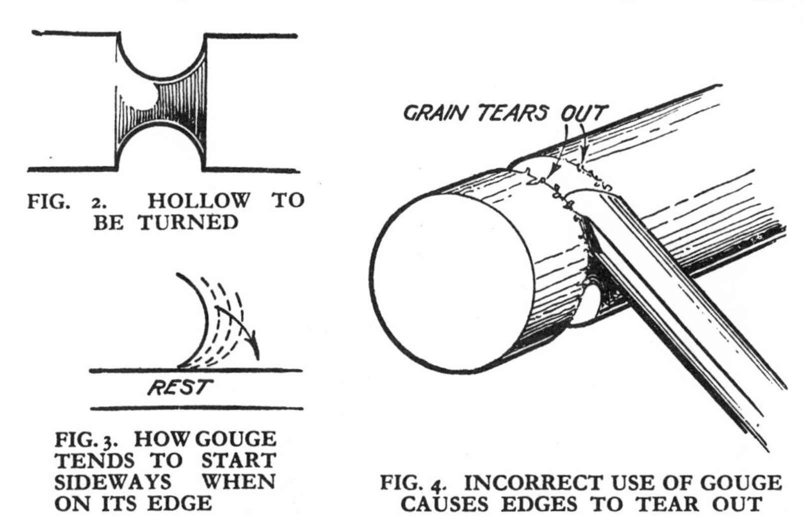

FIG. 2. HOLLOW TO BE TURNED

FIG. 3. HOW GOUGE TENDS TO START SIDEWAYS WHEN ON ITS EDGE

FIG. 4. INCORRECT USE OF GOUGE CAUSES EDGES TO TEAR OUT

in. When rubbed on the hone keep approximately to the same angle with a tendency to rub towards the point.

The skew chisel is given at (B), and it will be seen that both sides are sharpened because it has to be used for traversing in either direction. The bevels are flat. Scraping tools are given at (C). They are flat at the top, and the shape can be practically anything to suit the work. Many of them are ground from old files. They can generally be used direct from the grinding wheel. The angle 75–80 deg.

Using the Gouge—The best way of getting experience is to put a piece of wood in the lathe and try some practice cuts. Pick a piece of softwood about 2 in. square and fix it between centres. Put a spot of oil at the dead centre to reduce friction, and begin by roughing down the work to a cylinder. The gouge can be taken end to end quite rapidly. Point it slightly in the direction in which it is moving, and continue until all flats have been taken out.

The first sign of trouble when using the gouge is when an attempt is made to turn a hollow such as in Fig. 2. If the gouge is presented to the wood square on, the sides will inevitably tear out the grain as in Fig. 4 because they tend to lift the fibres. You need a slicing cut, and the method is to turn the tool on its side and take it in with a sort of twisting movement. Each side of the hollow is thus cut separately, the cut being inwards in each case. That is the theory, but what usually happens in the case of

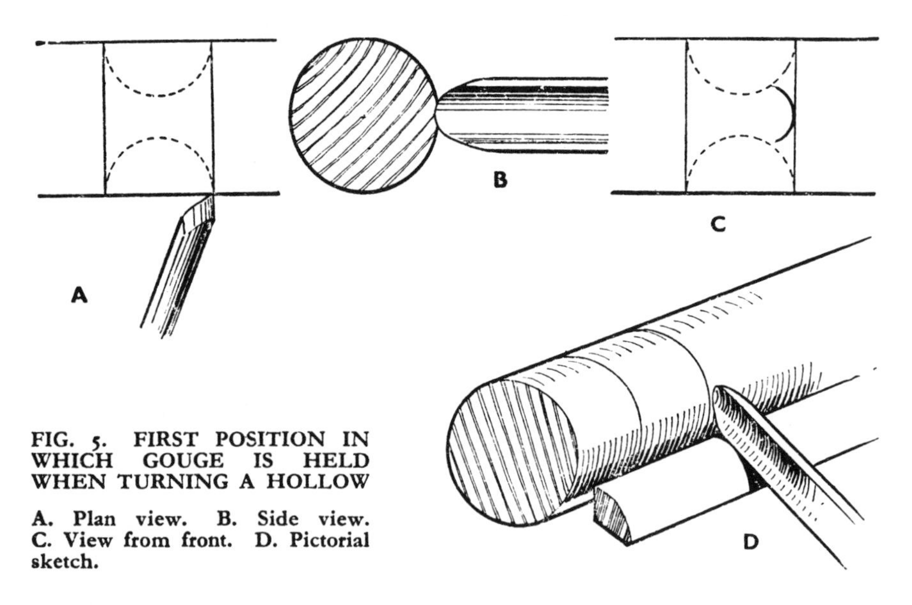

FIG. 5. FIRST POSITION IN WHICH GOUGE IS HELD WHEN TURNING A HOLLOW

A. Plan view. B. Side view. C. View from front. D. Pictorial sketch.

the beginner is that the tool immediately starts sideways and makes a gash in the wood.

To avoid the trouble place the gouge so that in plan its bevel is practically at right angles with the axis of the turning as shown in Fig. 5 at (A). In side elevation the tool is horizontal (B), and from the front the gouge is on its side, as at (C).

Offer the tool up to the wood so that it nicks in a line around the revolving wood. Once you can do this successfully the battle is half won, because, after the gouge has entered the wood, the bevel, in bearing against the wood it has cut, prevents it from moving sideways. This, in fact, is the secret of gouge work.

Keep the back or bevel rubbing on the wood. If it does this it cannot start sideways ; the bevel prevents it. That is why the initial start is always the difficult part. There is nothing on which the bevel can rub until after it has entered the wood a reasonable distance.

If you find great difficulty in this you can make preliminary nicks in the wood with the chisel. Then when the gouge is pressed forwards it already has something in which the back can rub.

Movement of the Gouge—Fig. 6 shows what happens as the

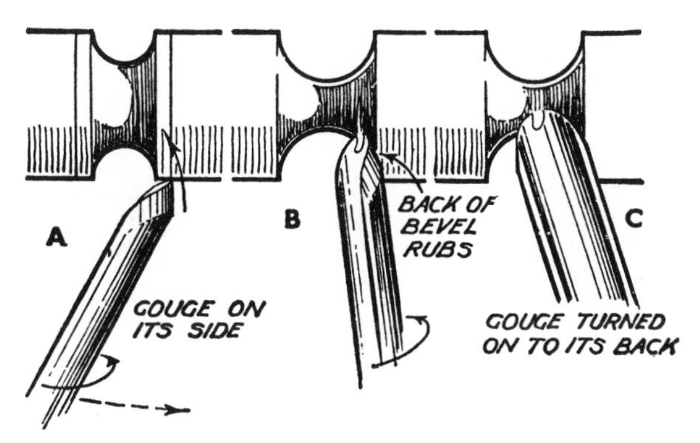

FIG. 6. STAGES IN MOVEMENT OF GOUGE
The movement is continuous, and consists of shifting the handle over to the right and lowering it at the same time. In addition the gouge is turned over on to its back.

gouge continues its cut. At (A) is the preliminary entry of the tool forming a nick all round. As it is pressed in the handle is pushed over to the right so that the curvature of the hollow is followed, and in doing so keeps the back rubbing against the edge. At the same time as it is pushed to the right it is lowered, and is twisted so that the gouge begins to turn over on to its back as at (B). The last stage (C), shows the gouge completely over on its back, and the handle has been so lowered that it has emerged above the turning. The other half of the hollow is dealt with in the same way.

The Chisel—The skew chisel is used for cutting, not scraping and is held across the wood at an angle. Do not be discouraged if you make a mess of it the first time. What invariably happens

FIG. 7. ROUGHING DOWN CYLINDER WITH LARGE GOUGE

FIG. 8. FINISHING CYLINDER WITH LONG-CORNERED CHISEL

FIG. 9. TURNING HOLLOW USING SMALL GOUGE

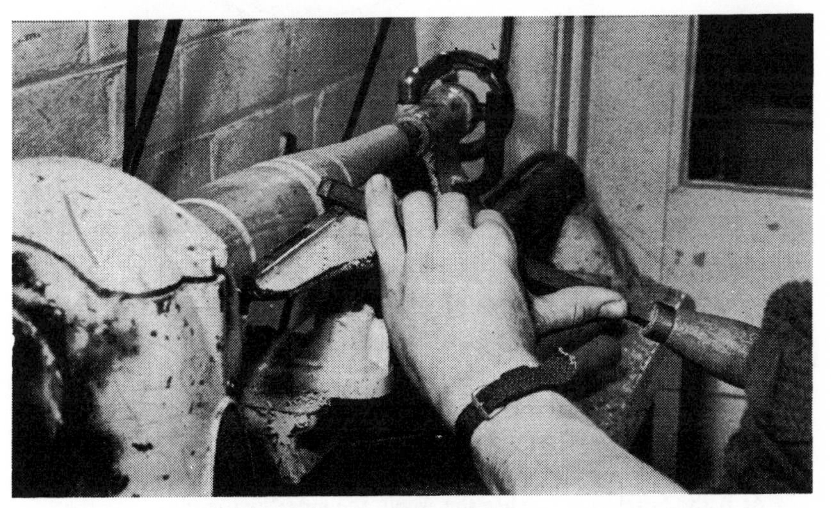

FIG. 10. BEAD BEING TURNED WITH NARROW CHISEL
Note that only the corner of the chisel is used.

is that the point digs in, resulting in a nasty gash in the wood. There are two things to keep in mind.

Keep the acute point of the tool clear of the work. Cutting is done at about the middle of the edge, but if the lower obtuse corner touches the work it will not do any harm. It is only when the acute point touches the work that it immediately digs in and spoils it. The second detail is to keep the bevel of the tool rubbing on the wood (just as in the case of the gouge).

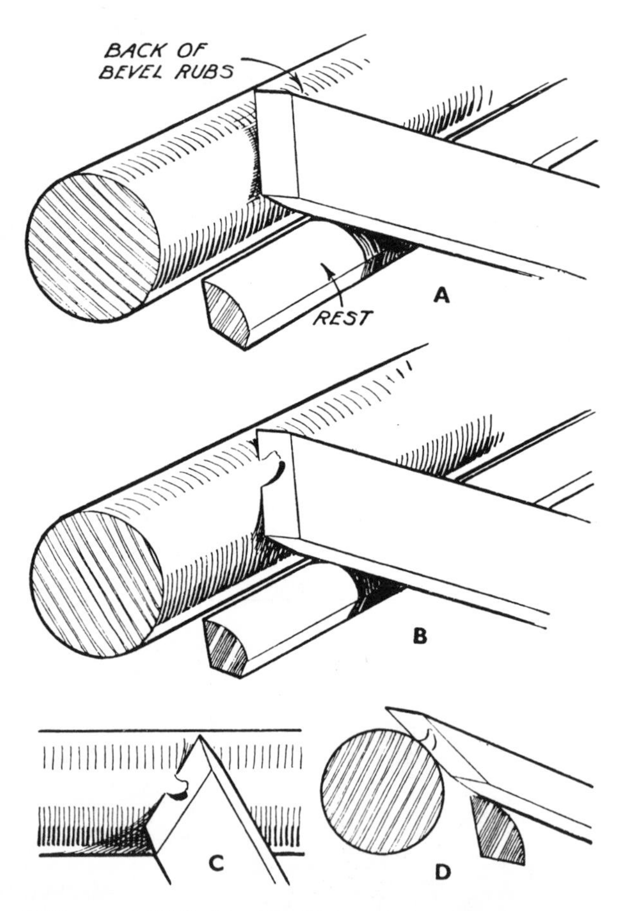

FIG. 11. METHOD OF USING THE SKEW CHISEL

At A the bevel only touches the wood, the chisel not cutting. As the handle is raised the edge begins to cut as at B. C and D are side and end views.

Place the chisel at an angle on the work with only the bevel touching it, not the actual edge, as at (A), Fig. 11. Obviously nothing will happen. The tool cannot cut. Now gradually tilt it over to the left until it is clear that the edge is down on the wood and is actually cutting. You can tell this by sliding the tool to the left when it will remove a shaving if the edge is right down (see (B)).

Do not tilt it any more. Only a light skimming cut is needed, the roughing having been done with the gouge. In this way the bevel continues to rub on the wood and there is no tendency to dig in. A cylinder being turned with the chisel is shown in Fig. 8.

One of the chief reasons why the point catches is that, in taking a heavy cut, the chisel is momentarily caught in the wood and is

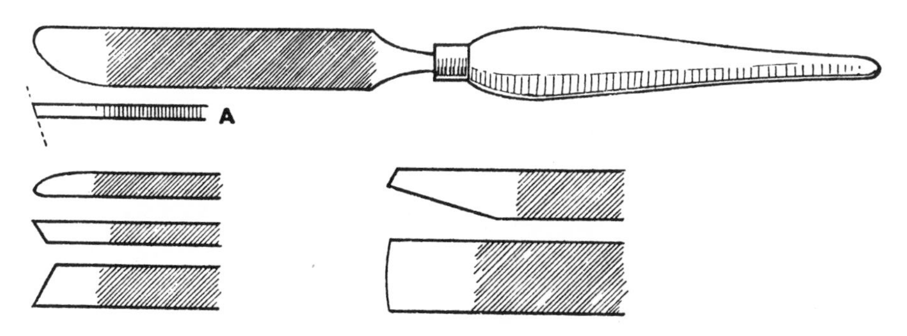

FIG. 12. SCRAPING TOOLS MADE FROM OLD FILES

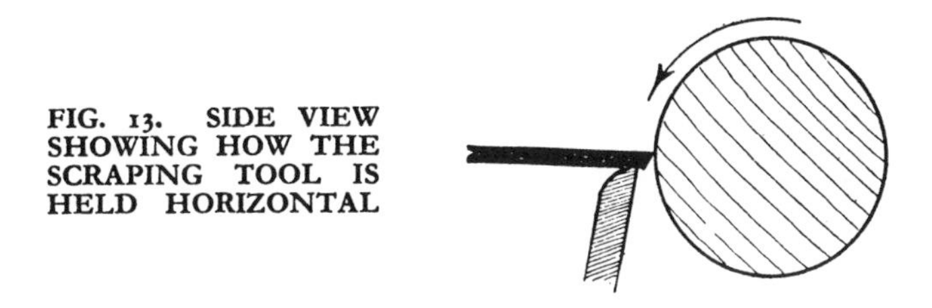

FIG. 13. SIDE VIEW SHOWING HOW THE SCRAPING TOOL IS HELD HORIZONTAL

drawn downwards so that the point catches in. Remember then, keep the bevel rubbing ; cut with the middle or lower part of the cutting edge ; use a wide chisel on large work ; and take only a skimming cut.

Scraping—Although special scraping tools can be bought they can be made perfectly well from old files. The serrations are ground away, and the edge is ground at about the angle shown in Fig. 12 at (A). The shape of the edge can be made to suit the job, and you will find that you eventually have a large number of varying shapes. As a rule the tool is best used straight from grinding, especially such woods as elm. Having ground away the serrations the edge is ground and the resulting burr is not removed. It does in fact help the cut.

Fig. 13 shows how the tool is horizontal or points downward slightly and approaches the wood at about the level of the centre. In the case of a bowl in which the grain runs crosswise the final cuts must be extremely fine, otherwise the grain will tend to tear out where the cut is made against it.

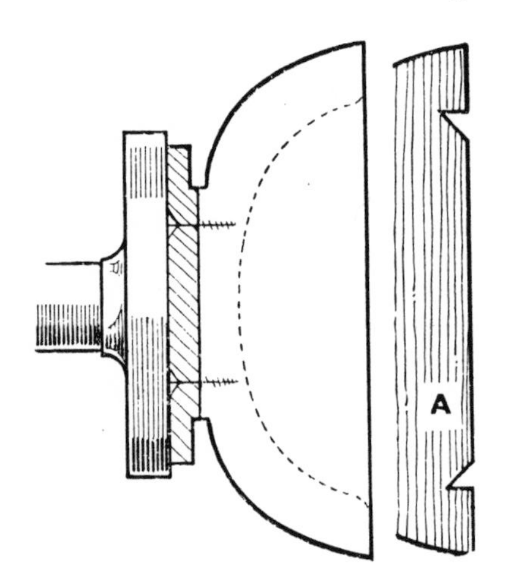

FIG. 14. PRELIMINARY NICK MADE WITH SCRAPING TOOL BEFORE GOUGE IS USED WHEN TURNING A BOWL

In work of this kind the gouge can be used for all roughing out operations both inside and outside. For the former a preliminary entry can be made with the scraping tool as at (A), Fig. 14, as otherwise the gouge may tend to run off, but after this there is no difficulty providing that the bevel of the tool rubs on the wood. As already mentioned the angle of the bevel should be not less than about 45 deg.

These few notes explain the general principle of wood turning, but it is an involved subject, and readers who seek fuller information should see *The Practical Wood Turner* by F. Pain, which deals with every branch of the subject.

CHAPTER XIII

TIMBER AND MATERIALS

THE range of timbers runs into thousands, and here we can deal with only the relatively few in common use. Those seeking fuller information should see *Timbers for Woodwork*.

To make a broad distinction timbers may be divided up under two headings: hardwoods and softwoods, the former referring to deciduous broad-leaved trees which shed their leaves in winter, and the latter to coniferous trees which have needle-pointed leaves. The terms are purely of convenience and frequently bear little reference to actual hardness. The hardest of the softwoods are heavier and harder than the lightest of the hardwoods.

Hardwoods—For general cabinet-making oak is one of the most popular woods. English oak when suitable boards are available has a fine figure, but frequently it is unreliable owing to bad seasoning and is liable to shakes and warping. An excellent alternative is Japanese oak, which, properly seasoned, is sound, well-figured, works well, and is available in good sizeable boards. Slavonic oak also is frequently available in sound boards, and is a fine timber. American oak is not often seen nowadays, presumably owing to exchange difficulties, but when it is found is in fine standard boards. There are two kinds; red and white, the latter being invariably of better quality.

Much of the attractiveness of oak is due to the figure derived from the medullary rays which radiate from the heart. A board cut parallel with these exhibits the largest figure and makes the most reliable wood. The more the board departs from the parallel the smaller the figure until the rays pass through it at right angles and appear only as minute specks on the surface.

Silky oak which perives from Australia is not a true oak at all, but gets its name from the pronounced figure it has. It works well and is quite suitable for cabinet making as it is capable of a good finish and polishes well.

As a substitute for oak, chestnut is frequently used. It has no figure derived from the medullary rays, but resembles plain oak closely in both grain and colour. Beech is often available in squares and is thus suitable for turned legs, etc. It has a good figure, though smaller than oak. Owing to the shortage of walnut it is often used for turned parts, the rest of the job being walnut veneered.

Mahogany is an excellent cabinet wood, though the finer wide boards are becoming difficult to obtain. Practically the only true American mahogany available is the Honduras kind; Cuban is almost unobtainable. African mahogany is frequently used, and, although it has not the same fine figure, is considerably cheaper.

Sapele is sometimes referred to as a mahogany, and has something of the colour and marking of true mahogany. Its chief characteristic is the stripy roe figuring consisting of narrow stripes of light and dark wood. Both rauli and niangon have something of the general appearance of mahogany, but boards vary enormously. Some are entirely plain, whilst others have a most attractive figure. There are many substitutes for mahogany, of which gaboon is quite common. It is not a true mahogany, but is a useful secondary hardwood for drawer sides, cabinet backs, etc. It is often used in the manufacture of multi-ply.

Walnut is a fine cabinet wood, but is generally difficult to obtain. Both English and French walnut are occasionally seen but stocks of the plainer American or black walnut are seldom available. Australian walnut makes a good cabinet wood, manv of the boards being finely figured.

There are also many other imported hardwoods, supplies of which fluctuate. They vary considerably in quality and the best plan is to consult a text book for their characteristics, or to see whether the timber merchant has any information to offer.

Softwoods—Of the softwoods the chief timber for carpentry is red Baltic pine. Quality varies widely, the chief drawback of the poorer grades being the presence of knots, but better boards can be reasonably free from larger knots. It is used widely for structural timber—roofs, flooring, doors, etc., but needs care in selection when used for joists, rafters, and similar purposes, as knots in bad positions can reduce the strength enormously. For back frames, concealed rails, etc., it is frequently used in furniture making, though the poorer grades should be avoided.

Yellow or white pine from North America is a delightful wood, but is most difficult to obtain, but when once-used timber is available it is excellent for veneer grounds, etc. Parana pine (South America) is in good supply and is a first-rate timber, often entirely free from knots, and is reliable once properly seasoned.

When Western red cedar can be obtained it makes an excellent joinery timber, wide, long boards free from knots being available. It is suitable for both indoor and outdoor use. For the latter no

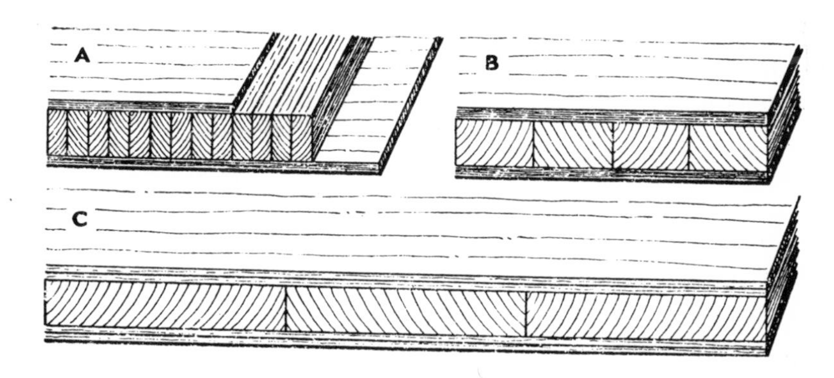

FIG. 1. EXAMPLES OF LAMIN BOARD, BLOCK BOARD AND BATTEN BOARD

preservative is needed, and is often used for roofing for this reason.

Plywood—Qualities vary enormously. The cheap tea chest is useless for work of any reasonable quality; the layers have probably not been properly dried out, the gluing may be faulty, and there are most likely blemishes, such as gaps in the middle layer, or even overlaps. A properly made ply by a reliable manufacturer, however, is quite sound and can be used for the carcase of a veneered job. Fuller information on this appears in the chapter on veneering. Thinner plies have three layers, the centre one often being thicker than the others and known as stout heart. When more than three layers are used it is termed multi-ply. Various woods are used in the manufacture—birch, alder, ash, pine, and gaboon. The latter when made up as multi-ply makes a good ground for veneered flush doors.

[*This chapter is concluded on page* 159.

CHAPTER XIV

WOOD FINISHING

THE following are the chief finishes for wood, choice depending upon the position in which the item is to be used, the wear it will have, the kind of wood, and personal preference.

Paint Used for most outdoor items, kitchen furniture, and some general furniture. It seals the grain effectively, keeping out damp, and enables mixed woods to be used.

Varnish Used mostly over paint in furniture, but is sometimes used over bare wood in joinery.

French Polish Probably the most popular finish for furniture made in hardwood. The wood can be stained first or left in natural colour. It seals the grain well but is liable to heat marks. A table top polish is available.

Polyurethane lacquer Tough heat-resistant polish suitable for table tops. Some are ready for use straightaway, others require addition of a catalyst.

Wax Polish Gives an eggshell gloss and is easy to apply. Can be used on almost all woods, though its most usual application is oak.

PAINT

To give best results at least three coats should be applied; priming, undercoat, and finishing coat. It is advisable to obtain all three from the same manufacturer, as this ensures that they are safe to use together.

Priming—Having cleaned up the wood go over any knots with painter's knotting. Leave for half an hour and give a second application. Really bad knots should be cut out and plugged. Any nails should be punched in. Rub smooth with glasspaper, and give the coat of priming. This is usually of a grey or pink colour, though for white or cream paint it is frequently white. It should be comparatively thin, and should be applied evenly, and brushed well into the wood. Work in the direction of the grain to finish off. Brush the paint into cracks, etc.

Leave for 12–24 hours to harden.

Undercoating—All nail holes, cracks, etc., should be filled with putty, the latter pressed well in and the surface made smooth by drawing the flat of the knife across it. Incidentally, in the case of glazed windows, etc., the rebates should have a coat of priming before the putty is used. Otherwise it will fail to adhere properly.

Rub down any roughness or unevenness with wet-dry glass-paper used over a cork rubber, damping the surface beforehand so that all dust is kept down. Any nibs or runs that may have formed should be smoothed, though they should be avoided altogether as far as possible.

The undercoating invariably approximates in colour to the finishing coat, though there is usually a slight difference so that it is easy to see whether every part has been covered. The application is similar to that of the priming coat. Work well into awkward places first, avoiding the filling in of detail, and laying-off with long, even strokes in the direction of the grain. Again leave for 24 hours to harden.

Finishing Coat—Once again rub down with glasspaper as before, and brush away any dust. As gloss paints have the property of flowing out and eliminating brush marks no more re-crossing is necessary than that needed to give an even coat—in fact prolonged working is inadvisable because an initial set takes place early. Work towards edges as far as possible so that fat edges and runs are avoided. If there are any runs at adjoining edges work them out straightway.

All paint should be well stirred before use, and if a skin has formed on the surface cut it round with a knife and remove it. Old paint which has stood for some time should be strained through old silk before use. Brushes which are to stand overnight for use next day can be placed in a jar of water. When finished with altogether they should be cleaned with turps, and finally washed in warm soapy water.

VARNISH

Apart from general decorations, varnish is used chiefly for special jobs in woodwork. For instance oil varnish is often valuable for finishing toys which have been painted with either oil or water poster colours. A special heat-resistant variety is also handy for items which may be subjected to heat.

On small items oil varnish can generally be applied directly over the painted or bare wood, though two or more coats are then essential. Sinking is inevitable, especially on end grain. On large surfaces it is advisable to give a coat of glue size over the bare wood. This saves a great deal of sinking. On wood which has been oil painted the varnish can be used directly without size, though the last coat of paint should be flat, not glossy.

Spirit varnishes, which include the various french polishes, are not so durable for outside work, and are more generally used for finishing indoor items, either by themselves, or in combination with french polishing.

FRENCH POLISH

As this popular finish generally involves staining, we begin with this. You can either use proprietary stains, or you can make up your own. The choice depends to an extent upon the wood to be finished.

Staining—For oak the most useful basic stain is made from vandyke crystals dissolved in warm water, the quantity depending upon the depth of colour required. Stir thoroughly and strain through muslin. The usual plan is to make a concentrated solution and dilute as required. Immediately before use add a little ·880 ammonia as this helps drive it into the grain.

Mahogany crystals can also be obtained, these giving a much redder shade. The two can be mixed together (after making up separately) to obtain any special shade. Another material useful for warming up a stain is eosin powder which, dissolved in water, gives a bright red stain. It is seldom used as a stain by itself but is handy for adding to others. Be careful not to overdo its use.

To darken mahogany bichromate of potash is generally used. The crystals are steeped in water which becomes bright orange in colour. Its effect on the wood is chemical, however, and it turns the mahogany a brown shade, the depth depending on the strength. It is widely used in the reproduction trade. It can also be used on oak which it turns a slightly greenish brown. By adding it to vandyke crystals and ammonia a variety of shades can be obtained.

Sulphate of iron, or green copperas, dissolved in water will turn oak a bluish grey tone (avoid using it too strong or you may end with a bright Air Force blue colour). It is sometimes used to make mahogany match up to walnut. As its effect becomes noticeable chiefly when it dries out it should be used with care. It should be practically water-clear, and the effect should be tried on spare wood and allowed to dry out. Sycamore is often treated with it to turn it a grey colour.

Ammonia has a darkening effect on oak. In the best way the liquid is not applied to the wood, but the latter is exposed to its fumes. The whole is placed in an air-tight container, all glue and grease being removed from the surface, and all doors, drawers, etc., opened. The liquid is poured into a couple of saucers, and the container sealed. If an inspection glass is not practicable a hole should be bored and a piece of the same kind of oak inserted. The time taken may range for ten minutes to several hours in accordance with the depth of colour required, and the size of the container. As some varieties of oak are more readily affected than others, the same kind should be used in any one job.

Take care not to bend over the fumes as they are powerful, and may have unpleasant results. Do not directly handle ammonia as it can be painful to the fingers and may turn them yellow.

Oil Stains—These are usually bought ready made. They have the advantage of not raising the grain, but are not so transparent as water stains, and their effect is different in that they leave a dark deposit in the open grain. After drying they should be given two coats of french polish before any wax polish is applied, as otherwise the stain may be lifted unevenly in patches.

Spirit Stains—These again do not raise the grain, but, owing to the rapid evaporation, they require deft and confident handling. On large surfaces it is difficult to keep the edge alive. They are obtained ready made, or in powder form for mixing with spirit.

Aniline Dyes—Owing to the colours being bright and somewhat unorthodox from the woodwork angle, the anilines should be used with care. Frequently they are used to add to other stains for toning purposes. Generally the most useful are vandyke brown, a somewhat cold brown used chiefly for oak, black for ebonizing, and Bismarck brown, a powerful red used chiefly to tone brown stains. A wide range of colours is available, green, blue, yellow, etc., and they can often be used in finishing toys, etc.

Aniline dye is in powder form and can be obtained soluble in either water or oil. The former can be dissolved in either water or spirits, and if a binder is necessary add a little glue size to water, or white french polish to the spirits. This spirit-soluble type is often useful to add to french polish to make colour polish. Oil-soluble aniline is dissolved in turps substitute, and in the event of a binder being required a little gold size can be added.

Application of Stain—Either a brush or rag can be used. In all cases keep the edge alive to avoid unsightly joining marks, and finish off along the grain. Before water stain is used the surface of the wood should be damped with warm water, allowed to dry, and glasspapered flat. Then when stain is applied the grain will not rise unduly. As end grain soaks up the stain more readily and is inclined to turn darker in consequence, the stain should be diluted for these parts. To avoid dribbling at the ends work the brush towards the edges. When it has dried go over the surface twice with french polish. This serves to fix the stain.

Filler—Oak is usually polished just as it is, but hardwoods such as mahogany and walnut generally have the grain filled. Various fillers are available, but that most widely used in the trade is plaster of paris. Use *superfine* grade. For light woods it is used just as it is, but for medium or dark woods and when stain has been used it is desirable to tone it with powder colour, mixed with the plaster powder. Vandyke brown is suitable for walnut or stained oak, and rose pink for mahogany.

In the case of dark woods a good plan is to damp the rag with which the plaster is applied with water stain. On dark oak for example use stain made with vandyke crystals. This will remove any risk of the plaster showing up light in the grain.

Applying the Plaster—Shake the plaster into a saucer and mix with it the colouring powder. Choose a piece of loosely woven canvas, wet it with water (or water stain), and dip it into the plaster. Apply to the wood with a circular movement, using moderate pressure. Allow a few seconds for it to set and rub across the grain with a piece of clean canvas to remove the surplus. Remember that plaster sets rapidly. Clean out all corners, mouldings, etc., well and allow to dry out thoroughly.

The surface will have a light film all over it. Soak a piece of cotton wool in raw linseed oil, and go over whole surface, leaving a thin film of oil. This will kill the whiteness. Now rub down with glasspaper held in the fingers. This will cause the oil and surplus plaster to combine and form a thick paste which can be wiped away with a rag. Do this thoroughly and again set aside to allow the oil to dry out.

Paste Fillers—Most users of paste fillers buy a proprietary ready-made filler. It can be obtained natural (grey) or in various tones to suit the wood. In any case it can always be toned with an oil stain. If too thick, thin out with turpentine. Keep the lid well pressed down as the filler will otherwise harden.

Its application is similar to that of plaster, being applied with a circular movement, and rubbed off across the grain as soon as it goes dull. No oil is used. Finally as soon as it is clear of all surplus, the surface is rubbed vigorously with a piece of clean rag, and the whole set aside to harden for about twenty-four hours.

For softwoods the usual plan is to use glue size. This can be ordinary glue thinned down until it no longer feels tacky. Thick size remains on the surface, whilst a thin size soaks into the grain and seals the pores. When thoroughly dry it is glasspapered smooth, and the work is ready for polishing. Incidentally, size cannot be applied over work which has been oil stained. In this case the paste filler must be used.

Stages in French Polishing—The wood having been stained and the grain filled in, the polishing proper is begun. This has four main stages : fadding, colouring, bodying, finishing. Sometimes the colouring stage can be omitted altogether.

The polish used for general bodying up depends upon the job. The four chief polishes in order of their colour are : garnet, a dark and somewhat greenish brown ; button, a yellowish tone ; orange, golden yellow shade ; white, made with bleached shellac, a creamy colour. For dark work garnet is generally used as it

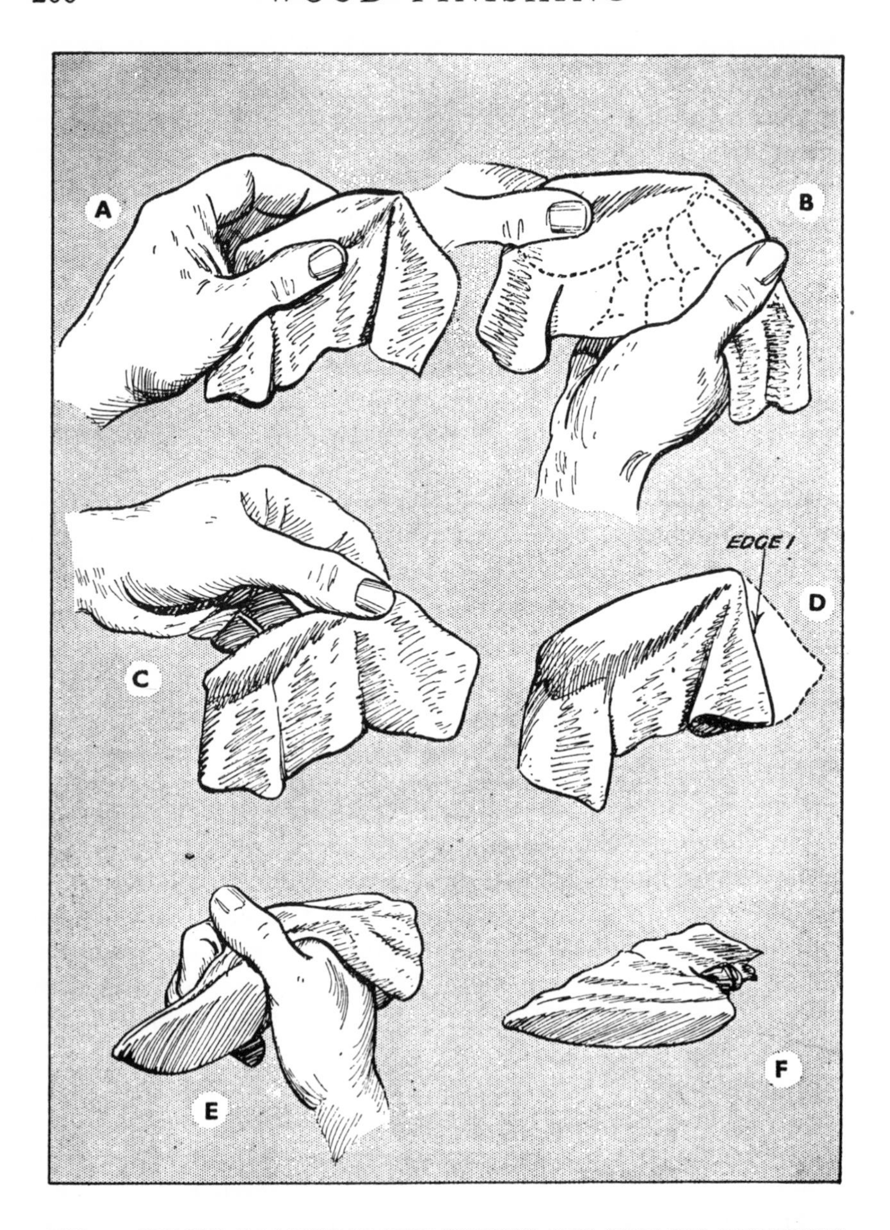

FIG. 1. STAGES IN MAKING THE RUBBER FOR FRENCH POLISHING

Unbleached cotton wool is used for the body of the rubber, this being moulded to a pear shape. After charging with polish this is wrapped in a piece of fine linen.

deepens the already dark wood. Light polishes (white, button, or orange) should not be used over a very dark wood, or one which has been stained dark, because it tends to give a cloudy appearance. Garnet polish is useful to deepen the tone of work which is not dark enough. Whenever the rubber is charged it should be placed over the mouth of the bottle and the latter inverted once or twice.

The Rubber—To make rubbers and fads use unbleached wadding. Medicated cotton-wool is useless. For the covering rag use a material free from fluff—fine linen is ideal. Cut a piece of wadding about 9 in. square, soak it in polish, and allow to dry out. It will then be hard and stiff. Soften with methylated spirit, squeeze out the surplus and mould to a pear shape. This is best done by following the stages in Fig. 1. Charge it with polish fairly freely and knock flat on the back of a piece of glasspaper laid on the bench. This distributes the polish evenly. The reason for dipping up the wadding and allowing it to dry out is that it prevents hairs from becoming detached and sticking to the work.

Fadding—Start at one edge and work straight along with the grain, gradually covering the entire surface once only as in Fig. 2. Allow a few minutes to dry out, and rub over the surface with a piece of fine glasspaper. This will expose any traces of filler on the surface, and these should be at once rubbed off.

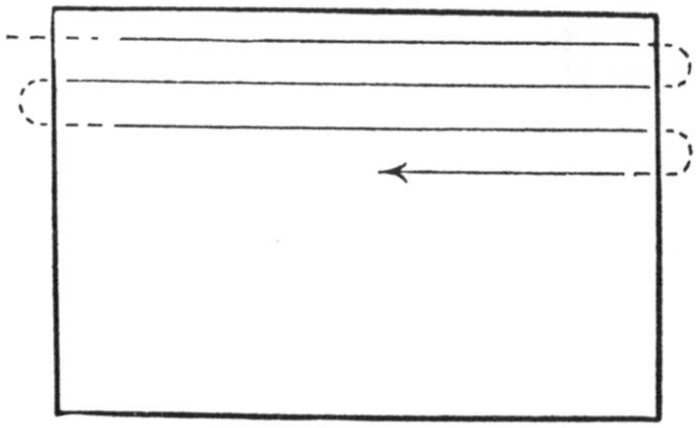

FIG. 2. HOW WOOD IS FADDED
This is the first stage of actual polishing.

Charge the fad once again and repeat the process twice more. If only a little polish is used the fad will not tend to stick, especially if a reasonable time is left between each application. No oil is used in this early stage, the purpose being to seal the wood. Otherwise oil may be trapped beneath the polish and cause sweating later on. After three or four fads of polish a dull shine will have been built up, and the next step is to convert this into a fair body. It is an early stage of bodying as much as a last stage of fadding.

Colouring—This is not always needed, but it sometimes happens that the work turns out to be of a different tone from that intended. For instance, bichromate of potash is an excellent stain for mahogany, but some consider it rather cold. The particular polish used affects the final result, but it is in the colouring process that any main correction is given.

Materials—A brush is needed for some colouring, and an artist's camel hair (No. 6 or 7) is excellent. Soak the new brush in polish for a couple of days, the hairs suspended in the polish. Squeeze out the polish between the fingers, bringing the hairs to a point, and allow to harden. This sets the hairs. When required for use soften the hairs in methylated spirits—except for the first week or so when polish should be used, this being less likely to soften the polish which has been worked into the roots.

Powder colours are chiefly used in colouring, and various colours are needed according to the job ; gas black, Bismarck brown, vandyke brown, brown umber, red ochre, yellow ochre, etc. Spirit dyes are also sometimes useful. These are mostly aniline—brown, scarlet, green, yellow, and so on. They should be used with great care as the colours are somewhat unorthodox so far as woodwork is concerned.

Stand before the work, note the light places, and go over them with the fad, following the grain where possible, and avoiding touching places which are already on colour. Some places will be too small for the fad, and for these the brush is needed.

General Correction—Having brought the whole to a generally even tone you can consider how far the work may need a general correction. It may want darkening or warming, and if so you can go over the whole with the colour fad, using either black or red in the polish, or a combination of both. When colouring has been completed go over the surface with a rubber of clear polish applied quickly and lightly. This will fix the colouring.

Bodying—This consists of building up the film of shellac to an appreciable thickness, evenly and clearly. Rub two pieces of *flour* grade glasspaper together to take off the extreme cut, and go over the whole surface to remove any roughness. Make up the rubber as in Fig. 1 and charge it so that it is fairly wet. The polish should exude when the sole is pressed with the finger, but it must not be anything approaching dripping wet. As it is used it should leave its path of polish without clearly defined, built-up edges. The latter always occur with an overcharged rubber.

A certain amount of oil is necessary during bodying to act as a lubricant as otherwise the pull of the rubber would be too great. Use raw linseed oil. Put a spot on the sole of the rubber. Avoid too much oil because in any case it has all to be got rid of later on, and excessive oil may result in the polish remaining soft. Work at first with a circular movement as at (A), Fig. 3, covering every part of the surface, and paying special attention to the corners and edges. Work over the whole surface, then back again until the rubber works out almost dry. When the rubber is re-charged the pressure is fairly light, but this is increased as it gradually dries out.

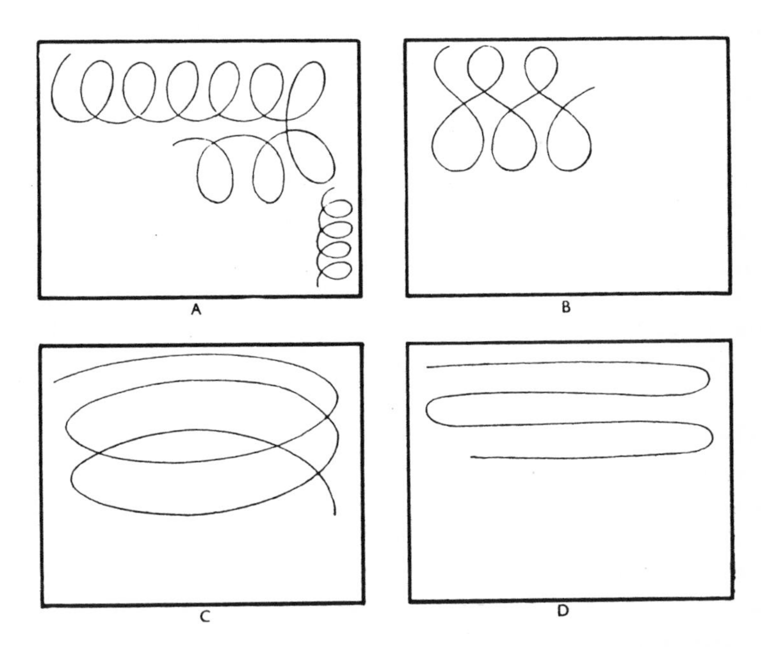

FIG. 3. MOVEMENT OF RUBBER WHEN FRENCH POLISHING

The oil will show itself as a well defined smear, and the presence of this is essential. To see it properly keep the head well down and look towards the light.

Having given three or four rubbers with the circular movement, a fair thickness of polish should have been built up, and this should now be improved with another rubber. In order to level the work more, however, the movement should be changed for large figures of eight as at (B), Fig. 3. This again should be changed for the long ovals at (C), and finally this should merge into the straight strokes at (D). If there is a tendency for the ends to be starved, the rubber can be taken straight across once or twice from front to back, but do not overdo it as the path may show up.

There are three main ways of finishing off a polished surface ; stiffing, spiriting off, and the acid finish.

Stiffing—Dip the rubber half strength and flatten out the face by dabbing on to the back of a piece of old glasspaper. There should be enough polish to exude when pressed with the finger, but not enough to run.

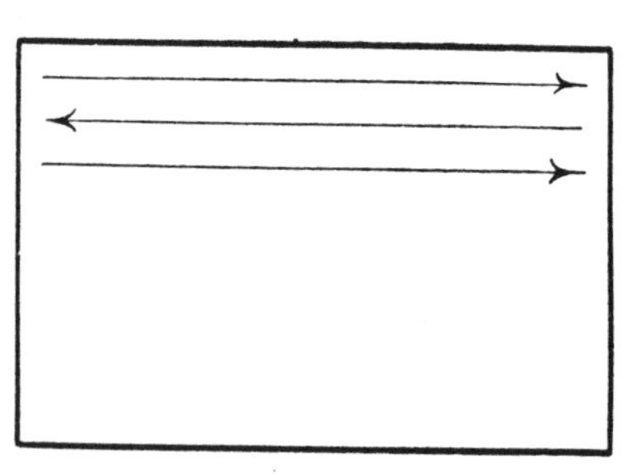

FIG. 4. MOVEMENT OF RUBBER WHEN STIFFING

Glide on the rubber at the top at one end and pass straight to the other corner in a straight stroke and glide off. Start just below with the rubber overlapping about half an inch, and take straight back, as in Fig. 4. Go over the whole surface in this way once, and then start at the top again, repeating the process. About three rubbers will have reduced the oil smear to practically nothing. There may be a few stress marks caused by the path of the rubber, but these will soon disappear. As the oil is gradually taken off you will find that the pull on the rubber becomes stronger until finally there is a definite stiffness.

Spiriting Off—The bodying stage having been completed the work will appear with a good depth of polish but with a distinct oil smear running from end to end in straight strokes. Make a fresh rubber. Cover with the rag and test by touching the lips. There should be no suggestion of any liquid, but just a distinct coolness, the result of evaporation. It is most important that only the driest of rubbers should be used.

Apply to the surface in large circles or figures of eight, changing gradually to straight strokes. As the rubber dries completely out the pressure can be increased until it acts as a burnisher as well as a means of lifting the oil. You will find that the face of the cloth will become greasy with the oil as it is removed, and you can change to a clean part. Eventually all oil smear should be gone.

Acid Finish—Body the work as before and allow to harden. Prepare the acid by adding one part sulphuric acid to seven of cold water. Shake thoroughly and spread it over the work with a piece of muslin. Fill a pounce bag with Vienna chalk and dab over the moist surface. If you cannot get Vienna chalk use precipitated chalk. Now burnish the work with the palm of the hand, or a piece of chamois leather, working *with* the grain. As it dries dust off the chalk, so leaving a bright, clear surface.

POLYURETHANE LACQUER

Use a paste filler, and when dry apply lacquer with the brush. Two–three coats are needed with drying intervals. When hard after 2–3 days give matt finish by use of fine steel wool and wax polish, or finish by burnishing with any fine powder abrasive such as whiting and wax.

WAX POLISH

This is simple to use, and can be renewed at any time. If an oil stain has previously been used it is essential that it is first fixed with at least two coats of french polish. Otherwise it may be lifted unevenly in patches. In any case it is a good plan to body up the wood, using white french polish for a job to be in natural colour. It not only helps to keep out dirt, but it builds up a preliminary shine.

You can use any good proprietary wax polish, or you can make your own from beeswax shredded into turps. Best American turps is the most satisfactory, but a good grade substitute (white spirit) is cheaper and may have to be used. The absorbing process is quickened by heating the mixture in a can of hot water (do not use a naked flame). To harden the polish add a small proportion of rosin whilst molten and stir in well. When cold the polish should be the consistency of butter in summer time.

Apply freely with a brush (boot brush type) and leave to harden for 12–24 hours. Polish with a similar brush and finish with a rubber. No shine can be built up until the turps has evaporated.

An invaluable handbook on the subject is *Staining and Polishing*, published by Evans Brothers Ltd.

SECTION II.

DESIGNS FOR SMALL THINGS

AFTERNOON TEA TRAYS

Details in all three trays are largely interchangeable.

Design (A)—The edging finishes 1 in. by $\frac{5}{8}$ in. and is either dovetailed or mitred at the corners. The inlay groove is worked with the scratch stock, and the joining positions of the boxwood and ebony lines squared across in pencil. Rub in the inlay with the cross-pene of the hammer after gluing. The base, $\frac{3}{8}$ in. thick, stands in $\frac{3}{16}$ in. all round and is screwed from beneath. To work the grooves for the inlay on the base use a narrow chisel or bradawl worked against a straight-edge cramped to the base. Alternatively a tenon or dovetail saw can be used against a straight-edge. Finish all grooves sloping in one direction and glue in the inlays. Scratch the remaining grooves right across the others after the glue has set. The shaped handle is held with screws driven into cups.

Design (B)—Here the base projects and is moulded. The edging also is moulded and is mitred at the corners. Handles are cut in and held with recessed screws.

Design (C)—This is similar to design (A) but with projecting base. The handles can be strengthened with small cross-pieces dovetailed into the edging as shown by the dotted lines.

Design (D)—Prepare the four edging pieces, and trim the ends of the long sides to about 30 deg. The end edgings must be wide enough to include the bottom slope and the handles. Glue to the outer side at the centre a thicknessing piece to enable the scrolled handle to be worked, and dovetail the corners. Cut the handles, leaving the ends proud so that the joint can be levelled after assembling. The slope of the bottom edges of the end edgings is best planed after gluing up.

The base stands in a trifle and is bevelled at the ends to agree with the slope of the edging. It is screwed on.

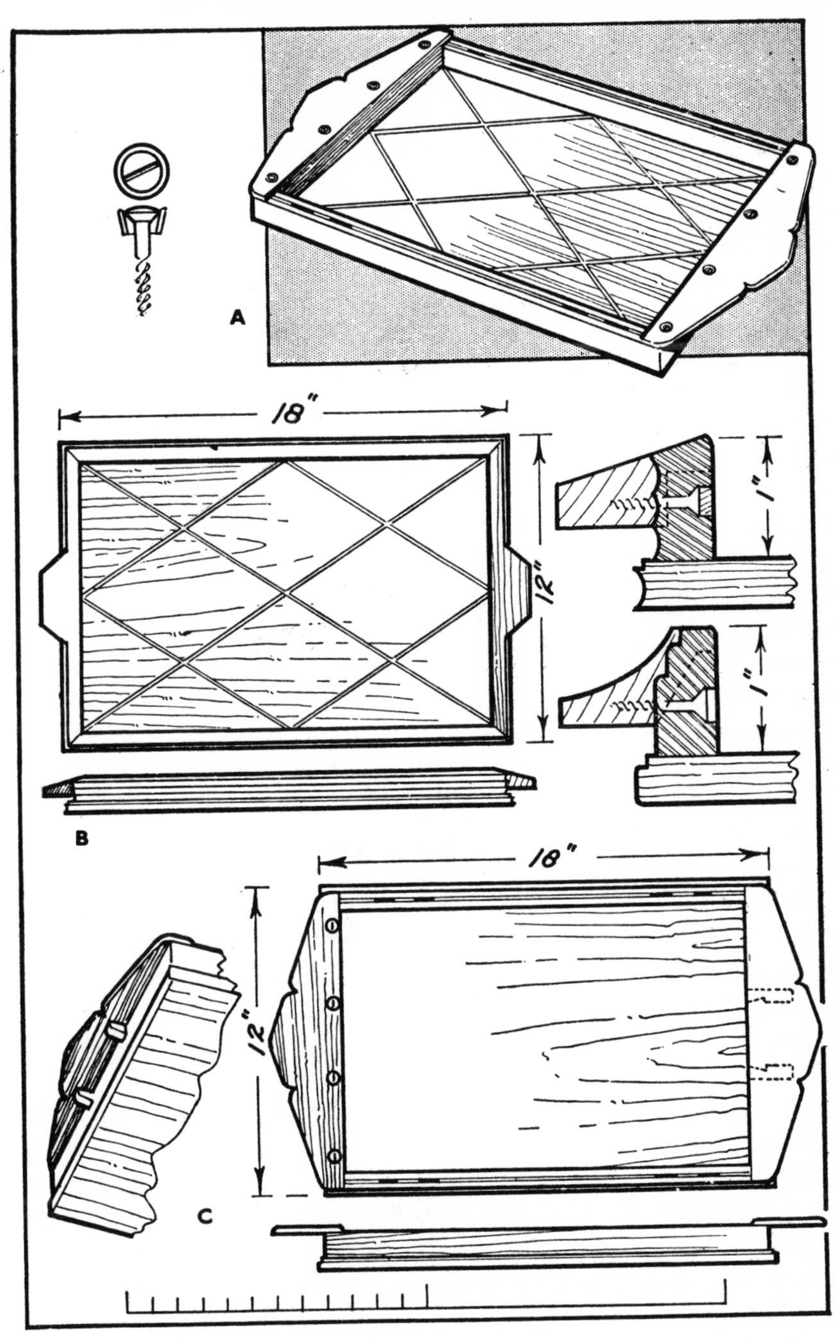

FIG. 1. DESIGNS FOR SIMPLE TEA TRAYS. DESIGNS A, B, C.

Design (E)—Prepare the base to the shape shown by the dotted lines to the left in Fig. 2. The edging is in six pieces mitred together in two sets of three, and screwed through the base. There is a gap between them opposite the handles. Note that the short end edgings are narrower than the long sides by the handle thickness; also that notches are cut at the ends of the long sides to receive the handles. Fret out the handles (in 4 mm. ply) and glue down. As the tray is to have a painted finish, one or two panel pins can be driven in and punched home.

CUTTING LISTS

Design (A)	Long	Wide	Thick
1 Base	1 ft. 6 in.	12 in.	3/8 in.
2 Edgings	1 ft. 7 in.	1 1/8 in.	5/8 in.
2 „	1 ft. 1 in.	1 1/8 in.	5/8 in.
2 Handles	1 ft. 1 in.	3 1/4 in.	3/8 in.
Design (B)			
1 Base	1 ft. 6 1/2 in.	12 1/4 in.	3/8 in.
2 Edgings	1 ft. 6 1/2 in.	1 1/8 in.	1/2 in.
2 „	1 ft. 0 1/2 in.	1 1/8 in.	1/2 in.
2 Handles	4 in.	1 3/8 in.	3/4 in.
Design (C)			
1 Base	1 ft. 6 1/2 in.	12 1/4 in.	3/8 in.
2 Edgings	1 ft. 6 1/2 in.	1 1/8 in.	5/8 in.
2 „	1 ft. 0 1/2 in.	1 1/8 in.	5/8 in.
2 Handles	1 ft. 0 1/2 in.	3 1/4 in.	3/8 in.

Design (D)	Long	Wide	Thick
1 Base	1 ft. 8 1/2 in.	13 1/4 in.	3/8 in.
2 Edgings	1 ft. 10 1/2 in.	1 1/2 in.	5/8 in.
2 „	1 ft. 1 1/2 in.	3 in.	5/8 in.
2 Handle pieces	6 1/2 in.	3/4 in.	5/8 in.
Design (E)			
1 Base	1 ft. 8 1/2 in.	12 1/4 in.	3/8 in.
2 Edgings	1 ft. 6 1/2 in.	1 1/4 in.	1/2 in.
4 „	4 1/2 in.	1 1/4 in.	1/2 in.
2 Handles	1 ft. 0 1/2 in.	4 1/2 in.	4 mm. ply

Working allowance has been made in lengths and widths. Thicknesses are net.

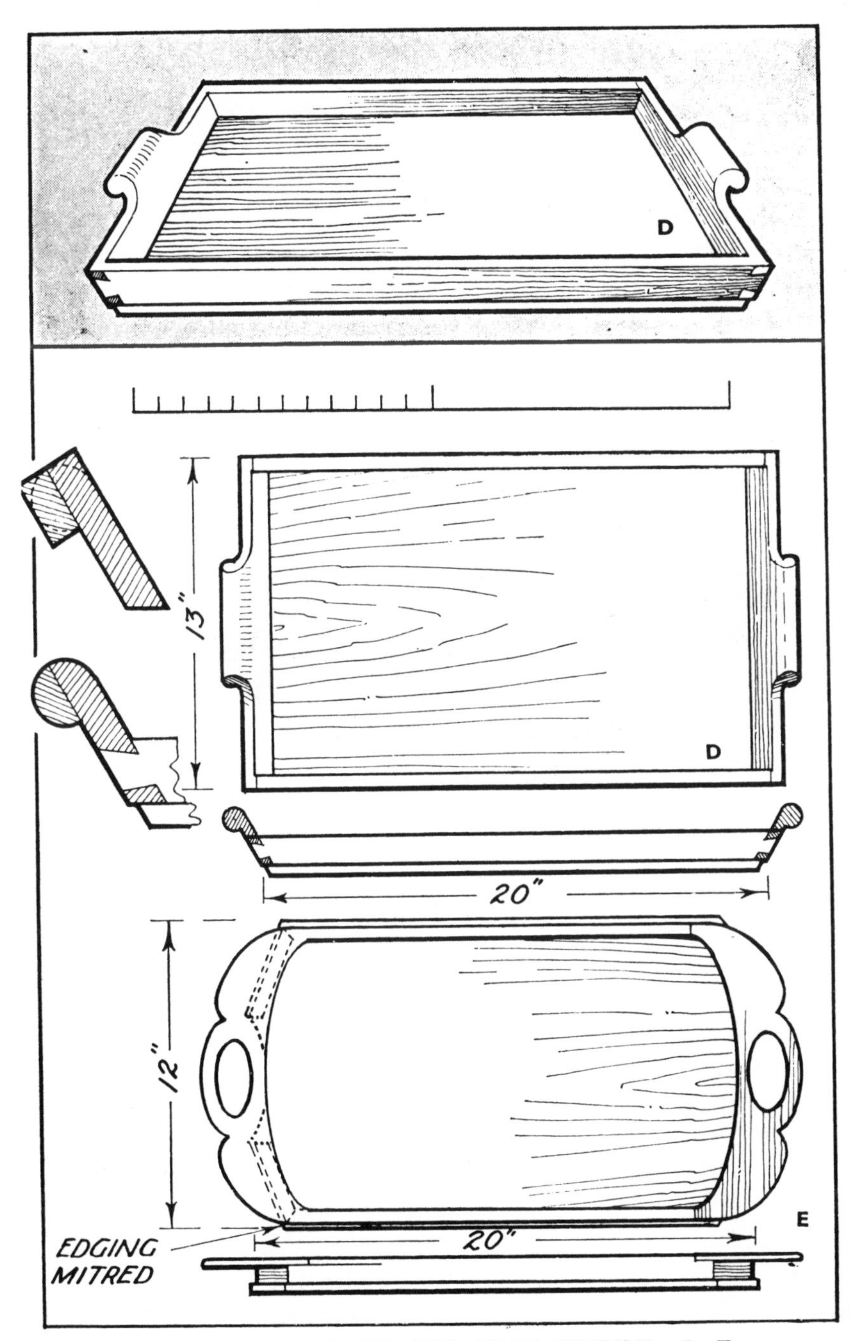

FIG. 2. ALTERNATIVE TEA TRAY DESIGNS. D, E

FOLDING STRIPWOOD ITEMS

These look extremely well if made in contrasting hardwoods. Failing this stains can be used for some of the members. The method of making the gifts is obvious from the illustrations. The strips are prepared to standard size and are bored at each end to take a wire. The strips are threaded on, and at the open ends little lengths of dowels, *Systoflex*, or other coloured wire covering are inserted to keep the strips the required distance apart.

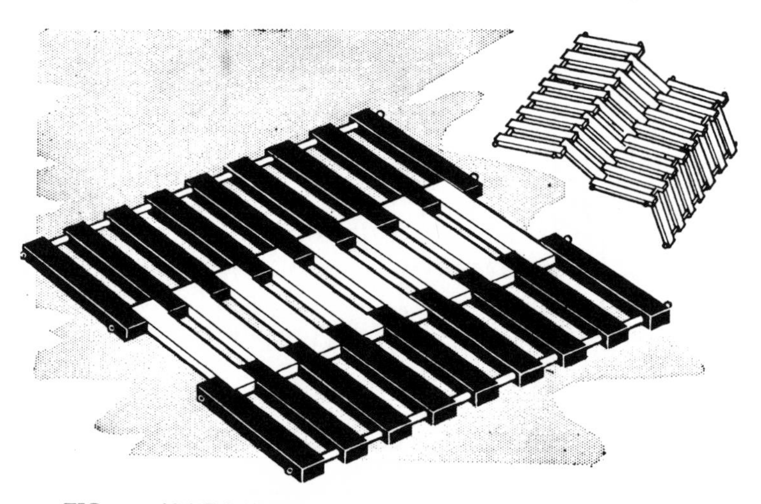

FIG. 1. ATTRACTIVE 3- AND 4-FOLD TABLE MATS
Natural woods of contrasting colours are best, but stained woods can be used.

Table Mats—Whatever object is made up the system is the same. Taking the 3-fold mat in Fig. 1, the strips are prepared in long lengths and are planed and glasspapered. It is advisable to take off the edges with glasspaper. A convenient size for the strips is 2¼ in. by ⅜ in. by a full ⅛ in., but this can be varied to suit the object being made or the material available. To cross-cut the strips to length the simple jig in Fig. 2 can be used. It is a block of wood nailed to the bench hook at the required distance from the saw kerf.

Having cut all the pieces the ends can be drilled. If an electric drill on a stand is available the drilling is simple. A jig is arranged so that the wood is in the right position for the hole. It is then merely a matter of putting each block in position in turn and lowering the drill. If this cannot be done the ordinary breast drill will have to be used, and the simple jig in Fig. 2 made up. The end of the wood is pushed into the notch and the drill inserted in the top hole. This not only gives the correct position, but it ensures the hole being upright. The only point to watch is that the notch does not fill up with dust and so give an inaccurate position. A $\frac{1}{16}$-in. drill is the right size, the wire being slightly smaller than this.

Now round over the end edges slightly with glasspaper, and if

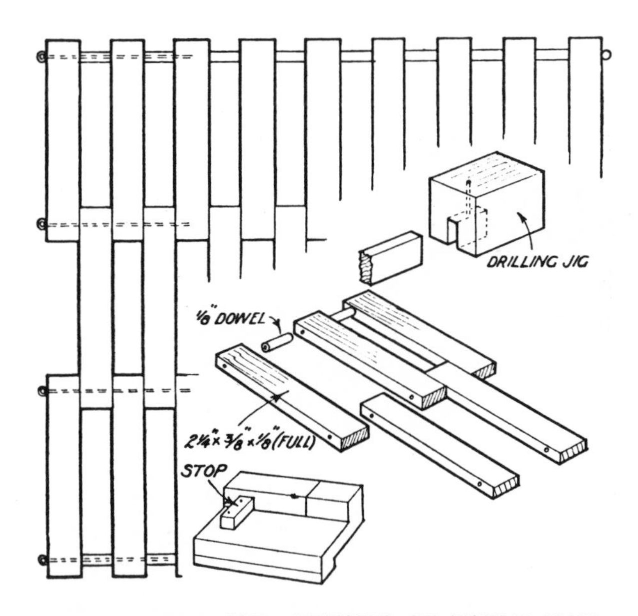

FIG. 2. SIZES AND DETAILS OF TABLE MAT

any staining is necessary do this. Any finish can also be given. For most purposes wax is suitable. Apply liberally and leave to set until the following day when it can be polished. Incidentally if an oil stain has been used it should be fixed with a coat of french polish before any wax polish is applied.

An alternative is clear cellulose lacquer to be brush applied. In this case the strips will have to be suspended by a wire passed through one of the holes to allow them to dry. Those who have the facilities could apply the lacquer by the dip method.

To thread the strips loop one end of the wire, see that it is reasonably straight, and cut it off to length. Thread through the strips and loop the other end. For the open ends the pieces of *Systoflex* can be cut off to standard size and threaded. This is required for open-ended objects only, such as the table mats.

Other Items—The method of making other items is the same, but it is necessary to make special parts such as the top of the lamp shade, and the bottoms of the wastepaper basket and flower pot cover.

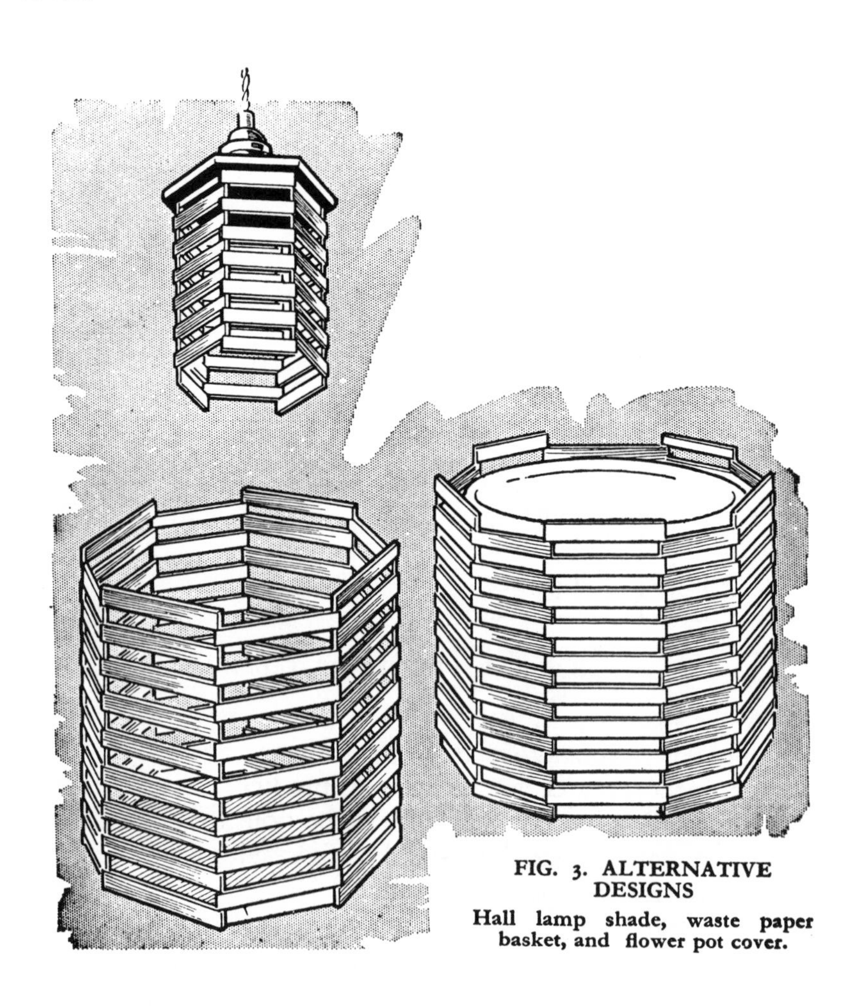

FIG. 3. ALTERNATIVE DESIGNS

Hall lamp shade, waste paper basket, and flower pot cover.

BELLOWS

Apart from its obvious usefulness, a pair of bellows is an attractive fireside feature. Those in Fig. 1 are of the long-handle type, the advantage of which is that it saves a great deal of stooping. Oak is the most suitable wood to use.

Back and Front—These are almost identical in outline, but the front is short at the end where the hinge occurs. The back has a hole cut in it to receive the valve. Use ½ in. stuff for both, and mark out the front, working from a centre line. Cut it out and mark the back from it. Except for the curve at the end of the handle the entire thing can be cut with the panel saw. Trim the edges using the block plane. If a bullnose plane is available this will be found handy to finish off near internal corners, though the chisel will have to be used at the extreme corner. A file is also handy in places. Finish with glasspaper held around a flat block of wood. The front can either be inlaid as Fig. 1 or carved, Fig. 2.

Valve—Fig. 2 shows the rectangular hole cut in the back for the valve. It is about 3 in. by 2½ in. Just above it nearer the handle is a square strip of ½ in. wood which prevents the bellows

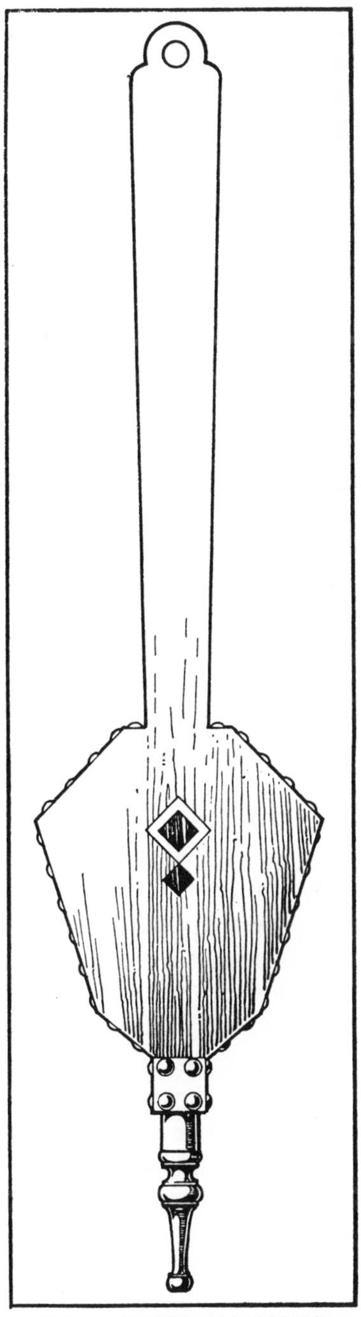

FIG. 1. LONG HANDLED BELLOWS

from over-closing, and provides a certain stiffening. It is screwed on.

Details of the valve itself are given in Fig. 2. The main plate (F) is some 4 in. by 3½ in. and is rebated to fit into the hole in the back. The rebate might be ⅜ in. deep, leaving a ⅛ in. lap through which screws can be driven into the back. A ¾ in. or ⅞ in. hole is bored right through the plate as shown by the dotted line in Fig. 2, and a piece of fairly stiff leather is cut to fix on the inside. A wood block (G) is glued to one side to form a stiffening, and the whole thing secured by the small strip (H) screwed to the plate. Small round-head brass screws are used to fix the plate to the back.

Nozzle—The example in Fig. 1 is in brass, and at one time was freely available. There has been a shortage, however, and it may be necessary to substitute a brass tube, or possibly sweat two tubes together one inside the other to give a stepped effect, a decorative pattern being turned afterwards. Another plan might be to turn the main portion in wood and fit a brass tube at the end only.

To provide a seating for it the arrangement in Fig. 2 is followed. Block (D) (½ in. thick) is glued above the square portion of the back, and above this another short piece (C) of ½ in. stuff is glued. This last named is later cut to receive the hinge. A ⅞ in. hole is bored about halfway in from the end, and the circular plug (E) glued into it. This plug (E) has a ¼ in. or $\frac{5}{16}$ in. hole right through it. It should preferably be turned, but can quite easily be shaped by hand, the centre hole being bored first. When the glue has set the hole is continued right through the block (D), so allowing the air to emerge. The nozzle is fixed with small round-head screws.

The front is pivoted by means of a stout brass back-flap hinge. It has the knuckle downwards, and this necessitates counter-sinking on the reverse side.

Leather Work—To prevent the bellows from opening too far a piece of cord is fixed to the inside. Either two round-head screws can be used for a fixing or a couple of screw eyes can be driven in. The cord will be just inside the bellows opposite the handles. Another piece of cord can be passed across the valve with a loose fit to prevent the valve itself from dropping in too

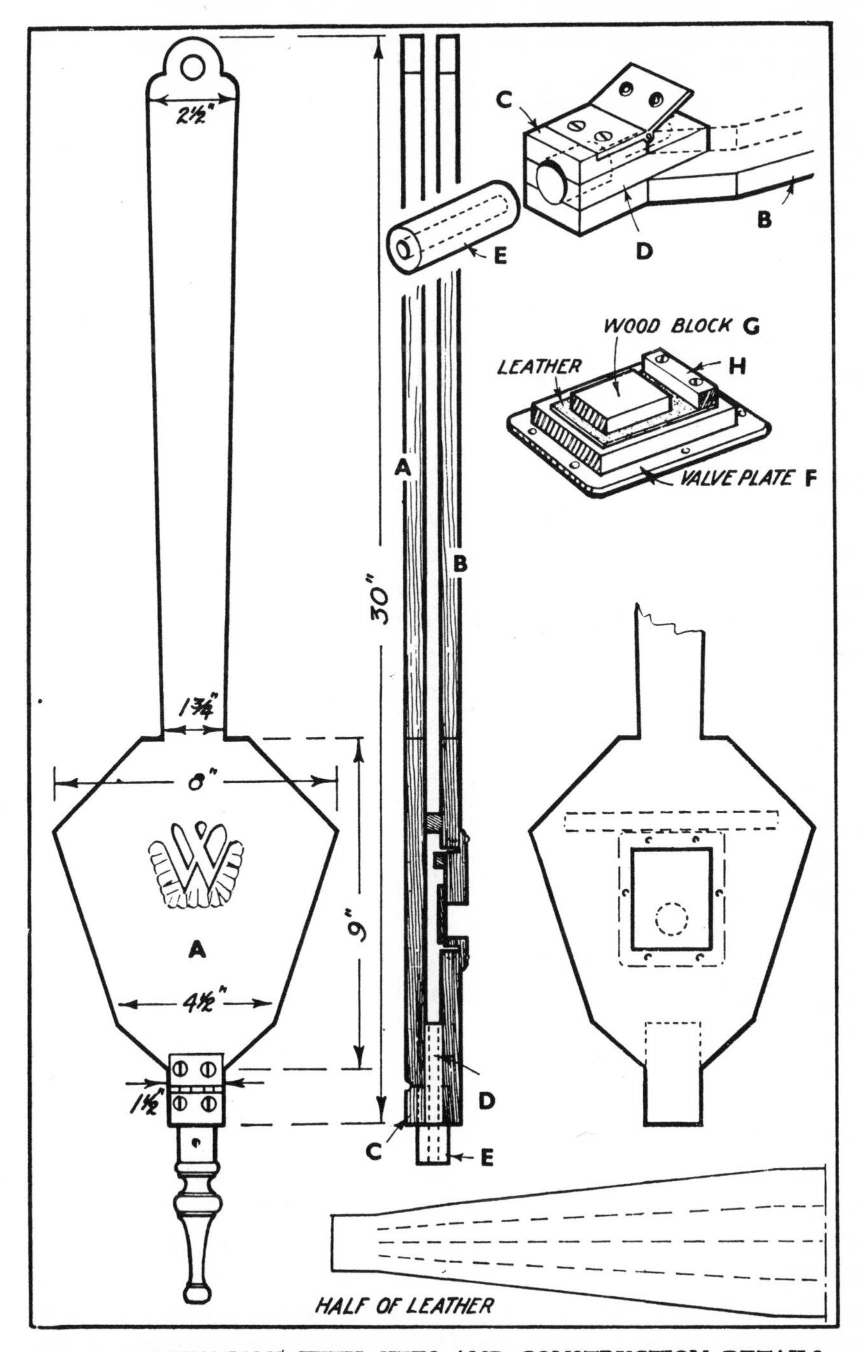

FIG. 2. ELEVATIONS WITH SIZES AND CONSTRUCTION DETAILS

far and failing to function in the event of the leather being too pliable.

It is essential to cut out a pattern in paper before cutting the actual leather. This can be fitted up to the bellows and definite marks made for folding. The pattern in Fig. 2 is approximately correct, but a little paring here and there may be needed. A single join is made at the handle end, but this is done after fitting both sides. Try the folds in the paper first and then do the leather. Damp the latter first, fold it exactly in two, and press it. Fold up the $\frac{3}{8}$ in. edging where it fits in the rebate of the front and back, and fold midway between this and the centre fold. Finally fold straight across at the two corner positions. By careful manipulation you can then find the diagonal folds, holding the leather in both hands.

When satisfactory, glue the two pieces together, having first marked the exact size, and glue and tack to the bellows. Begin at the handle, fixing to both front and back and work gradually to the nozzle end, paring and fitting as may be necessary. Remember to fix with the bellows in the open position. Follow with strips of gimp held with brass-head nails. Another piece of leather is bound right over the hinge.

CUTTING LIST

	Long	Wide	Thick
(A) 1 Front	2 ft. $5\frac{1}{2}$ in.	$8\frac{1}{4}$ in.	$\frac{1}{2}$ in.
(B) 1 Back	2 ft. $6\frac{1}{2}$ in.	$8\frac{1}{4}$ in.	$\frac{1}{2}$ in.
(C) 1 Block	$1\frac{1}{4}$ in.	$1\frac{3}{4}$ in.	$\frac{1}{2}$ in.
(D) 1 ,,	$3\frac{1}{4}$ in.	$1\frac{3}{4}$ in.	$\frac{1}{2}$ in.
(E) 1 Plug	$4\frac{3}{4}$ in.	$\frac{7}{8}$ in. diam. finished	
(F) 1 Valve Plate	$4\frac{1}{4}$ in.	$3\frac{3}{4}$ in.	$\frac{1}{2}$ in.
(G) 1 Block	$1\frac{1}{4}$ in.	$1\frac{1}{4}$ in.	$\frac{1}{4}$ in.
(H) 1 Strip	7 in.	$\frac{1}{2}$ in. square finished	

TRAY WITH EASY-DUST CORNERS

For the base of this a piece of solid $\frac{3}{8}$ in. stuff can be used providing it is flat and seasoned. Probably it will be necessary to joint two pieces together to make up the width. If plywood or one of the veneered boards is used it will be necessary to add a

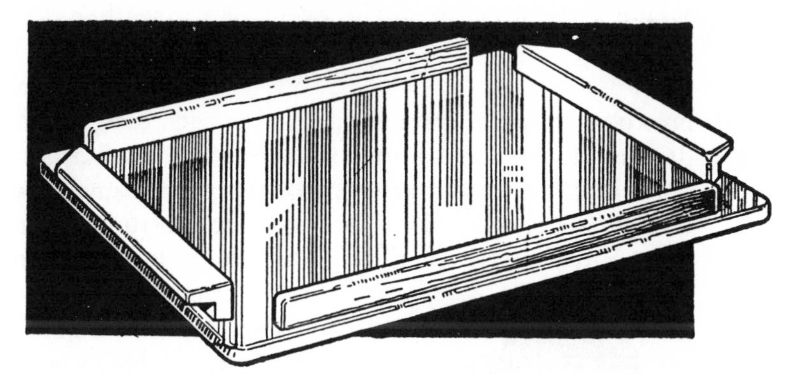

FIG. 1. TRAY THAT IS EASILY KEPT CLEAN
This would look well if the edgings were of a light coloured wood to show in contrast with the base.

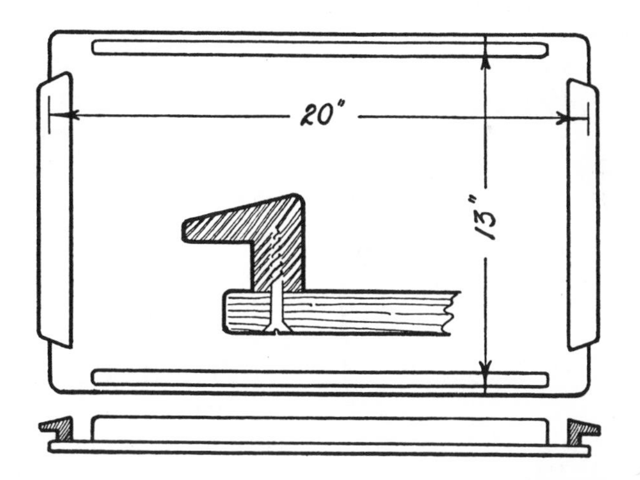

FIG. 2. PLAN, ELEVATION, AND HANDLE SECTION

lipping. The long edgings are rectangular in section except that the top corners are lightly rounded. Short edges are worked to the section shown to form handles. All are screwed in position.

CUTTING LIST

	Long	Wide	Thick
1 Base	1 ft. 8¼ in.	13¼ in.	⅜ in.
2 Edgings	1 ft. 5½ in.	1 in.	½ in.
2 "	10⅛ in.	1¼ in.	⅞ in.

MUSICAL CIGARETTE AND TRINKET BOXES, TOYS, ETC.

A simple clockwork movement is fitted in each case, this having a stop device which comes into operation when the lid is closed. A piece of wire is bent round the small lever, and a small rounded wood block is attached to the other end. It protrudes slightly at the top, and is depressed when the lid is closed, thus stopping the mechanism.

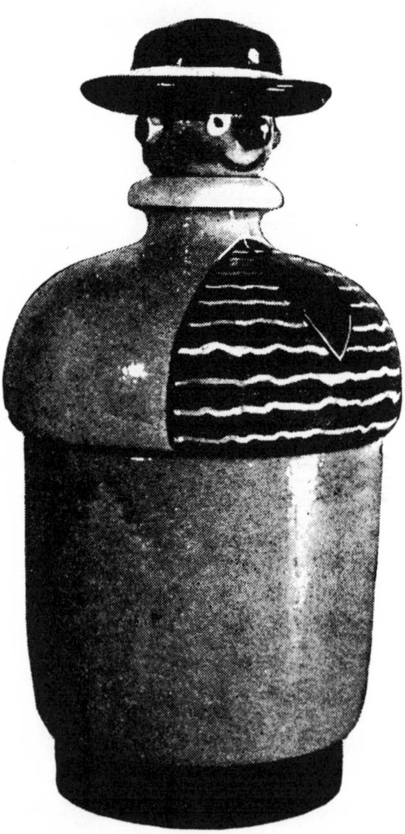

The musical-box movement should be mounted on a stout soundboard. This should be in a close-grained wood such as beech and at least ½ in. thick. Apart from this the box or container can be in practically any form. There is no need to follow the exact sizes providing that there is space for the movement. The latter is covered over inside. It has what amounts to a separate compartment.

FIG. 1. CHILD'S BOX IN THE FORM OF A TURNED FIGURE

The upper part lifts off as in Fig. 2, so releasing the mechanism. The box could be used for sweets, trinkets, marbles, etc.

Turned Doll Box — A photograph of this is given in Fig. 1, whilst Fig. 2 shows a sectional view drawn to scale. The whole thing is turned in two parts. Taking first the box, turn a cylinder to finish 3½ in. diameter and about 5 in. long. This is turned between centres, after which it is held in the three-jaw chuck as at (A), Fig. 3. Bore a hole about 4 in. deep, using the largest drill you have—say ½ in. It can be held

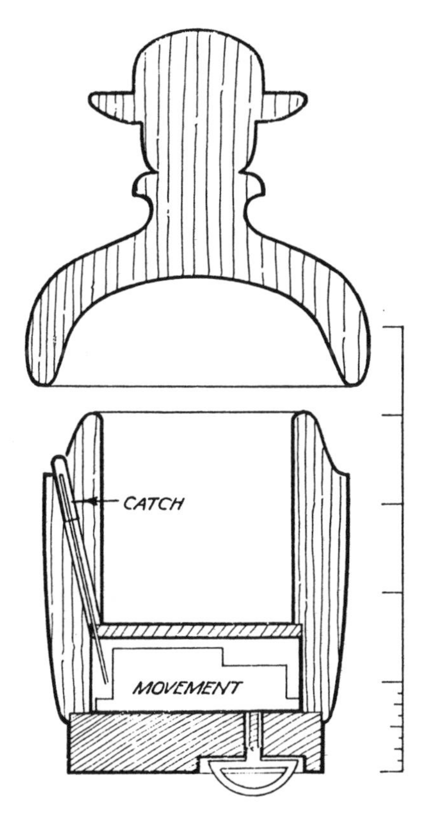

FIG. 2. SECTIONAL VIEW WITH SCALE

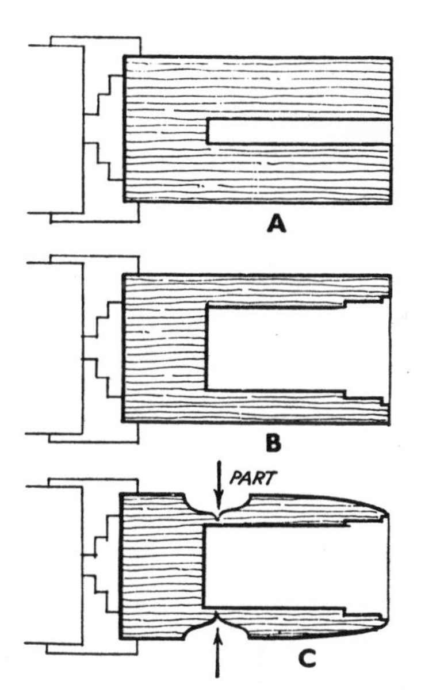

FIG. 3. STAGES IN TURNING BOX

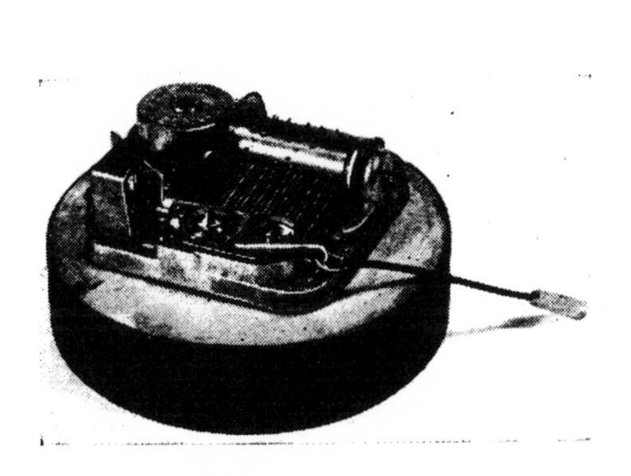

FIG. 5. VIEW OF THE MECHANISM

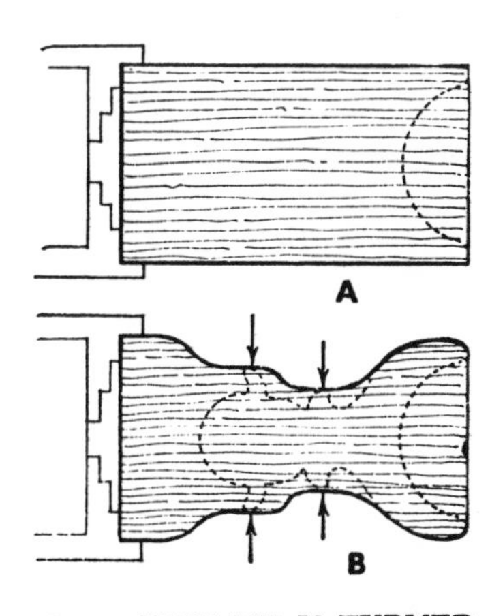

FIG. 4. HOW LID IS TURNED

with pliers or with a hand screw, and can be started centrally if an indentation is formed with the chisel held on the rest. If the back of the drill is held against the back centre, it will run in alignment. Enlarge this hole, using a flat tool worked with a scraping action. As the hole deepens the rest can be taken into it so that the tool has close support. Only light cuts should be taken. Two steps are needed, so that there are three internal diameters of $2\frac{7}{8}$ in., $2\frac{3}{8}$ in., and $2\frac{1}{8}$ in. as shown at (B), Fig. 3. Afterwards turn the outside shape. Finish to the shape given at (C), including the glasspapering, and then part off. If the work is reversed in the lathe and held lightly, the end just parted can be rounded over and cleaned.

Fig. 4 shows the stages in turning the lid. Hollow out the inside to make a fit over the box (A), and turn the outside, cutting down to the main over-all shape (B) and putting in the detail lastly.

A hole to receive the stop is drilled through the side as in Fig. 2. The drill is held in the chuck and the box pressed up to it. It is quite easy to find the correct direction by holding a short rod such as a pencil against the back centre and pointing centrally along the lathe. The box is held so that the desired hole is in alignment with the rod. The hole should emerge at the upper

FIG. 6. TRINKET OR CIGARETTE BOX AND OTHER ITEMS. THESE MAKE DELIGHTFUL GIFTS

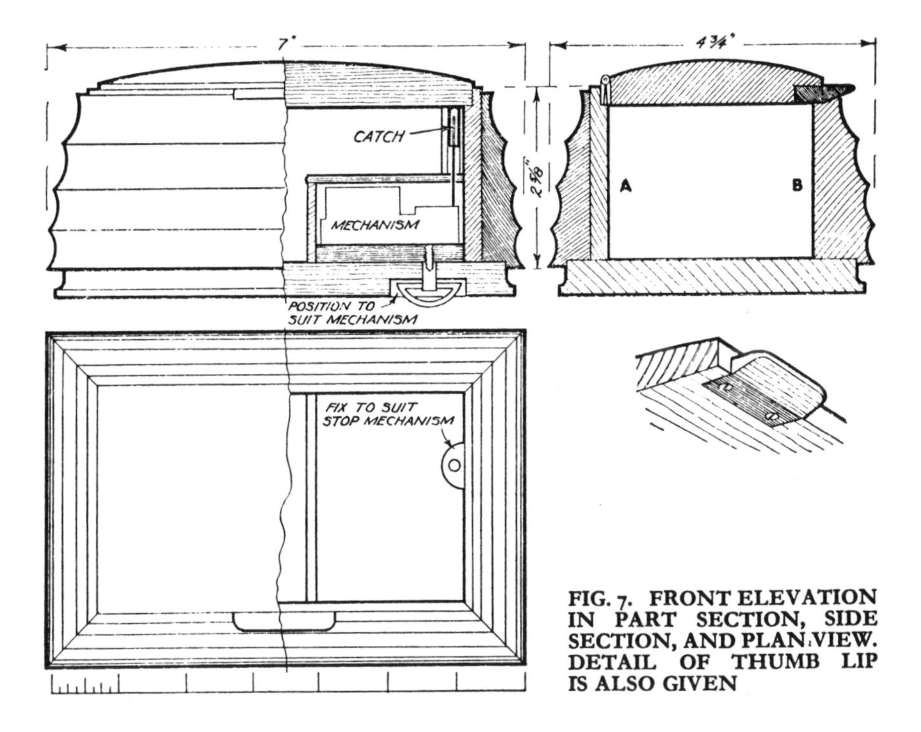

FIG. 7. FRONT ELEVATION IN PART SECTION, SIDE SECTION, AND PLAN VIEW. DETAIL OF THUMB LIP IS ALSO GIVEN

step as in Fig. 2. A ⅛ in. platform is glued at the upper step and held with a couple of pins. A notch cut in this will enable the catch to pass through. The base is turned to fit the bottom step, and a hole drilled in it to receive the winding-handle. At the lower side a large hole is bored so that the handle can be bent over and so be flush. The bottom is screwed on. The catch is a piece of wire bent to fit around the catch of the stop. At the top a little block of hardwood is fitted with a friction fit.

An excellent finish is poster water-colour followed by clear oil varnish, though if preferred oil colours can be used.

Cigarette or Trinket Box—This is shown in Figs. 6 and 7. The mechanism is fitted inside a small inner compartment, and the lid stops it by depressing the catch shown in the sectional view in Fig. 7. The main box itself is fluted, and it can be made by either of the methods at (A) and (B). In the simpler (B) the parts are just mitred at the corners and glued. The stronger way is to make a main box of ¼ in. stuff, through-dovetailed at the corners, and mitre and glue the fluted portion around this. When gluing, the best way is to assemble the whole thing dry with cramps. Then, removing one side at a time, glue and cramp up. In this way the already cramped pieces act as a guide in positioning the pieces being glued. Unless this is done the parts are liable to float out of position on the wet glue. Remember to work the rebates at both top and bottom edges before assembling.

The bottom fits in the rebate and has a hole and recess for the winding-handle. It is moulded before being fixed. Prepare the lid to equal thickness first and fit it. The opening edge will have to be at a slight angle so that it clears the rebate as it opens. The top side is rounded as shown. The simplest way is to work a broad equal chamfer all round, then gradually round it, using a spokeshave followed by a flat file and glasspaper.

A thumb lip is cut into the lid (Fig. 7), and the top edge of the box cut away to receive it. The use of contrasting woods would improve the appearance.

BLACKBOARD AND EASEL

If it can be obtained a sheet of $\frac{3}{8}$ in. or $\frac{1}{2}$ in. plywood or lamin board is ideal for the board. Failing this a board built up as shown here can be used. It consists of two sheets of fibre board glued to a series of battens. For a board of the size given there should be battens around the edges, and two intermediate ones, the whole butted together. No special joints are needed as the fibre boards bind the whole together. An alternative would be to use a piece of chip board.

Easel—This is a framework of 2 in. by $\frac{3}{4}$ in. strips put together with mortise-and-tenon or halved joints. As the legs splay outwards towards the base the shoulders will have to be cut at an angle. If a sliding bevel is available this should be used. Otherwise a piece of card can be marked to the required angle and this used. To obtain the angle it is necessary to set out the shape in full size. Note that both frames are identical except that, whereas the front uprights project at the top and are rounded over, the back ones finish flush with the top rail. All the uprights can be put together and the joint marks squared across them all. The positions for the peg holes can also be put in. When assembling test for truth by using a diagonal strip.

Having cleaned up the frames they are hinged together at the top. A length of chain serves to prevent their opening too far. A little box for chalk about 8 in. long is nailed together and is screwed to the bottom front rail. Pegs are preferably turned, but

FIG. 1. COMPLETED TOY AND CONSTRUCTION OF BOARD

dowel rods lightly tapered with the plane and finished with glass-paper can be used.

To finish the blackboard give a coat of ordinary paint priming. When dry apply a coat of the special blackboard composition made specially for the purpose.

As an alternative, though not so satisfactory as the above, give a coat of black priming. When dry, add about two tablespoonfuls of fine pumice powder to a pint of the same black priming and apply a coat.

Another method is to stain with black water or spirit stain. Allow to dry and give a second coat. Thin out some drop-black with turps so that it works freely without becoming too pale, and add to it two tablespoonfuls of finely ground carborundum powder or fine pumice powder, and a dessertspoonful of gold size. Stir well and give a coat, following with a second after it has dried out.

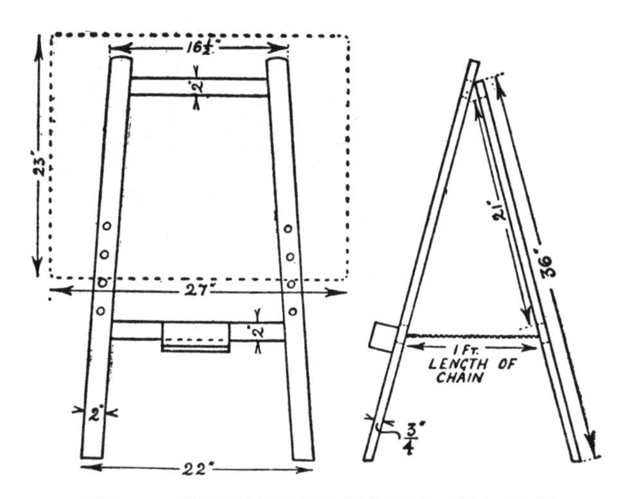

FIG. 2. ELEVATIONS WITH MAIN SIZES

CUTTING LIST

Board	Long	Wide	Thick
2 Panels	2 ft. 3½ in.	23¼ in.	$\frac{3}{16}$ or ¼ in fibre board
2 Battens	2 ft. 3½ in.	2¼ in.	⅜ in.
2 ,,	1 ft. 11½ in.	2¼ in.	⅜ in.
Easel			
2 Uprights	3 ft. 2½ in.	2¼ in.	¾ in.
2 ,,	3 ft. 0½ in.	2¼ in.	¾ in.
2 Rails	1 ft. 9½ in.	2¼ in.	¾ in.
2 ,,	1 ft. 4½ in.	2¼ in.	¾ in.

Trimming allowance has been made in lengths and widths. Thicknesses are net. Small parts extra.

ITEMS FROM LAMINATED WOOD

All these items are best made from bent and laminated wood. The latter can be between $\frac{1}{16}$ in. and $\frac{1}{8}$ in. thick, and will bend quite well without steaming or heating if beech, birch, or similar woods are used. Items liable to become damp should be put together with resin or casein glue. A former of the shape is needed so that the laminæ can be cramped to it whilst the glue sets. Solid

FIG. 1. USEFUL PLATE RACK OF ATTRACTIVE APPEARANCE
The hoops are made from three layers of wood glued together to make a thickness of $\frac{1}{4}$ in.

wood $\frac{1}{4}$ in. thick can be bent if steamed but results are not generally so satisfactory as the work is liable to bend unevenly in steps from the cramp positions unless supported by formers at both sides. Another point is that glue cannot be used on damp wood. Consequently the latter must dry out completely before any glue can be applied. A similar method of construction is used for all these items.

Plate Rack (Fig. 1)—A jig around which the laminæ can be assembled is required. Mark out a piece of $\frac{3}{4}$ in. wood to the shape in Fig. 4 and bore a series of holes right through to take the fixing cramps (see Fig. 6). The laminæ are prepared in strips about 18 in. long by full $\frac{3}{8}$ in. by full $\frac{1}{16}$ in. Both sides and edges should be planed.

There is no need to steam or damp the strips as they will bend easily around the curve, especially if in beech. Rub the edge of the jig with candlegrease to prevent glue from sticking—also grease a spare strip which will be fitted at the outside to prevent the cramps from marking the hoops. Scotch glue is unsuitable owing to the rack being liable to become damp. Resin glue is

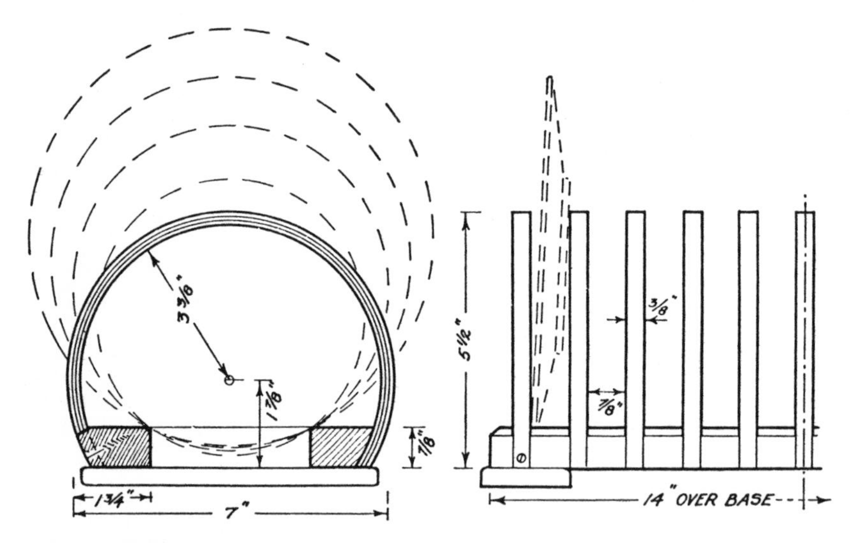

FIG. 2. SECTIONAL END VIEW FIG. 3. HALF SIDE ELEVATION

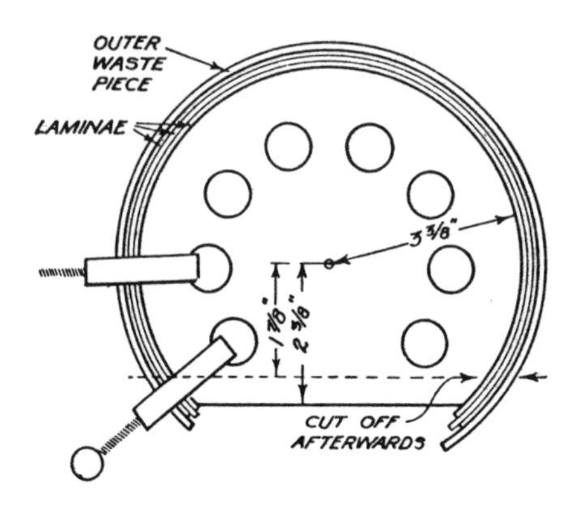

FIG. 4. JIG FOR LAMINÆ

FIG. 5. FIXING OF HOOPS

ideal, but failing this casein can be used. It is far more water-resistant than Scotch glue.

Put the three thicknesses level at one end, place the spare strip over them and tighten the end thumbscrew. Press the parts down and add the next thumbscrew, and so work right round. Take care to keep the parts level and parallel with the jig. The same jig can be used for all the hoops, but of course it means waiting a day for each to set before the cramps can be removed and the next hoop assembled. When all are finished clean up the edges with a smoothing plane and cut off the ends as in Fig. 4.

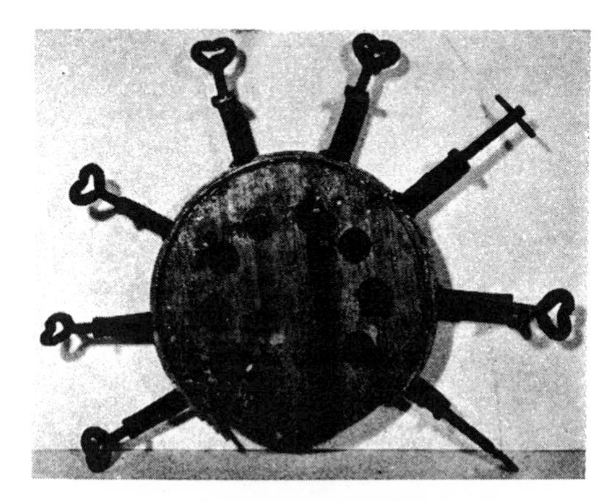

FIG. 6. HOW LAMINÆ ARE BENT TO SHAPE

The base portion consists of two long sides fixed together with cross-pieces. The sides of the former are bevelled and the top corners chamfered. A series of notches is cut in to take the hoops, and the last named fixed with raised-head brass or nickelled screws. It will be found an advantage to file little half-round nicks along the inner top edges (Fig. 1) as they help to prevent smaller plates from slipping. For the same reason the ends are filled in with cross-pieces (Fig. 1). The rack is best left as it is in the white.

CUTTING LIST

	Long	Wide	Thick
33 Strips	1 ft. 6 in.	½ in.	$\frac{1}{16}$ in. full
2 Base pieces	1 ft. 2½ in.	2 in.	⅞ in.
2 Cross pieces	7½ in.	1¾ in.	⅜ in.
2 " "	4 in.	1 in.	⅜ in.

Cut a few extra strips for the cramping pieces and to allow for failures.

Toast Rack—Only two thicknesses are required for these strips as the hoops can be quite thin. As before, cut them extra long to allow for trimming. A jig is required, and this will require holes bored through it to enable thumbscrews to be tightened. It might be an advantage to have one large hole in the centre large enough for all the cramps to go in rather than a number of small holes, one for each cramp. Proceed as in the case of the plate rack, greasing both the jig and the top cramping strip. Begin at one end and work gradually round, tightening the cramps as you go,

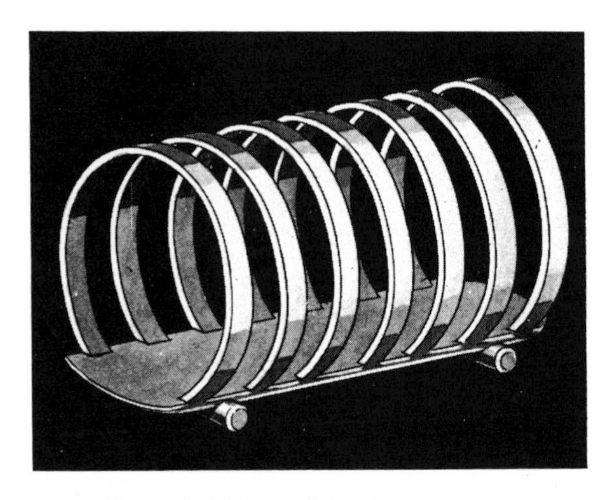

FIG. 7. EASILY MADE TOAST RACK
Items of this kind have a touch of novelty which breaks away from the ordinary run of things.

and being careful to keep the strips level. The glue having set, trim the edges and cut off to length.

The base is $\frac{3}{8}$ in. thick by $2\frac{3}{4}$ in. wide, and a wide chamfer is worked on the underside to align with the hoops. The top corner is rounded over. To give a neat finish the ends are slightly rounded as in Fig. 8. Notches cut along the sides hold the hoops which should be a firm fit. Brass raised-head screws make a strong fixing.

Dowel rods $\frac{1}{2}$ in. thick are used for the feet. The ends are rounded over or lightly chamfered, and a flat is cut along the top to enable the dowel to bed against the base. Countersunk screws are used for fixing. The handle screwed to the middle hoop is not essential but is quite useful. It is simply a piece of ¼ in. stuff shaped as shown and fixed with screws. Paint could be used to finish the rack, or it could be left in the white. Some may prefer to stain the dowels dark or use a dark wood for them.

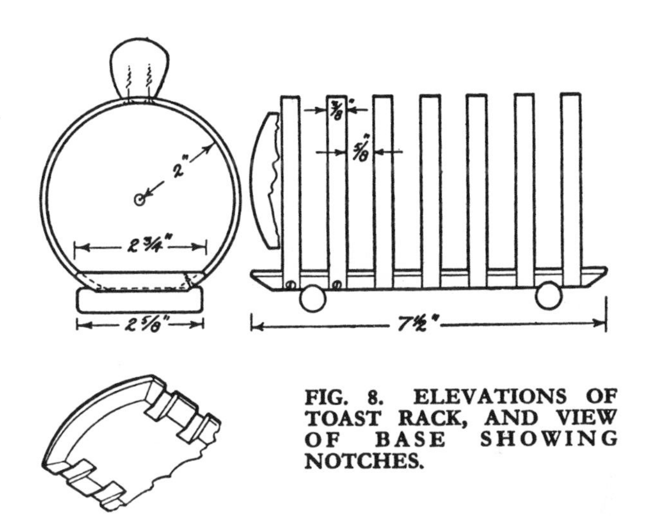

FIG. 8. ELEVATIONS OF TOAST RACK, AND VIEW OF BASE SHOWING NOTCHES.

CUTTING LIST

	Long	Wide	Thick
14 Hoop strips	1 ft. 1 in.	½ in.	1/16 in.
1 Base	8 in.	3 in.	3/8 in.
2 Dowels	3 in.	½ in. diam.	

Extra strips should be cut to allow for the cramping strips, and for possible breakage.

Book Trough—The bentwood strips are assembled in two sets, each to its own particular curve, and are then glued together at the lower part where the curves coincide. Two jigs are therefore required as shown in Fig. 11. The dotted lines at right angles show the extent of the curve required for the strips, and it will be seen that the wood is continued well beyond to allow for trimming.

Cramp the three layers to the jigs as in the previous examples, starting at one end and working round. When the glue has set, put the smaller shape back on its jig and glue the larger shape to it. Be sure not to put cramps beyond the point where the two shapes separate (Fig. 10). Trimming to length and cleaning up the edges follows when the glue has set.

The parts forming the trough are put together with a grooved joint and are glued and screwed (Figs. 10 and 11). Cut them to the shape shown and clean up the edges. Assemble them, and, laying the shaped ends in them, mark their positions. Notches are cut in as given in Fig. 10. Fix them with glue and screws. Practically any finish can be given—paint or polish. In the latter case it is advisable to polish the parts before they are assembled.

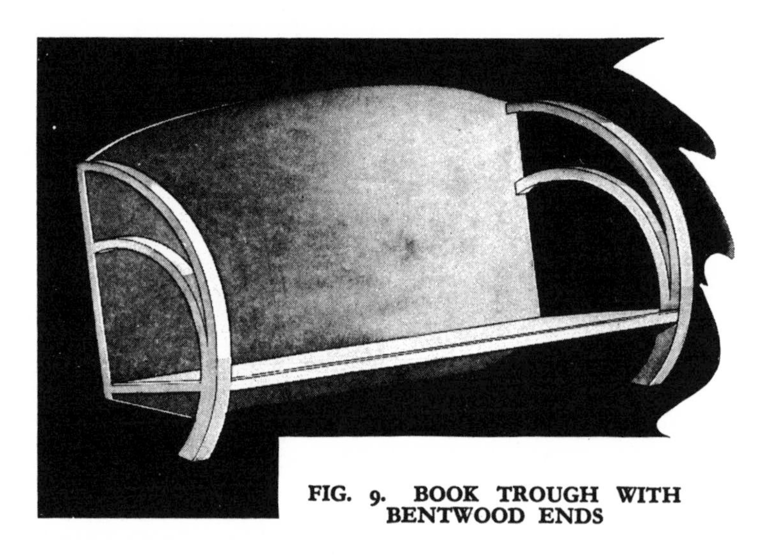

FIG. 9. BOOK TROUGH WITH BENTWOOD ENDS

CUTTING LIST

	Long	Wide	Thick
12 Strips	1 ft. 4 in.	5/8 in.	1/16 in. full
1 Back	1 ft. 1½ in.	8½ in.	3/8 in.
1 Base	1 ft. 1½ in.	5¼ in.	3/8 in.

Cut extra strips to allow for cramping strips and possible breakage.

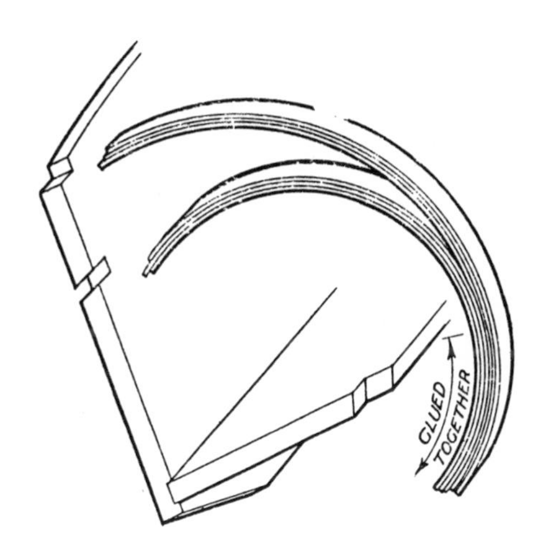

FIG. 10. FIXING OF BENTWOOD ENDS

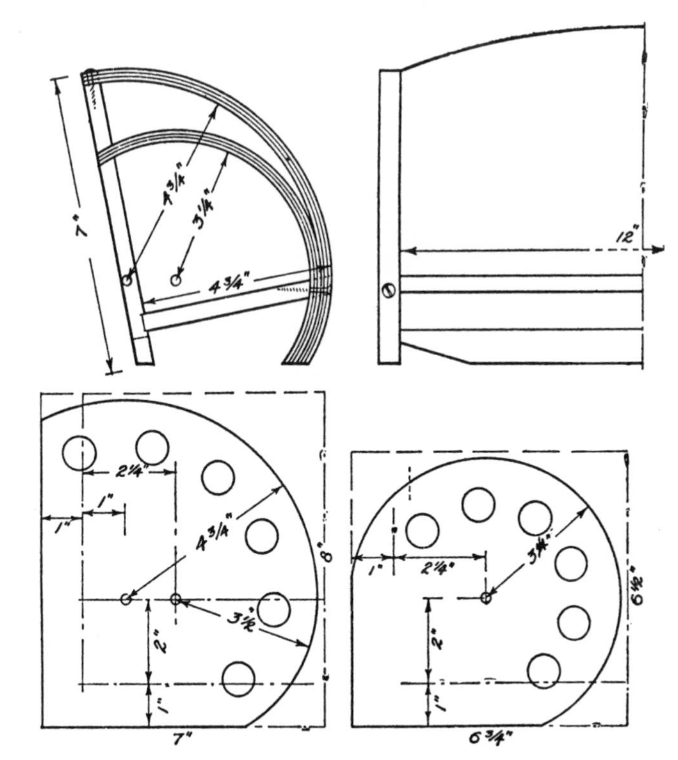

FIG. 11. ELEVATIONS AND JIG DETAILS

AMUSING DISC TOY

This gives children endless fun building up figures and shapes of all kinds with varying heads and hats. The simplest way of making the toy is to turn the main part in one, and separate the individual discs afterwards. Extra heads and hats can be turned separately ; also the stand. The drawing in Fig. 2 shows the thing as actually turned with $\frac{1}{8}$ in. gaps between the items, this being the width of the parting tool to be used.

FIG. 1. THIS WILL APPEAL TO THE MAN WITH A LATHE

All these discs are separate and fit over the peg of the stand. The discs are brightly coloured.

Main Figure—Prepare a block of wood about 10 in. long and of sufficient section to hold up to $3\frac{1}{8}$ in. diameter. Place in the lathe between centres and turn to a cylinder of $3\frac{1}{8}$ in. diameter. On this mark the positions of the main members whilst the work is revolving as shown at (A), Fig. 3. Cut into the depths of the hat, face, etc., as at (B). The main outline follows as at (C).

To separate the discs a $\frac{1}{8}$ in. parting tool is used. This will be found to give a cleaner finish if the cutting edge is sharpened slightly hollow so that the corners cut before the centre. For a start take the tool in to a depth of no more than $\frac{1}{4}$ in., and round over the sharp edges with the small chisel. Clean up with glass-paper, and take in the parting tool so that only about $\frac{1}{4}$ in. is left uncut in the middle. If this is done beforehand there will be too much whip when the corners are rounded.

Remove from the lathe and saw the parts to separate them. Each is then put individually in the self-centering chuck and the $\frac{1}{2}$ in. hole bored. To do this make a small hole first with the ordinary morse drill, and press a $\frac{1}{2}$ in. chisel into the work, holding the chisel on the rest. The holes pass right through all the pieces except the hats and these are stopped short. Whilst still in the lathe round over the edges, and finish all surfaces with glasspaper.

Spare hats and faces can either be held in the self-centering

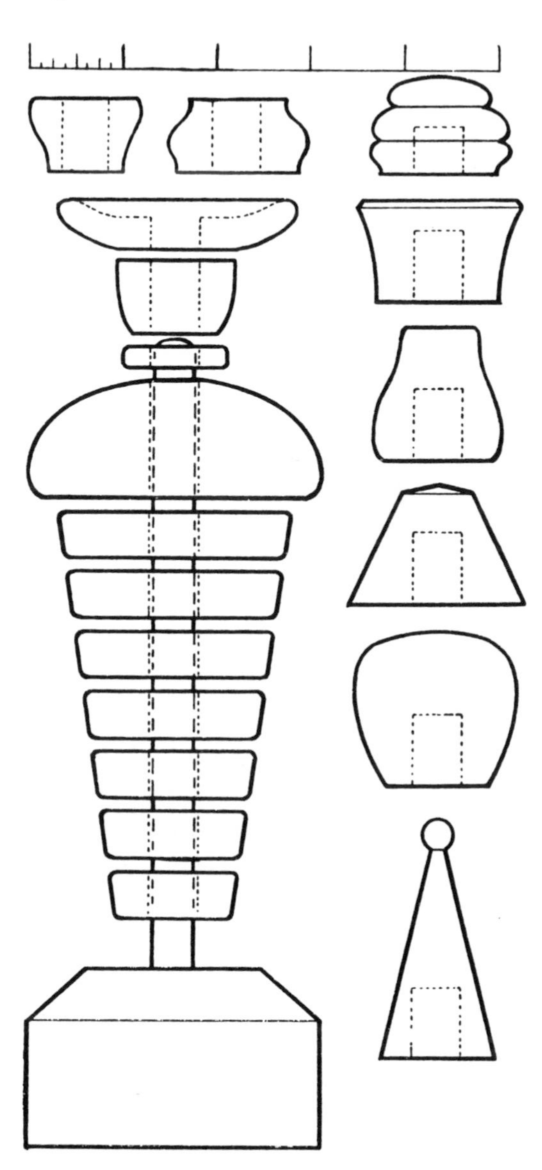

FIG. 2. ELEVATION WITH SCALE

chuck, or made a wedge fit in a chuck with tapered hole. If the wood tends to slip rub a piece of chalk over the surface first.

Stand—This can either be turned in a single piece, or a stout, heavy base can be turned and a hole bored in it to receive a $\frac{1}{2}$ in. dowel rod.

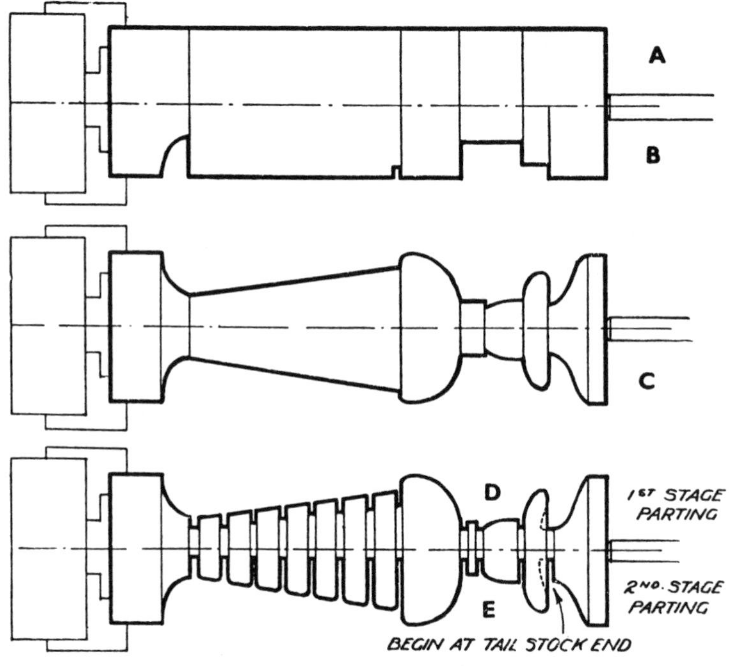

FIG. 3. STAGES IN TURNING DISCS OF THE MAIN FIGURE

Finish—An excellent finish is poster colour paint, decoration and face detail being added as required. When dry give a coat of copal varnish. Probably a second coat will be needed, especially on end grain.

CIGARETTE BOX

Box and lid are made in one, and sawn apart after assembling. The corners are put together with a simple lapped joint, glued and pinned. Lid has a rebated joint. After sawing apart the edges are trimmed, and corners rounded over. Bottom is screwed on, and is preferably in a dark contrasting wood. The same applies to the handles which fit and are screwed into notches cut in the underside. Lining pieces of thin wood mitred at the corners and projecting slightly at the top keep the lid in position.

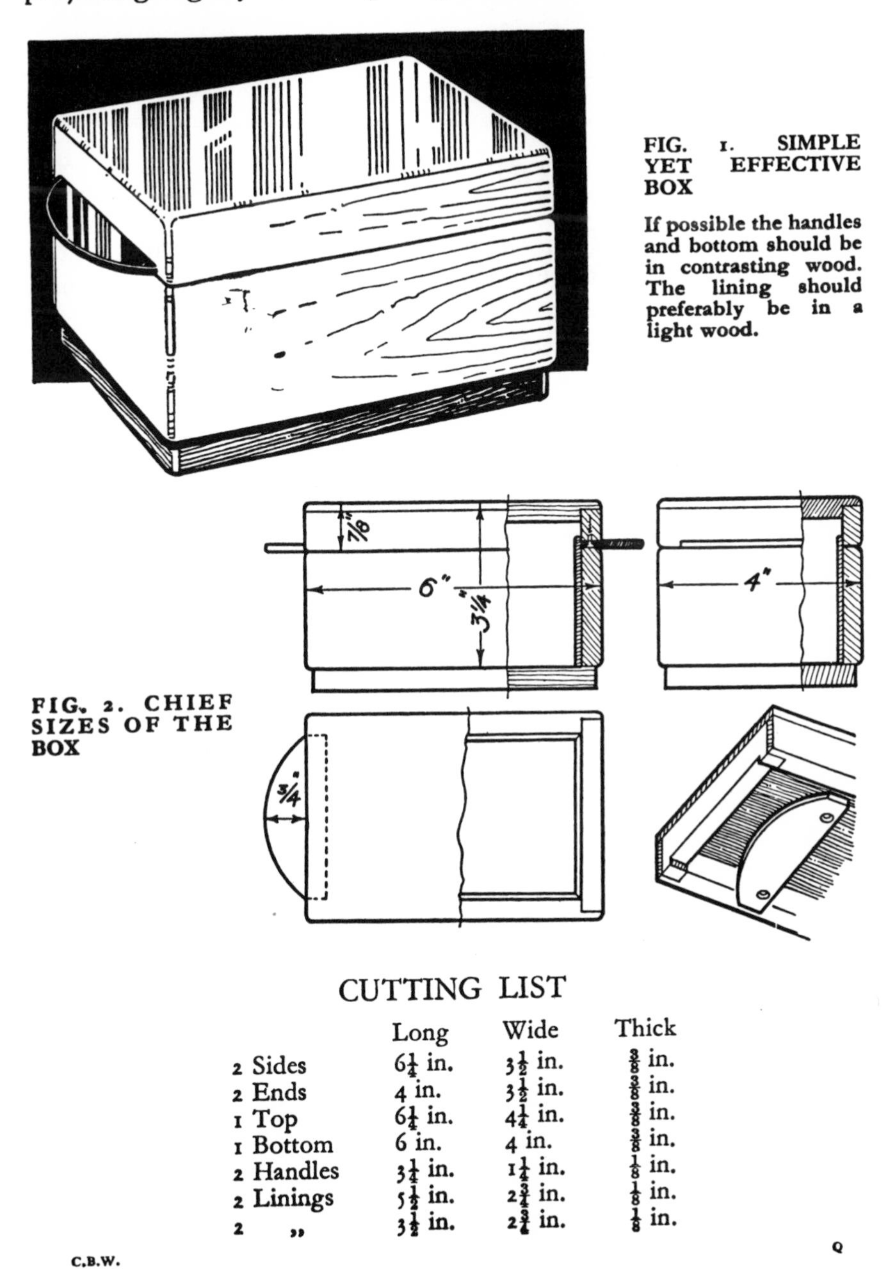

FIG. 1. SIMPLE YET EFFECTIVE BOX

If possible the handles and bottom should be in contrasting wood. The lining should preferably be in a light wood.

FIG. 2. CHIEF SIZES OF THE BOX

CUTTING LIST

	Long	Wide	Thick
2 Sides	6¼ in.	3½ in.	⅜ in.
2 Ends	4 in.	3½ in.	⅜ in.
1 Top	6¼ in.	4¼ in.	⅜ in.
1 Bottom	6 in.	4 in.	⅜ in.
2 Handles	3¼ in.	1¼ in.	⅛ in.
2 Linings	5½ in.	2¾ in.	⅛ in.
2 "	3½ in.	2⅜ in.	⅛ in.

SECTION III.

FURNITURE DESIGNS

COFFEE TABLE

This breaks away from the conventional form of construction. There is no under-framing of the kind usually used in tables. Instead the legs are through-tenoned to cross rails, these in turn being screwed beneath the top. Assuming that solid wood is

FIG. 1. ATTRACTIVE SMALL OCCASIONAL TABLE
The legs are tenoned into battens screwed beneath the top.

used for the latter it is necessary to use screw shrinkage plates for the rails, because the grain of the top runs crosswise, and, unless allowed to shrink freely, the top would be liable to split. These shrinkage plates are available in various forms, but fundamentally they are metal plates with slots in them, the slots allowing movement of the screw heads as the top shrinks or swells. Oak or any of the home-grown hardwoods would look very well for this table.

Top—It is necessary to joint two or more pieces together to get the required size. Use either $\frac{3}{4}$ in. or $\frac{7}{8}$ in. stuff, and having planed the joints put three $\frac{3}{8}$ in. dowels in each. When set level the joints and clean up. The shape is best set out by bending a lath of wood. The latter should be tapered towards its ends as otherwise there will be too much shape in the middle. Cut on the bandsaw or with the bow saw, and clean up with plane and spoke-shave. The chamfer on the underside is worked with the same

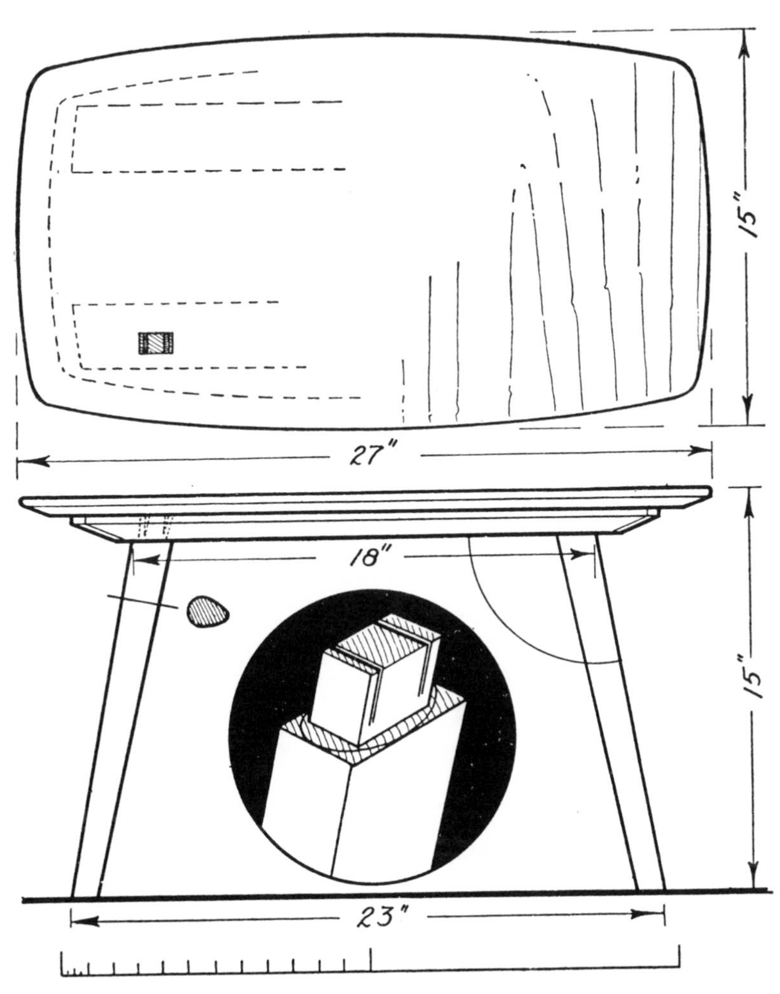

FIG. 2. PLAN OF THE TABLE TOP AND SIDE ELEVATION WITH SCALE

tools. Note how it gives an appearance of lightness.

Legs—At the top these are 1½ in. by 1¼ in. in section, and they taper to 1 in. by ¾ in. at the bottom. They can be sawn economically from a board by marking them out side by side, top to toe. Prepare them in square form to the required taper, and mark the top tenons, using a sliding bevel with the stock held against the inside of the legs so that all slope to the same extent. The angle is about 100 degrees. Saw the tenon joint, not forgetting the saw kerfs which are to receive the wedges. Lastly plane the section to the egg or stream-lined section shown in Fig. 2, and finish off with glasspaper wrapped round a specially shaped rubber.

Cut the rails to finish 23 in. by 2½ in. by ⅞ in. Mark out the mortise positions, using the sliding bevel at the same setting as for the shoulders of the legs to mark across the edges. The mortises should be ⅛ in. longer at each end at the top to allow for the wedges.

Bevel the rails and glue the legs in position. If possible use two cramps to each leg so that the end of the tenon is not covered. This enables the wedges to be knocked in, after which the cramps can be removed. Lastly screw the rails beneath the top using the shrinkage plates as already described.

A table of this kind is best finished with special table-top french polish which is both heat and water-resistant.

CUTTING LIST

	Long	Wide	Thick
1 Top	1 ft. 3½ in.	27½ in.	¾ or ⅞ in. (make up width to suit)
4 Legs	1 ft. 3 in.	1¾ in.	1¼ in.
2 Rails	2 ft. 0 in.	2¾ in.	⅞ in.

If preferred the grain of the top could run along the length. In this case cross-pieces should be halved to the rails. Alternatively veneered blockboard or multi-ply could be used.

OCTAGONAL COFFEE TABLE

This makes an attractive yet simple table for the fireside. It consists of an octagonal top supported by two simple frames halved together. The legs can be either reeded as at (V), Fig. 2, or they can have the stream-lined shape at (W). In the latter case the rounded section is started below the rails. Almost any hardwood could be used.

Top—Use either lamin board or multi-ply for the top. Veneer it both sides, the grain of the veneer at right angles with that of the outer layer of the groundwork. An edging is added all round, the corners being mitred. Any of the sections (X, Y, Z), Fig. 2, can be used. Of these (Z) is the simplest, being merely glued and pinned on. For (X) a groove is needed in the plywood, but the edging

FIG. 1. LOW COFFEE TABLE WITH OCTAGONAL TOP
If preferred the top could be left loose so that it could be used as a tray.

itself is rather awkward to work with hand tools. On this score (Y) is rather simpler. The addition of the edging after veneering serves to protect the edges of the veneer. Hand grips can be cut in opposite sides if desired, but they are not essential. If they are cut the simplest plan is to bore 1 in. holes at each end and saw away the wood between them.

Stand—The legs could be cut out economically by marking them out toe to head. Prepare them to rectangular section and mark out the joints. Note that the mortises have to be cut at a

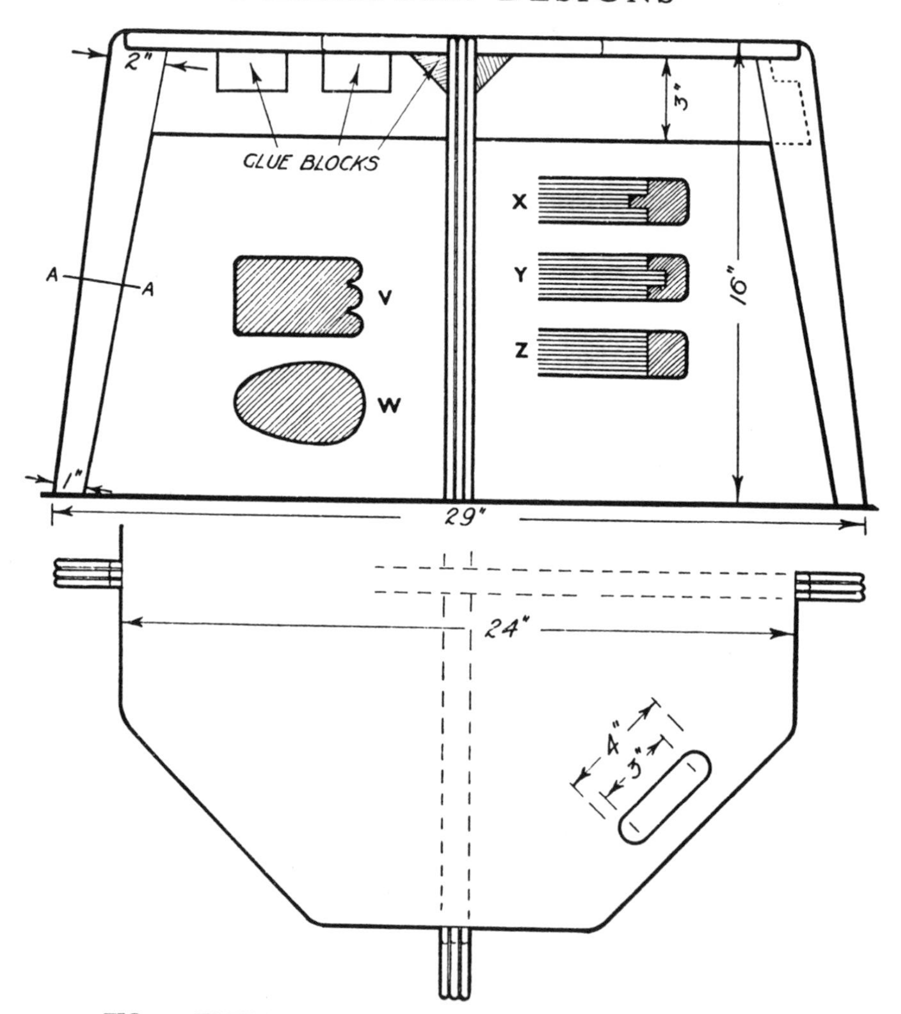

FIG. 2. ELEVATIONS AND HALF PLAN WITH MAIN SIZES

slight angle, and it is a guide if the sliding bevel as used for the shoulders of the rail is used, a pencil line being drawn across the side. When satisfactory work either the reeds or the ovoid section.

Set the bevel to about 100 degrees when marking the shoulders of the rails. At the centre the rails are halved. After assembling rub a stout glue block into each of the four corners of the halving joint. These are a great help in preventing whip in the stand. The top itself is pocket-screwed and glued blocks are rubbed all round as in Fig. 2. If preferred the top could be left loose so that it is free to be lifted off as a tray. In this case extra wide glue blocks should be rubbed in the corners of the halving joint, and they can be strengthened by screwing through into the rails as well.

CUTTING LIST

	Long	Wide	Thick
1 Top	2 ft. 0¼ in.	24¼ in.	½ in. (lamin board or multi-ply)
4 Legs	1 ft. 5½ in.	2¼ in.	⅞ in.
2 Rails	2 ft. 1 in.	3¼ in.	⅞ in.

CHAIR-SIDE COFFEE TABLE

This type of table has become popular in recent years owing to the way in which it fits close to the fireside chair. The sizes given are a good average, but they could be adapted within a little if necessary. Construction is of the simplest kind, the legs being through-tenoned to discs, and these in turn screwed beneath the ply or lamin board top. As the latter is chamfered at the underside and shows only a thin edge, there is no need to use any lipping.

Top—Cut the top to the shape in Fig. 2. If a bandsaw is available it gives the best means of cutting ; otherwise use a fine-toothed bow saw or coping saw to avoid any tendency for the under layer to split out. Clean up with spokeshave, and mark the extent of the chamfer by running a pencil round, using the finger and rule as a gauge. The plane can be used for chamfering if set fairly fine and with the back iron advanced to minimize all tendency for the grain to tear out (it is complicated by the varying direction of the grain in the layers). At the square notch it is necessary to use the spokeshave and file at the extreme corner.

Legs—Fig. 2 shows how the legs are tenoned into the discs. Note that the wedges are entered at right angles with the grain. If a lathe is available they can be turned ; otherwise they are sawn and spokeshaved. Tenons are marked out and cut before the ovoid section is worked. Assemble each individually, using two cramps if possible so that the end of the tenon is left clear for the wedges to be knocked in. They can be taken off immediately afterwards. It is a good plan to complete the polishing of all parts before assembling as it enables the rubber to be used freely.

FIG. 1. TABLE WHICH FITS UP CLOSE TO AN EASY CHAIR
The legs are tenoned to round blocks which are secured beneath the table top.

Table top polish is the most suitable as it is not liable to mark if wet glasses or hot cups are placed upon it. When completed screw the discs beneath the top, taking care that the legs slope outwards radially in every case as in Fig. 2.

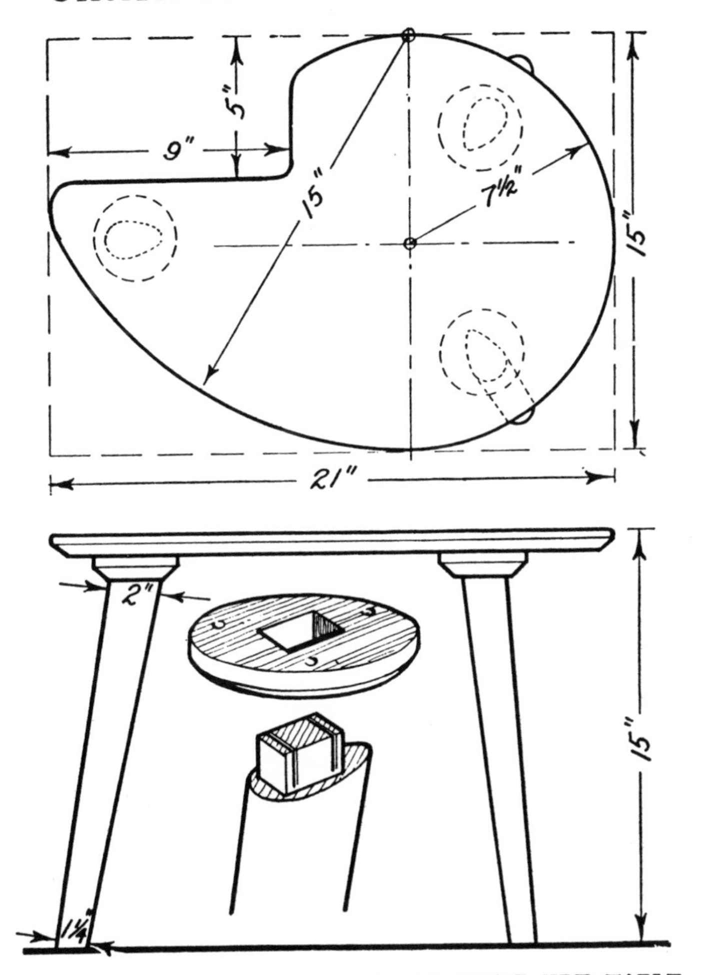

FIG. 2. PLAN AND ELEVATION OF CHAIR-SIDE TABLE

CUTTING LIST

	Long	Wide	Thick
1 Top	1 ft. 9½ in.	15¼ in.	¾ in. ply or lamin board
3 Legs	1 ft. 3 in.	2¼ in.	1¼ in.
3 Discs	3½ in.	3¼ in.	⅞ in.

LADY'S WORKBOX ON STAND

The main box and its trays are made separately from the stand, the two being screwed together. To enable small items such as cotton reels, scissors, etc. to be stored conveniently the top trays are pivoted on arms which keep the trays in a horizontal position when shifted.

Box—Simple through-dovetails are used for this. If neatly

FIG. 1. COMMODIOUS WORKBOX WITH PIVOTED TRAYS
The tops of this could be used for holding small items, or they could be used for the afternoon cup of tea.

cut they have a decorative value. Since the bottom fits in a rebate, it is necessary to allow for this at the bottom corner, otherwise a gap will show. This can be done either by cutting a mitre, or by allowing a projection on the one piece to fill in the rebate. Unless this is done the gaps will have to be filled in with little blocks. The same thing applies to the bottom corners of the trays. Take care to make the last named a neat fit with the box, taking particular care to see that they are square. Note also that the facing ends are narrowed by the thickness of the lid.

Some may prefer to cut lapped-dovetails though the wood is rather thin for this. For a really simple alternative a plain lapped joint can be used. It is, however, necessary to nail as well as glue this. If the nails are entered from the side and are punched in they will be scarcely noticeable providing stopping coloured to match the wood is used.

Fig. 2 shows how the centres are found. Mark the open and

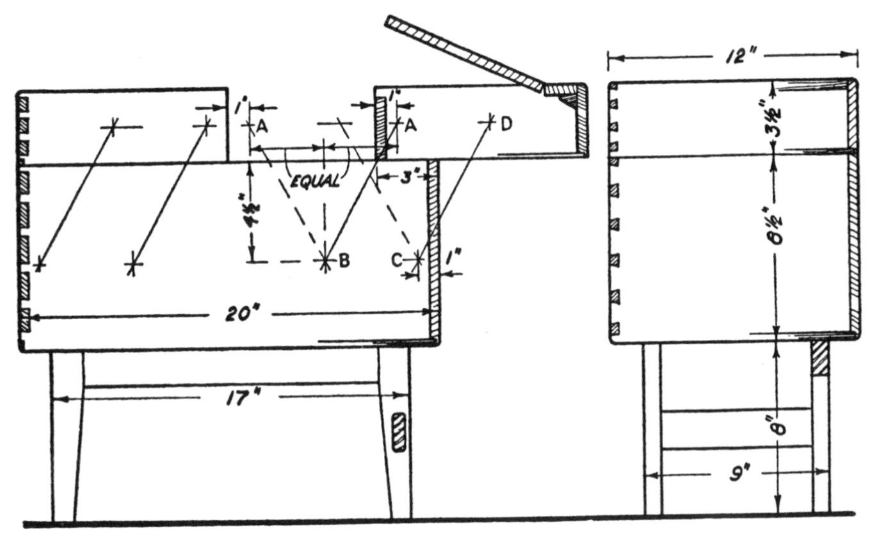

FIG. 2. FRONT ELEVATION IN PART SECTION AND SIDE ELEVATION

closed positions of the box, and put in the position of the top centre 1 in. from the end in both (A). Midway between the two draw a vertical. Lower pivoting position can be anywhere along this, though the lower it is the easier the action. A distance of 4½ in. is about right. Position (C) is 1 in. from the edge, and (D) is found by making (A–D) equal to (B–C).

Strips of hardwood about ¾ in. wide by ¼ in. thick are used for the arms, care being taken to make the holes exactly the right distance apart. Round-head brass screws are used as pivots. In

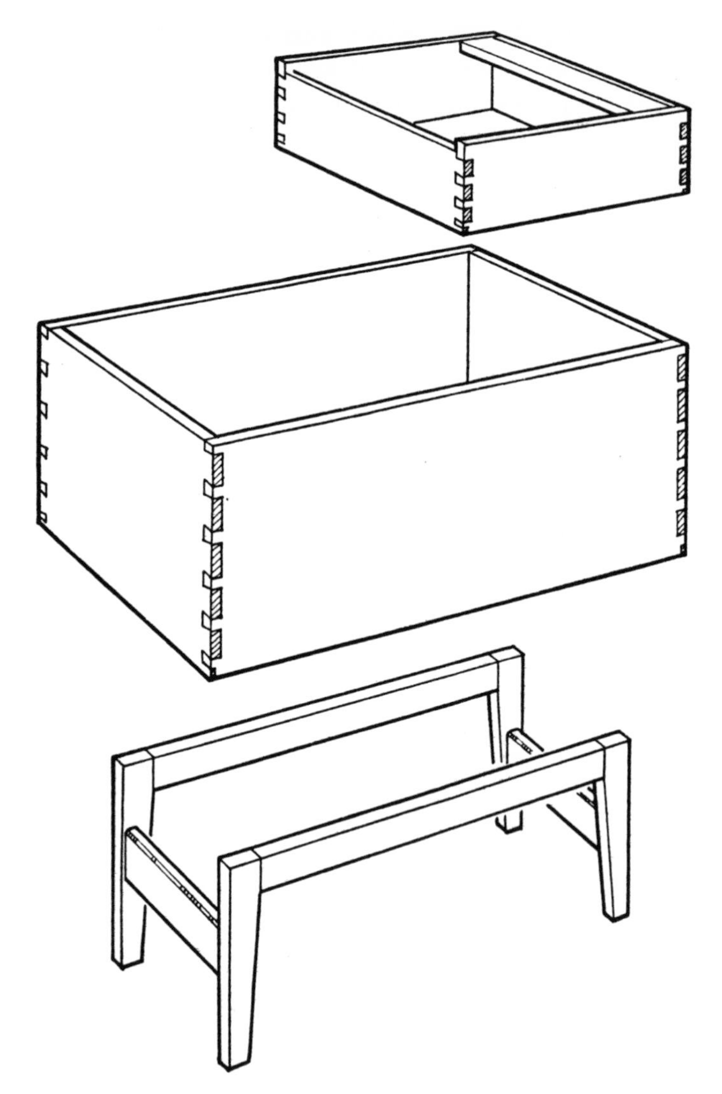

FIG. 3. HOW BOX AND STAND ARE MADE

order to keep the arms from rubbing the box and tray sides, washers are placed between the two.

It is convenient to add fixed pieces to the outer ends of the trays and hinge the lids to these as shown in section in Fig. 2, though they can be omitted if preferred and the lids hinged directly to the tray sides. All outer edges and corners of box should be pencil rounded as it gives a neat appearance.

Stand—Fig. 3 gives details of this. Note that the taper of the legs begins below the rails, enabling square shoulders to be cut. Front and back long rails are tenoned in normally, but the end rails are set down as shown. An advantage of this is that it enables the tenons to be of maximum length since they are at different levels. Put the two opposite sides together independently and allow the glue to set before adding the remaining rails.

Having levelled the joints the stand can be screwed on by counterboring through the rails. Wooden handles screwed on at the ends are convenient for lifting the whole. Finish with transparent or white French polish or use polyurethane lacquer. The latter looks well if brought to a bright gloss then dulled down with the finest grade steel wool lubricated with wax polish.

All parts should be separated as far as possible before polishing as it enables the rubber to be used freely. Those who prefer a dark finish can stain the wood first with Vandyke crystals in the case of oak, or with bichromate of potash for mahogany.

(Cutting list appears on next page.)

CUTTING LIST

Box	Long	Wide	Thick
2 Sides	1 ft. 8¼ in.	8¾ in.	½ in.
2 Ends	1 ft. 0¼ in.	8¾ in.	½ in.
1 Bottom	1 ft. 8 in.	12 in.	¼ in. (ply)
Trays			
4 Sides	10¼ in.	3¾ in.	½ in.
2 Ends	1 ft. 0¼ in.	3¾ in.	½ in.
2 Ends	1 ft. 0¼ in.	3¼ in.	½ in.
2 Bottoms	10 in.	12 in.	¼ in. (ply)
2 Lids	11½ in.	8¼ in.	½ in. (ply)
2 Lid pieces	11½ in.	1¾ in.	½ in.
Stand			
4 Legs	8½ in.	1¾ in.	⅞ in.
2 Rails	1 ft. 4½ in.	1⅞ in.	⅞ in.
2 Rails	9 in.	2 in.	⅝ in.

RECORD STORAGE CABINETS

Sliding doors can be ¼ in. thick plate glass or 6 mm. thick good-quality plywood veneered with equal thickness on both sides. Plywood partitions can be inserted as shown in Fig. 1, or plastic record racks may be fitted. Each holds 50 records and stands quite loose within the cabinet. (A) and (C) designs will each take four of these racks, i.e. 200 records. (B) design will take six racks with

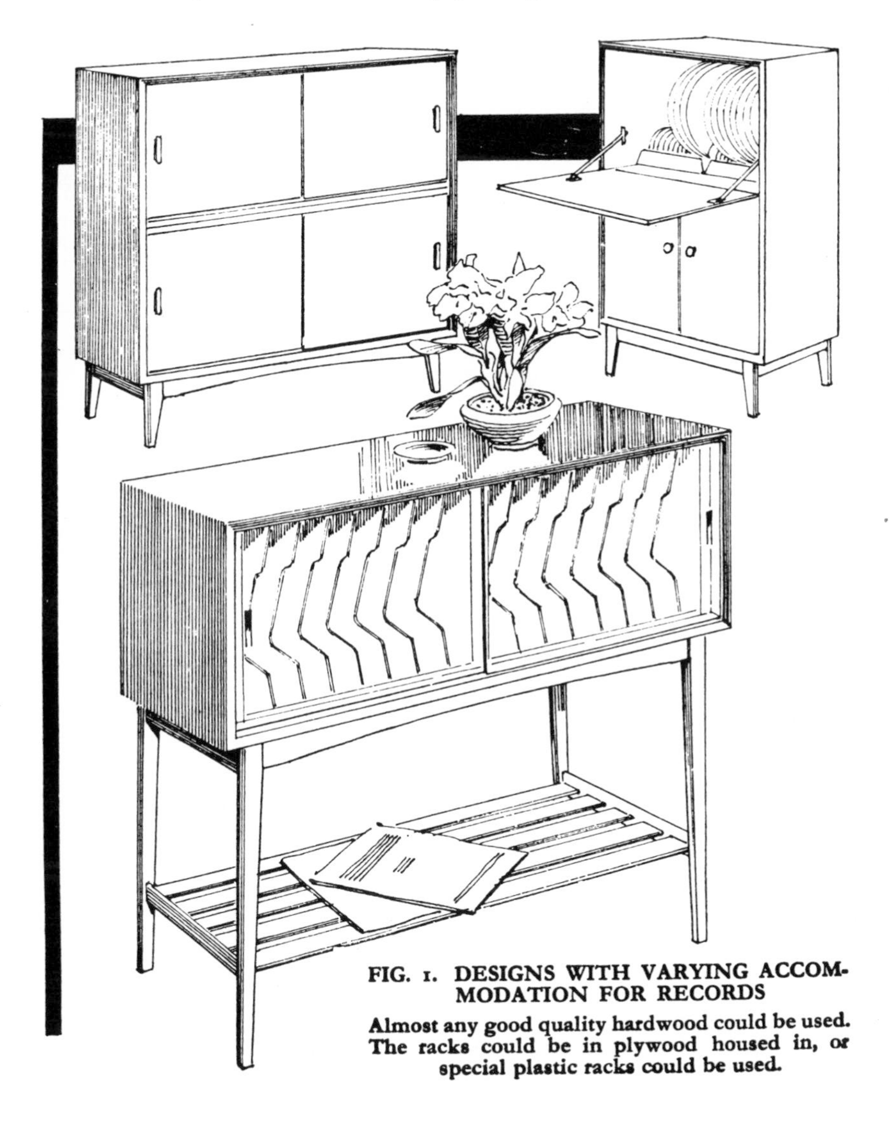

FIG. 1. DESIGNS WITH VARYING ACCOMMODATION FOR RECORDS

Almost any good quality hardwood could be used. The racks could be in plywood housed in, or special plastic racks could be used.

a capacity of 300 records. Accommodation would be less with plywood divisions and the records in cardboard containers or in albums. Construction is standardized in all designs, the method employed in making the carcases largely depending upon the material used.

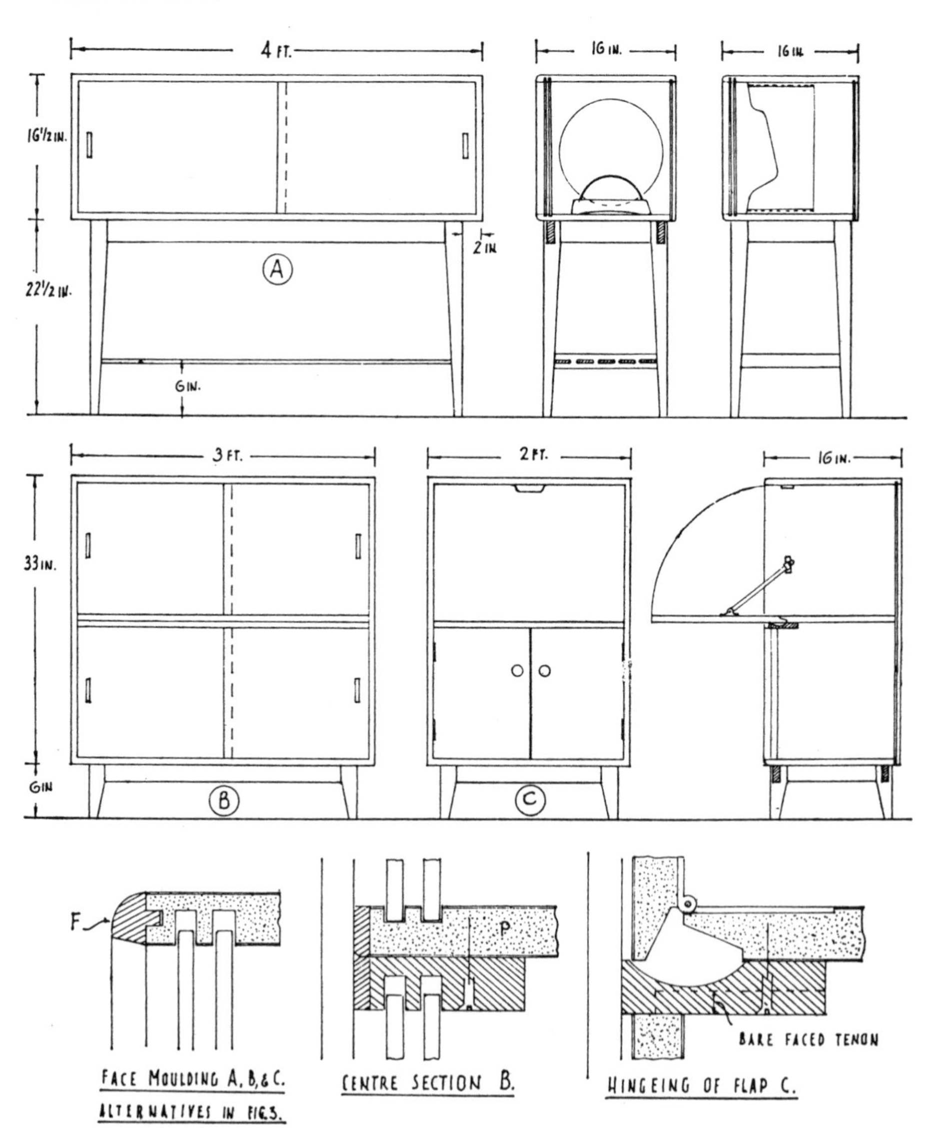

FIG. 2. ELEVATIONS OF THE THREE DESIGNS WITH MAIN SIZES AND ENLARGED SECTIONS

Design (A)—The carcase top (C), ends (D), and bottom (E) can be in solid wood or in blockboard, plywood, or chipboard, the top and ends being veneered on both sides. The awkward joint for those not very skilled is that of top to ends. The strongest joints are the secret mitre dovetailed or the secret lap-dovetailed joints shown in Fig. 3. These are only possible with solid wood. Blockboard and plywood would have to be mitred and tongued, Fig. 3. The carcase bottom (E) could be lap-dovetailed if in solid wood or glued and screwed to rebated ends if blockboard or chipboard is used.

Partition and Door Grooves—If plywood partitions are being put in directly, trenches for these should be cut across top and bottom, stopping at the front clear of the grooves for the doors. Procedure is to assemble the carcase dry and true up the front and rear. Knock down and groove top and bottom for the sliding doors commencing about ½ in. from the front edges. This will clear the grooves to be made for the face mouldings (F), see section, Fig. 2. Top grooves are ½ in. deep, bottom grooves ¼ in. deep. They should be wide enough to allow the doors to be inserted and to slide freely.

Top cover to the sliding doors is $\frac{3}{16}$ in. full which enables them to be lifted in and out.

The front edges of top, ends, and bottom are now grooved ¼ in. deep for the tongued face mouldings, three alternative sections of which are shown in Fig. 3. These mouldings can be glued and pinned straight on if desired although it is not so satisfactory as the method shown. Pins should be punched in and the holes filled. These should not be so long as to penetrate into the sliding door grooves at the top.

Finally groove or rebate the top and ends to receive the carcase back (M). Where divisions are run into grooves in the top and bottom the back should be screwed into rebates.

Assembling—The carcase work is now ready to assemble and when gluing up test for squareness. This is important when glass sliding doors are fitted. The dead space at centre can be filled in by running in vertical edge divisions about 2 in. apart at centre and the gap filled between with (H) on list. See sketch of cabinet, design (A) in Fig. 1.

Alternatively, separate cases can be through-dovetailed together with partitions suitably spaced run into grooves across top and bottom. These cases should fit into the carcase freely, and need not be carried the full depth, see end section, Fig. 2. Screw into place after fitting the doors, and before fixing the back.

When ordering the $\frac{1}{4}$ in. thick plate glass sliding doors it is advisable to make plywood templates, running them in, to ensure a correct and easy fit. Specify the ground-out finger slots in pair

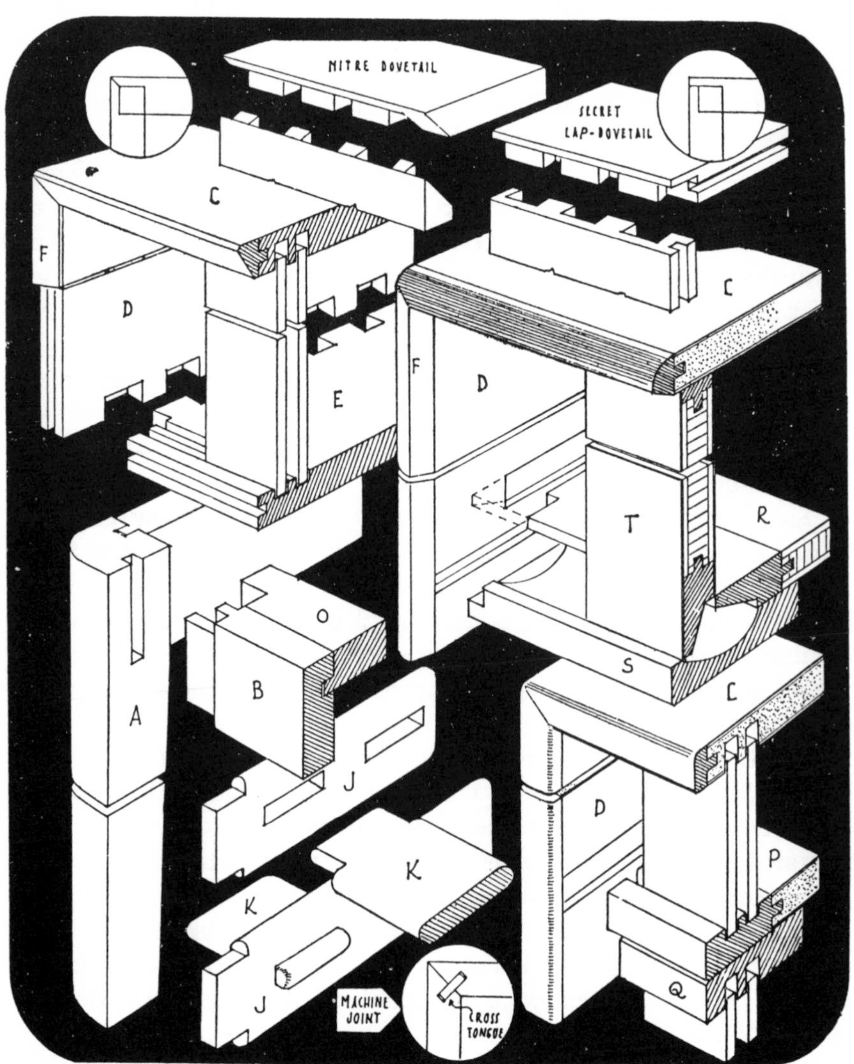

FIG. 3. CUT-AWAY VIEW SHOWING JOINTS AND SECTIONS

at opposite sides. The centre lap should be about 1 in. and each door stopped when open about 1¼ in. from the end by filling in the groove.

Stand—The legs (A) are prepared and mortised for the frame rails which should be stoutly tenoned as the stool has to carry considerable weight. When mortising for the end stretcher rails (J) allow for the inside taper to the legs. The outside corners of all legs are nicely rounded, Fig. 3. The slats (K) of the magazine rack are through-tenoned for strength, the ends being proud and rounded as shown in Fig. 3. Alternatively, stub tenons give an appearance as shown in Fig. 1. The carcase is fixed by screwing up through the stool framing, and, to avoid screws entering the sliding door grooves, add a block (O) to the front rail (B), Fig. 3, and screw through the block.

Design (B)—Main carcase construction as for design (A). The position of the midboard or shelf (P) can be adjusted to suit. A little extra height may be required in the lower section for 15 in. records in plastic holders, enough being left above for 12 in. and 10 in. records. The midboard (P) may be slip-dovetailed or housed to the carcase ends ¼ in. deep. If in plywood or chipboard it should be clamped (P), Fig. 3, or lipped (P), Fig. 2.

The lining piece (Q) is butted to the ends and screwed up to the midboard both of which are grooved for the doors to correspond with those in top and bottom. Bevel off the meeting edges very slightly to form a Vd joint. Procedure is as for design (A). The low stool is mortised and tenoned together and the height increased somewhat if preferred.

Design (C)—Main carcase as previously described for (A) and (B) designs. The midboard (R) and flap (T) are in chipboard, blockboard, or multiply clamped at the hinged joint as shown in Fig. 3. The top and side edges of the fall require lipping or clamping. A good quality hard core chipboard may not require this, section, Fig. 2. It is advisable to work the joint and hinge together with a pair of odd sided hinges cut in before fitting the midboard to the carcase, as the joint can then be tested with ease.

The midboard should be housed in ¼ in. deep and the hollowed rail (S) beneath base-faced tenoned to the ends and screwed up to the board as shown in Fig. 3. The lower pair of doors are hinged with 2 in. brass butt hinges and fitted with ball catches engaging the rail or the carcase bottom. The stool is similar to design (B), but the legs should have less set-under; about 1 in. at the ends.

Avoid the use of blockboard or plywood for the carcases unless the use of machinery is available for the mitred and tongued corner joint which is the only one possible to give satisfaction.

Should the use of plastic racks be contemplated it is advisable to obtain these before commencing work. Sizes may vary.

CUTTING LISTS OF RECORD CABINETS

Design (A)		Long	Wide	Thick
(A)	4 Legs	1 ft. 11 in.	2 in.	2 in.
(B)	2 Stool rails	3 ft. 8 in.	2½ in.	⅞ in.
	2 ,, ,,	1 ft. 2 in.	2½ in.	⅞ in.
(C)	1 Top	4 ft. 0½ in.	15¾ in.	¾ in.
(D)	2 Ends	1 ft. 5 in.	15¾ in.	¾ in.
(E)	1 Bottom	4 ft. 0 in.	15¼ in.	¾ in.
(F)	2 Facings	4 ft. 0½ in.	1 in.	¾ in.
	2 ,,	1 ft. 5 in.	1 in.	¾ in.
(H)	1 Facing	1 ft. 3½ in.	2½ in.	¾ in.
(J)	2 Stretchers	1 ft. 2 in.	2 in.	½ in.
(K)	5 Slats	3 ft. 8 in.	2 in.	½ in.
(M)	1 Back	3 ft. 11½ in.	16¼ in.	¼ in.
(N)	16 Divisions	1 ft. 4 in.	13 in.	¼ in.
(O)	1 Stool block	3 ft. 6½ in.	2 in.	¾ in.

Cut glass doors to fit cabinet. They should have $\frac{3}{16}$ in. cover in top ½ in. grooves. This allows them to be raised and lifted out or in.

DESIGN (B)		Long	Wide	Thick
	4 Legs	6½ in.	2 in.	2 in.
	2 Rails	2 ft. 8 in.	2½ in.	⅞ in.
	2 ,,	1 ft. 2 in.	2½ in.	⅞ in.
	1 Top	3 ft. 0½ in.	15¾ in.	¾ in.
	2 Ends	2 ft. 9½ in.	15¾ in.	¾ in.
	1 Bottom	3 ft. 0 in.	15¼ in.	¾ in.
	2 Facings	3 ft. 0½ in.	1 in.	¾ in.
	2 ,,	2 ft. 9½ in.	1 in.	¾ in.
(P)	1 Midboard	2 ft. 11½ in.	15¼ in.	¾ in.
(Q)	1 Lining	2 ft. 11 in.	2¾ in.	¾ in.
	1 Back	2 ft. 11½ in.	32¾ in.	¼ in.

Cut doors to fit cabinet, allowing $\frac{3}{16}$ cover at the ½ in. grooves at the top.

DESIGN (C)		Long	Wide	Thick
	4 Legs	6½ in.	2 in.	2 in.
	2 Rails	1 ft. 8 in.	2½ in.	⅞ in.
	2 „	1 ft. 2 in.	2½ in.	⅞ in.
	1 Top	2 ft. 0½ in.	15¾ in.	¾ in.
	2 Ends	2 ft. 9½ in.	15¾ in.	¾ in.
	1 Bottom	2 ft. 0 in.	15¼ in.	¾ in.
	2 Facings	2 ft. 9½ in.	1 in.	¾ in.
	2 „	2 ft. 0½ in.	1 in.	¾ in.
(R)	1 Midboard	1 ft. 11½ in.	14¾ in.	¾ in.
(S)	1 Rail	2 ft. 0 in.	2¾ in.	¾ in.
(T)	1 Flap	1 ft. 11 in.	16 in.	¾ in.
(U)	2 Doors	1 ft. 3½ in.	11¾ in.	¾ in.
	1 Back	2 ft. 9 in.	23¼ in.	¼ in.

Trimming allowance has been made in lengths and widths. Thicknesses are net.

TEA TROLLEY WITH LOOSE TRAY

The legs (D) are shaped and mortised at the top for the rails (E). These rails are cut away centrally for the tray handles to pass over, Fig. 5. The legs are notched away for the twin stretchers

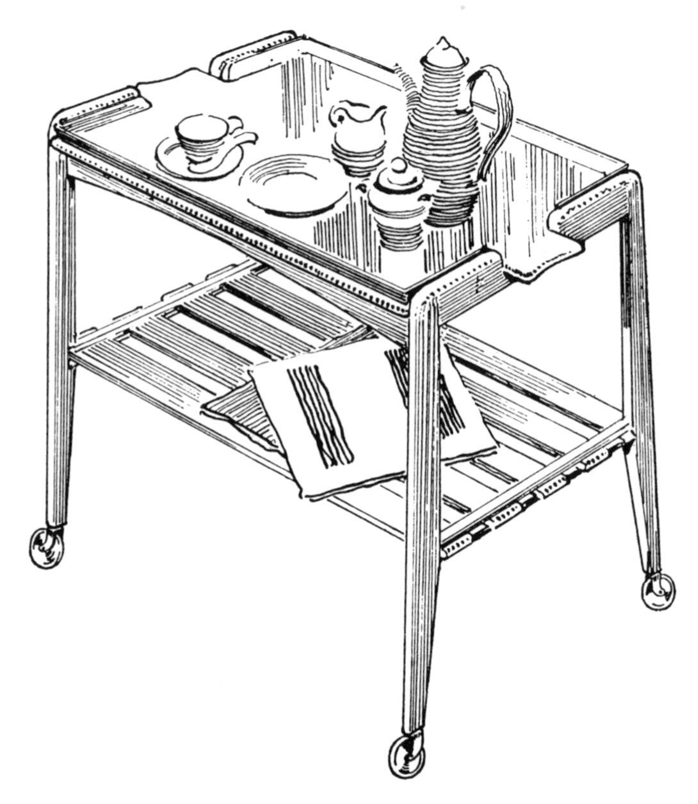

FIG. 1. INVALUABLE IN LOUNGE OR THE GARDEN

carrying the slats, the notching being stopped near the outside face and not carried through. Glue together and round afterwards. Side rails (G) may be shaped as shown in Fig. 2. They are tenoned to the legs (D). For additional strength the inside corners could be braced below the tray bottom.

The slats (K) have rounded edges and ends and are held by a couple of stretchers (J) at each end, the slats projecting slightly. Glue and pin from below. When the complete slatted shelf is

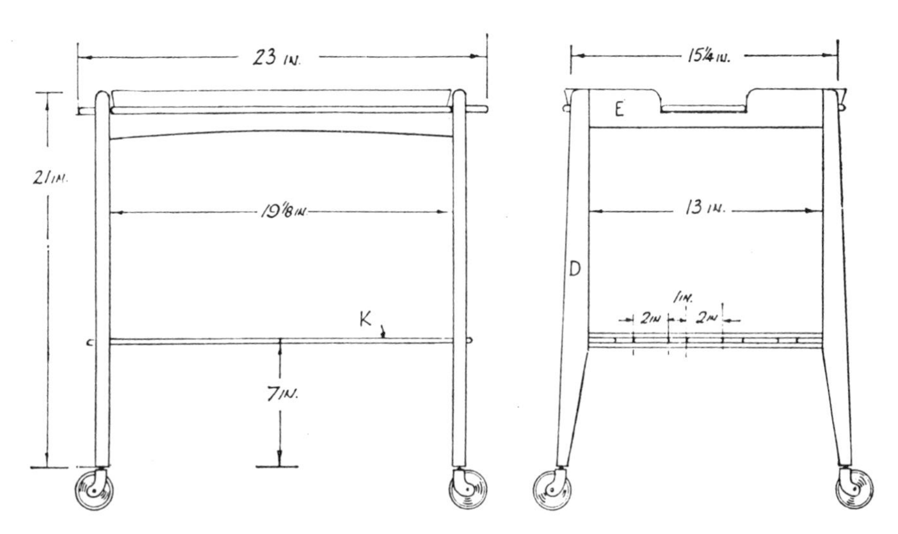

FIG. 2. FRONT AND END ELEVATION WITH MAIN SIZES

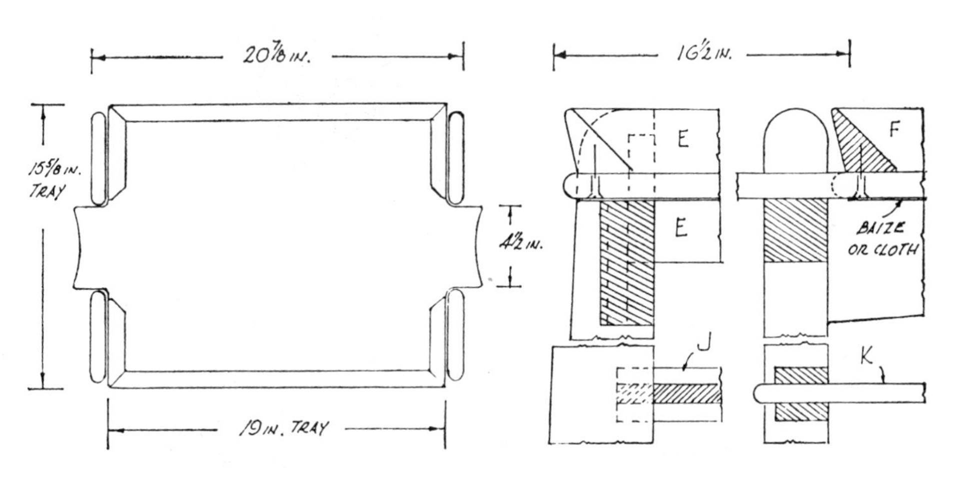

FIG. 3. PLAN OF TOP WITH TRAY SIZES

FIG. 4. TOP AND SHELF SECTIONS

housed and glued into the legs drive good stout panel pins in diagonally from below into the legs.

An alternative for the shelf is to use a piece of $\frac{3}{8}$ in. plywood, this fitting between stretchers (J). In some ways this is better in that cups, glasses, etc. are not liable to fall off. The real purpose of the shelf, however, is to hold a spare tray. It is advisable to use $\frac{3}{8}$ in. thick plywood for the tray, rounding the edges. Solid wood may be used but it should be firm and dry.

The rim mouldings (F) are bevelled from a wide piece and split

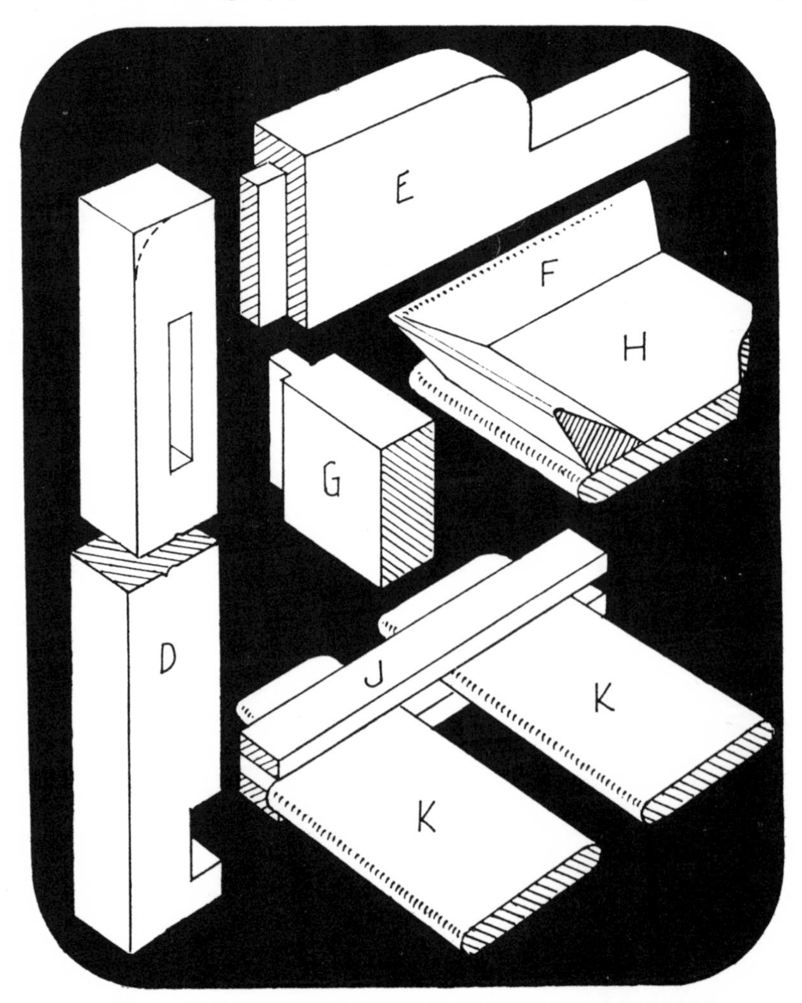

FIG. 5. EXPLODED VIEW SHOWING CONSTRUCTION

down. If the bevelled faces are held temporarily together with pins the opposite edges can be bevelled off with the plane. Attach the moulding by screwing up through the tray bottom, mitreing the corners and slightly rounding them off outside.

CUTTING LIST

		Long	Wide	Thick
(D)	4 Legs	1 ft. 9½ in.	1¾ in.	⅞ in.
(E)	2 Rails	1 ft. 2¼ in.	2⅜ in.	⅞ in.
(F)	1 Tray Moulding	2 ft. 7 in.	2¼ in.	⅞ in.
(G)	2 Rails	1 ft. 9 in.	2 in.	¾ in.
(H)	1 Tray	1 ft. 11½ in.	15⅞ in.	⅜ in.
(J)	4 Stretchers	1 ft. 2½ in.	1 in.	¼ in.
(K)	5 Slats	1 ft. 10 in.	2¼ in.	¼ in.

Allowances: ½ in. on lengths; ¼ in. on widths. Thicknesses net.

SIDEBOARD

Its small size makes this sideboard suitable for the modern house, and its clean lines give it a dignified appearance without being austere. Construction follows the system largely followed

FIG. 1. ATTRACTIVE MODERN DESIGN WITH CLEAN LINES
The effectiveness of this sideboard is largely due to the use of plain straight-grained veneer such as sapele.

in the modern factory, in which plywood, lamin board, and chipboard are largely used. A point to note in this connection is that the grain of the veneer is invariably at right angles with that of the outer layer of the ply. Unless this is done there is danger of hair cracks appearing on the surface. A striped veneer such as sapele would look well. In the case of the doors, which have

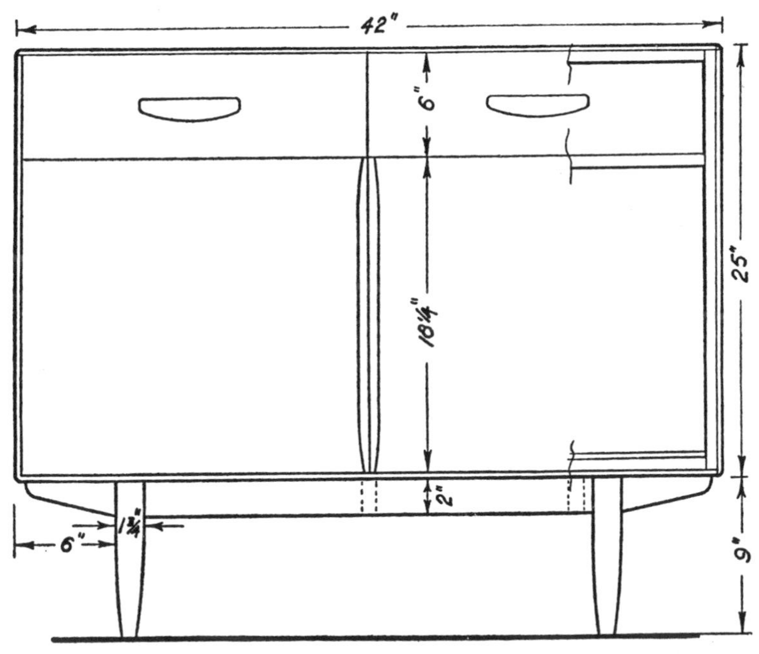

FIG. 2. FRONT ELEVATION WITH MAIN SIZES SHOWING PROPORTIONS

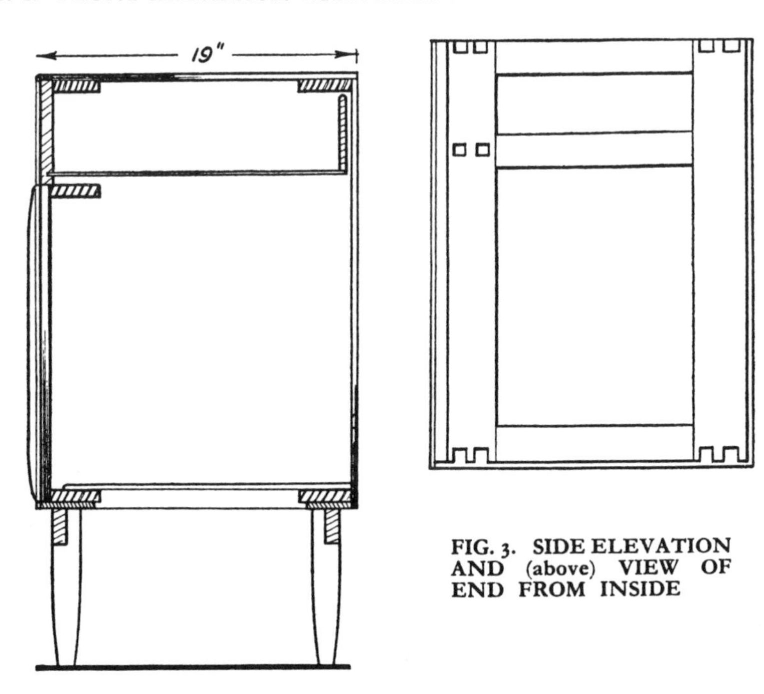

FIG. 3. SIDE ELEVATION AND (above) VIEW OF END FROM INSIDE

nothing but their own construction to keep them flat, it is strongly advisable to veneer both sides so that any pull is equalized.

Ends—Fig. 4 shows how the main framework is made. It will be seen that the ends consist of $\frac{3}{8}$ in. plywood panels to which a series of rails and uprights is glued. In the best way these rails

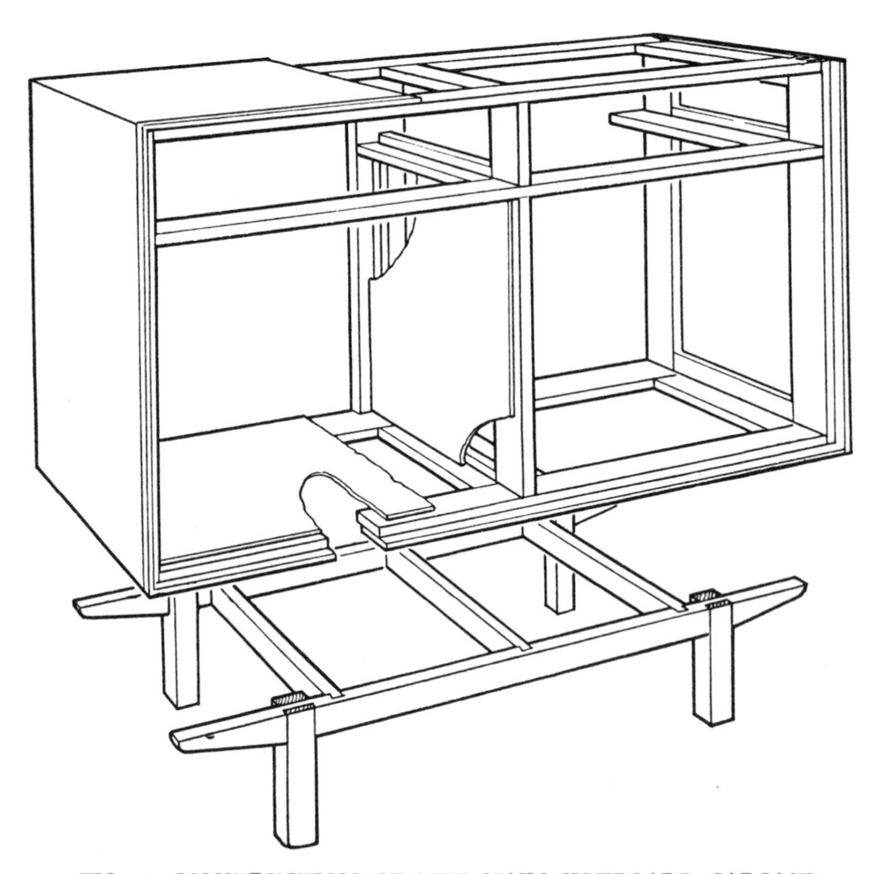

FIG. 4. CONSTRUCTION OF THE MAIN SIDEBOARD CARCASE

and uprights are fitted together to form a framework, the corners being halved. Frequently this jointing is omitted, the parts being butted together and glued direct to the panels. The panels should be lipped at the front edge to give a neat finish.

Before putting them in position, however, it is desirable to cut the joints for the rails—dovetails for top and bottom, and mortises for the drawer rails. These are shown in Fig. 3. Having cut them they can be glued to the panels. The last named are trimmed to size, and, since close positioning is essential, gauge marks are made to the inside of the panel. Pins put in on these marks give the exact position. A single pin driven through each member into the panel will prevent risk of movement when cramps are applied. If there are not enough cramps available the two ends can be assembled independently, placed together, and cramps tightened over both. If this is done it is advisable to use a cold glue as otherwise hot glue may chill before the assembling can be completed. If Scotch glue is used work in a warm shop, heat the parts beforehand, and if possible have assistance to speed up the work. Any glue which may have crept into the dovetails should be removed before it sets.

Screws are driven through the rails, etc., into the panels, and readers may prefer to drive these in at time of assembling, relying on the screws to draw the parts together, and it should certainly economize in cramps. Note that the rails are flush at the top but stand in at the bottom as in Fig. 3.

Front and Back—Front and back rails are now prepared and jointed. At front the three rails run right through, and the centre uprights are contained between them. When all have been fitted the whole can be assembled. Watch the order when assembling. Fit the mid rail to the ends, add the centre upright, and glue the bottom rail. Put in the short upright which divides the drawers, and follow with the top rail. Back parts are added similarly, but there is no drawer rail. There is, however, a centre upright, and this must be put in after the bottom rail is in position, but before the top rail is added. Test for truth and set aside.

Runners, bottoms, and partition follow. Note that a guide is required above the wide middle runner. Kickers are also needed. Add the top panel, this being glued and cramped down over the whole carcase. Afterwards it is also screwed from beneath. The front edge should be lipped similarly to the ends. At the corners hardwood strips are glued in, the outer corners being pencil rounded.

Stand—Fig. 4 gives details of this. The legs are rounded towards the bottom and are fixed to the front and back rails with bridle joints. They stand in from the ends, the rails being tapered at the ends as in Fig. 2. Cross rails are slot-dovetailed into the rails (Fig. 4). It may be convenient to fix these to the front and back rails before adding the legs.

Drawers and Doors—As the fronts necessarily project beyond the sides, the last named are joined to them with slot-dovetails. The fronts stand up at the top also because they close in front of the top rail. The dovetail slots are therefore stopped at the top by an amount equal to the top rail thickness. Normal through-dovetails are used at the back. Bottoms are fitted in the usual grooved drawer bottom moulding.

Doors are simply pieces of multi-ply or lamin board lipped at the edges and veneered both sides. A neat fit is essential. It is advisable to make the outside lippings extra wide to provide a suitable grip for the hinge screws. These lippings must be tongued to make a strong joint.

The handles look well if in a contrasting hardwood. Finish is best in white or transparent french polish or with polyurethane lacquer. The latter has the advantage of being mark resistant. It needs about three brush-applied coats, each being lightly rubbed smooth. Leave for 2–3 days and rub down with the finest grade steel wool lubricated with wax. This will leave a matt finish which some may prefer, or it can be burnished with one of the fine-grade abrasive compounds. Whiting and wax can be used.

CUTTING LIST

Main Carcase	Long	Wide	Thick
2 End panels	2 ft. 1 in.	19 in.	3/8 in. (ply)
1 Top panel	3 ft. 6 in.	19 in.	3/8 in. (ply)
4 Uprights	2 ft. 1 in.	3¼ in.	¾ in.
6 Rails	1 ft. 6½ in.	2¼ in.	¾ in.
5 Rails	3 ft. 6 in.	3¼ in.	¾ in.
1 Upright	2 ft. 1½ in.	2¾ in.	¾ in.
1 "	1 ft. 7 in.	3¼ in.	¾ in.
1 "	7 in.	3¼ in.	¾ in.
2 Bottoms	1 ft. 8 in.	17½ in.	3/8 in. (ply)
1 Partition	1 ft. 6 in.	17½ in.	3/8 in. (ply)
2 Runners	1 ft. 3½ in.	2¼ in.	¾ in.
1 Runner	1 ft. 3½ in.	3¼ in.	¾ in.
3 Cross rails	1 ft. 1 in.	2¼ in.	¾ in.
1 " "	1 ft. 1 in.	3¼ in.	¾ in.

	Long	Wide	Thick
1 Back	3 ft. 6 in.	25 in.	$\frac{3}{8}$ in. (ply)
2 Doors	1 ft. 9 in.	$18\frac{1}{2}$ in.	$\frac{1}{2}$ in. (ply)
2 Drawer fronts	1 ft. 9 in.	$6\frac{1}{4}$ in.	$\frac{3}{4}$ in.
2 ,, backs	1 ft. 8 in.	5 in.	$\frac{3}{8}$ in.
4 ,, sides	1 ft. 6 in.	$5\frac{1}{2}$ in.	$\frac{3}{8}$ in.
2 ,, bottoms	1 ft. $7\frac{1}{2}$ in.	18 in.	$\frac{1}{8}$ in. (ply or hardboard)
Stand			
4 Legs	$9\frac{1}{2}$ in.	—	$1\frac{3}{4}$ in. (sq.)
2 Rails	3 ft. 6 in.	$2\frac{1}{4}$ in.	$\frac{7}{8}$ in.
3 ,,	1 ft. 5 in.	$2\frac{1}{4}$ in.	$\frac{7}{8}$ in.

Lippings and the small parts extra. Note that all plywood lengths and widths should be decided in accordance with proposed direction of grain of veneer. If for instance, grain of veneer of ends is to be horizontal length and width measurements as given should be reversed. Plywood lengths as given are reckoned as the direction of the grain of the outer layers.

EXTENDING DINING TABLE

The draw-leaf system is one of the oldest methods of extending a table, and is still one of the most satisfactory. The main top, although prevented from lateral movement, is free to rise to the extent of about an inch. This enables it to lift as the leaves are drawn out. These leaves are fixed to tapered bearers which cause them to rise by an amount equal to the thickness of the top as they are pulled out.

It will be seen from Fig. 3 that the legs are set askew and are separate from the main framework. The latter is dovetailed together and the legs are slotted to fit the corners. Top and leaves are curved at the ends as given in the plan in Fig. 2, but those who prefer could make them straight. Veneered laminated board should be used for the tops, and it should be noted that the edging is applied after veneering as this protects the edges of the veneer, always the most vulnerable part.

Main Frame—This is 27 in. square by $4\frac{1}{2}$ in. deep, and the corners are through-dovetailed together. After assembly the corners are taken off at 45 deg. to the extent of the dovetails as shown in Figs. 2 and 3. A centre rail is slot-dovetailed in across the centre, this stopping short at the bottom by 1 in. and standing up at the top by the thickness of the top. In it holes are cut to receive the tapered bearers, and corresponding notches are

FIG. 1. DINING TABLE WORKING ON THE DRAW-LEAF PRINCIPLE
The main framework is made up as a complete unit dovetailed at the corners. If preferred the tops could have straight end edges.

cut in the end rails. One pair of bearers runs immediately inside the other, and the holes must be positioned accordingly. Furthermore the holes must slope at the same angle as the bearers. The only way of making them accurate is to set out a side section of the job in full size.

Above the main frame is a fixed frame (Fig. 3) of the same thickness as the leaves and top. It is tenoned together, and is screwed down. In the best way it would be shaped to correspond with the curvature of the leaves, but it is not essential, and the square frame in Fig. 3 is satisfactory and simpler. To prevent the sharp corners of the leaves from being damaged when the last named are closed, the fixed frame can be made about 1 in. over width and the extreme corners cut at an angle to line up with the curve.

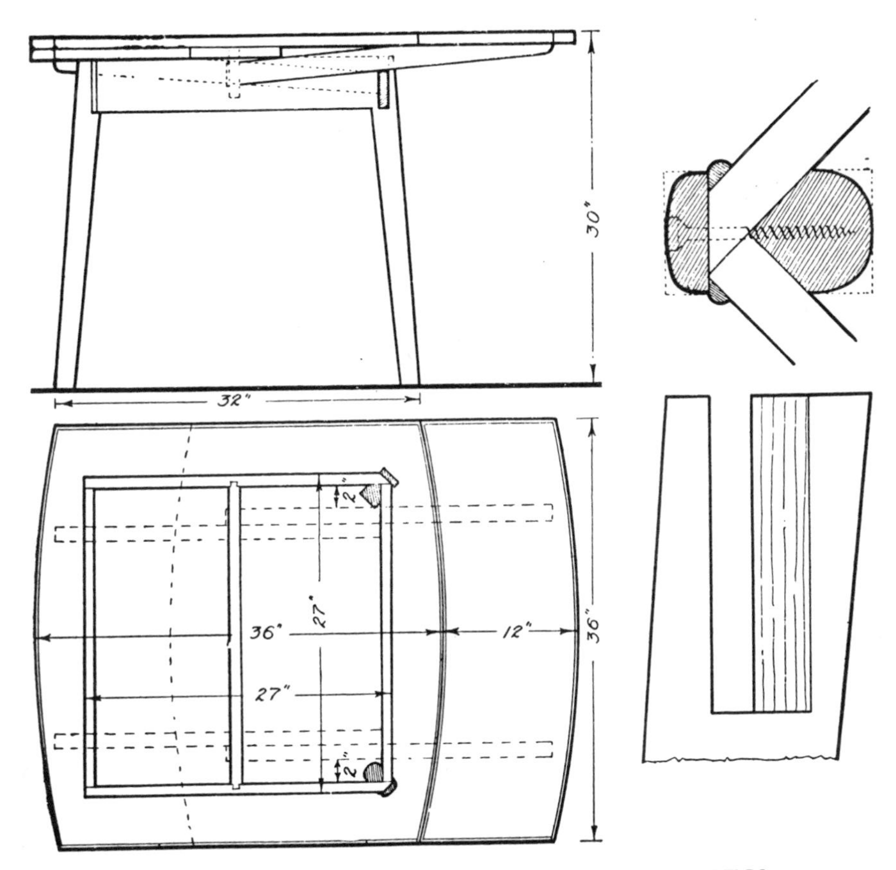

FIG. 2. ELEVATION, PLAN, AND DETAILS OF LEGS

Legs—At this stage the legs can be put in hand. They are prepared in rectangular section and measure 3 in. by $1\frac{3}{4}$ in. at the top, tapering to $1\frac{3}{4}$ in. by $1\frac{1}{4}$ in. at the bottom. A slotted joint is cut at the top to fit the corner of the framework, and it is strongly advisable to set it out in full size as shown in the enlarged view, Fig. 2. Note the spread of the legs which brings them to 32 in. at the bottom (Fig. 2).

The front square surface of the notch can be sawn, but it is possible to reach down with the saw only part of the way when sawing the surfaces at 45 deg. The rest will have to be chiselled away. Matters are helped by boring a hole at the bottom of the slot right through. A close, accurate fit is essential if the joint is to be strong.

When satisfactory round the legs to the approximate egg

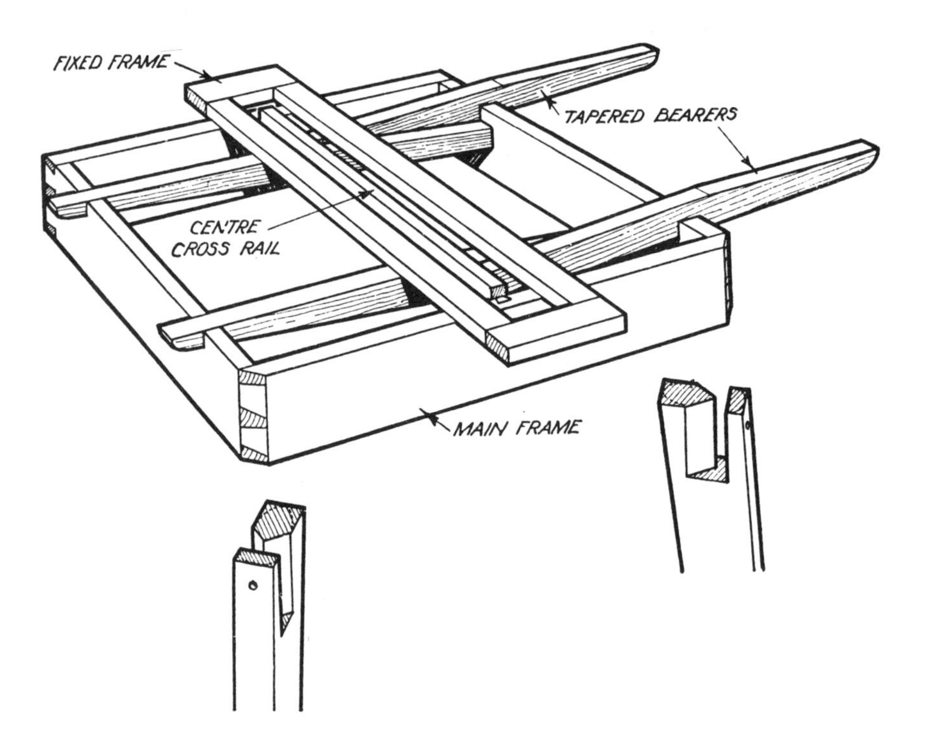

FIG. 3. EXPLODED VIEW SHOWING CONSTRUCTION AND WORKING

section, clean up and glue. A stout screw is driven in from the front, the head being slightly recessed and the hole pelleted as in the sectional view in Fig. 2. Note that there is no need for the curved section to run right through to the top of the inside. There is in fact an advantage in leaving it square here in that it enables strengthening glue blocks to be rubbed in.

It will be found that awkward notches are left at each side of the legs, and these are filled with special beads cut at an angle as in the enlarged plan in Fig. 2. Clean them up and glue in. After levelling the top surfaces the job is ready for the tops and bearers.

Top and Leaves—Laminated board is the best material for the top and leaves, and, assuming that the surface is to be veneered, the grain of the outer layers should be at right angles with that of the veneer. Otherwise there may be trouble owing to hair cracks developing in the surface. The edges should be lipped all round, and the most suitable section is of *T* formation in which the edge of the laminated board is grooved to take the leg of the *T*. It will go quite easily around the flat shape.

The simplest way of holding the main top in position is to fit four dowels in the underside to pass through holes bored through the fixed frame. The dowels might be ½ in. to ¾ in., and the clearance holes in the fixed frame should be about $\frac{1}{16}$ in. over size to allow free movement and to enable the top to tilt slightly.

Work to the full size setting out of the table to obtain the taper of the bearers. They are screwed beneath the leaves, care being taken to keep them parallel. Before screwing them make sure that they work freely in the main framework. When satisfactory rub candlegrease over all bearing surfaces.

The leaves have to open a trifle beyond the open position to enable them to be pushed home against the main top, and stops must be fixed to the sides to prevent their being pulled right out. The clearance inside the frame fixes their length, and they should not be cut down unnecessarily as otherwise it may be found that they will pull right out of the holes in the centre cross rail.

Several tests are needed apart from easy opening. All three parts must be in alignment when open, and either leaf must be true when opened independently. Then again the parts must be level along the joints when open. When the tops are made in the solid there is no difficulty because a shaving or two can be taken off where necessary. There is also no problem when the tops are veneered after the edging is fixed because again they can be levelled after fitting before being veneered. In the present case, owing to the tops being veneered before the edging is applied, any correction will have to be made in the bearers or in the main table framework. It is therefore essential that special care is taken in the entire construction.

For the top of the table one of the special heat and water resisting polishes should be used, or alternatively it should be oil-polished. For the main framework ordinary french polish gives a good finish, though the table top polish could be used throughout if preferred.

CUTTING LIST

	Long	Wide	Thick
1 Top	3 ft. 0 in.	36 in.	7/8 in. lamin board
2 Leaves	3 ft. 0 in.	14 in.	7/8 in. " "
4 Frame rails	2 ft. 3½ in.	4¾ in.	7/8 in.
1 Cross rail	2 ft. 3 in.	4¾ in.	7/8 in.
4 Legs	2 ft. 5 in.	3¼ in.	1¾ in.
2 Fixed frame rails	3 ft. 0 in.	2¼ in.	7/8 in.
2 " " "	9 in.	2¾ in.	7/8 in.
4 Bearers	2 ft. 5 in.	2¼ in.	1⅜ in.

Lippings and small parts extra.

DIVAN BED

It is assumed that a 30 in. mattress of 6 ft. 2 in. length will be used with the box framing. If the mattress to be used varies the sizes will have to be adapted accordingly. A double-size bed could be made in the same way, and using the same weight materials, but it would be as well to add a few extra corner brackets between the main frame and the spring slats. In particular two brackets should be used at each end, these connecting the rails and the two end spring rails. They could bridge across the gap between the two. The headboard is a separate extra and could be omitted altogether if preferred. It has uprights which fit into metal sockets screwed to the main framework.

Main Frame—Sizes are given in Fig. 2, and Fig. 3 shows construction. The four main sides are through-dovetailed together, and after assembly the spring rails are dovetailed in beneath. They should be screwed as well as glued. To stiffen the whole corner brackets can be screwed to the two mid spring rails. A note about extra brackets for a double divan has already been given.

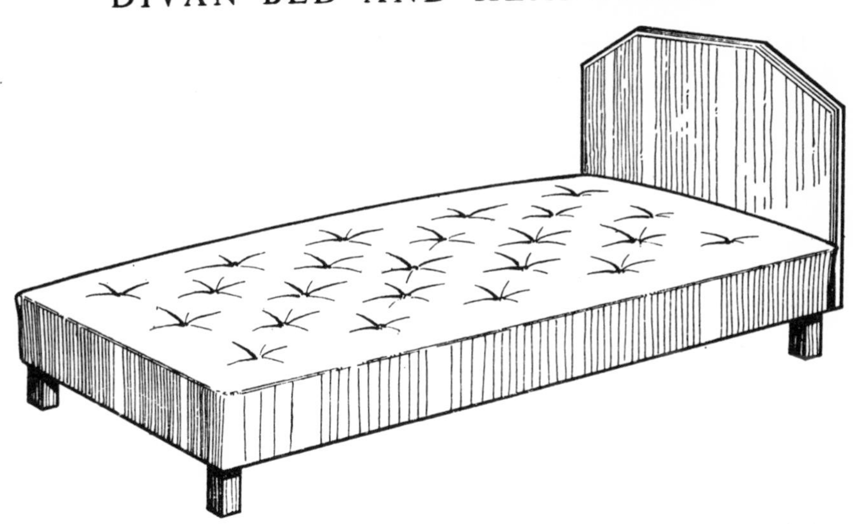

FIG. 1. DIVAN BED WITH DETACHABLE HEADBOARD (OPTIONAL)

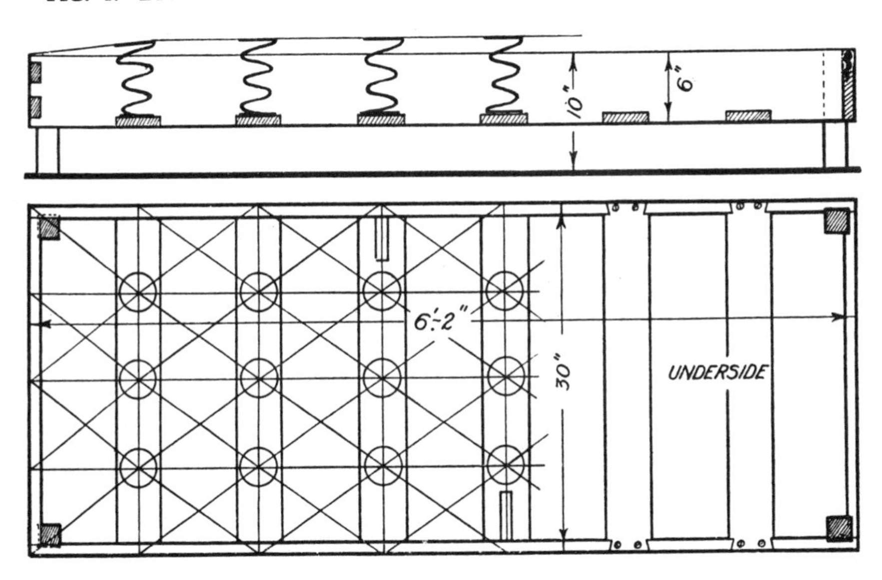

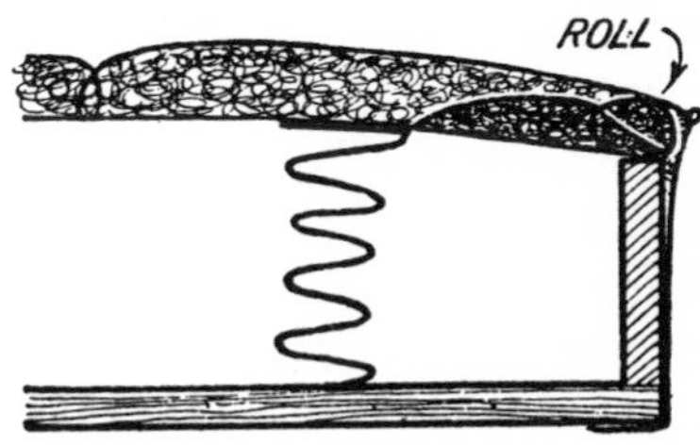

FIG. 2. SECTIONAL ELEVATION. PLAN SHOWING SPRINGS, AND ENLARGED SECTION THROUGH STUFFING

Fig. 3 shows how the legs are slightly notched (about $\frac{1}{8}$ in. deep) to fit in the angles. They are screwed in position. Without the notches all the weight would be taken directly by the screws. The legs should be polished before fixing. Gliders fitted to the legs enable the bed to be moved easily. Having levelled the joints take off all sharp edges and corners.

Springing—To prevent noise tack a strip of hessian to the tops of all spring rails. Use 7 in. by 10 gauge springs and fix them with staples, three to each spring. Using strong laid cord lash

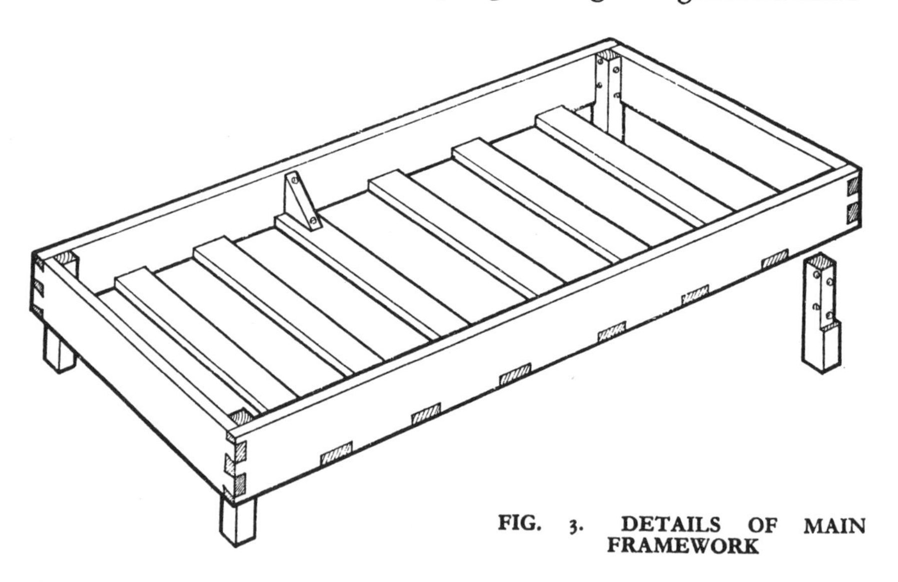

FIG. 3. DETAILS OF MAIN FRAMEWORK

the springs to the frame and to each other. Tack the cord to the frame, and take to the first spring. Knot it around the wire, take to the next spring, and so on to the other side. Lash in both directions in this way as in Fig. 2, and have the outer springs leaning outwards at a slight angle (Fig. 2). In the best work the springs are also laced diagonally as well. Where the cords cross each other it is as well to hitch the one around the other.

Stuffing—Cut a piece of strong hessian to cover the whole, allowing for a turn-in, and tack it temporarily to the underside of the frame. Even it out and tack finally in position, doubling in the raw edge. If the springs have been laced diagonally there is no need to stitch the canvas to them.

A roll is necessary all round as shown in the enlarged illustration in Fig. 2. Stitch a length of canvas all round about 5 in. from the edge and parallel, turning in the edge. Stuff some hair beneath this canvas to bring it about level with the middle of the bed and tack temporarily to the sides. Regulate the stuffing to make it even and tack down finally. A double-pointed needle is required for stitching. Start at one end, passing the needle in close to the frame, nearly out at the top, and taking in about 1½ in. of scrim. Pull through and make a slip knot. Draw tight, take the needle about 1½ in. along, and insert as before, taking the needle through

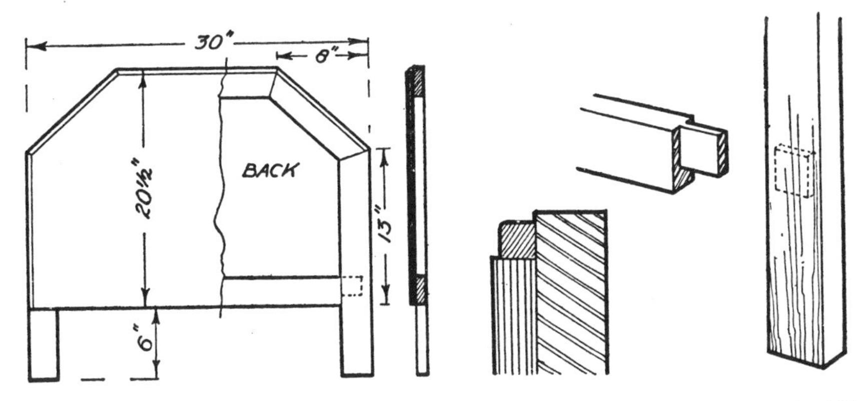

FIG. 4. HEADBOARD ELEVATION AND DETAILS OF CONSTRUCTION

until the eye almost appears, then push back, but this time about 1¼ in. behind the point of entry. Take a turn around the needle as it emerges and pull tight. Proceed in this way all round, forming an even edge or roll.

Cut out the mattress ticking, and sew the top to the sides with a piped edge. Run a few loops of twine a few inches in all round, and pick the stuffing beneath them. Put a layer of hair, fibre, or wool over the whole evenly, place the sewn cover over the whole, and pull down. Make sure the piped edge is even all round and tack down temporarily to the underside.

Tufting follows. Pass the straight needle through, and return about ¾ in. from its first point. Tie a slip knot and cut off a few inches from the knot. Do all tufting similarly before placing the tufts beneath the slip knots. Pull all tight, knot the twine and cut off. Finally tack the hessian permanently beneath, doubling the edge, and tack a bottom cover of hessian over the whole.

Headboard—This is shown in Fig. 4. It consists of a piece of veneered multi-ply or laminated board, with framing rails screwed all round. The ply stands in to enable an edging fillet to be inserted in the rebate so formed. The bottom rail is tenoned to the uprights as shown by the dotted lines, but plain mitred joints are used at the top as there is no strain. Glue and screw the parts in position. Sockets to hold uprights are screwed to the head of the bed.

CUTTING LIST

Bed	Long	Wide	Thick
2 Sides	6 ft. 3 in.	6¼ in.	⅞ in.
2 ,,	2 ft. 7 in.	6¼ in.	⅞ in.
6 Spring rails	2 ft. 7 in.	4¼ in.	⅞ in.
4 Legs	10½ in.	2 in. sq. finished	
Headboard			
1 Panel	2 ft. 6 in.	20½ in.	½ in.
2 Uprights	1 ft. 8 in.	3¼ in.	¾ in.
1 Rail	2 ft. 5 in.	3¼ in.	¾ in.
1 ,,	1 ft. 3 in.	3¼ in.	¾ in.
2 ,,	1 ft. 0 in.	3¼ in.	¾ in.

Edgings and small parts extra.

Headboard should be cut so that grain of outer layers is at right angles with required direction of veneer.

KIDNEY SHAPED DRESSING TABLE

The simplicity of this table is due to its carcase portion being rectangular in plan. Only the top is kidney-shaped. The flounce is fitted with runners at the top which travel around a metal track of the type used for window curtains, thus enabling it to be drawn back at the front to reveal the drawer and shelves. The track is quite pliable, so that it can bend around the curve easily. If preferred only the front portion need be on runners.

Top—Although it is possible to mark out the top geometrically, it does not produce a pleasing shape, having a disjointed appearance. It is far better to draw it in free hand. As a guide the shape is shown plotted out in squares in Fig. 2, and if 1 in. squares are drawn on a sheet of paper the shape can be plotted in map fashion. A good plan is to mark out one half and reverse this to complete the whole.

The strongest top is made in plywood or block board, but solid wood could be used. Alternatively it could be in chip board. If a bandsaw is not available, the bow saw will have to be used. Clean up with spokeshave and lightly round over the edge.

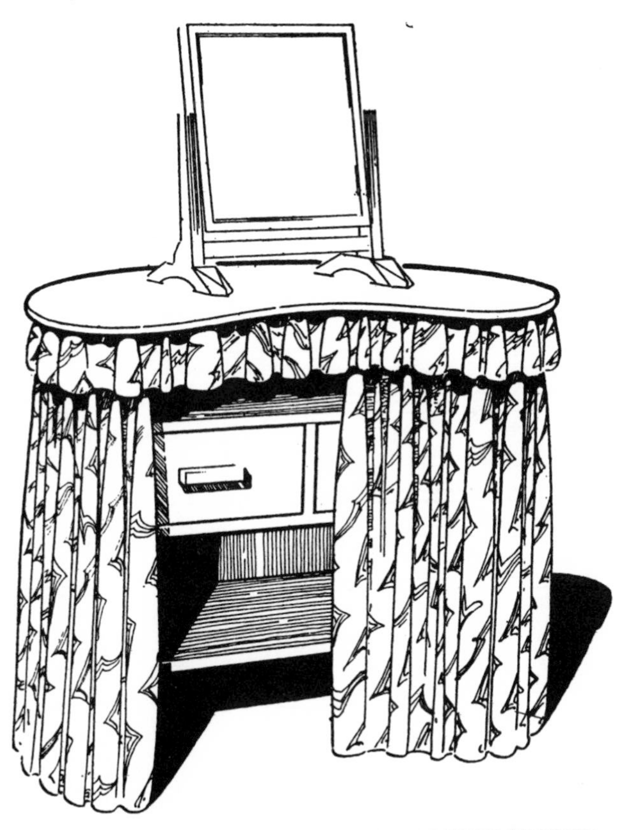

FIG. 1. DRESSING TABLE WITH KIDNEY-SHAPED TOP

The main carcase, concealed by the curtains is square in form, thus making its construction simple.

Carcase—Fig. 3 shows how the lower carcase is made. Sizes can be taken from Fig. 2. The strongest form of joint for the shelves is the through tenon in Fig. 3. This is wedged from the outside. The two upper shelves could be housed, the housings being stopped at the front. Top rails are dovetailed. Either two narrow drawers could be fitted as Fig. 1, or one wide one as in Fig. 3.

To increase the stability of the job projecting feet are glued on at front and back edges as shown. Note how the bottom edge is cut away in a hollow curve. This helps to ensure that the table stands evenly. Holes bored through the top rails enable the top to be screwed on.

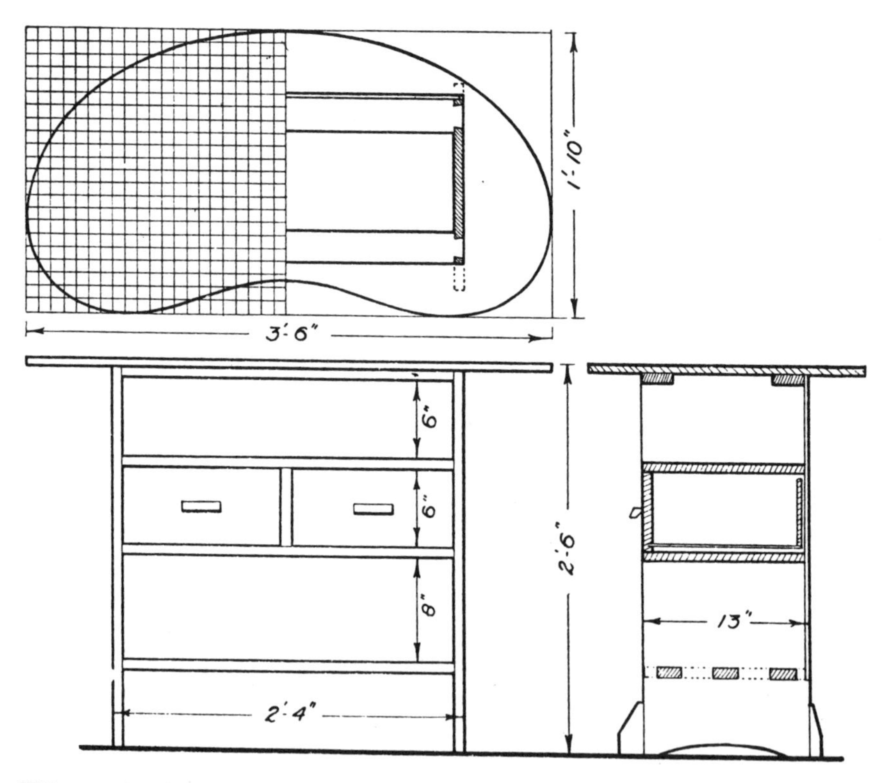

FIG. 2. SHAPE OF TOP SET OUT IN 1 IN. SQUARES, AND ELEVATIONS

A back is fitted, and this can be screwed or nailed into rebates worked in the uprights, the shelves finishing level with the rebates. In a simpler way it could be fixed straight to the back edges.

The drawer follows the usual construction (see p. 128). If preferred the lower space could have a drawer as well, but the top shelf should be left open as it would be awkward to reach into a drawer owing to the overhanging top. If two drawers are used in the centre space a short upright will have to be fitted, this being stub-tenoned between the shelves. A guide is fitted behind it to extend back about 6 in.

Paint is the usual finish for a table of this kind, though if preferred a veneered ply or chip board top could be used, this being polished.

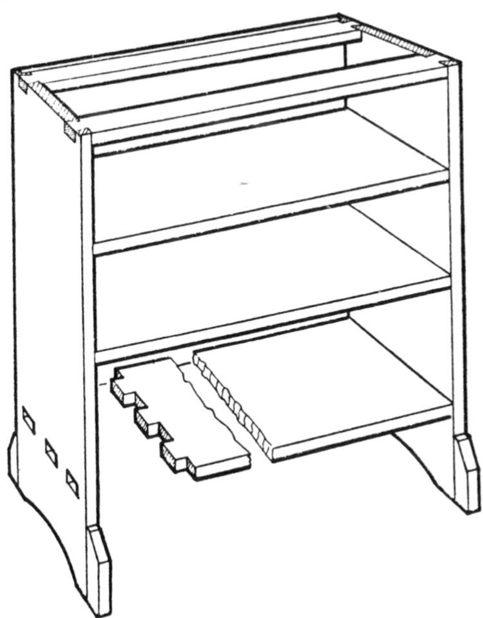

FIG. 3. HOW MAIN CARCASE IS MADE

CUTTING LIST

	Long	Wide	Thick
1 Top	3 ft. 6½ in.	22¼ in.	½ in. ply, block, or chip board, or ¾ in. wood.
2 Ends	2 ft. 6 in.	13¼ in.	¾ in.
3 Shelves	2 ft. 4½ in.	13¼ in.	¾ in.
2 Rails	2 ft. 4½ in.	2¾ in.	¾ in.
1 Back	2 ft. 4¼ in.	24 in.	¼ in. ply
1 Upright	8 in.	2¾ in.	¾ in.
2 Drawer fronts	1 ft. 1½ in.	6¼ in.	¾ in.
4 " sides	1 ft. 1 in.	6¼ in	⅜ in.
2 " backs	1 ft. 1½ in.	6 in.	⅜ in.
2 " bottoms	1 ft. 1 in.	12½ in.	¼ in. ply

Small parts extra.

COT WITH DROP-SIDE

As commercial mattresses vary in size it is essential that this is obtained before commencing work. A home-made article is shown on the plan, Fig. 2. This consists of a wood frame with interlaced upholsterer's 2 in. wide webbing stretched across

FIG. 1. ATTRACTIVE COT TO HOLD STANDARD 4 FT. BY 2 FT. MATTRESS

The cot would look well finished in gloss or eggshell paint, and decorated with nursery rhyme transfers.

End Frames—Set out the tapered posts (A) upon plywood to obtain the length and angle of the shoulders to the top rails (E). Prepare the posts in width and thickness, leaving the length till later, and taper on the inside above and below the bottom end rail (E), Fig. 2. Sink mortises for the tenoned rails.

Cut the rail shoulders, the top one being angled. Sink ½ in. square mortises, 4 in. centre to centre, in the rails for the sticks. The edges of these are well rounded off as shown in the enlarged section, Fig. 2, being cut back at top and bottom and bare-faced tenoned to the rails.

If it is decided to do the scalloping this should be completed before assembly. Limiting pencil lines should be gauged upon the side and edges of the rails. Remove most of the wood with carving

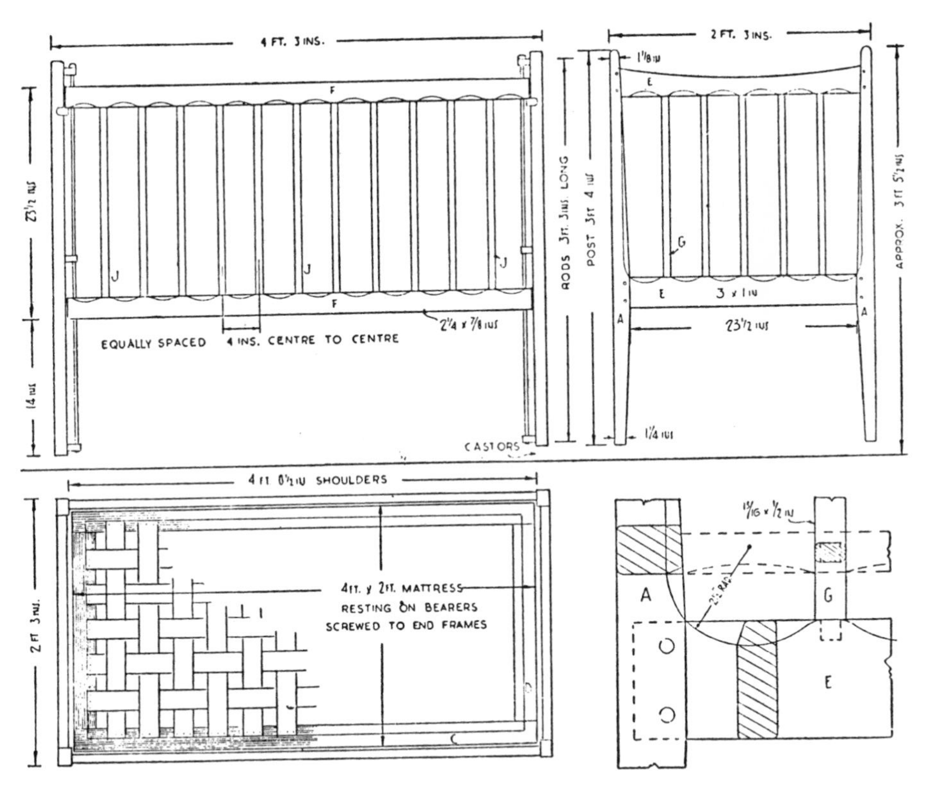

FIG. 2. ELEVATIONS, PLAN, AND DETAILS

tool or spokeshave, finishing with cabinet file and glasspaper wrapped round a shaped rubber. Well soften all edges.

The chamfered posts are treated similarly and by removing the widest part at the bottom the remainder could be worked with a bull-nosed plane. Sticks should be inserted upon assembly and, after gluing together, the tenons in the legs are pegged with hardwood dowels driven through the posts, Fig. 2.

Drop and Removable Sides—These are identical but, in the final fitting, the top and bottom rails (F) of the drop side will require shortening slightly to clear the posts and pivoted supports, Fig. 2. Metal fittings are available ready-made. The rod length fixes the positions of the brackets.

CUTTING LIST

		Long	Wide	Thick
(A)	4 Posts	3 ft. 4½ in.	2 in.	1¼ in.
(B)	2 Mattress bearers	2 ft. 0 in.	2¼ in.	1¼ in.
(C)	2 Mattress frame	4 ft. 0½ in.	2½ in.	1⅛ in.
(D)	2 " "	2 ft. 0½ in.	2½ in.	1⅛ in.
(E)	4 End rails	2 ft. 2¾ in.	3¼ in.	1 in.
(F)	4 Side rails	4 ft. 1 in.	2½ in.	⅞ in.
(G)	10 End sticks	1 ft. 7½ in.	1 1/16 in.	½ in.
(J)	22 Side sticks	1 ft. 9 in.	1 1/16 in.	½ in.

Working allowance has been made on lengths and widths. Thicknesses net.

If a commercial mattress is being obtained, items C and D are omitted.

KITCHEN CABINET

In the best way this cabinet should be made in Parana pine or one of the plainer reliable hardwoods. For economy it may be necessary to use ordinary Baltic pine, and this is satisfactory if reasonably free from knots. It is assumed that the whole thing will be finished with paint.

The whole thing is made in two carcases, these being fixed together with screws. It is immaterial which is made first, though when the lower one is together it provides a structure on which the other can be placed.

Lower Carcase—Fig. 3 gives the main construction. It will no doubt be necessary to joint two or more pieces together to obtain the width of the ends and bottom, and this should be done first. If good joints are made they need only be rubbed together. Fix the ends together in the relative positions they will occupy, and square them to size. As the job is being painted it will not matter if they are nailed temporarily, though cramps can be used if preferred. Prepare also the two top pieces, bottom, and centre upright. They are narrower than ends by the thickness of the back ($\frac{1}{4}$ in.). Mark out the joints, taking the shoulder length of the centre upright from the dovetail gauge lines on the ends. Drawer rails are stub-tenoned in, and the mortise positions should

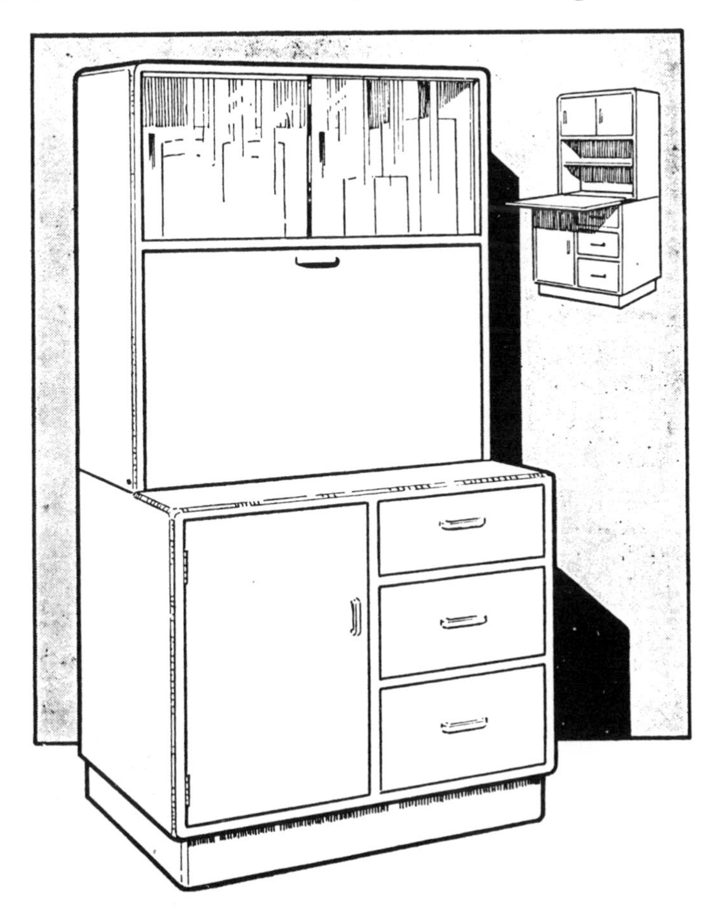

FIG. 1. KITCHEN CABINET WITH GOOD ACCOMMODATION
The internal arrangement could be left to personal requirements. Sizes, too, could be adapted within a little.

be squared across the right-hand end and centre upright, the parts being hand-screwed together temporarily. Note the grooves which are continued back behind the rail mortises. They need be only $\frac{1}{8}$ in. or $\frac{3}{16}$ in. deep.

A rather special spacing of the dovetails at the top is necessary to allow for the hollowed groove in which the fall of the top carcase turns. It is necessary to allow a gap between two dovetails wide enough to contain the groove. The back top is fixed flush with the rebate. For a simpler job the front top could fit in rebates and be nailed in, but it does not make so strong a job.

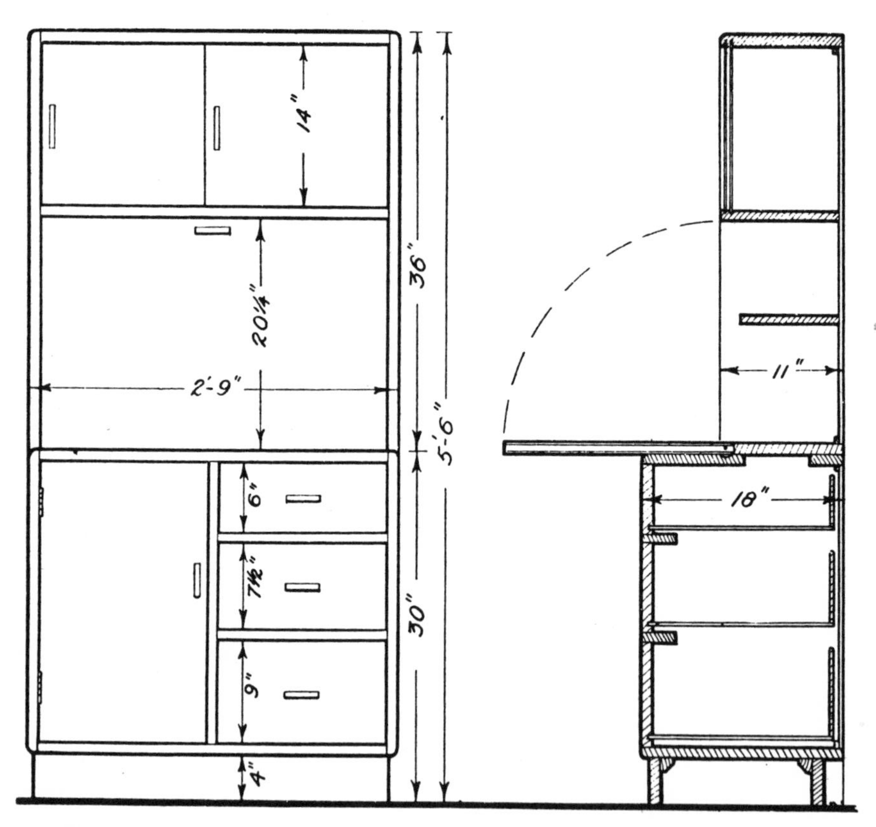

FIG. 2. FRONT ELEVATION WITH SIZES, AND SIDE SECTION

A simple stopped housing is used for the joint between centre upright and top and bottom.

When assembling glue the bottom to the ends and add the centre upright. Pass in the drawer rails (the upright can be pushed over to allow this), and add the two top pieces. Test for squareness and set aside to harden.

Plinth—In the best way the front corners are mitre-dovetailed, but many will no doubt prefer to use a plain mitre and glue-block the inner angles. At the back a slot dovetail is used. Fix the whole thing by pocket-screwing through the plinth into the carcase bottom. At the front the fixing is rigid, but at the sides and back the holes should be made large to allow for movement. In a better way the back and sides could be grooved inside and the whole thing fixed to the carcase with buttons.

Door and Drawers—For the door either a piece of multi-ply or laminated board could be used. It would probably be cheaper, however, to make a simple square-edged frame and glue a sheet of thin ply or hardboard to it. A stop should be fitted to the cabinet along the closing edge.

Drawers are dovetailed in the usual way, and the bottoms are fitted in the special drawer bottom moulding made for the purpose. Either ply or hardboard can be used for the bottoms. Notes on drawer construction appear on p. 128. Runners for the drawers fit in the grooves cut across the ends. At the front they are stub-tenoned into the rails. Glue them at front only, and drive in a screw at the back. The hole should be generous to allow for movement.

Upper Carcase—This again is lap-dovetailed together, and the shelves fit in stopped housings or slot dovetails. The general procedure is much as in the case of the lower carcase, the opposite parts being held together temporarily when being planed to ensure their being alike. Note that the top and upper shelf both finish flush with the ends at the front, whereas the bottom and lower shelf stand in.

A hollow groove is worked along the front edge of the bottom to enable the fall to pivot as shown in Fig. 4. The hollow is of the same section as that in the top of the lower carcase. It is best worked with round moulding plane, but failing this a square channelling will have to be worked to give the clearance. It is not so neat, but it is not seen. Grooves to take the sliding glass doors are also needed in the top and upper shelf. Those in the former are double the depth of the others to enable the glasses to be raised and dropped into the grooves (see Fig. 5). In this way they can be removed at any time by merely raising them and drawing the lower edges forward. When having the glasses made remember to have finger grips ground in them.

Fall—The fall is pivoted with long, stout round-head screws

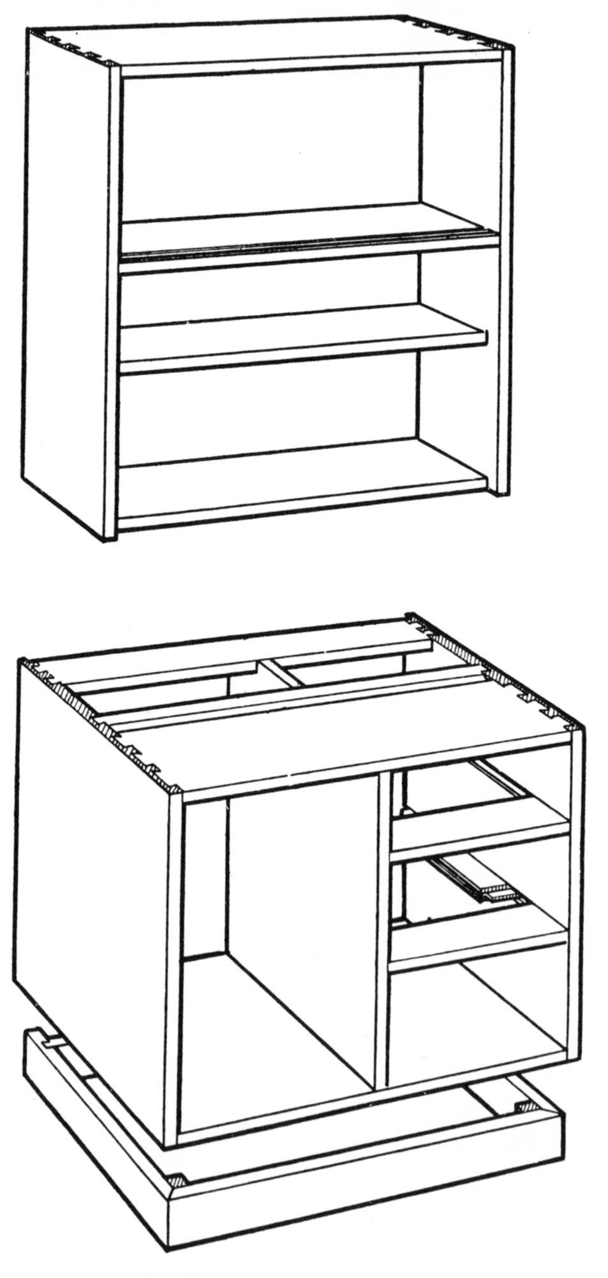

FIG. 3. HOW THE TWO CARCASES ARE MADE

passed through a clearance hole in the cabinet end and made a tight fit in the fall itself. To minimize wear metal sleeves could be fitted to the clearance holes, these being made a fairly tight fit in holes in the cabinet sides. A strong job is essential because the fall is used for pastry making and has to withstand considerable pressure.

Fig. 4 shows how the fall can be made, a framework of ½ in. stuff being halved together, and a sheet of plastic board cemented

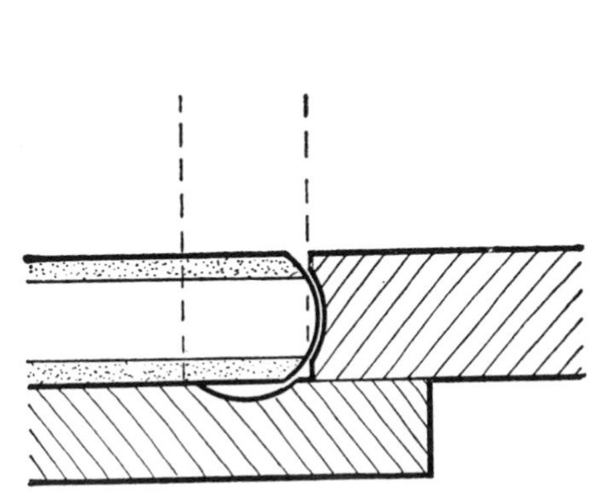

FIG. 4. SECTIONAL VIEW THROUGH FALL

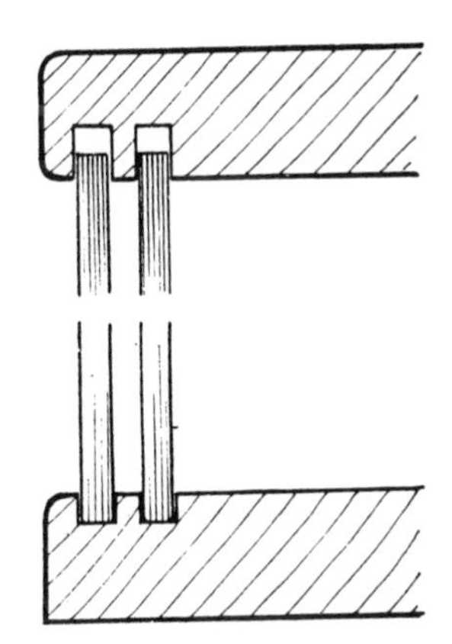

FIG. 5. GLASS DOORS

to the inside, and fibre board to the outside. To prevent any tendency to sag, and to provide good working support at least three cross rails should be fitted to the frame. One of the synthetic resin adhesives is suitable for fixing the plastic board, and there are several special adhesives sold for the purpose.

It will be seen from Figs. 1 and 2 that rounded edges are suggested everywhere. These not only look better but wear better in that there are no sharp corners to be easily battered. Before any paint is applied go over any knots with two coats of knotting with a two-hour interval. Give a coat of priming and when dry fill in all nail holes, gaps, etc., with putty or *Alabastine*. Follow with an undercoat, and lastly the gloss coat. If the undercoat does not leave a really light, even coat it would be advisable to give a second coat. This is specially true of cream paint.

Ball catches are fitted to door and fall, and chromium or wood bar handles.

CUTTING LIST

Lower Carcase	Long	Wide	Thick
2 Ends	2 ft $2\frac{1}{2}$ in.	$18\frac{1}{4}$ in.	$\frac{7}{8}$ in.
1 Upright	2 ft. $1\frac{1}{4}$ in.	18 in.	$\frac{7}{8}$ in.
1 Bottom	2 ft. 9 in.	$18\frac{1}{4}$ in.	$\frac{7}{8}$ in.
1 Top	2 ft. 9 in.	$9\frac{1}{2}$ in.	$\frac{7}{8}$ in.
1 ,,	2 ft. 9 in.	$3\frac{1}{4}$ in.	$\frac{7}{8}$ in.
2 Rails	1 ft. 5 in.	$3\frac{1}{4}$ in.	$\frac{7}{8}$ in.
4 Runners	1 ft. $3\frac{1}{2}$ in.	2 in.	$\frac{7}{8}$ in.
1 Back	2 ft. $0\frac{1}{2}$ in.	32 in.	$\frac{3}{8}$ in. ply
1 Drawer front	1 ft. $3\frac{5}{8}$ in.	$6\frac{1}{4}$ in.	$\frac{7}{8}$ in.
1 ,, ,,	1 ft. $3\frac{5}{8}$ in.	$7\frac{3}{4}$ in.	$\frac{7}{8}$ in.
1 ,, ,,	1 ft. $3\frac{5}{8}$ in.	$9\frac{1}{4}$ in.	$\frac{7}{8}$ in.
2 ,, sides	1 ft. 5 in.	$6\frac{1}{4}$ in.	$\frac{3}{8}$ in.
2 ,, ,,	1 ft. 5 in.	$7\frac{3}{4}$ in.	$\frac{3}{8}$ in.
2 ,, ,,	1 ft. 5 in.	$9\frac{1}{4}$ in.	$\frac{3}{8}$ in.
1 ,, back	1 ft. $3\frac{5}{8}$ in.	$5\frac{3}{4}$ in.	$\frac{3}{8}$ in.
1 ,, ,,	1 ft. $3\frac{5}{8}$ in.	$7\frac{1}{4}$ in.	$\frac{3}{8}$ in.
1 ,, ,,	1 ft. $3\frac{5}{8}$ in.	$8\frac{3}{4}$ in.	$\frac{3}{8}$ in.
3 ,, bottoms	1 ft. $3\frac{1}{2}$ in.	$17\frac{1}{2}$ in.	$\frac{1}{4}$ in. ply
2 Door stiles	2 ft. 2 in.	$3\frac{1}{4}$ in.	$\frac{7}{8}$ in.
2 ,, rails	1 ft. 3 in.	$3\frac{1}{4}$ in.	$\frac{7}{8}$ in.
1 ,, panel	2 ft. 1 in.	$15\frac{5}{8}$ in.	$\frac{1}{4}$ in. ply
2 Plinths	2 ft. 9 in.	$4\frac{1}{4}$ in.	$\frac{7}{8}$ in.
2 ,,	1 ft. 6 in.	$4\frac{1}{4}$ in.	$\frac{7}{8}$ in.

Upper Carcase	Long	Wide	Thick
2 Ends	3 ft. $0\frac{1}{2}$ in.	$11\frac{1}{4}$ in.	$\frac{7}{8}$ in.
1 Top	2 ft. 9 in.	$11\frac{1}{4}$ in.	$\frac{7}{8}$ in.
1 Bottom	2 ft. 9 in.	$10\frac{3}{4}$ in.	$\frac{7}{8}$ in.
1 Shelf	2 ft. 9 in.	11 in.	$\frac{7}{8}$ in.
1 Shelf	2 ft. 9 in.	10 in.	$\frac{3}{4}$ in.
1 Back	2 ft. 11 in.	33 in.	$\frac{3}{8}$ in. ply
2 Fall rails	2 ft. 9 in.	3 in.	$\frac{1}{2}$ in.
5 ,, stiles	1 ft. 9 in.	3 in.	$\frac{1}{2}$ in.
1 ,, panel	2 ft. 8 in.	$20\frac{3}{4}$ in.	$\frac{1}{4}$ in. ply
1 ,, ,,	2 ft. 8 in.	$20\frac{3}{4}$ in.	$\frac{1}{4}$ in. plastic board
2 Glass doors	1 ft. 4 in.	$14\frac{1}{2}$ in.	$\frac{1}{4}$ in. (finished but make to suit actual job).

BENCHES

A firm bench is a necessity to anyone who proposes to do any extent of woodwork. In many ways the plain, simple type is the best in that it is designed solely for the purpose of working at. On the other hand most home craftsmen have to work in limited space, and it becomes desirable to make a bench which will also store tools. Here we have a choice of two ; a simple bench, Fig. 1, and a cabinet bench with drawer and cupboard accommodation, Fig. 3.

SIMPLE BENCH

Essential requirements of a bench are that it is rigid, has a top which is straight and as thick as possible and which can be completely flush when necessary, and is provided with strong vice and planing stop. Size is largely decided by the space available, but the rule is to make it as large as the workshop will allow.

Details—In the bench in Fig. 1 rigidity is ensured by the wide top front rail which is notched over the legs. The top is dependent upon the material available, but assuming that only 1 in. stuff is used its freedom from bending is again helped by the wide front rail. If a thicker top is available it would certainly be better, and the sizes in Fig. 2 could be adapted accordingly.

A well is provided, as this enables everyday tools to be kept on top without fouling wide wood placed on the bench. In addition is a wide shelf for larger tools and appliances, and a tool rack at the back. The bench stop is a block of wood which can be tapped in flush. To help in cutting wood at the rear end of the bench an end stop is provided, this again folding down flush. To support long work when held in the vice a series of ½ in. holes is bored in the right hand leg, a dowel placed in one of these affording a useful resting place.

Framework—For the legs 3 in. by 2 in. stuff is used. Hardwood such as beech, birch, or ash is preferable, but softwood is frequently used with success. Square to section and mark out the joints. The back legs are shorter than those at the front to allow for the tool well, and the top end rails are notched accordingly (Fig. 2).

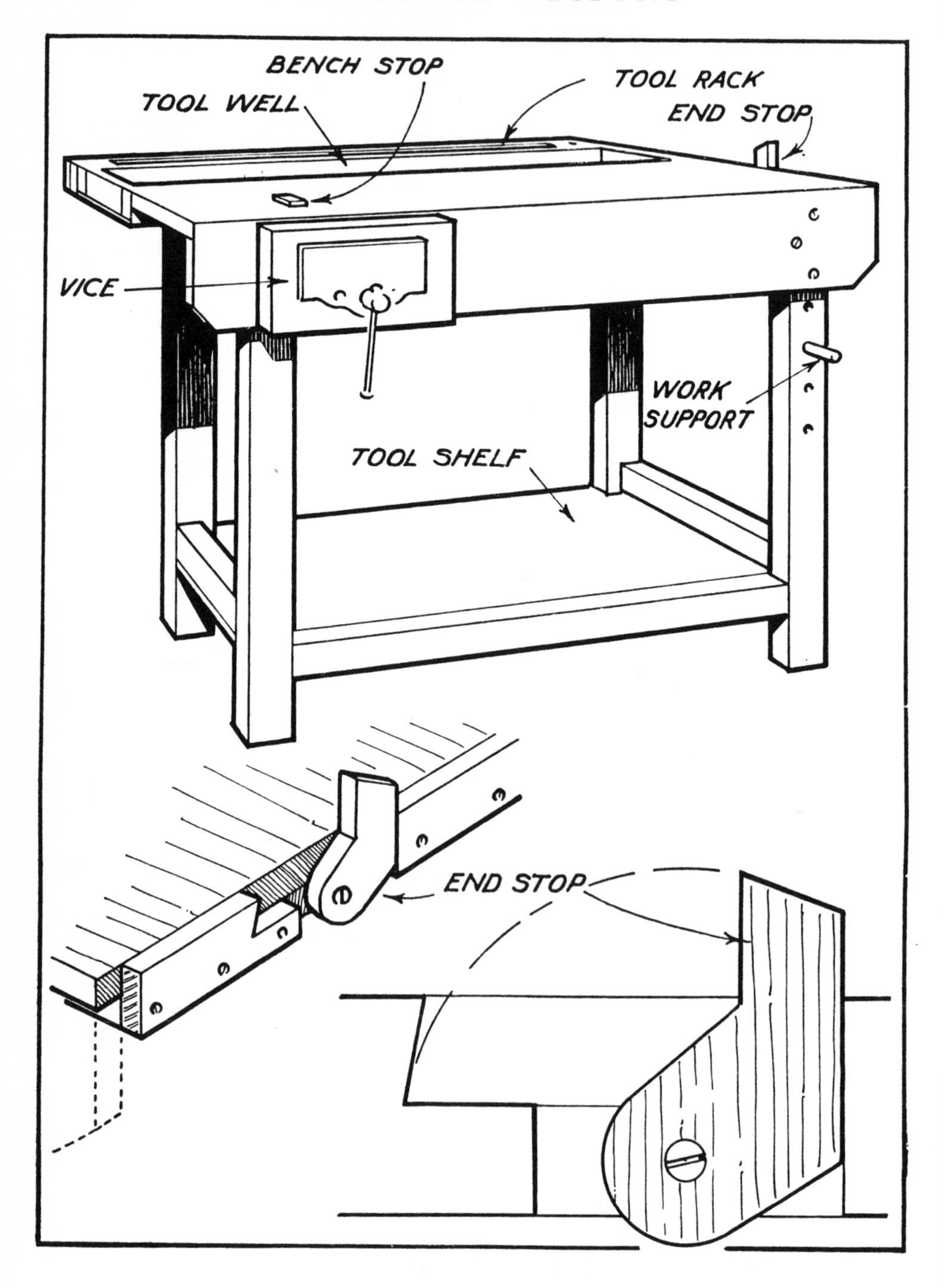
BENCH STOP
TOOL WELL
TOOL RACK
END STOP
VICE
WORK SUPPORT
TOOL SHELF
END STOP

Side rails are tenoned in, those at the top being haunched as in Fig. 2. Bottom and back top rails are also tenoned, and to avoid weakening the wood unduly the bottom rails are staggered, those at front and back being immediately below those at the ends. Top front or apron rail (Fig. 2) is not tenoned but is grooved to fit over the face of the legs. A close-fitting joint is essential here as the chief function of this wide rail is to prevent racking.

Glue the two end frames together independently. It is a good plan to draw-bore them. It not only saves having many cramps, but helps to keep the joints tight. The peg hole is driven through the mortise, the tenon cramped in position, and marked by passing the bit into the hole. The parts are separated and the tenon bored about $\frac{1}{16}$ in. nearer the shoulder. The pegs should be slightly pointed to enable them to enter easily. The parts are glued when assembling, of course.

The glue having set the front and back rails are added, these again being preferably draw-bored. Finally glue and screw on the apron rail.

Top—If possible use a hardwood such as beech for this. A thickness of $\frac{7}{8}$ in. the minimum ; if possible it should be 2 in., in which case the top end and back rails would be cut and positioned to suit. Fix it with screws driven downwards into the front rail, recessing the screws and plugging the holes. At the sides pocket screwing is the simplest method, but the holes should be generous in size to allow for possible movement caused by shrinkage.

The tool tray is like a simple shallow box with edgings nailed or screwed together with a plywood bottom screwed beneath. It is screwed in position, and a tool rack added at the back, this being simply a batten screwed at the back with three distance pieces interposed to enable tools to pass through.

Stops—To receive the bench stop a rectangular hole is cut through the top. The stop itself (of hardwood) is made a tight friction fit in the hole. Fig. 1 shows how the pivoted end stop

FIG. 1. SIMPLE BENCH FOR SMALL HOME WORKSHOP

The length of 4 ft. can be increased if preferred and the cutting list adapted accordingly. Either metal or wood vice could be used.

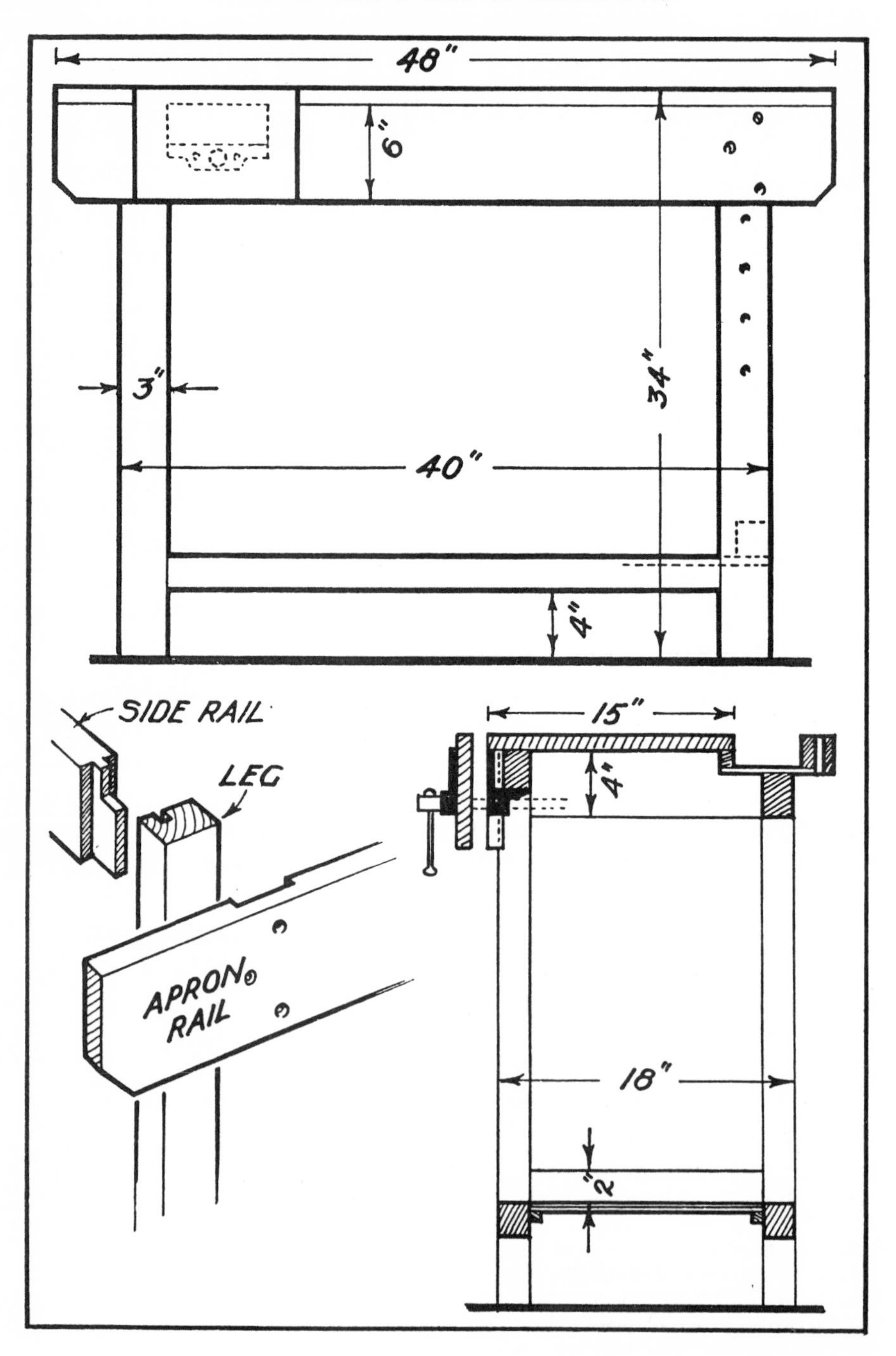
48"
6"
3"
34"
40"
4"
SIDE RAIL
LEG
APRON RAIL
15"
4"
18"
2"

can be added. It is shaped so that it folds down flush when not in use. Hardwood should be used for it, and an edging should be screwed to the end of the bench as shown. It is not an essential feature and can be omitted if preferred, the bench hook being used for all cross cutting.

Vice—This will certainly require a packing block beneath the top, the thickness depending upon the casting of the vice and the thickness of the top. Quite possibly too the apron rail will have to be recessed to take it, and slots may have to be cut—certainly holes to receive the screw and guide bars will be needed. It is impossible to give exact details since the vice casting varies in different makes. A strong rigid fixing is essential, and the face of the vice must be in line with the edge of the bench. In some cases it may be better to fix the casting to the back of the apron rail rather than in front. A wood cheek is screwed to the movable jaw.

The addition of the tool shelf completes the bench. It is screwed beneath the side rails, and fillets are added inside front and back rails to support it as in the side section in Fig. 2.

CUTTING LIST

	Long	Wide	Thick
2 Legs	2 ft. 10 in.	3¼ in.	2 in.
2 ,,	2 ft. 9 in.	3¼ in.	2 in.
1 Apron rail	4 ft. 0½ in.	6¼ in.	⅞ in.
1 Rail	3 ft. 4 in.	3¼ in.	2 in.
2 ,,	3 ft. 4 in.	2¼ in.	2 in.
2 ,,	1 ft. 6 in.	2 in. square finished	
2 ,,	1 ft. 6 in.	4¼ in.	2 in.
1 Top	4 ft. 0½ in.	15¼ in.	⅞ in.
1 Shelf	3 ft. 4½ in.	14½ in.	½ in. ply or chipboard
1 Well bottom	4 ft. 0½ in.	6¼ in.	¼ in. ply
1 Well rail	4 ft. 0½ in.	1 in.	⅞ in.
1 ,, ,,	4 ft. 0½ in.	2 in.	⅞ in.
2 ,, ,,	4½ in.	2 in.	⅞ in.
1 Tool rack	4 ft. 0½ in.	2¼ in.	½ in.

Small parts extra.

FIG. 2. DIMENSIONED FRONT ELEVATION, SIDE SECTION, AND JOINT

The wide apron rail gives rigidity to the top and helps to prevent side racking during planing or sawing.

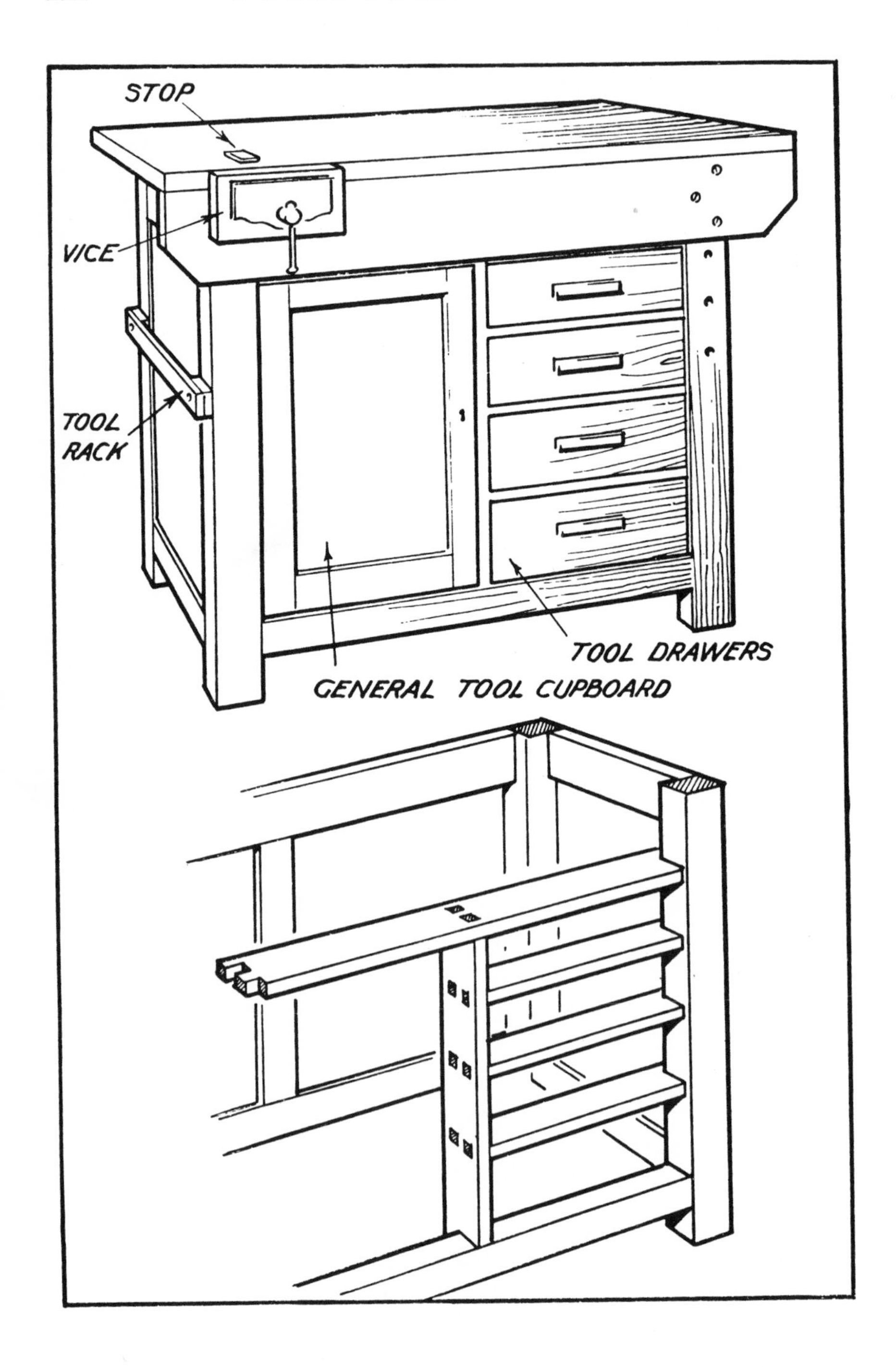
STOP
VICE
TOOL RACK
TOOL DRAWERS
GENERAL TOOL CUPBOARD

CABINET BENCH

In many ways this is the better proposition for the home craftsman in that it provides accommodation for the kit of tools, except the larger items. Construction of the main frame is much the same as the simple bench in Fig 1, but with additional rails, etc., for drawers, door, etc. The length of 42 in. as given in Fig. 4 is rather short, but could be increased if more space in the workshop is available.

Main Framework—Square up the legs and mark out on them the mortise positions. Fig. 3 shows how these are arranged. To ensure that all are marked alike they should be cramped together and the marks square across them all. Preferably the panels of side and back should be grooved into rails and legs, and this will necessitate haunches being cut in the top rail tenons to fill in the ends of the grooves. In a simpler way the panels could be screwed or pinned directly over the rails, in which case no haunches are cut (Fig. 3). The method has to be decided early on since the grooving necessarily cuts away the sides of the tenons, and this has to be allowed for in the mortises.

Note from Fig. 3 how the drawer rails are double-tenoned to the centre upright. This is better than a single tenon in that the rail is more easily kept square. At the legs the rails are necessarily cut away as shown. The top front rail is wide and extends the full length of the top. It is grooved at the back to fit over the legs and is screwed. Its width helps to prevent the top from bending in use, the grooves help to prevent side racking.

As there are several rails at the front, it is advisable to put this and the back together independently first. If the back panels are grooved in remember to insert them during the assembling. It makes a rather stronger job if the main tenons are draw-bored as described for the bench in Fig. 1. When completed add the side rails and panels, testing for squareness in both plan and elevation. Finally add the front top rail, gluing and screwing it.

FIG. 3. CABINET TYPE BENCH WITH ACCOMMODATION FOR TOOLS

This is an advantage in the small workshop as the space of separate tool cupboard or chest is saved.

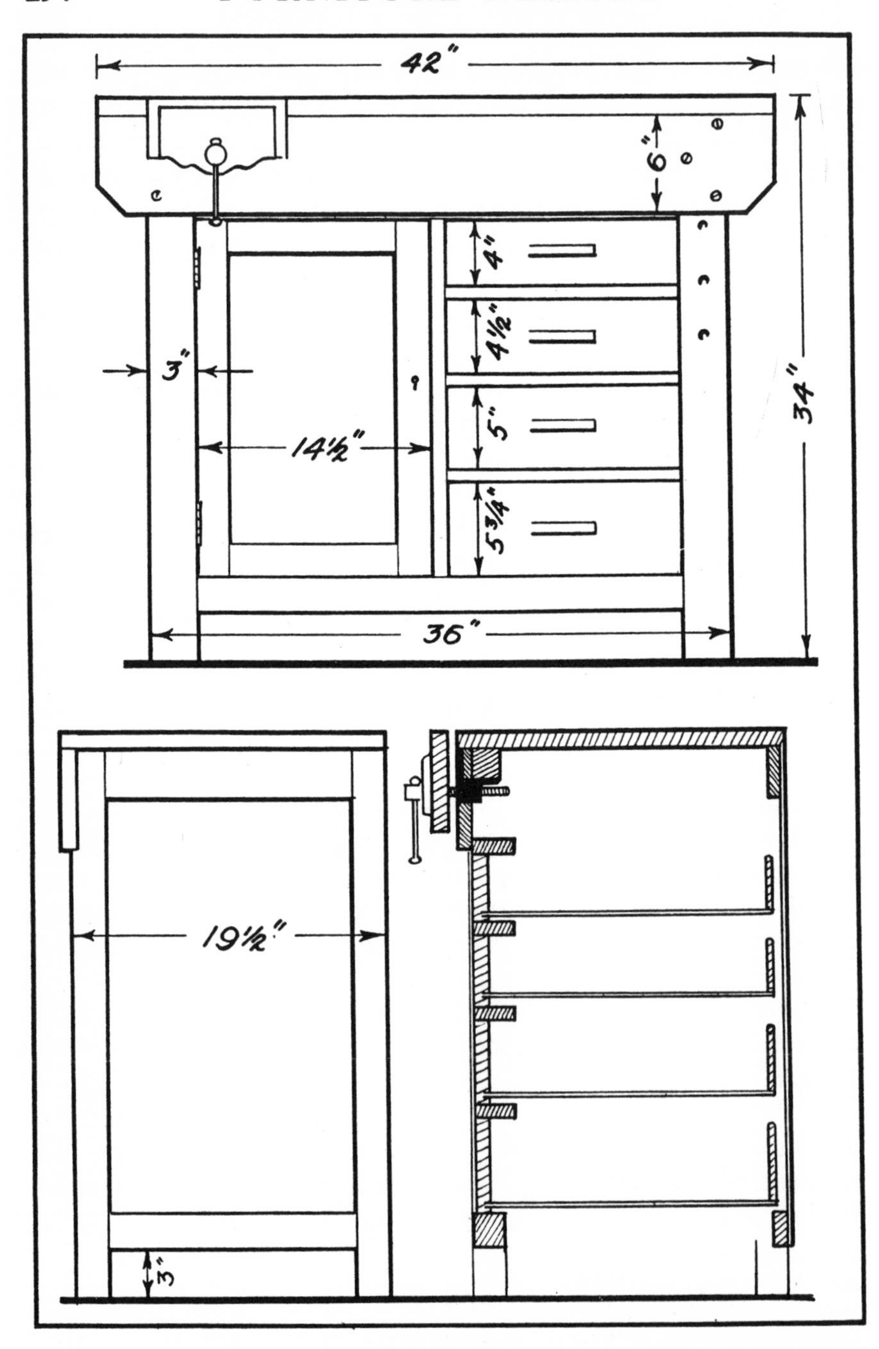

FIG. 4. ELEVATIONS AND SECTION OF CABINET BENCH WITH SIZES

Interior Fitting—Runners are obviously needed, and these are stub-tenoned at the front into the rails. At the back they are notched to fit around the back legs and are screwed. A similar idea is followed at the middle, except that they are either fitted into notches cut in the centre upright, or are kept the right distance apart by ⅞ in. blocks. These are cut to length to equal the various drawer heights and are screwed or glued and pinned to the back upright.

A plywood partition is fitted to the left-hand side of the centre upright, being pinned in position. A plywood bottom is cut to

[*Continued on next page*

CUTTING LIST

	Long	Wide	Thick
4 Legs	2 ft. 10 in.	3¼ in.	2 in.
1 Top rail	3 ft. 6½ in.	6¼ in.	⅞ in.
1 Rail	3 ft. 0 in.	2 in. square finished	
1 ,,	3 ft. 0 in.	3½ in.	⅞ in.
1 ,,	3 ft. 0 in.	2¼ in.	⅞ in.
2 ,,	1 ft. 7 in.	3¼ in.	⅞ in.
2 ,,	1 ft. 7 in.	2¼ in.	⅞ in.
1 Top	3 ft. 6½ in.	20½ in.	1¼ in. (⅞ in. min.)
1 Back	2 ft. 7 in.	32½ in.	¼ in. ply
1 Upright	2 ft. 7 in.	3¼ in.	⅞ in.
1 Bottom	1 ft. 5 in.	19 in.	¼ in. ply
1 Partition	2 ft. 3 in.	18¾ in.	¼ in. ,,
1 Upright	2 ft. 1½ in.	2¾ in.	⅞ in.
1 Drawer rail	2 ft. 10 in.	2¾ in.	⅞ in.
3 ,, ,,	1 ft. 5 in.	2¾ in.	⅞ in.
1 ,, front	1 ft. 3 in.	4¼ in.	⅞ in.
1 ,, ,,	1 ft. 3 in.	4¾ in.	⅞ in.
1 ,, ,,	1 ft. 3 in.	5¼ in.	⅞ in.
1 ,, ,,	1 ft. 3 in.	6 in.	⅞ in.
1 ,, back	1 ft. 3 in.	3¾ in.	⅜ in.
1 ,, ,,	1 ft. 3 in.	4¼ in.	⅜ in.
1 ,, ,,	1 ft. 3 in.	4¾ in.	⅜ in.
1 ,, ,,	1 ft. 3 in.	5½ in.	⅜ in.
2 ,, sides	1 ft. 7 in.	4¼ in.	⅜ in.
2 ,, ,,	1 ft. 7 in.	4¾ in.	⅜ in.
2 ,, ,,	1 ft. 7 in.	5¼ in.	⅜ in.
2 ,, ,,	1 ft. 7 in.	6 in.	⅜ in.
4 ,, bottoms	1 ft. 2 in.	18½ in.	$\frac{3}{16}$ in. ply
2 Door stiles	2 ft. 0 in.	2¼ in.	⅞ in.
2 ,, rails	1 ft. 2½ in.	2¼ in.	⅞ in.
1 ,, panel	1 ft. 8 in.	11½ in.	¼ in. ply

fit on the bottom rails, the centre edge being supported by a wood fillet glued and pinned to the partition. Normal drawer construction is followed (see p. 128), and much the same applies to the door (p. 111).

Top—The top should be of hardwood and as thick as possible —$\frac{7}{8}$ in. is a minimum. It is screwed to the front rail, either by pocket screwing through the latter, or is held with recessed screws driven through the top, the holes being pelleted. At sides and rear it will either have to be held with buttons in which case the rails must be grooved inside before assembling, or pocket screwing again can be used, the clearance holes being large enough to allow for certain amount of movement.

A metal vice is fitted, and it will probably be necessary to fit a packing piece to take the main casting. The top rail too will have to be cut to take the casting, though in some cases it may be possible to fit the latter to the inside of the rail. Note the wood cheek fitted to the movable jaw of the vice. A wood stop passes through a hole cut in the top, being held by friction.

SECTION IV.

GARDEN WOODWORK

GREENHOUSE

THE greenhouse in Fig. 1 is sectional, and can be moved to a fresh site. Sizes could be adapted within a little to suit whatever may be required, but it is advisable to keep to the same bar spacing which gives 12⅛ in. rebate size, this enabling a 12-in. width of glass to be used.

There are two ways of setting about this job. One is to use square stuff and rebate and mould it as required. The other is to use the standard ready-machined sections which are normally

FIG. 1. ATTRACTIVE GREENHOUSE FOR THE SMALL GARDEN, ABOUT 10 FT. BY 7 FT.

As softwoods are free from control, readers should have no difficulty about making this. Sizes could be adapted within a little if required, but bar spacing should allow for 12-in. pane widths.

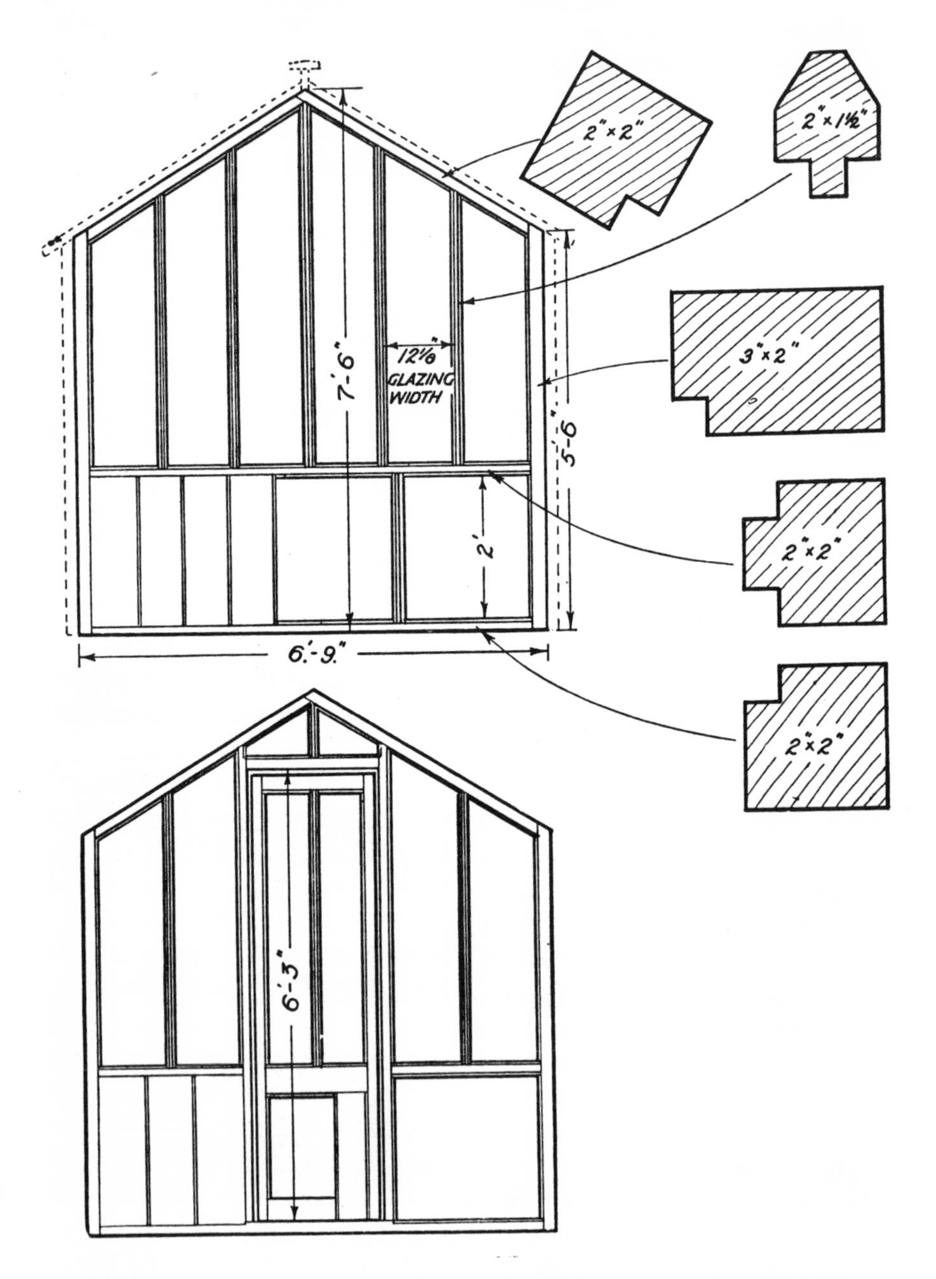

FIG. 2. MAIN SIZES OF THE TWO ENDS AND THE SECTIONS OF TIMBER USED

available. In Fig. 1 some of each have been used, the main members being square-edged stuff rebated where necessary, and the bars ready-machined. The procedure varies to an extent since it is usual to do all jointing before rebating and moulding are carried out, whereas with ready-machined stuff the jointing is obviously done afterwards.

Plain End—The apex ends are contained between the long sides, and are made to the sizes in Fig. 2. The uprights are of 3 in. by 2 in. stuff with single through rebate. Bottom rail and sloping rails are 2 in. by 2 in. also single through rebated, whilst the centre rail of 2 in. by 2 in. is double rebated. Both horizontal rails are tenoned into the uprights with long-and-short shoulders, the joints being similar to those in Fig. 4. For the bottom rail it is advisable to cut a haunch. A form of bridle joint is used where the sloping rails meet each other as in Fig. 5, and a similar joint is used where they meet the uprights. Note that the shoulders are unequal since the front one has to reach into the rebate.

Between the mid and bottom rails are two intermediate uprights, 2 in. by 2 in. They are double-rebated, and are tenoned in, the front shoulders being ½ in. longer than those at the back to enable them to reach into the rebate. This arrangement enables the matchboarding to be fitted into rebates all round.

The glazing bars are 2 in. by 1½ in. and are usually obtained ready made. Fig. 2 shows the section, though the inner sides could be moulded rather than chamfered if preferred. They are tenoned into the rails, the top tenons having both shoulders and ends cut at an angle as in Fig. 5.

In a simple way the mortise positions on the sloping rails can be marked out after the frames have been assembled temporarily. The bar positions are marked on the horizontal centre rails, and a straight-edge laid across the job level with each mark in turn. By keeping the straight-edge parallel with the uprights it is a simple matter to mark the sloping rails. The pencil should be drawn right across the outside of the rails as this gives the slope at which the mortise has to be chopped.

Door End—This is similar but two uprights are inserted to make provision for the door. These are rebated at their outer edges only, though two very short rebates are cut later with the chisel at the extreme top for the two small panes above the door.

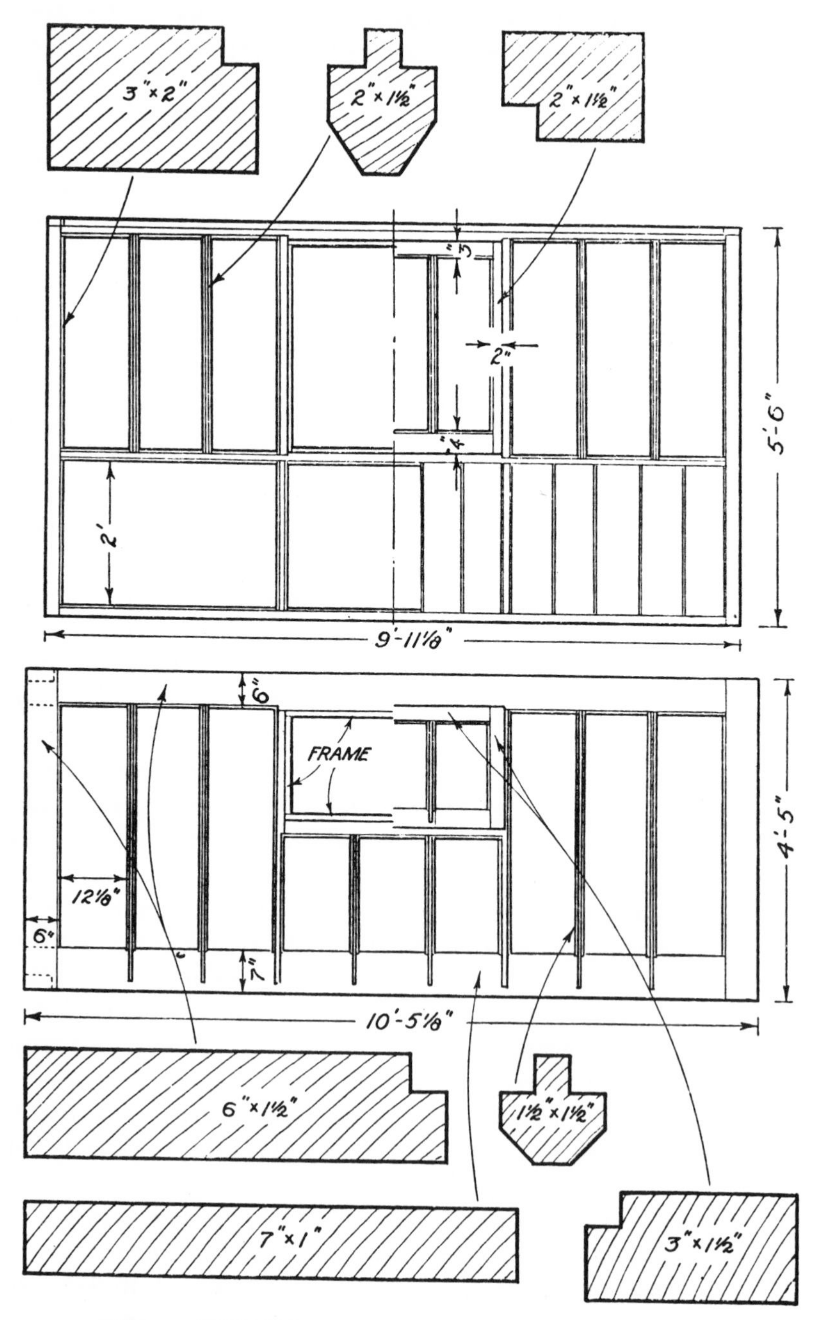

FIG. 3. DETAILS OF SIDES (top), AND ROOF (below)

One other slight difference compared with the plain end is that the bottom rail has its rebate stopped at the centre where the door occurs. The door posts are tenoned into the sloping rails similarly to the bars (Fig. 5). For preference they should be taken right through and wedged.

Sides—Details of these are given in Fig. 3 (top). The 3 in. by 2 in. outer uprights are through rebated. Intermediate uprights are in two pieces, the top one being rebated at one edge only. Of the horizontal rails the top one (3 in. by 2 in.) is rebated at the underside at the sides only, the centre window portion being left square. After jointing it is bevelled to allow for the slope of the roof. The centre rail is through rebated at the underside, the top being stopped similarly to the top rail. The bottom rail is through rebated at the top edge only. Fig. 4 gives details of the joints. The tenons are taken right through and are wedged.

Roof—Fig. 3 (below) shows this. The top rail is of the same section as the ends, and is rebated similarly except that the rebate is stopped at the middle where the skylight occurs. It will be noted that the bottom rail is thinner by the depth of the rebate, and this necessitates the use of bare-faced tenons. Both this and the top joint are similar to those used in the skylight frame, these being shown exploded in Fig. 6. The thin bottom rail is necessary because the glass passes right over it, thus avoiding trapping water.

To allow water from condensation to escape the bottom rail can be thinned to leave a gap between it and glass, or tapered grooves can be cut across the rail.

There are two rails of 2 in. by 1½ in. section, one each side of the skylight, these being tenoned in at the top, whilst at the bottom a sort of notched joint is cut. Again this is similar to the bar joints of the skylight shown in Fig. 6. Note that the inner rebates are stopped where the skylight occurs. Into the opening a lining is nailed as shown.

Assembling—All parts should be put together with thick paint. Assemble each frame independently on the ground, preferably on a couple of stout battens. Test for squareness by using a diagonal strip. Test also to see that the frames are free from winding.

As the sections will probably have to stand in the open it is advisable to give a coat of priming as soon as possible. Remember to do the rebates as otherwise the putty is liable to come away.

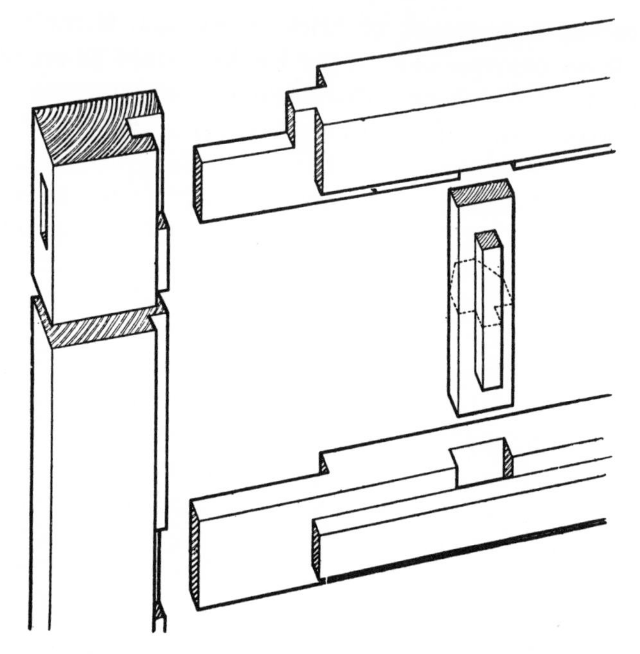

FIG. 4. JOINTS USED IN SIDE FRAMES

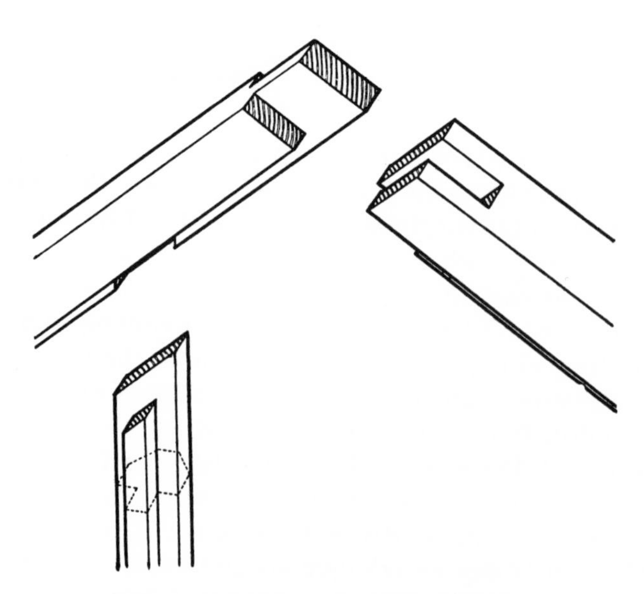

FIG. 5. DETAILS OF END FRAMES

A footing of concrete or of brick is essential if rot is to be avoided. If no concrete is used the bricks should be set on firm, undug soil to avoid sinking. Place two adjacent sections together and hold with a cramp. Bore for bolts and enter the latter, tightening the nuts over washers. Add the remaining sections, and fit a ridge board. To do this the extreme point of the apex can be taken off, and the ridge board notched over it. A capping piece chamfered at each side and with weather grooves beneath is nailed down on top.

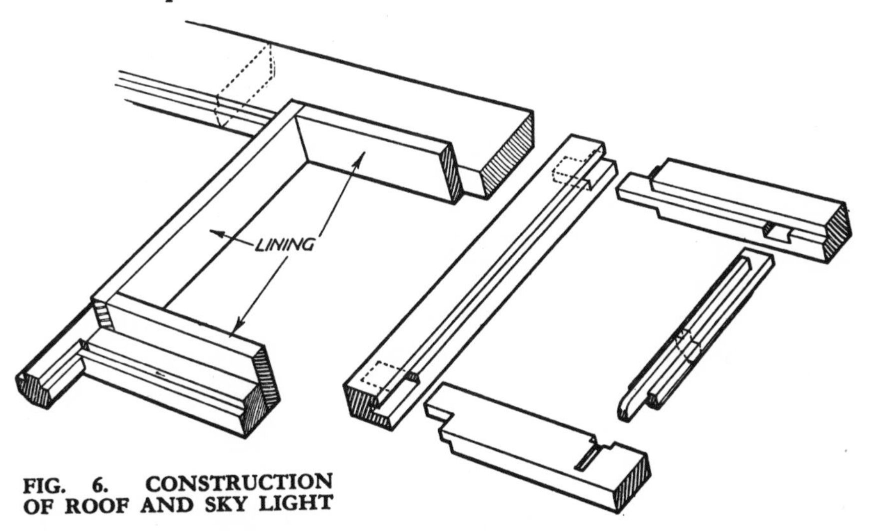

FIG. 6. CONSTRUCTION OF ROOF AND SKY LIGHT

Bevel the upper edges of the roofs to fit up to the ridge board and hold in position with a couple of cramps. Fix with a few screws driven upwards through the side and end frames, and also screw into the ridge board.

Skylight construction is given in Fig. 6. Windows are plain rebated frames with bars set to align with the roofing bars. Hinge at the top, and add weather strips all round at the inside to form a rebate. It is more satisfactory if the mid rail is bevelled locally and the window frame made to correspond.

Glazing and Painting—The wood being primed, putty all holes and cracks, and finish the glazing, setting the glass in a bed of putty and finishing neatly with a bevel. As soon as it is reasonably firm (a day or so) give an undercoat followed by the finishing coat.

Approximate Quantities—The following is roughly what is needed, but the exact feetage must be calculated in accordance with the lengths available. Some lengths will cut up more economically than others.

CUTTING LIST

Long	Wide	Thick
50 ft.	3 in.	2 in.
140 ft.	2 in.	2 in.
46 ft.	6 in.	1½ in.
45 ft.	3 in.	1½ in.
40 ft.	2 in.	1½ in.
22 ft.	7 in.	1 in.
30 ft.	4 in.	1 in.
85 ft.	2 in.	1½ in. bars
60 ft.	1½ in.	1½ in. bars
100 ft. run	8 in.	½ in. T.G.

GARDEN LIGHTS

The light can either be made single as in Fig. 1, or a two-frame light can be arranged as in Fig. 2. Sizes can be adapted within a little, but it is wise to keep to the 12⅛ in. between the rebates as

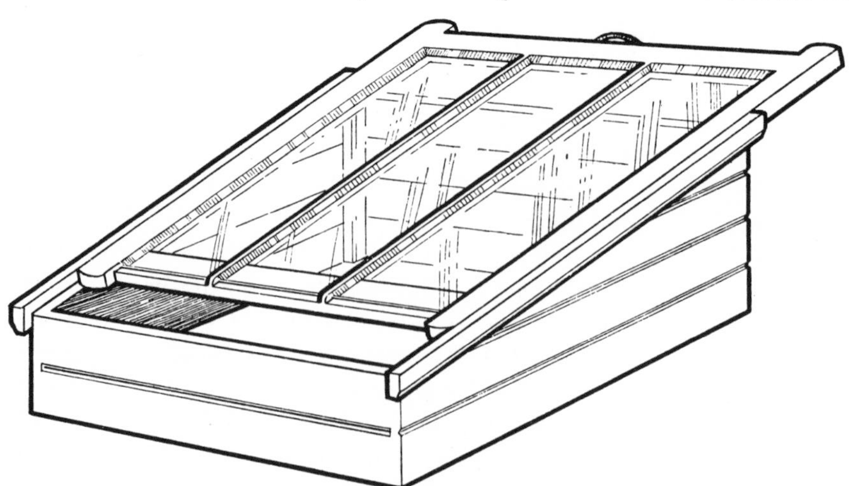

FIG. 1. LIGHT WITH SLIDING GLASS FRAME. STANDARD SIZE GLASS IS USED

If preferred the double-frame light could be made, as in Fig. 2.

this enables the standard 12 in. width of glass to be used. Sometimes the glasses are arranged two or three to an opening, in which case an overlap should be allowed.

Body Portion—Construction is given in Fig. 2, sizes being made to suit the frame. Tongued-and-grooved boarding is used, and it is as well to arrange height so that an even number of boards is used front and back, allowing for the unwanted tongues or grooves to be planed away. Put the front and back together independently, screwing corner posts flush with the ends and (in the case of the double light) cross pieces at the centre. It is advisable to paint all joining edges before fixing.

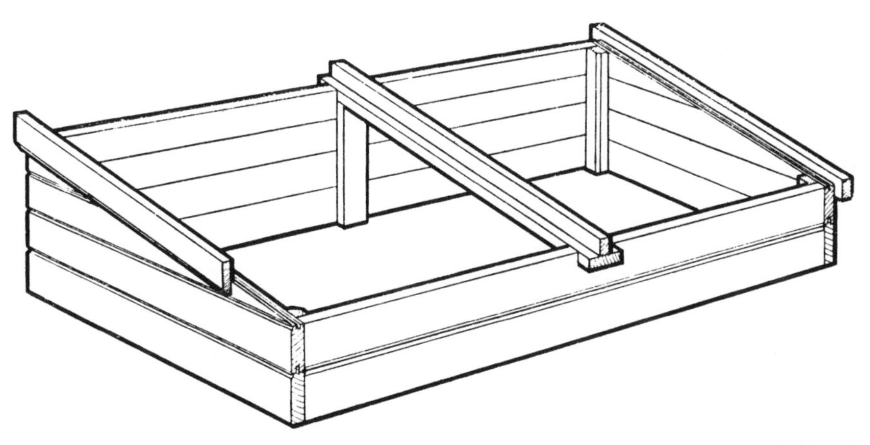

FIG. 2. BODY CONSTRUCTION FOR LIGHT WITH TWO SLIDING FRAMES

The ends are added to these, the two bottom complete boards being fixed first. Place the two top boards in position above them, mark a line across with a straight-edge to give the slope, and cut away the unwanted parts. Screw the sides through the posts at the back, and add the guide pieces. The last named stiffen the whole, though centre uprights can be added if there appears to be any weakness. It is advisable to cut draining grooves along the top sloping edges of the sides. For the two-light frame an inverted *T* section is made by nailing or screwing two pieces together as in Fig. 2. Notches are cut in front and back to receive it. Punch in all nails as the work proceeds. The holes are not stopped, however, until after the priming coat has been given.

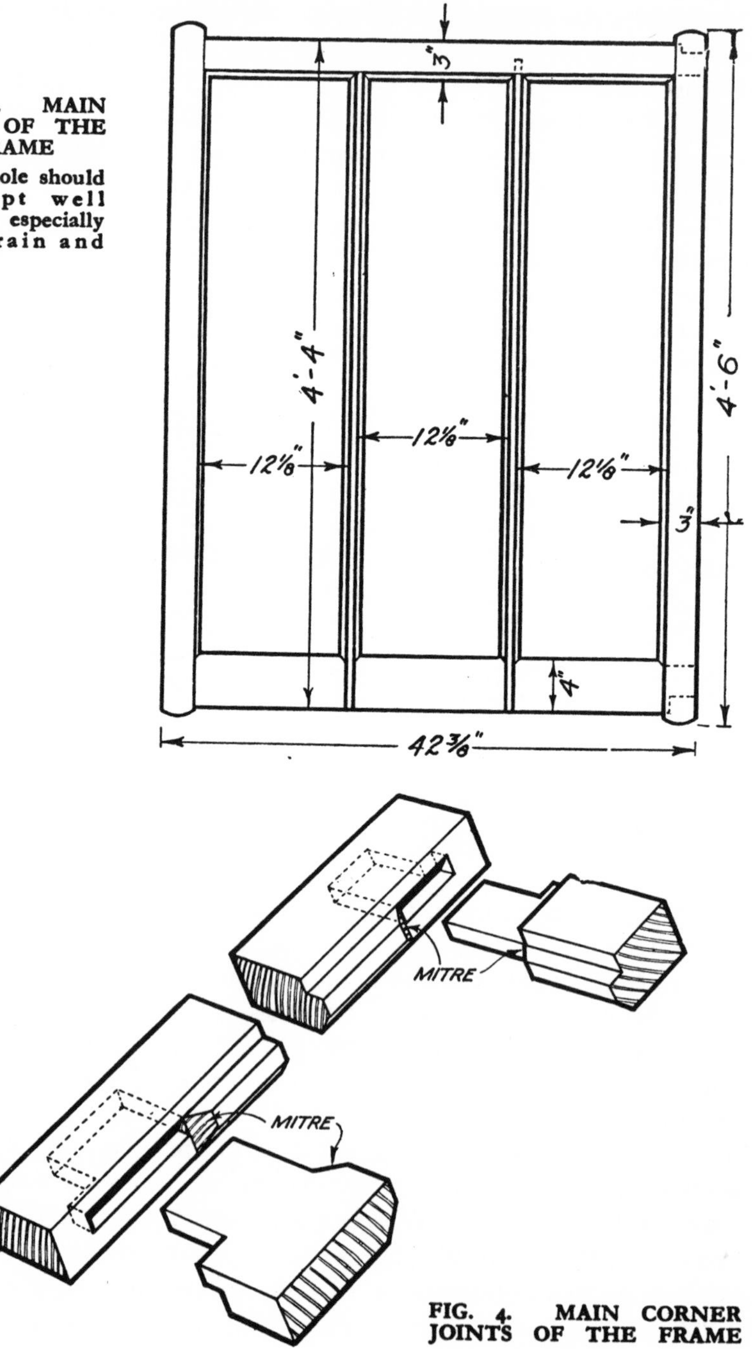

FIG. 3. MAIN SIZES OF THE FRAME

The whole should be kept well painted, especially end grain and joints.

FIG. 4. MAIN CORNER JOINTS OF THE FRAME

Frame—Sizes are given in Fig. 3. If preferred standard section timber can be used, especially in the case of the bars. If this is done it may be necessary to adapt the sizes to suit. Joints of the main frame are given in Fig. 4, and it will be seen that the bottom rail is thinner than the others since the glass has to lie over it. Consequently a bare-faced tenon is needed. A haunch is cut at the lower end as shown. Note that in all the joints mitres are cut and the wood cut away locally opposite the mortise level with the rebate. The advantage of this is that it enables level shoulders to be cut. In all cases the tenons are taken right through and are wedged from outside.

Fig. 5 shows how the bars are joined to the frame. At the lower end a notch is cut in the rail to receive the projecting portion, and mitres are cut as before. It is advisable to work a drip groove along the underside of the upper rail to prevent moisture from running down inside. Assemble the whole thing with thick paint or resin glue if preferred. The main tenons of the frame are wedged from outside.

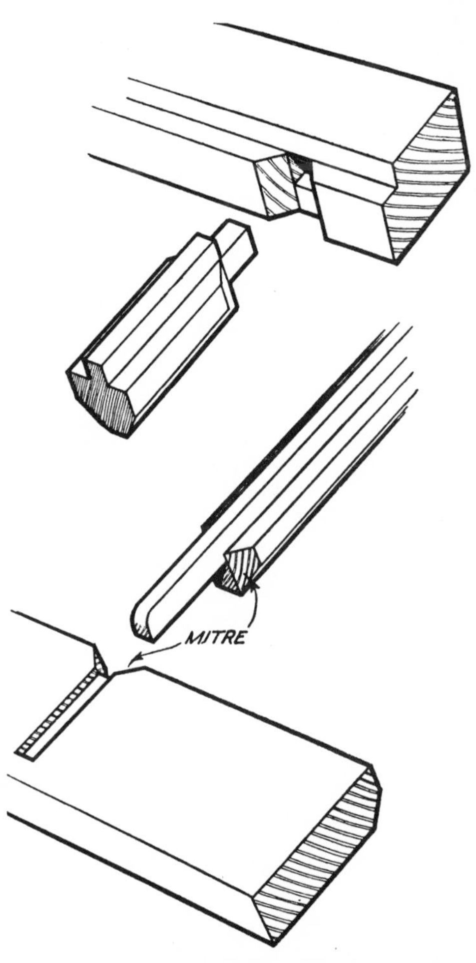

FIG. 5. JOINTS OF THE BARS TO FRAME

Having levelled the joints go over any knots with knotting. Give the whole a coat of priming including all rebates, and when dry fill in all nail holes, cracks, etc., with putty and carry on with the glazing. Thumb a fillet of putty into the rebate and press in the glass so that it beds evenly, and work an even filling of putty all round. Finish with an undercoat followed by a finishing coat, and keep well painted, paying special attention to end grain, corners, etc. It increases the life of the light if it rests upon a row of bricks all round, or a fillet of cement.

CUTTING LISTS

Single Light

Body	Long	Wide	Thick
6 Pieces	3 ft. 6 in.	6 in.	⅞ in. T. & G.
8 ,,	4 ft. 6 in.	6 in.	⅞ in. T. & G.
2 Posts	2 ft. 1 in.	2 in.	2 in.
2 ,,	1 ft. 1 in.	2 in.	2 in.
2 Guides	4 ft. 7 in.	4¼ in.	⅞ in.
Frame			
2 Stiles	4 ft. 7 in.	3¼ in.	2 in.
1 Rail	3 ft. 7 in.	3¼ in.	2 in.
1 ,,	3 ft. 7 in.	4¼ in.	1½ in.
2 Bars	4 ft. 6 in.	1¾ in.	2 in.

Double Light

Body			
6 Pieces	7 ft. 2 in.	6 in.	⅞ in. T. & G.
8 ,,	4 ft. 6 in.	6 in.	⅞ in. T. & G.
2 Posts	2 ft. 1 in.	2 in.	2 in.
2 ,,	1 ft. 1 in.	2 in.	2 in.
2 Guides	4 ft. 7 in.	4¼ in.	⅞ in.
1 T Piece	4 ft. 7 in.	3¼ in.	⅞ in.
1 ,,	4 ft. 7 in.	2¼ in.	⅞ in.

Frames. As single light but double quantities.

GARDEN WORKSHOP

The shed in Fig. 1 is made in sections to be bolted together. The sizes are given in Fig. 2, but these could be adapted within a little to suit any special requirements.

Framework—For the main framework 2 in. by 1½ in. stuff is used, though 2-in. squares would make a more rigid structure. Cut off the various members to length, and fit the uprights into the horizontals with notched joints. This is stronger than plain butted joints since the notches resist side thrust. Test for squareness with a diagonal rod, and fit the sloping struts.

Covering—The boarding should be from $\frac{1}{2}$ in. to $\frac{7}{8}$ in. thick. For thin stuff the rebated joint shown in Fig. 4 is effective. Thicker boards could be tongued and grooved. Cut off the boards

FIG. 1. SECTIONAL WORKSHOP WITH TIMBER FRAME AND BOARDING

Well-painted timber is a good insulation against climatic conditions, especially if the shed can be lined. Softwood is perfectly satisfactory.

full to allow a plane to be run along after fixing. The boarding of the short gable ends finishes flush at the ends, but that of the long sections projects by an amount equal to the thickness of the framing (see enlarged section in Fig. 2). The fixing of the boarding to finish flush is obvious, but for the long sides it is advisable to have an odd piece of the framing material handy to use as a guide for the projection at the end. Nail to the framework and punch the nails in straightway.

At the window openings the boarding at the sides finishes at

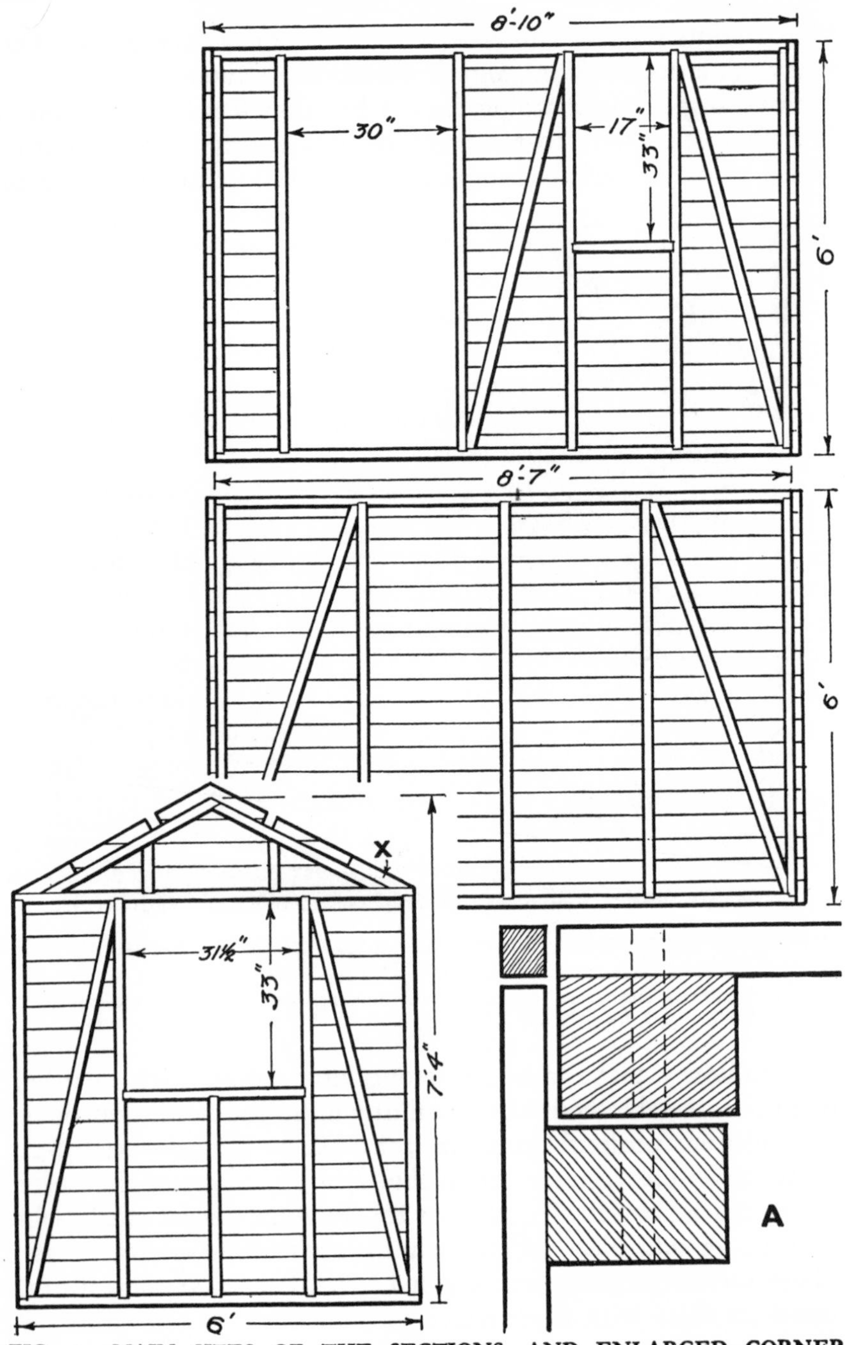

FIG. 2. MAIN SIZES OF THE SECTIONS, AND ENLARGED CORNER SECTION (A)

the middle of the upright framework member (see Fig. 4). This enables the square fillet (B) to be nailed in afterwards. At top and bottom of the window opening the boarding finishes flush, and it may be necessary to trim the boards back locally. At the bottom a sill with sloping edge and drip groove is cut in and nailed on (Fig. 4), and at top a similar member is fixed. Finally the fillets (A) are nailed all round to make the windows weather-proof. They are set back by the thickness of the window frames.

At the door aperture the boarding finishes at the middle of the uprights similarly to the windows. This allows finishing fillets to be nailed on. To make the door weather-proof fillets are nailed around the opening. The boarding of the door stands in front of the bottom rail of the framework.

Floor—The side frames having been put together the floor should be made. Tongued and grooved $\frac{3}{4}$ in. or $\frac{7}{8}$ in. boards are desirable. They are nailed down on to five joists at least 2 in. square in section. It would make a stronger job to have 3 in. by 2 in. stuff. If a concrete base is to be laid the floor can rest directly on it. Otherwise a number of brick piers should be used to keep the timber away from the ground. Every joist should be supported at both ends, and preferably at the centre also.

Dig holes for the bricks and consolidate by tamping. Make all as level as possible, using a long straight-edge and spirit level. Lay the floor in position, and erect the sides. Later it may be necessary to carry out some adjustment of the level, and a convenient method is to make pairs of folding wedges in oak and drive these between the joists and bricks at any point where the floor sags. If you stoop down level with the floor and look along, any sag will be at once obvious.

Erecting—Put two adjacent sections together, knock in a couple of temporary nails, and bore two holes right through to receive the bolts. These should be $\frac{5}{16}$ in. or $\frac{3}{8}$ in. round-heads with square shoulders. Oil the threads, and put washers beneath the nuts.

When all four sections are together the top boarding of the long sides can be bevelled to align with the slope of the ends. Note also that blocks (X) in Fig. 2 are nailed in on the sloping ends. They serve to strengthen the gable end. The outer corners of the shed are filled with fillets nailed in. Fix them to one side or the other, not both.

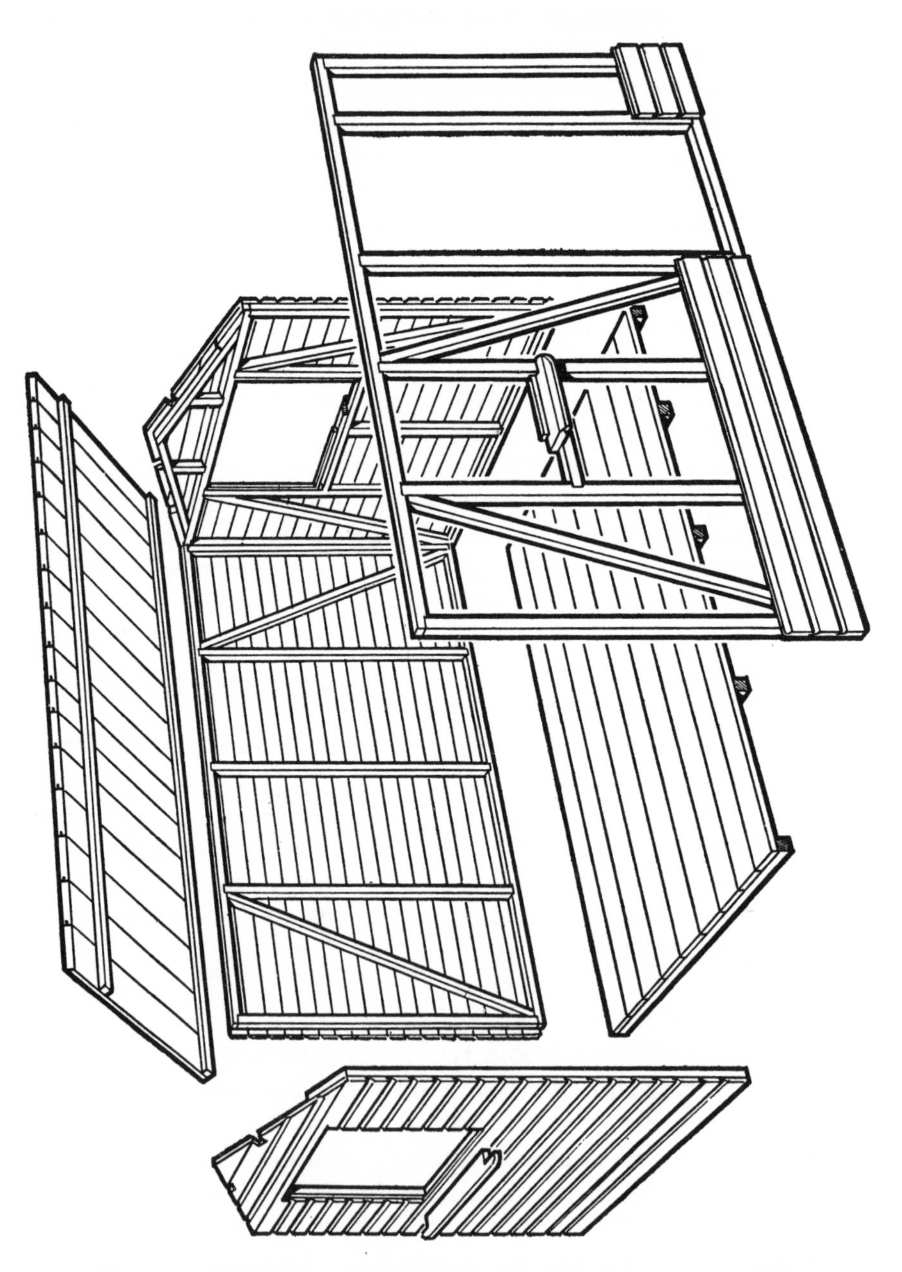

FIG. 3. EXPLODED VIEW SHOWING THE SEPARATE SECTIONS

Roof—One section of this is shown in Fig. 3. It consists of a series of ½ in. tongued boards nailed to two purlins. Cut all the boards to length and nail the whole together. The ridge edge is planed at an angle so that a mitre is formed when the two sections are in position. To receive the upper purlin a notch has to be cut in both gable ends. This is essential because, apart from making a close fit, the notch serves to hold the purlin rigidly. The two roof sections should just drop into position.

To hold the roof down screws can be driven upwards through the sloping framing rails of the gable ends into the purlins. Also two battens are fixed to the lower side of the roof with screws driven from the outside. These battens should be level with the inside of the framework. Screws driven through them into the latter hold the roof firmly. When it is not intended that the shed shall ever be dismantled the whole roof can be nailed down.

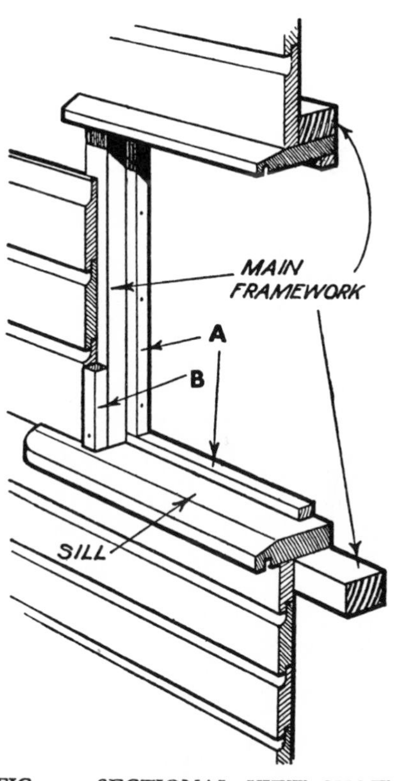

FIG. 4. SECTIONAL VIEW SHOWING WINDOW DETAIL

Three strips of roofing felt run along the length. Allow overlap for it to be turned under all round, and fix the two lower strips first. Hold in position temporarily with a couple of tacks each, and lay the centre strip which will lie right over the apex and overlap those below by several inches. Tack along the bottom edge using galvanized roofing nails.

The addition of barge boards nailed on at the ends completes the roof.

Windows—These are best made from standard sash material put together with the usual wedged mortise and tenon joint as in Fig. 5. The double windows can both be hinged, or one can be made a close fit and nailed in position. The centre join is made weather-proof by rebating the joining edges and inserting a bead in the moving frame. The glass is puttied in, but the rebate must be primed before the putty is applied.

Door—In the simplest way this can be the simple ledged and braced type shown in Fig. 5. Note that the ledges stand in at the edges so that they clear the framework.

FIG. 5. LEDGED AND BRACED DOOR, AND WINDOW ELEVATION WITH JOINT USED

Painting—Three coats of paint are needed, priming, undercoat, and gloss coat. The former should be given before any of the nail holes, etc., are filled with putty. The first step, however, is to go over all knots with two coats of knotting with a drying period of at least half an hour between.

CUTTING LIST

The covering boards will have to be varied in accordance with the width of material available.

Gable Ends	Long	Wide	Thick
12 Uprights and struts	6 ft. 0 in.	2 in.	1½ in.
4 Horizontals	6 ft. 2 in.	2 in.	1½ in.
2 Uprights	3 ft. 2 in.	2 in.	1½ in.
4 Roof rails	3 ft. 2 in.	2 in.	1½ in.
4 Uprights	1 ft. 0 in.	2 in.	1½ in.
2 Window rails	2 ft. 10 in.	2 in.	1½ in.
Long Sides			
15 Uprights and struts	6 ft. 0 in.	2 in.	1½ in.
4 Horizontals	8 ft. 10 in.	2 in.	1½ in.
1 Window rail	1 ft. 7 in.	2 in.	1½ in.

About 500-ft. run of 4 in. (sight) by ½ in. to ⅞ in. rebated or T. & G. boarding for covering all four sides. This should be in lengths which will cut economically into 8 ft. 10 in. and 6 ft. lengths.

Door			
6 Pieces	6 ft. 1 in.	5½ in. (sight)	⅞ in.
3 Ledges	2 ft. 6 in.	4 in.	⅞ in.
2 Braces	3 ft. 7 in.	4 in.	⅞ in.
Windows			
4 Sills and drips	3 ft. 0 in.	4½ in.	⅞ in.
2 " " "	1 ft. 10 in.	4½ in.	⅞ in.
10 Stiles	3 ft. 0 in.	sash mould	
8 Rails	1 ft. 4 in.	"	"
2 "	1 ft. 6 in.	"	"
Floor			
9 Boards	8 ft. 10 in.	8 in.	⅞ in.
5 Joists	6 ft. 0 in.	2 or 3 in.	2 in.
Roof			
32 Pieces	3 ft. 7 in. (or equiv.)	7 in.	½ in.
4 Purlins	9 ft. 2 in.	2 in.	1½ in.

Lengths allow for cutting. Widths and thicknesses are nominal. If the board widths vary the foot run will have to be corrected accordingly.

GARDEN GATES

Of the designs given here all could be made in oak and left natural colour for weathering or given a coat of creosote or a stain—preservative ; designs (B) and (C) could be painted if preferred. If the gate is to be in natural oak it is a good plan to give a coat of a clear preservative.

Construction is similar in all cases, though modification will be necessary in accordance with the particular design selected. The sizes can be adapted within reasonable limits.

Design (A) (Figs. 1 and 5)—This could be hinged at either side providing the strut is positioned accordingly. Its lower end should be near the hanging stile. Note that the bottom rail is

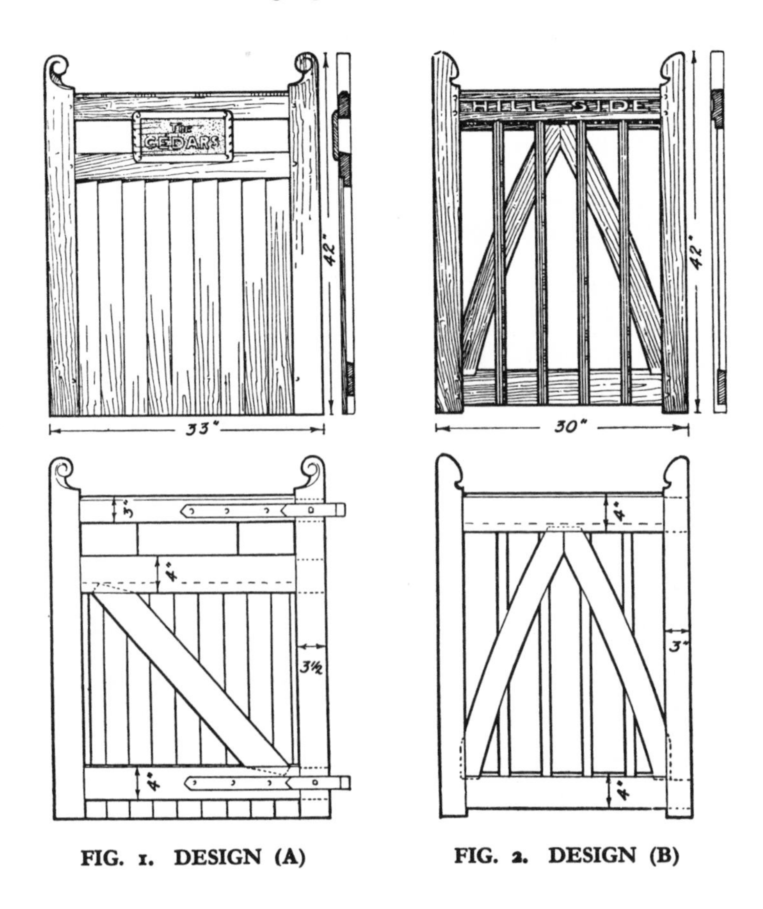

FIG. 1. DESIGN (A) FIG. 2. DESIGN (B)

thinner than the others so that the weather-boarding can be nailed directly to its face. To give support at the sides fillets are nailed to the stiles as in Fig. 6, whilst the mid-rail is rebated to take it.

Plane the stiles to finish $3\frac{1}{2}$ in. by $1\frac{3}{8}$ in., and mark out the mortise positions. In every case the tenons are cut back at the top as shown by the dotted lines, and the mortises are made accordingly. The bottom rail is $\frac{7}{8}$ in. thick and is flush at the back. It has bare-faced tenons (Fig. 6), and consequently the mortises are $\frac{1}{2}$ in. in from the face side. It is convenient to set all the mortises in the same distance. Square the marks round on to both edges and chop in about half way from each side. In these designs the mortises are cut square throughout, because wedges are notoriously liable to work loose. The joints are draw-bored and pegged. When jointing is complete the top scrolled shaping can be worked.

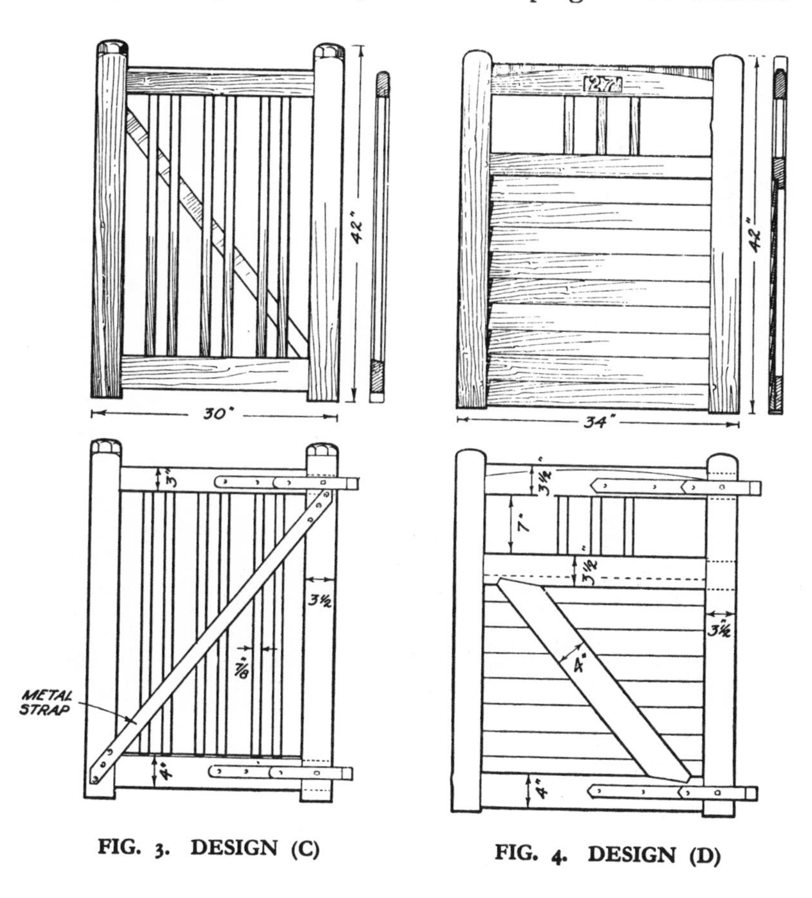

FIG. 3. DESIGN (C)

FIG. 4. DESIGN (D)

Prepare the rails and cut the tenons. The rebate for the weather-boarding can then be worked on the mid-rail. Note that the top rail has a double chamfer, whilst the other two are bevelled to allow water to drain away. Try the gate together, test for winding and squareness, and, laying the strut in position, make pencil marks where it crosses the rails. Sloping notches are cut in the rails to receive the bare-faced tongues of the strut.

If the wood is dry the joints can be put together with resin glue. The draw-boring will pull the joints home tight. Remember to drop in the strut during the assembling. Nail on the fillets and

FIG. 5. ATTRACTIVE WEATHER-BOARDED GATE SUITABLE FOR MAKING IN OAK

If it is desired to give a weathered oak effect the wood should be left unstained. It will gradually take on a fine grey tone. It is advisable to go over it first, however, with a clear preservative. This will not affect the colouring.

add the weather-boarding. The name-plate is screwed on with brass screws. All nails should be galvanized to prevent staining.

Design (B) (Fig. 2)—Construction is similar, but two struts are used. As these pass right into the corners it is necessary to cut notches to receive them above the bottom mortises in the stiles. Shallow notches to take the bars are cut across the bottom

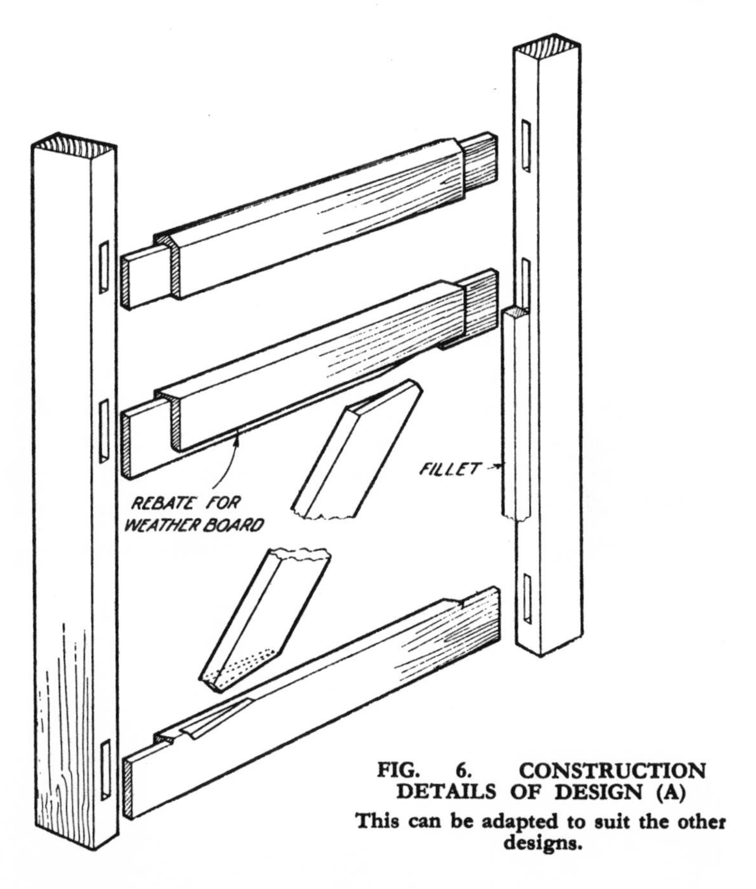

FIG. 6. CONSTRUCTION DETAILS OF DESIGN (A)
This can be adapted to suit the other designs.

rail and the rebate of the top rail. Sloping notches are also needed on the struts, and the positions of these are found by assembling the main framework and putting a straight-edge across the struts, keeping it in alignment with the notches in top and bottom rails. The bars are chamfered at the front, and are held with brass screws driven in from the rear. The name can be carved in the top rail.

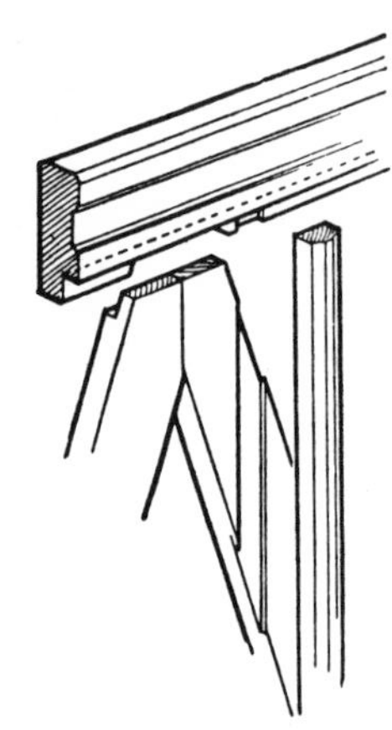

FIG. 5. STRUT DETAIL OF DESIGN (B)

Design (C) (Fig. 3)—In this design there is no wood strut, and a metal strap is used instead. Since this is more effective when in tension it is hung from the top of the hingeing stile. The $\frac{7}{8}$ in. uprights are lightly shouldered to fit in $\frac{5}{8}$ in. square mortises. At the top of the stiles a decorative touch is given by the chamfer, having the effect of an irregular octagon.

Design (D) (Fig. 4)—This is similar in many ways to design (A). The top rail has rounded chamfers worked along its top edge, and there are short bars between it and the mid-rail. A slight variation is in the jointing as the notches for the strut are taken right through. This is simpler to cut but is not quite so satisfactory as that in Fig. 1.

Whatever the design of the gate, it is essential that the hingeing posts are sound and firmly secured in the earth. In the best way they are jointed by a buried horizontal rail with struts. This may not be practicable, and an alternative is to well tamp the earth around and fill in with stones and broken bricks, ramming them well in, and pouring in concrete. The latter should be rammed hard so that the spaces are all filled in. Work a neat fillet of cement and sand at the top to stand about 1 in, above the ground level.

CUTTING LISTS

Design (A)	Long	Wide	Thick
2 Stiles	3 ft. 7 in.	$3\frac{3}{4}$ in.	$1\frac{3}{8}$ in.
1 Rail	2 ft. $9\frac{1}{2}$ in.	$3\frac{1}{4}$ in.	$1\frac{3}{8}$ in.
1 ”	2 ft. $9\frac{1}{2}$ in.	$4\frac{1}{4}$ in.	$1\frac{3}{8}$ in.
1 ”	2 ft. $9\frac{1}{2}$ in.	$4\frac{1}{4}$ in.	$\frac{7}{8}$ in.
1 Strut	2 ft. $8\frac{1}{2}$ in.	$4\frac{1}{4}$ in.	$\frac{7}{8}$ in.
1 Name-board	1 ft. $0\frac{1}{2}$ in.	$6\frac{1}{4}$ in.	$\frac{3}{4}$ in.
9 Weather-boards	2 ft. $4\frac{1}{2}$ in.	$3\frac{1}{2}$ in.	$\frac{5}{8}$ in.

Design (B)			
2 Stiles	3 ft. 7 in.	$3\frac{1}{4}$ in.	$1\frac{3}{8}$ in.
1 Rail	2 ft. $6\frac{1}{2}$ in.	$4\frac{1}{4}$ in.	$1\frac{3}{8}$ in.
1 ”	2 ft. $6\frac{1}{2}$ in.	$4\frac{1}{4}$ in.	$\frac{7}{8}$ in.
2 Struts	2 ft. 9 in.	$4\frac{1}{4}$ in.	$\frac{7}{8}$ in.
4 Bars	2 ft. 10 in.	$1\frac{1}{8}$ in.	$\frac{3}{4}$ in.

Design (C)

2 Stiles	3 ft. 7 in.	3¾ in.	1⅜ in.
1 Rail	2 ft. 6½ in.	3¼ in.	1⅜ in.
1 ,,	2 ft. 6½ in.	4¼ in.	⅞ in.
6 Bars	2 ft. 10 in.	1 in.	⅞ in.
1 Strap	3 ft. 10 in.	1¾ by ⅛ in. (iron)	

Design (D)

2 Stiles	3 ft. 7 in.	3¾ in.	1⅜ in.
2 Rails	2 ft. 10½ in.	3¾ in.	1⅜ in.
1 ,,	2 ft. 10½ in.	4¼ in.	⅞ in.
1 Strut	2 ft. 10½ in.	4¼ in.	⅞ in.
3 Bars	9 in.	1 in.	⅞ in.
9 Weather-boards	2 ft. 3½ in.	3½ in.	⅝ in.

Allowance has been made in lengths and widths. Thicknesses are net.

GARDEN SEAT

This makes a dignified seat and the size will suit the average small garden. If possible it should be in oak or chestnut, and, left to weather naturally, it will develop a fine grey tone. It would help to preserve it if a coat of clear preservative were given immediately on completion. It will not affect its natural toning.

The only parts which cut into any great extent of timber are the back legs which require sections of 4 in. by 2 in., but this is inevitable because of the rake.

Legs—It is a good plan to mark out and cut the shape of the back legs in a piece of card or hardboard. As, however, a full size drawing of the whole seat end is desirable in order to give the various shoulder lengths and angles, this should be put in hand. A thin lath of wood is handy for marking out sweeping curves. Start by marking the position of the seat rail as the front edge of the leg is vertical at this point. Mark in the various sizes as in Fig. 2, bend the lath to the various points, and run a pencil along the edge.

Place the template on the wood and mark round. If a wide

board is available it may be economical to mark the one shape within the other, but remember to allow for cutting out in accordance with the facilities available. Clean up the edges and mark out the positions of the mortises. One point to note is that, in order to retain square tenons and mortises, the top and mid back rail must be drawn in alignment with each other as shown by the

FIG. 1. ATTRACTIVE GARDEN SEAT MADE PREFERABLY IN OAK
An alternative to oak is chestnut which also weathers to a fine grey shade. If softwood is used frequent treatment with preservative is essential.

dotted lines in Fig. 2. This means that they are not lined up with the curve of the back itself. To ensure that both legs are marked alike they should be fixed together temporarily and the marks squared across both.

Front legs are straight. When cutting out remember to allow sufficient length at the top for the tenons which enter the arms. Mark out the tenons, taking the positions from the full size drawing. The front outer corner is chamfered, but this should be left until after the joints have been cut and fitted.

End Rails, etc.—The necessity for the full size drawing becomes

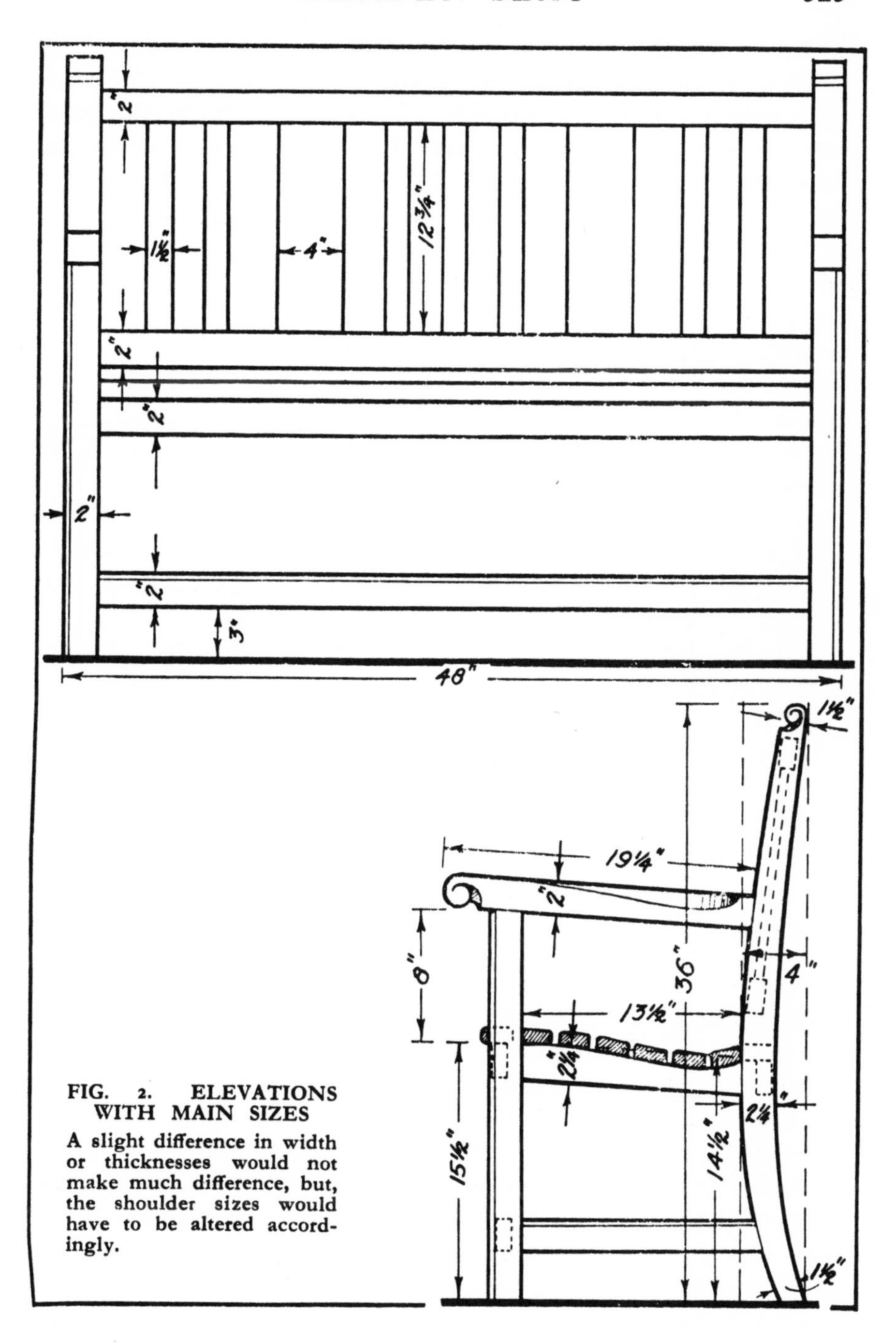

FIG. 2. ELEVATIONS WITH MAIN SIZES

A slight difference in width or thicknesses would not make much difference, but, the shoulder sizes would have to be altered accordingly.

obvious when cutting these. Not only is the shoulder length made obvious, but the shoulder angles become clear. The seat rail is shaped, but the curve should not be cut until after the joints have been cut. In the same way the arms have a curved decorative chamfer and a scroll. These again are worked after jointing (but before assembling).

Try the complete ends together, and if satisfactory assemble with either resin glue or thick paint. In any case all joints should be pegged and draw bored. The latter saves the use of many cramps. Bore the hole right through the mortised piece, and cramp the joint. Enter the bit in the hole so that the centre point marks the tenon. Separate the parts and bore the hole in the tenon about $\frac{1}{16}$ in. nearer the shoulder. When the peg (which should be slightly pointed) is knocked home it will pull the shoulder tightly home. The pegs can either be levelled or left slightly projecting. Even if levelled they will probably stand up a trifle after a short time owing to shrinkage in the surrounding wood.

Back—The two upper back rails are put together with their slats and panels as a whole. They are then entered into the legs at the same time as the other rails. Note that the tenons of the seat rails and stretchers meet in the thickness of the legs as shown in Fig. 3, this giving them maximum length. Carry out any decorative touches and clean up all surfaces before assembling. All joints are draw-bored as already described. Test for squareness in plan as well as in front elevation. Although not essential a centre back-to-front rail strengthens the seat and prevents undue sagging of the seat slats.

Seat—This consists of a series of slats screwed down to the rails. Brass screws should be used, and the heads should be recessed as in Fig. 3 and the holes pelleted. These pellets are made to a taper section, the grain running crosswise. They can be turned in a length of eight or nine and separated. They are glued into the holes and levelled. The advantage of the cross grain is that they do not eventually stand up owing to shrinkage as they would do if dowels were used.

[*Cutting List on page* 326

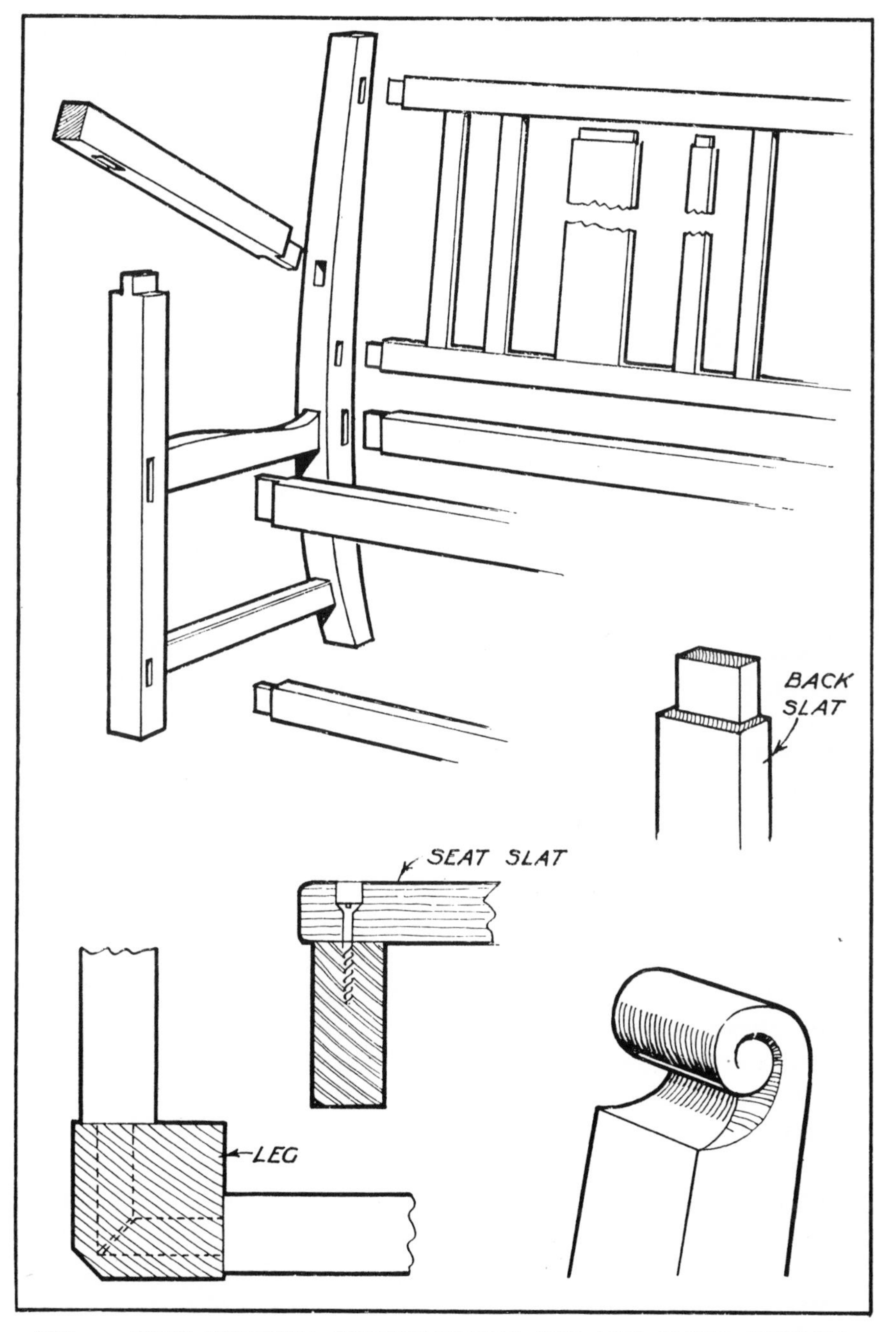

FIG. 3. VIEW SHOWING CONSTRUCTION AND ENLARGED DETAILS

CUTTING LIST

	Long	Wide	Thick
2 Legs	3 ft. 1 in.	4¼ in.	2 in.
2 „	2 ft. 1 in.	2 in. square finished	
5 Rails	3 ft. 11 in.	2¼ in.	1 in.
2 „	1 ft. 4½ in.	2½ in.	1 in.
(3 „ if centre rail used)			
2 „	1 ft. 6 in.	2¼ in.	1 in.
2 Arms	1 ft. 9 in.	2¼ in.	2 in.
2 Panels	1 ft. 2½ in.	4¼ in.	¾ in.
7 Slats	1 ft. 2½ in.	1¾ in.	¾ in.
8 Seat slats	4 ft. 0½ in.	2¼ in.	1 in.

GARDEN SWING

Chief sizes are given in Figs. 2 and 3. The uprights and cross-bar are 4 in. by 3 in. in section, and are sawn from one piece of 6 in. by 4 in. stuff, a size widely used for fencing timbers. A little variation would not matter, though it would not be wise to reduce the section seriously. If large knots are present it would be advisable to regard 4 in. by 3 in. as a minimum.

Posts—These will probably be obtained straight from the saw and will need to be planed. Use the trying or jack plane, and if there is any bow in the length arrange them to balance. Do not use pieces which are really badly out, however. Mark out the joints at both ends ; also put in a line marking the top of the joint where the struts enter. At this stage there is no need to mark this joint more fully.

The tenons should be 1 in. thick, and at top they do not pass right through the top cross-rail. Saw them, but do not cut the shoulders at present because otherwise they are liable to be damaged when completing other processes.

Cross-bar—Mark out and cut the mortises about two-thirds into the thickness. The ends are shaped as in Figs. 2 and 6, and a decorative touch is given by carving the simple scroll device. The shape (assuming that a large bandsaw is not available) is best cut by wasting away. Cuts across the grain are made with the saw, and the bulk of the waste chopped with chisel and mallet, followed by a coarse rasp. The file used afterwards will take out the deep rasp marks, and the whole can be finished with spokeshave and scraper. The scroll is cut at least $\frac{1}{2}$ in. deep at its lowest part

FIG. 1. AN ITEM THAT WILL APPEAL TO THE READER WITH A YOUNG FAMILY

Although the obvious purpose is to provide something that the children will get a lot of fun from, a swing of this kind makes an attractive item for the garden. Height above the ground is 7 ft. 11 in., width over posts 4 ft.

with carving tools. Between the mortises a stopped chamfer is worked on each lower edge.

Although the three parts are not assembled at this stage, it is as well to fit the bolts which will subsequently be added. As shown in Fig. 6 a hole is bored through the cross-bar into the end of the tenon about 3–4 in. beyond the shoulders. A recess is chopped at the inner side of the upright and a nut slipped in.

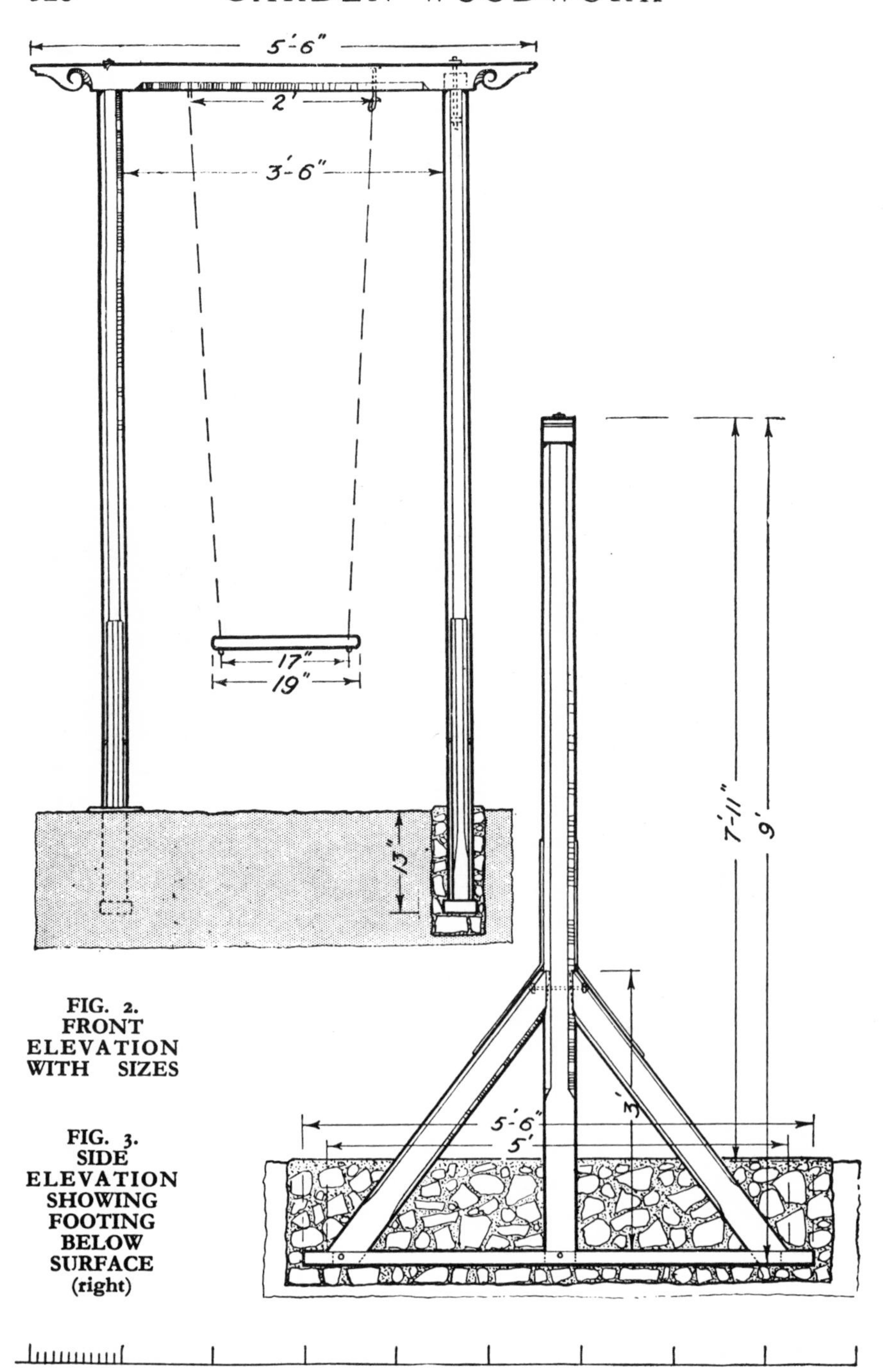

FIG. 2. FRONT ELEVATION WITH SIZES

FIG. 3. SIDE ELEVATION SHOWING FOOTING BELOW SURFACE (right)

The hole should continue about an inch beyond the recess. If a long bolt is not available, studding can be substituted as shown. It is advisable to cover it with thick grease or paint to prevent corrosion. This is done when the whole is assembled.

Footing and Struts—Mark out the centre mortise position, and at each side square a line giving the outer position of the struts (they are 5 ft. apart as shown in Fig. 3). Chop the centre mortise and fit the joint. Make sure that it is square, and lay one strut in position opposite the marks on footing and post (its joints are not yet cut, of course). Mark with pencil the slope on the edge of the footing, and on the post note the point where the lower edge cuts the post. This enables the joints to be marked out

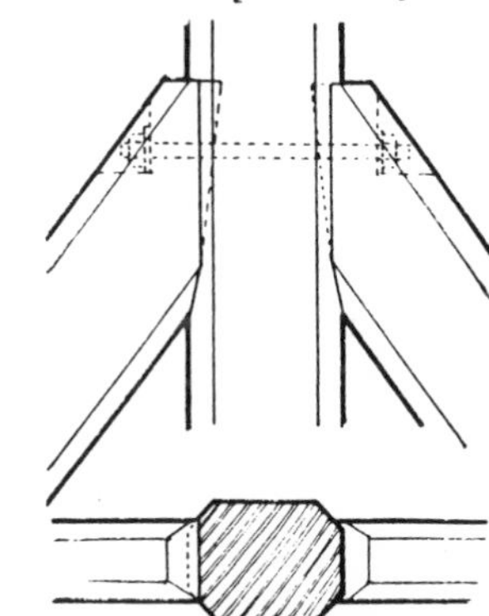

FIG. 4. ENLARGED ELEVATION SHOWING STRUT JOINT

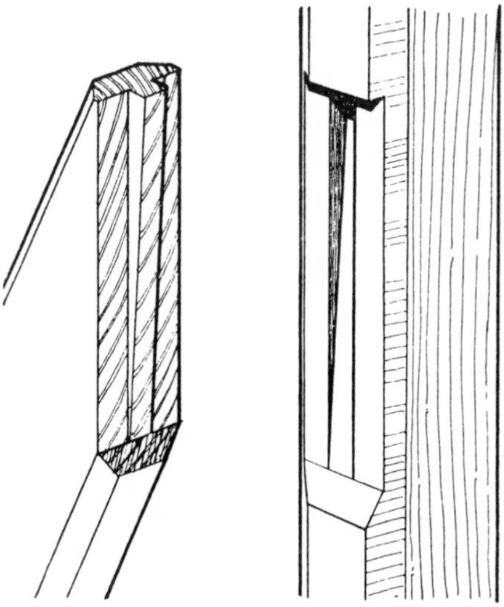

FIG. 5. JOINT BETWEEN POST AND STRUT

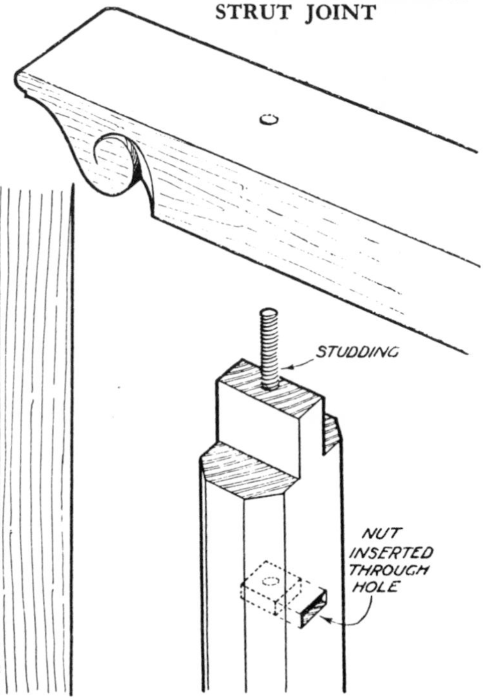

FIG. 6. DETAIL OF CROSS-BAR AND POST JOINT

and cut. It is as well to reverse the strut to the opposite side to see that the same length is registered. Theoretically it should be the same, but English oak has a knack of twisting, and it is as well to check up. If it is out at all it is advisable to make both the same and spring the footing so that it flattens out. An exception is when rough twisted stuff is used for the footing, in which case it is as well to set it as square with the post as possible and cut the struts to suit it.

Note that the outer side of the mortise is cut down square, whilst the inner side slopes at an angle which agrees with the slope of the strut. This is marked on the lower side from the sloping line drawn across the edge of the footing.

Fig. 5 gives details of the joint at the top of the struts. The post is notched back equidistantly from the surface, the top end being square, and the lower end at an angle which forms a mitre with the strut (see enlarged diagram in Fig. 4). In this notch a sloping blind mortise is chiselled, and the struts are cut to suit it. Finally bore a $\frac{3}{8}$ in. hole for the bolt, boring in half-way from each side.

When the fitting has been completed cramp one strut in position by fixing a triangular block to the outer edge to provide a seating for a sash cramp. The bit can then be entered through the post and the hole continued through the strut. Take care when it emerges not to splinter out the wood unduly. Repeat the process with the other strut. To enable the nuts to bed chop recesses in the outer edges of the struts as shown by the dotted lines in Fig. 4. When finally screwing up grease them well or coat with paint. Work the chamfers, and clean up all surfaces with plane and scraper.

Assembling—The two ends are put together independently first. Note that pegs pass through the bottom tenon joints, and it is advisable to draw-bore these.

As the footings are 4 in. wide the troughs to receive them should be about 8 in. wide and 16 in. deep. This allows a 3 in. layer of bricks or stones beneath the footings. The troughs being dug, place a 3 in. brick at each end, and lower the whole ends into position. See that they are approximately the correct distance apart, and drop on the top cross-bar and bolt it. This will keep the whole thing from falling sideways. Carry out tests to see that the structure is true. With a plumb bob make sure that one post is upright, and if necessary wedge up the footing at one end with thin stones to make it true. Take a sight to see that the other post is not in winding with it, again wedging with stones if necessary. Test also the front elevation with the plumb bob, and put a spirit level on the top cross-bar. In all probability one side or the other will require packing up. Finally test to see that the posts are equidistant throughout their length.

Pack stones beneath the footings and ram in a coarse concrete mix. Finally throw in old bricks and stones so that the space is filled. Concrete could be used entirely but is not essential though it is as well to dress the surface with a mix of cement and sand. It is a wise precaution to go over the whole of the woodwork with a preservative, especially the parts being buried.

Ropes—Special curved hooks are available to hold the rope thimbles. Holes to take them are bored through the cross-bar, and recesses are chopped in the top side to enable the nuts to be let in flush. Having entered the hooks they should be burred over so that there is no risk of the hooks becoming unscrewed. This can easily happen as the ropes tend to untwist in use. The seat can be a plain board about 10 in. wide, but it is stronger if it has cross-pieces beneath at each end. The rope passes through a hole, beneath the seat, up through a corresponding hole, and is spliced. If splicing is difficult the only plan is to bind the top tightly. Rope is classified by circumference, and a 3 in. is about right. Sisal rope is satisfactory.

CUTTING LIST

	Long	Wide	Thick
2 Posts	9 ft. 0 in.	4 in.	3 in.
1 Cross-bar	5 ft. 7 in.	4 in.	3 in.
2 Footings	5 ft. 7 in.	4 in.	1½ in.
4 Struts	4 ft. 1 in.	4 in.	2 in.
1 Seat	1 ft. 7½ in.	10 in.	1 in.

Allowance has been made in lengths. Other sizes are nominal. If parts finish slightly under it will not matter.

PORTABLE BIRD HOUSE

There is frequently an advantage in a house that can be moved from place to place. That shown in Fig. 1 is preferably in oak or possibly chestnut. Well made in the first place, and given an occasional coat of preservative it will last for years.

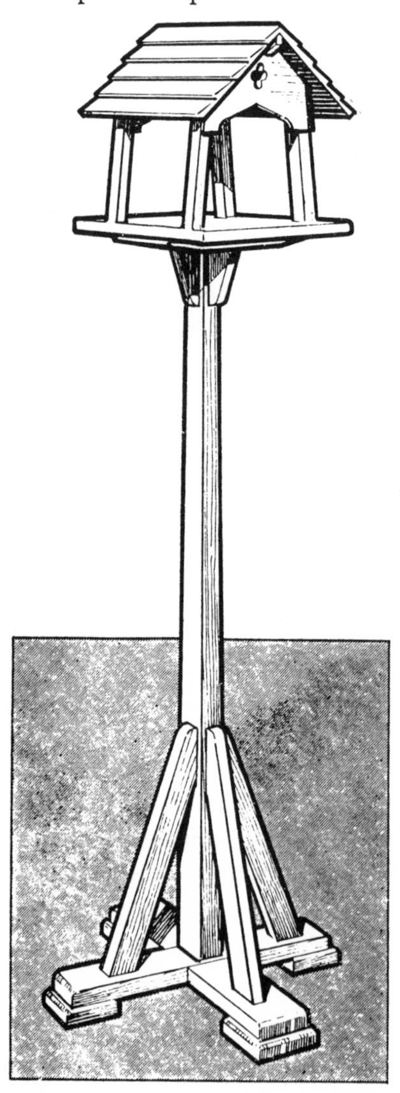

FIG. 1. ATTRACTIVE HOUSE IN OAK

Height to table is 5 ft. The base should be fairly heavy to give stability.

Post—The main post is made from a 2 in. square, and is 58 in. long, including the tenons at both ends. Plane it straight and mark out the joints. Both tenons pass right through, that at the bottom being square in plan (Fig. 3), whilst the top one is in alignment with the grain of the cross-piece in which it fits (Fig. 4). The taper starts just above the struts.

For the feet use 3 in. by 1 in. stuff, halving them together. Blocks 4 in. square are screwed on beneath at the ends. Cut the mortise right through the halving, splaying out in one direction beneath so that wedges can be knocked in. The struts are also tenoned to the feet, but join the post itself with a form of sloping notch joint as in Fig. 3. Assemble the whole thing in one operation, fixing the struts to the post, and adding the base. Resin glue, which is water resistant, can be used, but it is advisable to peg the top strut joints.

At the top fit the cross-piece, enlarging the mortise at the top

CUTTING LIST

	Long	Wide	Thick
1 Post	4 ft. 11 in.	2 in. square finished.	
2 Feet	2 ft. 0½ in.	3¼ in.	1 in.
4 Struts	1 ft. 9½ in.	2¼ in.	1 in.
4 Blocks	4¼ in.	4¼ in.	1 in.
1 Table	1 ft. 2½ in.	12¼ in.	1 in.
4 Brackets	4¾ in.	3¼ in.	1 in.
1 Cross-piece	1 ft. 0 in.	6½ in.	1 in.
4 Uprights	1 ft. 0½ in.	1 in. square finished	
2 Gables	10½ in.	7½ in.	½ in.
1 Ridge	1 ft. 2½ in.	2¼ in.	¾ in.
10 Weather boards	1 ft. 2½ in.	3 in.	½ in.

so that there is room for expansion when the wedges are knocked in. Fig. 4 shows how the brackets fit in sloping notches. If cut as shown they can be added after the cross-piece is in position.

House—This is made up complete in itself. Notches are cut in the edges of the floor to receive the uprights which are screwed in. Remember that the inner surfaces must be at a slight angle. Shallow notches at the top receive the gables. The top slope is not cut until later, when it is made to agree with the gable slope. A halved joint is used where the ridge joins the gables. Details of the shaping and decorative holes in the last named appear in Fig. 2.

Put the parts together with

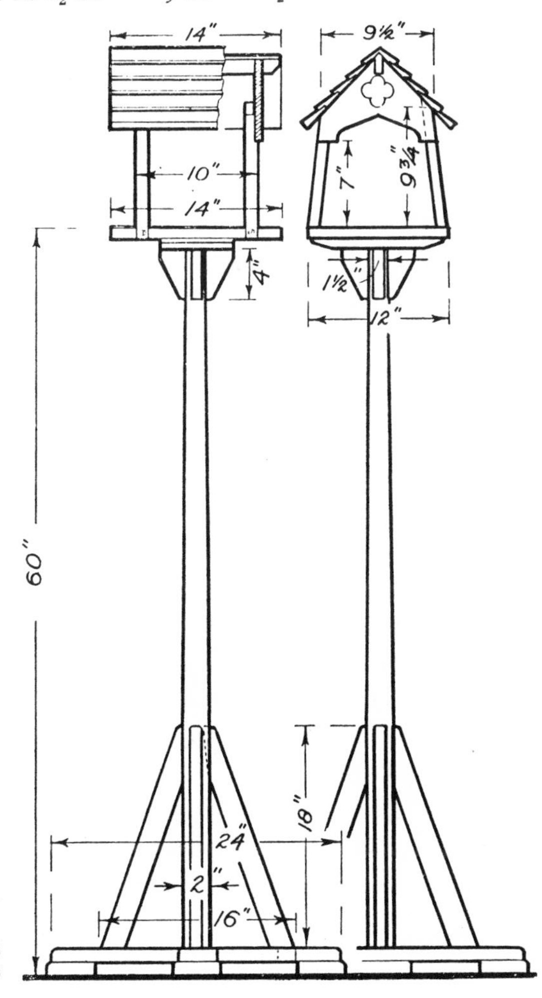

FIG. 2. ELEVATIONS WITH DIMENSIONS

resin glue, screwing or nailing where required. Screws through the cross-piece hold it in position. For the roofing use either plain tapered boarding or the rebated kind.

Assuming that the house is to be natural colour, give a coat of clear preservative and leave to weather naturally. If preferred, a combined stain and preservative can be used.

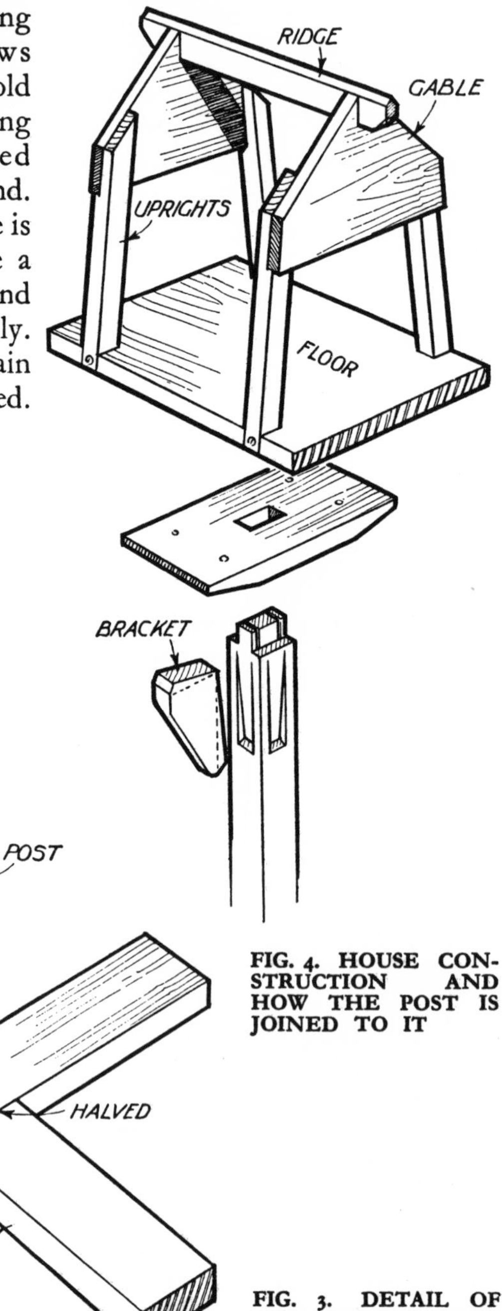

FIG. 4. HOUSE CONSTRUCTION AND HOW THE POST IS JOINED TO IT

FIG. 3. DETAIL OF THE POST AND FEET JOINTS

LYCH GATE

This makes an attractive entrance feature when the front garden and house are of reasonable size. Erected in front of a small house it would appear out of place, but in suitable surroundings it looks extremely well. Oak should be used preferably, not only because it looks well, but also because it is a durable wood. If softwood is used it should be given two coats of preservative, and re-treated periodically.

To suit special circumstances the sizes in Fig. 2 and 3 could

FIG. 1. DELIGHTFUL ITEM FOR THE FRONT GARDEN OF FAIR SIZE
Oak is the obvious choice of wood, with chestnut as an alternative. Softwood calls for repeated treatment with preservative.

be adapted to a reasonable extent, but they give good proportions as they stand.

Posts—These are 4 in. squares tenoned at the top into the main cross beams, and into the cross footing at the bottom. Straight struts are let into the footings and posts with a sort of sloping notched joint to ensure that the whole thing is rigid. A depth of about $\frac{3}{4}$ in. only is required in the post notches. Do not cut them unnecessarily deep because the post is otherwise weakened. To prevent their working loose a $\frac{3}{8}$ in. bolt can be passed horizontally through all three members, the nut being recessed in flush. If a long bolt is a difficulty a length of studding (which is a rod threaded throughout its length) can be used, a nut being used at each end. Washers beneath the nuts prevent biting into the wood. At the footings the notches pass right through, and pegs are used to hold them.

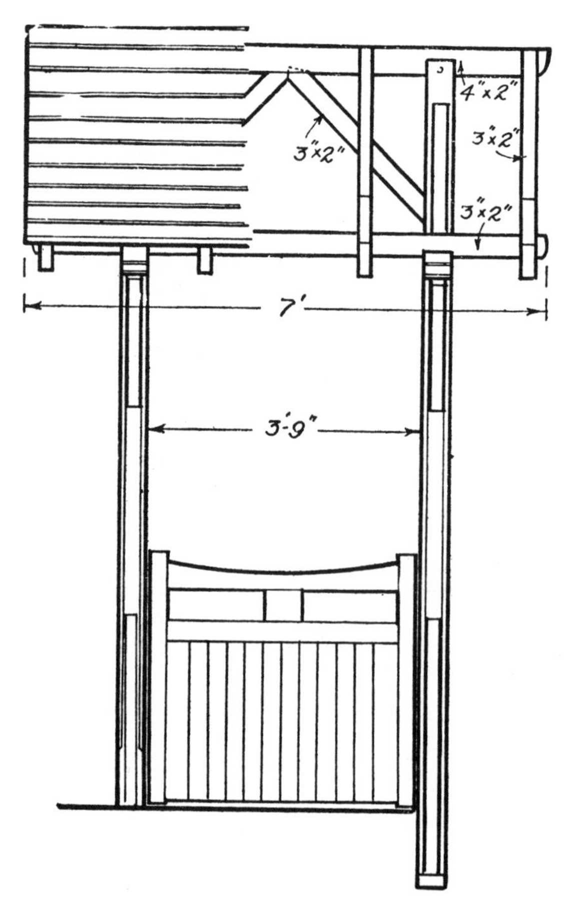

FIG. 2. FRONT ELEVATION WITH SIZES

The shoulder lengths of the struts could be worked out theoretically or taken from a drawing, but in practice it is better to place the footing in position, make sure it is square, and place the struts in position to obtain the size. The reason is that much English oak is not straight, and it is better to accept the curvature (if reasonable) and cut the braces to suit.

The top braces are

curved, but it is advisable to cut the joints before the outer edge is shaped. The straight edge enables the sliding bevel to be used for marking the shoulders. Both cross-beams and posts should be reasonably straight, and consequently the shoulder length of all the braces is theoretically the same. If there is any slight curvature anywhere, however, it will be necessary to calculate each brace individually. Fig. 4 shows the notched joint used for the braces. Note that the mortises in the cross-beams pass right through as the upper posts are also tenoned in. The tenons should have a gap of about $\frac{1}{4}$ in. between them as shown by the dotted lines in Fig. 3.

Rafters — These are jointed similarly to the braces. Again it is advisable to mark each individually, though there should not be any serious discrepancy in size. Short uprights are fitted between the rafters and cross-beams, these being stub-tenoned in as shown by the dotted lines in Fig. 3.

At the top the upper posts are notched to receive the ridge as in Fig. 4. At the inner face of each is also a notch or sloping mortise to receive the ridge brace. This should be cut at this stage; also the grooves at

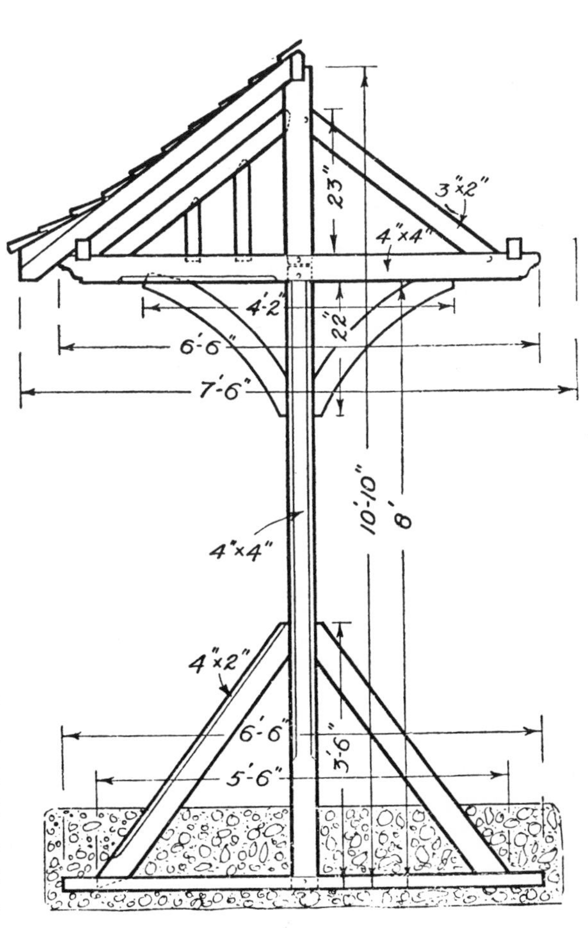

FIG. 3. END ELEVATION INCLUDING BASE

the ends of the cross-beams to receive the plates (Fig. 4).

Assembling—All joints being cut, any decorative touches such as the chamfering can be given, and all surfaces cleaned up. Each post and its parts is assembled independently on a piece of flat ground. Start by fixing the footing and its struts to the post and knock in the pegs. Put in the bolt, covering it with a thick coat

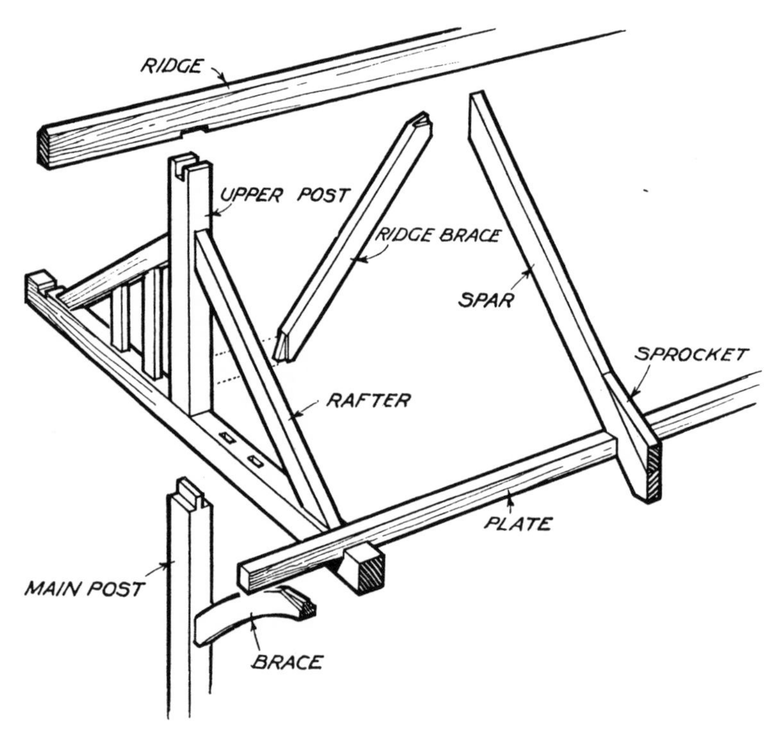

FIG. 4. PARTS OF THE ROOF AND THE JOINTS USED

of vaseline and tighten the nuts. To make all secure rivet over the ends.

The cross-beam follows, all joints being pegged except where the braces join the post where a bolt is used. Above this the rafters and upper post are erected, the short uprights being placed in position as the whole goes together.

Erecting—At this stage the troughs to receive the footings should be dug. They should be about 16 in. deep, this allowing for old bricks, stones, etc., to be passed beneath. Place a brick at each end and drop the completed truss into position. Add the ridge and its braces but do not peg for the moment. Now carry out all tests for accuracy. The posts must be upright and free of winding one with the other. They must be equidistant throughout their length, and the cross-beams must be the same distance apart at both ends. Furthermore the ridge must be horizontal, a test

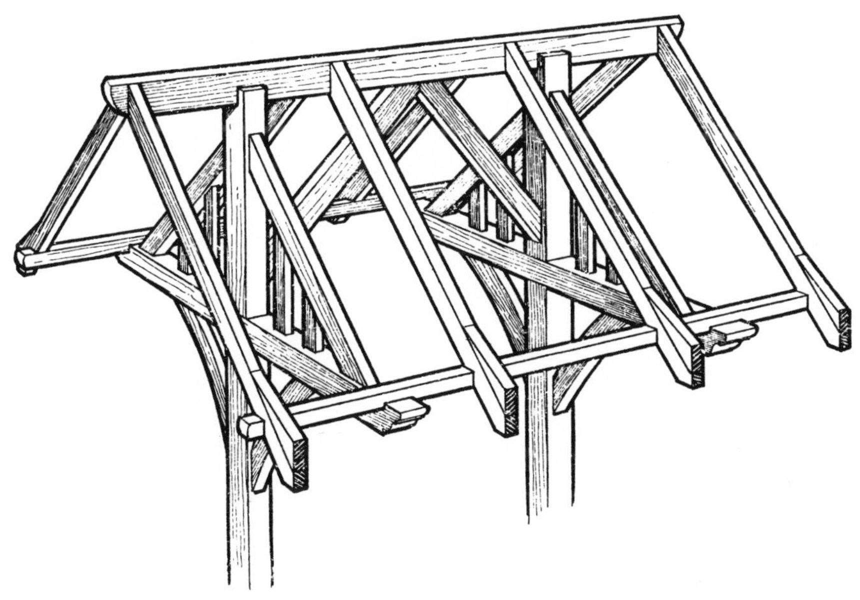

FIG. 5. APPEARANCE OF ROOF WITH COVER BOARDING REMOVED

being made with the spirit level. It may be necessary to wedge up one or both ends of the footings, or shift them away from or towards each other.

When all is satisfactory drive in the pegs of the ridge braces and ridge, and press in old bricks and stones beneath the footings so that they have ample support. Again pile in rubble, pour in some coarse concrete, and tamp well. Finish with a surface of concrete made with sand and cement, finishing above the general surface of the ground. Incidentally all parts below ground should be given a generous coating of preservative before erection.

Roof—Now follow the plates and spars. The former can be screwed from above or be nailed. Spars are notched over the plates and are nailed. To the spars the rebated weather boarding is nailed. Remember to use galvanized nails throughout as otherwise the wood will stain badly.

If preferred shingles could be used for the roofing, in which case a series of 4 in. by 1 in. battens is nailed horizontally to the spars with 1 in. spacing. The shingles are nailed to these, all joints being staggered and a gap of about $\frac{1}{8}$ in. left between each to allow for movement. Use two nails to each shingle, boring holes first to avoid splitting. There should be three thicknesses of shingles in all positions.

If the lych gate is to be in natural colour it should be given a coat of clear preservative solution of which proprietary brands are available.

CUTTING LIST

	Long	Wide	Thick
2 Main Posts	8 ft. 3 in.	4 in.	4 in.
2 Upper posts	2 ft. 10 in.	4 in.	4 in.
2 Footings	6 ft. 7 in.	4 in.	2 in.
4 Struts	4 ft. 6 in.	4 in.	2 in.
2 Cross beams	6 ft. 7 in.	4 in.	4 in.
4 Braces	3 ft. 0 in.	7 in.	2 in.
4 Rafters	3 ft. 4 in.	3 in.	2 in.
4 Uprights	1 ft. 5 in.	2½ in.	1 in
4 "	11 in.	2½ in.	1 in.
1 Ridge	7 ft. 1 in.	4 in.	2 in.
2 Ridge Braces	3 ft. 0 in.	3 in.	2 in.
8 Spars	5 ft. 0 in.	3 in.	2 in.
8 Sprockets	1 ft. 6 in.	2 in.	2 in.
2 Plates	7 ft. 1 in.	3 in.	2 in.

About 150 ft. run rebated weather boarding in 7 ft. lengths and 7 in. widths. Quantity to be revised in accordance with width.

Working allowance has been made in lengths. Widths and thicknesses are net.

INDEX

Drake Woodworking Books

Suppliers of Materials

Albert Constantine & Sons
2250 Eastchester Road
Bronx, N.Y. 10461

Craftsman Wood Service
2727 S. Mary Street
Chicago, Illinois 60608

Minnesota Woodwork Supply Co.
925 Winnetka Avenue
Minneapolis, Minnesota 55427

Woodcraft Supply Co.
313 Montvale Avenue
Woburn, Massachusetts 01801

Holz Machine & Tool Corp
43 Mercer Street
New York, N.Y.

Boice-Crane Power Tools
16 Hudson Street
New York, N.Y.